"That's just the way I am. I have a strong will
to be the best in the world. I drew a lot of
strength from that. To be No. 1 in the world.
To play on a championship team.
That's very important to me."

—Mario Lemieux

"Sports has been an excellent window through which to monitor changes in the rest of the society as we become more and more of an entertainment society. I do not know of any other venue that showcases the changes in American life and its values and the coming of the norms of entertainment more dramatically than sports.
We can learn about race from sports as almost any subject and we can learn what the coming of big money does to players and to lines of authority more from sports than anything else."

—David Halberstam
Pulitzer Prize-winning author

Books by Jim O'Brien

COMPLETE HANDBOOK OF PRO BASKETBALL 1970-71
COMPLETE HANDBOOK OF PRO BASKETBALL 1971-72
ABA ALL-STARS
PITTSBURGH: THE STORY OF THE CITY OF CHAMPIONS
HAIL TO PITT: A SPORTS HISTORY OF
THE UNIVERSITY OF PITTSBURGH
DOING IT RIGHT
WHATEVER IT TAKES
MAZ AND THE '60 BUCS
REMEMBER ROBERTO
PENGUIN PROFILES

Lowell MacDonald and Syl Apps pair up against New York Islanders in memorable 1975 Stanley Cup playoffs.

PENGUIN PROFILES

Pittsburgh's Boys of Winter

By Jim O'Brien

> *This book is dedicated
> to my family
> and to the memory of
> Michel Briere, Baz Bastien,
> Badger Bob Johnson
> and The Boys of Winter
> who are no longer with us.*

Copyright @ 1994 by Jim O'Brien

All rights reserved

James P. O'Brien — Publishing
P.O. Box 12580
Pittsburgh PA 15241
Phone (412) 221-3580

First printing, October, 1994

Manufactured in the United States of America

Printed by Geyer Printing Company, Inc.
3700 Bigelow Boulevard
Pittsburgh PA 15213

Typography by Cold-Comp
810 Penn Avenue
Pittsburgh PA 15222

ISBN 0-916114-17-1

To order copies directly from the publisher, send $24.95 for hardcover edition and $14.95 for softcover edition. Please send $3.50 to cover shipping and handling costs per book. Pennsylvania residents add 6% sales tax to price of book only, Allegheny County residents add an additional 1% sales tax, for total of 7% sales tax. Copies will be signed by author at your request. Discounts available for large orders. Contact publisher regarding availability of all books in *Pittsburgh Proud* series. Several of them are sold out.

Contents

- 8   Acknowledgements
- 10   Introduction
- 15   Lemieux: The Best
- 21   A New Day For E.J.
- 25   Les Binkley
- 39   Brian Spencer
- 46   Beer Debut At Arena
- 47   Welcoming Back Penguins
- 60   Red Fisher
- 69   E.J.'s Christmas Tree
- 78   Kevin Stevens
- 93   Bryan Trottier
- 104   Rick Kehoe
- 116   Where Are They?
- 117   Jack Riley
- 130   Penguins' Power Play
- 133   Mike Lange
- 144   Joe Mullen
- 162   Greg Malone
- 173   Tom Barrasso
- 190   Craig Patrick
- 203   Hometowns
- 211   Mario Lemieux
- 226   Ron Stackhouse
- 228   Jean Pronovost
- 239   Line Changes
- 242   Red Sullivan
- 245   Scoop Saulsbury
- 252   Hall of Famers
- 260   Gregg Sheppard
- 262   Duane Rupp
- 271   Greg Polis
- 274   Ulf Samuelsson
- 283   Syl Apps
- 294   Luc Robitaille
- 304   Paul Gardner
- 314   Red Kelly
- 316   Paul Martha
- 328   Jackie Powell
- 339   Val Fonteyne
- 340   Dave Burrows
- 347   George Ferguson
- 352   Jaromir Jagr
- 364   Ron Schock
- 369   Ron Francis
- 380   Orest Kindrachuk
- 382   Lowell MacDonald
- 388   Larry Murphy
- 398   Mario Sits Out Season

OTHER VOICES

- 402   Jimmy Jordan
- 404   Phil Musick
- 407   Roy McHugh
- 409   John Patterson
- 411   Ron Cook
- 414   Dave Ailes
- 416   Bill Heufelder
- 419   John Steigerwald
- 422   Paul Steigerwald
- 425   George Von Benko
- 428   Mike Prisuta
- 431   Guy Junker
- 434   Stan Savran
- 436   Goose Goslin
- 439   Doug Hoerth
- 442   Alby Oxenreiter
- 444   Readers Always Write
- 446   Words of Praise
- 448   About The Author

Acknowledgements

This is the seventh book in my "Pittsburgh Proud" series and, as always, I had great assistance and support from many special people in writing and publishing this tribute to the Penguins — Pittsburgh's Boys of Winter.

I want to thank all the members of the Penguins family who invited me into their homes and offices and shared their time and stories.

No one helped me more than Harry Sanders of the Penguins public relations staff, who was always there when I needed a name, an interview, some statistics, scrapbooks, files, pictures, a telephone number and, most of all, a generous smile.

The entire Penguins' publicity and marketing staff, from executive vice-president Bill Barnes and vice president Phil Langan, Cindy Himes, Steve Bovino, Renee Petrichevich and Mike Miller were helpful and came through when called upon. Executive assistant Elaine Heufelder always asked, "How's the book coming?" That helped to keep me at the task. It was nice to know someone cared.

Photos were provided by Denny Cavanaugh, the Penguins official team photographer, and Jim Cunningham, George Gojkovich and Bruce Bennett Studios.

Pittsburgh sports broadcaster George Von Benko provided me with many classic photos from his personal collection of early Penguins and NHL stars, as did former Penguins' minor official Tom "Scoop" Saulsbury. Von Benko and Glenn Barton provided photos of the Pittsburgh Hornets. Their enthusiasm about this book was also especially supportive.

I am appreciative of special permission granted to reprint articles about the Penguins that first appeared in *The Pittsburgh Press* and *Post-Gazette*, the *Tribune-Review,* and *McKeesport Daily News,* as well as by some free-lance writers.

Thanks to all the writers and broadcasters who follow the Penguins who provided us with special reflections. In their name, a designated share of the proceeds from *Penguin Profiles* will be donated to the Mario Lemieux Foundation and the Ashley Barrasso Cancer Foundation for cancer research.

Proceeds from past books in the "Pittsburgh Proud" series have been given to the Art Rooney Scholarship Fund, to special inner-city tutorial programs, and gifts have been given to many libraries and Pittsburgh charities and foundations.

Special thanks to Barbara Potter, a professional writer, editor and neighbor, and to my oldest daughter, Sarah O'Brien, a third-year premed student at the University of Virginia, for their proof-reading assistance and suggestions.

Gayland Cook and John Williams of Integra Bank Pittsburgh have been especially supportive of my book projects — Integra's theme of "for times like these. . ." is certainly appropriate to what I am doing — and Integra has provided a base on which to build a library about accomplishment and sports successes in Western Pennsylvania.

I wish to thank these patrons who have supported my writing and publishing projects through the years: Aeriss, Inc., Alcoa, Arco Chemical, L.D. Astorino & Associates, Ltd, Architects, Babb, Inc., Baierl Chevrolet, Black Box Corp., Blue Cross of Western Pennsylvania, Bowne of Pittsburgh, Chevrolet/Geo Dealers of Greater Pittsburgh, Christopher's Restaurant, Community Savings Bank, Compucom, Continental Design and Management Group, Daniell-Sapp-Boorn Associates, Inc., Eat'n Park Restaurants, E-Z Overhead Door & Operation Service, Ernst & Young, Feldstein Grinberg Stein & McKee, Bill Few Associates, Frank B. Fuhrer Wholesalers, The Gustine Company, F.E. Harmon Construction, Inc., Hawthorne Sports Marketing, H.J. Heinz Co., J&L Structural Inc., Johnson & Higgins, Ketchum Public Relations, Mascaro Inc., Meridian Exploration Corp., Merna Corp., Miles, Inc., North Side Bank, Nortim Corp., Pittsburgh Trane Sales Agency, PNC Bank, Reed Smith Shaw & McClay, Russell, Rea, Zappala & Gomulka Holdings, Inc., Sargent Electric Company, Slippery Rock University, Sutersville Lumber, Tedco, Inc., TRACO, Three Rivers Bank, Vista Resources, Waddell & Reed Financial Services, Westinghouse Electric Corp., Wheeling-Pittsburgh Steel Corp.

I wish to thank the following for their continued support: Larry Anlauf, Dennis Astorino, Bill Baierl, Eugene J. Barone, Walt Becker, Michael Berlin, Tom Bigley, Jeffery M. Boetticher, Howell Breedlove, Jim Broadhurst, Dave Brown, John Bruno, Everett Burns, Renny Clark, Ray Conaway, Carole Cook, Joe DeGregorio, Bill Eiler, John Fadool, Richard E. Farrell, Mike Fetchko, Gregory W. Fink, Patrick Fleming, Mike Ference, Barbara and Ted Frantz, Bob Friend, Frank B. Fuhrer, Lloyd Gibson, M. John Gaurneri, Bill Gormley, Frank Gustine Jr., Bob Gustine, Bill Haines, F. Edwin Harmon, Darrell J. Hess, James D. Hesse, Rolf Hilden, Karen Horvath, Dave Jancisin, Andy Komer, Angela Kremen, Ron Livingston, Robert Lovett, Laura Madonna, Ron Maser, Jack Mascaro, Del Miller, Don Miller, J. A. Miller, Carl R. Moulton, Richard J. Nesbit, Clark Nicklas, Thomas H. O'Brien, Ron Parkinson, Christopher Passodelis, Jack Perkins, Alex Pociask, Bill Priatko, Steve and Charlie Previs, Bob Randall, Jim Roddey, Art Rooney Jr., Patrick J. Rooney, Tim Rooney, Ed Ryan, Frederick B. Sargent, Vince Scorsone, Bob Scott, Gordon Small, Tom Snyder, Stanley M. Stein, Dick Swanson, Tom Sweeney, W. Harrison Vail, Larry Werner, Roy Werner and Earle Wittpen.

Pittsburghers who took tremendous pride in producing this series of books are Ed Lutz of Cold-Comp Typographers and Stan Goldmann, Bruce McGough and Tom Samuels of Geyer Printing. Goldmann officially retired this year, but has promised to keep an eye on my projects. All the work on this book was done in Pittsburgh, and that is a real point of pride.

—Jim O'Brien

Introduction
This is about beginnings

> *"There are some people in New York who would like to know it's raining in Minneapolis."*
> —Ike Gellis

My brother Dan and I decided to go to New York before they leveled the old Madison Square Garden. It was actually the third Garden and it replaced trolley car barns on a site between 49th and 50th Streets on Eighth Avenue in Manhattan.

This was in 1966, when there were only six teams in the National Hockey League, and the NHL was a year away from doubling its size with an expansion program that would bring the Pittsburgh Penguins into being. The Rangers and Knicks were less than two years away from moving to a new building bounded by Seventh and Eighth Avenues and 31st and 33rd Streets.

I had just come out of the U.S. Army after a 21-month stint, the last 10 months at the U.S. Army's Northern Warfare Training Center and Arctic Cold Weather Testing Center in Fort Greely, Alaska. I had gotten an early out to attend graduate school at the University of Pittsburgh, where I was a literature major that winter.

I wanted to go to New York by airplane. Dan decided we were going by bus. He was my big brother, five years older, so we went by bus. I remember I got sick to my stomach when I got off the bus in New York after a stifling 10-hour trip. I left a lasting impression on the sidewalks of New York.

We had lined up an ambitious doubleheader in our weekend sports pilgrimage: an NHL game between the Rangers and the Chicago Blackhawks, and then an NBA contest the following day pitting the New York Knicks against the Los Angeles Lakers. That night we stood up in the end zone of the highest balcony of the building that had been erected in 249 days in 1925 — the same year Pitt Stadium opened. We thought we were in heaven. We had purchased standing-room-only tickets. It was good enough. We just wanted to be in the building before the wrecking ball erased it. It was regarded as the mecca of indoor sports and other major events in this country. The building was packed to the rafters; it had great atmosphere.

The Rangers stars included Bob Nevin, Rod Gilbert, Eddie Giacomin, Jean Ratelle and Earl Ingarfield. The Blackhawks had Bobby Hull, Phil Esposito and Stan Mikita. Read those names again, and let them roll off your tongue slowly. They are still to be savored.

Dan and I had seen our share of games involving the Pittsburgh Hornets in the American Hockey League through the years, and we were struck by the difference in the speed and intensity in the frenzied action below us. It was a whole different game from what we were accustomed to watching in Pittsburgh. We'd never seen anybody who could play like Bobby Hull. Or been in a place like Madison Square Garden.

The next day we sat in the opposite end zone, on a lower level this time, and watched Jerry West, the one-time All-America at West Virginia University, "the Zeke from Cabin Creek," as he was called in one major sports magazine feature. He led the Lakers to victory over the Knicks, netting one long jump shot after another. He was facing us at our end of the court in the second half, and he was something to behold. He has always been one of my favorites.

West was joined by Elgin Baylor on that ballclub, and the Knicks included Walt Bellamy, Willis Reed and Tom Gola. They are all in the Basketball Hall of Fame.

I had no idea that weekend that within four years I would be back in Manhattan, working as a sportswriter for *The New York Post*, covering games on a routine basis involving the Rangers and the Knicks at the "new" Madison Square Garden which opened in February, 1968. It was there that I would have a ringside press seat to report on the first of the historic heavyweight championship boxing matches between Muhammad Ali and Joe Frazier in the most exciting sports event I ever covered. I have never been in a sports building that buzzed like The Garden, that had so much electricity.

This is a book about beginnings, about how people got started in sports, and about memories. One that comes quickly to mind involves the Rangers and my boss at *The Post*, sports editor Ike Gellis. He was a little guy who smoked big cigars, and reminded me of Edward G. Robinson. He was a great boss because he didn't care if he ever saw you, as long as your stories came in on time and at the proper length.

Ike Gellis liked the fight game, horse racing, football, baseball, basketball, anything you could bet on. When I called him from Minneapolis and mentioned that it was raining on the day of a Monday Night game involving the Vikings, he reprimanded me. "You know," he said, sternly, "there are some people in New York who would like to know it's raining in Minneapolis."

But Ike Gellis hated hockey. Someone at The Garden or at the office talked him into attending a playoff game between the Rangers and Toronto Maple Leafs in 1971.

Gellis had just been given a brand new Mercedes-Benz by local sporting interests, mainly the race tracks, at an "appreciation night" at a New York hotel. How's that for winning the affection of the sports editor of what was then the largest daily circulation afternoon newspaper in the nation?

"I wish they'd throw another night for me," Gellis told me a month or so later when I asked him how he liked his new wheels, "so they could give me the money to maintain this car. Damn, the upkeep is so expensive."

Gellis goes to the game at Madison Square Garden and asks a cop at the curb if it's OK for him to park his car in that block. The cop assures

Gellis that it's OK. Gellis had no idea what was in store for him that night as he entered the press gate.

The game went into three overtimes, for one thing. Here's a guy who hates hockey to begin with, and now he has to watch six periods worth of it. He looked like a man squirming in an electric chair. When, at last, he exited the building he found an empty space where his new Mercedes-Benz had been parked. The police had towed it to the city pound. Now Ike Gellis really hated hockey. And forever after.

I have already mentioned the first NHL game I ever saw live. I have vaguer memories of my first visit to the old Duquesne Gardens in Oakland, the first time I ever saw the Hornets play in the American Hockey League. A team called the Pittsburgh Pirates had played there and been members of the NHL back in the late '20s. The building seated about 4,500, maybe 4,800 when fans stood behind the seats. Duquesne Gardens also replaced a trolley or streetcar barn. It was located on Fifth Avenue, between Craig and Neville Streets. St. Paul's Cathedral, the bishop's church, was on the other side of Craig Street.

I remember a smoky haze in the building. I saw Duquesne University play basketball there, a boxing show, a Golden Gloves final, I think, and a few Hornets games. That's about it, as best I can recall. I remember getting there on my own by streetcar.

The cop at the door of the players' entrance was from my hometown of Hazelwood. He was white-haired and pot-bellied and nicknamed "Doughbelly." I'd been told to mention some names to him of mutual acquaintances, maybe Blue Martin, and he let me enter without a ticket. Right from the start, I liked that set-up. Later, I'd get a press pass.

I was 14 at the time and had just been named the sports editor of *The Hazelwood Envoy*, a bi-weekly tabloid where I got my first job in journalism. Unless you count delivering the *Post-Gazette* before school each morning.

I remember the cop from Hazelwood also got me a broken hockey stick and had it signed by Bobby Solinger, one of the stars of the Pittsburgh Hornets. It might have been my first sports souvenir. I have no idea what happened to it.

Those were the Hornets of goalie Gil Mayer, defenseman Frank Mathers and center Willie Marshall. I remember Mayer and Baz Bastien, the coach of the team, attending a sports banquet in the auditorium at St. Stephen's Grade School in Hazelwood. I still have their signatures in a red-jacketed autograph book from those days. Remember when people actually had autograph books?

There were two boys about my age in Hazelwood who loved hockey. Their names were Don Cherubin and Timmy Kyle. They were the only kids I knew who had hockey equipment and they used to play street hockey in front of Kyle's home on Glenwood Avenue. They used to go to Hornets games regularly.

They talked Andrew "Chief" Bennett, who looked after the Burgwin Field sports complex in our community, into flooding part of the ballfield each winter, and creating a crude outdoor hockey rink. I tried it a few times, but I was never good at it. I sneaked out of the house with my brother's figure skates, and got hell from him when I got home. I wore the black shine as well as some leather off the tips of his skates by using them as well as the jagged edge of the skate tips to stop myself. I also remember spending a lot of time standing in snowbanks at rinkside because it was easier to stand up that way. That wasn't good for the skates, either.

I tried to skate a few years back, at the Mt. Lebanon Recreation Center where the Penguins used to practice, and I still wasn't very good at it. I can roller skate now better than I ever could as a teenager — when it was important to look good at a high school skating party — but I still can't do more than one turn around the ice rink without having to sit down and rest my aching ankles.

It helps you appreciate how special the skills are of these Penguins and Blackhawks and Rangers.

I remember in the Hornets' last season, when they would win the AHL's Calder Cup championship, how I had lunch one day at Goldstein's Restaurant on Fifth Avenue in the Lower Hill. They had great bean soup and corned beef sandwiches. I took Doug Harvey there to interview him for *Pittsburgh Weekly Sports*, a tabloid I published and edited along with Beano Cook, who had been the sports information director at Pitt.

Harvey had been demoted to the minors by the Detroit Red Wings. He had been the best defenseman in the history of the National Hockey League. He had won the James Norris Trophy as the outstanding backliner in the league seven out of eight years, from 1955 to 1962 while playing mostly for the Montreal Canadiens and also one year with the Rangers. He had been runner-up for the award in 1954 to Red Kelly of the Detroit Red Wings, then won it the next four years. Now Harvey was holding on for a paycheck, playing out the string in Pittsburgh, of all places.

Harvey would be in the Hockey Hall of Fame within six years of our luncheon meeting. That winter he looked lost in Pittsburgh. He seemed happy to have someone to join him for lunch. I still treasure memories like that.

The Civic Arena opened in 1962, only it was called the Civic Auditorium then, as it was to house the Civic Light Opera, and that's why it was built so that the roof could open in the summer.

We started *Pittsburgh Weekly Sports* in 1963, my senior year at Pitt. I was still struggling to make a living when I began dating Kathleen Churchman, then a graduate school student at Pitt, in November of 1966. I took her to many Hornets games. I got free tickets and the price was right. I did some games on WEEP Radio during that championship season of 1965-66, with Beckley Smith Jr. doing the play-by-play. Kathie and I got married in August of 1967, so we share the same anniversary as the Penguins. We were there at the beginning.

I covered the New York Islanders in their infancy as well, and met most of the players who would eventually win four straight Stanley Cups. I got back to Pittsburgh in 1979 in time to see the Steelers win their fourth Super Bowl, the Pirates win their second World Series in the '70s, and to see the Penguins begin to put together the team that would win consecutive Stanley Cups in 1991 and 1992.

This book is a collection of stories and reminiscences, reflections and, of course, profiles. It's not meant to be the definitive history of the Penguins. It's meant to provide pleasurable reading, and to spark personal reminiscences, for anyone who ever pulled for the Penguins or hollered on behalf of the Hornets.

It's bits and pieces of the history of hockey in Pittsburgh. It's about beginnings. It's about how people, including the Penguins and members of the Pittsburgh sports media, got hooked on hockey. It's about Penguins past and present. It's about people who truly cared.

Bobby Hull   **Stan Mikita**   **Phil Esposito**
Chicago Blackhawks who played at Madison Square Garden

Rod Gilbert   **Jean Ratelle**
Two of the New York Rangers stars in '60s and '70s

*"At the age of six
I separated myself
from the others,
thanks to the way I could
handle a stick and puck,
and never did the idea
of doing anything else
other than playing hockey
ever cross my mind.
My life is one long
skating rink."*
—Mario Lemieux

Lemieux: The best I've ever seen

*"Mario amazes me every
time I see him play."*
—Craig Patrick

The hockey puck was flying past players about belly high. It had ricocheted like a cannon shot — thrack! — off the glass shields behind the goalie's cage at the north end of the Civic Arena and was the object of several players' attention.

Mario Lemieux lifted his hockey stick skyward and stopped the puck in flight. He dropped it deftly in front of his skates, and as quick as can be, Lemieux let loose a pass in front of the cage and teammate Rick Tocchet tipped it in for the go-ahead goal.

It was a thing of beauty to behold.

It broke a 2-2 tie in the second period of a game between the Penguins and the St. Louis Blues and was the first of five unanswered goals by the Penguins to spark them to an 8-4 victory.

"You have to be lucky to be good," Tocchet once said. "And with 66, we're already lucky."

It was just one play in one particular game, back on November 5, 1992, one of so many games in the regular season schedule of the National Hockey League. Singlehandedly, Lemieux made it a memorable game.

That particular moment was just one of the many incredible maneuvers and plays Lemieux would make on this one night. He turns a hockey stick into a magic wand. Everyone else seems to be playing with a simple stick. Lemieux seems to be cheating, like he is playing with a cesta that he borrowed from a Basque jai-alai player. He can catch a puck somehow with his stick.

Does he have fly paper instead of black tape wrapped around the blade of his stick? How does Lemieux manage to control the puck the way he does?

Lemieux moves his stick this way and that way, like he wants to barbeque the puck on both sides, interrupting its helter-skelter movement, has it under complete control and can slide it onto a teammate's stick so swiftly it's hard to see it. I am more amazed by his assists sometimes than by his goal-scoring. He can pass a puck as precisely as if he were playing shuffleboard in a neighborhood saloon.

I tire of the claims by so many sports writers and media mavens that the regular season games in the NHL are meaningless. Even Lemieux has bought into this at times, when he's hurting, and says he'll be back in time for the playoffs, when the team really needs him. But whenever Lemieux plays, every game has the potential to provide a lifelasting moment to remember, something of enduring splendor. Every fan has their own favorite. Lemieux does something mind-bending or unbelievable at least once a week.

Mario Lemieux

For playoffs, international play and all-star games, Lemieux usually lifts his game another notch or two. Such superstar efforts have contributed to his legendary status.

Penguins general manager Craig Patrick is an impassive man, not a man given to gushing, or too much emotion about anything, yet he offers, "Mario amazes me every time I see him play."

Former Boston coach Rick Bowness observed later that same 1992-93 season, "He's in a class by himself, no doubt about it."

Or, as Penguins' teammate Ron Francis put it, "He's the best player in the world. And people who refuse to recognize him as such are missing the boat."

If there is a sports arena in the country that should be required by law to have a big screen for instant replay it's the Civic Arena — and one was installed for the 1994-95 season. Once is not enough when it comes to admiring Lemieux's legerdemain, or antics on the ice.

It's often hard to see what happens in a hockey game, to begin with, which is one of the reasons it has always held limited appeal to the bigwigs at the television networks. But Lemieux, as well as his much-gifted teammate Jaromir Jagr, does so many subtle things, and they do them so quickly, that the human eye, or the mind, has a hard time taking it all in. Ask any opposing goalies.

There is no way Lemieux can be fully appreciated from the press box high above the Civic Arena, or from the super boxes, and the same is true of most NHL playing sites. Most press boxes are against the ceilings of the buildings, and none are any higher than the one at the Civic Arena.

Rest assured, Lemieux receives enough accolades from all who sit in those press boxes, but I still have to believe that they are missing something from their ivory tower viewpoints.

I was sitting behind the north goal in about the sixth or seventh row, the guest of a good friend, Bill Shields. His two seats cost $38 apiece then, and he's one of those fans who feels lucky to be able to pay it to see Lemieux light up the red beacon just behind and above that goal on a frequent basis.

The Penguins go after that goal only once in three periods, but the price is still a bargain, as Shields sees it. Critics complain that there are too many games that don't mean a great deal in the NHL, but every game is worth watching when Lemieux is at work. On any given night, Lemieux might do something you have never seen before. Then again, Lemieux has missed too many regular season games in recent seasons to suit most fans.

Another buddy of mine, a former sandlot soccer and hockey player named Jim Godwin, who has had Penguin tickets at the other end of the rink for over 20 years and saw them play in the beginning of their franchise (1967-68 season) shakes his head and smiles everytime somebody mentions Lemieux in his presence.

"Jimmy, I'm telling you," he'll say. "I've never seen anything like him — in soccer or in hockey. Pele might have come close in soccer. He's unreal!"

In this particular game against the Blues, Lemieux had a goal and three assists. It upped his totals to 19 goals and 23 assists for 42 points after 14 games. The Penguins had lost only one of those games, back in St. Louis against these same Blues in a game I had watched on TV.

The Penguins had gotten off to their best start in the 26-year history of the franchise with an 11-1-2 overall record and they were 7-0 at home. In their previous game, at the Civic Arena, Lemieux had a club-record 12-game goal streak stopped.

Afterward, he was critical of the ice, saying the surface that was established after the circus had come and gone from the Civic Arena, was soft and poor. Sure enough, in the next game, the revenge battle with the Blues, his linemate Kevin Stevens wrenched his knee on the first foray down the ice, catching the blade of his skate in a rut and twisting his knee. Stevens required orthoscopic surgery and was expected to miss a month of play. That hurt because Stevens was second only to Lemieux on the Penguins' scoring list. During a post-game interview, it was obvious that Lemieux was disappointed.

Lemieux had led the Penguins to back-to-back Stanley Cup championships, yet he was still seeking to set more standards. His back didn't appear to be bothering him that much and he was still hungry.

I had seen my share of hockey games over the previous 35 years, first as a 14-year-old sneaking past obliging policemen from my hometown to see the Hornets play at Duquesne Gardens. I saw the Hornets win the American Hockey League championship in their last season at the Civic Arena, and was there for the birth of the Penguins.

I covered the Islanders and the Rangers in New York when I worked there. At the Blues-Penguins game, I saw Bryan Trottier and Denis Potvin make appearances, and it brought back memories of reporting on them as young players with the Islanders, before they won four Stanley Cups. I had seen Wayne Gretzky and Bobby Hull and Bobby Orr and even Jean Beliveau in his last season, and I had never seen anyone play like Lemieux.

"He's the best I've ever seen in hockey," I gushed to Joe Gordon, the Steelers' publicity director, during a visit to his office one day at Three Rivers Stadium.

"He may be the best you've ever seen in any sport," came back Gordon, a guy who was the general manager for the Pittsburgh Rens of the American Basketball League, the publicity director of the Hornets and the Penguins after the Civic Arena was opened, and then the Steelers through four Super Bowl championships. Gordon played baseball at the University of Pittsburgh and has been a long-time fan of the Pirates. In short, he knows sports inside and outside as well as any observer in Pittsburgh.

He has seen them all up close: Connie Hawkins, Terry Bradshaw, Joe Greene, Franco Harris, Jack Lambert, Roberto Clemente, Bill Mazeroski, Dick Groat, Dave Parker, Barry Bonds, Tony Dorsett, Billy Knight, Norman Nixon, Arnold Palmer.

"Mario is unusual," said Paul Martha, who similarly had been involved with several sports in Pittsburgh through the years, as well as elsewhere. "And you tell people, and because I've been so involved with him and the Penguins, people take it with a grain of salt. But he's special. No doubt about it."

You had to see the Penguins play in their initial seasons to truly appreciate how far they have come, and what Lemieux means to the franchise.

In recent seasons, the Penguins had been the biggest and most talented team in the league, and they intimidated teams as soon as they skated onto the ice in their black and gold uniforms, just like the Steelers did in the National Football League in the '70s, just like the Pirates did in the National League in the '70s, and again in the early '90s.

Back in the beginning, ex-Ranger Red Sullivan was the first coach. His wife, Marion, used to sit at mid-ice with rosary beads in her lap and say prayers for the Penguins, and her husband, throughout the game. She prayed a lot.

So did the Penguins. They couldn't advance the puck up the ice by passing it to one another. More often than not, somebody would shoot the puck into the offensive zone and everybody would chase after it, hoping it might bounce in the Penguins' favor.

To see them in their Stanley Cup seasons, with Lemieux and Jagr juking here and there, controlling the puck like it was pastry, was a sweet sight. Led by Lemieux, the Penguins were playing this game better than anybody.

Jim Cunningham

A New Day For E.J.
Coach comes back to Civic Arena

"Things happen for a reason."

Eddie Johnston was eager to begin his job as coach of the Pittsburgh Penguins. Johnston was driving from his home in suburban Upper St. Clair to the Civic Arena in Uptown Pittsburgh. For the 57-year-old Johnston, things were definitely looking up.

This was Tuesday, June 22, 1993, and in a few hours Craig Patrick, the general manager of the Penguins and a former teammate with the St. Louis Blues, would be introducing Johnston at a press conference at the Civic Arena.

Johnston was wearing a dark blue double-breasted suit, a well-starched white shirt, a light-colored paisley tie, and a somber look more befitting a pallbearer.

It was not exactly a news conference, and his return had not thrown off many sparks. In a certain sense, his return was being taken for granted. Everyone who cared about the Penguins had known for weeks that Johnston was returning after a three-year absence to become the coach, or something significant, of the Penguins.

In fact, the Penguins had made efforts a year earlier to get Johnston, but could not work out a deal to pry him away from the Hartford Whalers, where Johnston had served as general manager since he departed Pittsburgh.

Johnston had been unsuccessful in his attempts to sell his home in Upper St. Clair when he went to Hartford, so he did not have to look for a place to live when he returned. "Things happen for a reason," he said.

Johnston knew his way around the Arena, and felt comfortable there. And, from top to bottom, the sentiment was shared by nearly everyone in the Penguins' organization.

"I have known Eddie Johnston for a long time and believe him to be not only a quality person," said Patrick in his introductory remarks, "but also a quality hockey person."

Everyone who has ever met Johnston knows he is a quality guy, a good guy, but it remained to be seen if he could coach and push and prod the Penguins to play to their abilities and capture a third Stanley Cup championship in four seasons.

Anything less would be considered a disappointment, by Johnston as well as the Penguins fans. Ticket prices had soared again, and the faithful felt they were paying for the best hockey team money can buy in the National Hockey League. "You better win," advised sports guru Beano Cook, who had worked in a p.r. capacity for the Penguins when Johnston was there the first time.

Johnston had never coached a team this talented before, and he knew the expectations. So he seemed solemn and even paler than usual.

In a positive sense, Johnston seemed perfect for the Penguins and Pittsburgh. Somehow, he looks like a Pittsburgher, the sort that used to carry his lunch in a metal box to work in the steel mills.

"I've always felt I'd be part of three Stanley Cups," said Johnston, who played for two Stanley Cup champions with the Boston Bruins during a distinguished 16 year NHL career as a gritty goaltender. "Hopefully, this is the next one."

Johnston was replacing Scotty Bowman, who was leaving to coach the Detroit Red Wings. During the three years Johnston had been away, the Penguins had won two Stanley Cup championships, under Bob Johnson in 1991 and — after Johnson stunningly died of cancer — Bowman in 1992, before faltering and getting upset by the New York Islanders in the playoffs in the spring of 1993.

"I had a case of the nerves last night," said Johnston, who had sliced melon, a muffin and coffee for breakfast before getting into his champagne-colored Nissan Maxima sedan, with Connecticut license plates, and heading for the Arena. "But it was good nerves. I really have a good feeling about this. It's a challenge, I feel, coming after a guy like Bob Johnson and a legend like Scotty Bowman.

"The players have to realize what happened to them. If they respond to the challenge, we can have quite a year. They didn't win 17 straight games and finish first in the league (record-wise) without having the best team in the league."

Johnston was a popular, if controversial choice, to coach the Penguins. People were comfortable with the idea of Johnston as coach, because everyone from Mario Lemieux to the media enjoyed Johnston when he last worked here. Lemieux said he loved the guy.

Lemieux lived near the same neighborhood where Johnston had grown up before him in Montreal, just a Lemieux slap shot away from the fabled Forum where the Canadiens once ruled the NHL. They understand each other, and they remember where they come from.

Whenever Johnston sees someone he knew from the past, he's apt to say, "Hey, let's get together for a beer." He was a 'Burg thing before there was such a slogan.

But Johnston's record as coach of the Penguins was suspect. He compiled an overall record of 79-126-35 in three seasons. He guided the team to the playoffs in his first two seasons, both times suffering heartbreaking losses in overtime in the deciding game.

He was named general manager of the Penguins in 1983, a position he held for five years. He spent one more season with the Penguins, as an assistant general manager, before heading for Hartford.

Johnston gets high marks, however, for hanging tough and rejecting all kinds of tempting offers for the Penguins' No. 1 draft choice — No. 1 overall in the NHL — when Lemieux was the leading amateur prospect available back in 1984.

He not only landed Lemieux, but he was also responsible for drafting Shawn McEachern, Paul Stanton, Jim Paek and Jeff Daniels, as well as former Penguins Zarley Zalapski, Doug Bodger, Bob Errey and

Rob Brown. He made trades that landed the likes of Kevin Stevens and Paul Coffey.

The Penguins never had a better power play than they did when they set a since-surpassed NHL record for efficiency during the 1981-82 season when Johnston was calling the shots.

He made another contribution to the Penguins' Stanley Cup champions, as the Hartford GM, when he traded Ron Francis and Ulf Samuelsson to the Penguins in 1991. He said he did that under a dictum from the owner, and did not feel it would be a sore point with the players now that he was their boss.

"I know the one thing Ronnie and Ulfie and I have in mind," Johnston said, "is to win the Stanley Cup."

In the recent past, the Penguins have been known to devour their coaches for breakfast. They convinced Patrick that they would perform better if Bowman were banned from practices, and Patrick and Bowman unbelievably obliged them.

Johnston is a tough customer. He still has some nicks and scratches from stopping slaps shots for 16 seasons, including the 1963-64 campaign when he was the last goaltender in the league to play every minute of a season.

Even so, there were some questions to be answered. The Penguins were going to be playing in the Northeast Division during the 1993-94 campaign with Montreal, Quebec, Boston, Buffalo, Hartford and Ottawa. Lemieux still had Hodgkin's disease and a balky back that flared up on him at the worst times. Stevens suffered such severe facial injuries in the 1993 playoffs that some insiders feared would haunt him and make him more cautious. Troy Loney, a winger who contributed to the special chemistry of the team for ten years, was lost in the expansion draft. Jaromir Jagr and Tom Barrasso would have to come up big in the playoffs if the Penguins were to win it all again.

Johnston had some help in returning the Penguins to their premier position in the league. Bryan Trottier had also returned, as an assistant coach. Trottier was a vital cog with four Stanley Cups winners with the Islanders, and two with the Penguins. He is an inspirational guy.

So is Johnston.

The streets of Pittsburgh were still familiar to him on that first day he reported to work at the Arena, but he was not always sure where to turn. "Do I turn left here?" he asked as he approached the intersection of Bower Hill Road and Cochran Road in Mt. Lebanon.

"You can go either way," he was told.

The same would be true of his comeback as coach of the Penguins.

As he emerged from the Fort Pitt Tunnel and took in the always-impressive skyline of Pittsburgh, he remarked, "It still looks great. Everybody who ever came to visit me always commented on the experience of coming out of that tunnel.

"That's the way I feel right now. There's light at the end of the tunnel. I'm like the Steelers; I want to win another Super Bowl."

Eddie Johnston joins Penguins mascot Iceburgh at team's Christmas party, 1993, and his family at their home in Upper St. Clair. From left to right, they are wife Diane, sons Joseph and E.J., daughter Michele and Eddie.

Les Binkley
The Original Penguin

"I don't think the players today have as much fun as we did."

Les Binkley looked a lot like the Les Binkley I knew when the Penguins first came into being. It had been over 20 years since I had last seen Binkley up close, but his face and smile had gracefully survived the passage of time.

It is a kind face, friendly and inviting, and given to grinning when he gets into his war stories. He is not really that visibly scarred for someone who had stopped more than his share of hockey pucks with his face, and taken 300 stitches, by his own count, to patch up facial wounds during his 21 years of playing professional hockey, twelve in the minors, five in the National Hockey League and four in the World Hockey Association.

The stitch marks somehow blend in with the age lines on a face that's as tough and leathery as an old goalie's glove. Seeing photos and newspaper stories from the early days of the Penguins, it still makes one shake his head to see Binkley blocking and catching shots with no protection on his head. There's one of him with a patch on his head, where he was struck earlier by a puck. The Penguins weren't as good as Binkley back then, and this is a tough customer who stood on his bare head to keep the Penguins in a lot of games, and to steal some games when they had no right to do so.

His crewcut was gone, the forehead went higher, the hair that remained was gray, neatly parted and combed to the sides. But Binkley was still Binkley, or Bink, as some call him, and he was still fielding slap shots, even if they were just verbal ones offered in jest by members of the Penguins party.

Binkley, by the way, was the original Penguin, and he is proud of that distinction. "The Penguins bought my contract a year before they came into the NHL, and put me in storage in San Diego for a year," he pointed out. "They wanted to make sure they had a goalie in the organization. Jack Riley was the Penguins' first general manager — he was a good hockey man — and he bought me in a deal that was scratched out on a napkin in a restaurant. He should have saved that napkin. It'd be a nice souvenir today."

Binkley is a better souvenir, one of the remaining relics from that first season, when the Penguins replaced the Hornets in the hearts of die-hard hockey fans in Pittsburgh. That was when the American Hockey League gave way to the National Hockey League.

Binkley wore a dark blue blazer and well-pressed gray slacks, a button-down white dress shirt with a burgundy paisley tie, and well-shined black shoes. He looked like he could have been a card-carrying member of the Fox Chapel Golf Club.

His stance was not that much different from the one he so often assumed in front of the home nets at the Civic Arena, starting with the inaugural 1967-68 National Hockey League campaign.

Now he was sitting in a white metal patio chair, his backside propped up by a four-inch black cushion seat. He was still wielding a stick, only now it was a dark-stained cane. He had undergone surgery over the summer for an artificial hip replacement. He had it done on July 8, 1993, in Toronto. He had been on the mend just over two months.

His knees were not as nimble as they once were. He mentioned that he had arthritis, and that he could feel all the nicks and cuts he incurred while stopping and slapping away shots at the goals he guarded so valiantly for so many years.

"You have to be a little strange to be a hockey goalie in the first place," said Binkley. "My teammates would say they couldn't believe I was a goalie because I was almost normal. Notice I said 'almost' normal.

"I was the type of goalie who didn't stare at someone if they made a mistake, or blame other people in the clubhouse, or in post-game interviews. I was the last man on the totem pole, and if it got by me I figured it was my fault."

At age 34 back in 1970, Binkley was one of the few holdouts who did not wear a mask while tending goal.

"Each time I get hit in the face, I get closer to wearing a mask," he told me at the time. "I keep saying to myself, 'If I get hit again, I'll wear it.'"

After his contact lenses were knocked out on one occasion when he was hit in the jaw by a flying puck, the team doctor said the inside of his mouth "looked like raw hamburger."

The durable Binkley was a no-nonsense type who shook off injuries that would have sidelined most goalies. There were two memorable occasions during the 1967-68 season, as recalled by NHL official Bill Friday.

The one incident occurred in Minnesota. Binkley was knocked out by a North Star shot that deflected off the stick of Penguin defenseman Al MacNeil and caught Binkley flush in the mouth.

"He was out cold when he hit the ice, face down," said Friday. "The shot knocked out two teeth and he needed a number of stitches for cuts around his mouth.

"Hank Bassen finished that period, but Bink was back on the job in the next one. He had a mouth that was swollen twice its normal size, but it didn't prevent him from playing a whale of a third period. That took a lot of guts.

"Then there was the night a Bobby Hull shot hit him on the leg above his pad. He went down, but the leg was numb and he couldn't move. Stan Mikita put the rebound past him because he was helpless. I thought he was through for the evening, but he shook off the injury and stayed in the game."

Friday didn't know how long and hard Binkley had worked to get an opportunity to play in the NHL. "I always hoped I would make it someday," said Binkley.

"We'd drink beer late into the night."
—Les Binkley

Binkley was sitting on a veranda at the Fox Chapel Golf Club, having a drink and a conversation with John Gill, a fellow talent scout in the Penguins' organization. This is one of Pittsburgh's most exclusive clubs, and it looks the part. Binkley had a great view of the golfers coming back to the clubhouse. Other scouts, like former Penguin Greg Malone and Charlie Hodge, would stop by and ask Binkley how his new hip was working out, and kid him about the throne he had set up to ease the pain. They wanted to know why he was not out there playing golf.

Dr. Peter Sheptak, who had performed back surgery on Mario Lemieux during the off-season, was among those playing golf. "How's the hip?" Dr. Sheptak asked Binkley.

Binkley had always been out on the course in past Penguins golf outings, but he had to sit this one out during the early days of the 1993 pre-season training camp. The Penguins had practiced for a few days at the Civic Arena, and now they were taking a day off for some fun in the sun, and to help raise funds for amateur hockey league teams in Pittsburgh.

Mario Lemieux was sitting out the exhibition schedule as well as the golf outing, but Kevin Stevens, who had smashed his face in a terrible freefall he took in the last game of the playoffs the previous spring, had gotten a positive report after undergoing a CAT scan exam that morning at Allegheny General Hospital. He had been given the green light to scrimmage with his teammates, and play in the upcoming campaign.

Stevens was all smiles as he sat next to me at dinner. Most of the Penguins were positive the team could bounce back and win their third Stanley Cup in four seasons. Eddie Johnston, who was a member of two Stanley Cup championship teams in Boston, and Bryan Trottier, who had contributed to four championships with the New York Islanders, and two more in as many seasons with the Penguins, were going to be coaching the team. There was a possibility Trottier might even make a successful comeback as a player after a year's layoff.

A Mideast peace resolution had been adopted and announced earlier in the day in a history-making assembly of world leaders at the White House. Israel and the PLO were in accord to make peace between their long-time rival factions. It was a day when anything seemed possible. It was a Monday when many Pittsburghers were brooding because the Pitt and Steelers football teams had been embarrassed that weekend by Virginia Tech and the Los Angeles Rams, respectively, and the way the Pirates had struggled against the Colorado Rockies, one of the new teams in Major League Baseball. So it was a good day to think about hockey, and think about the Penguins' prospects to grab their game's Holy Grail again.

It was an idyllic day in Pittsburgh. The sun was out, the sky was blue, and the weather was just right, with a slight breeze blowing through the thick, tall trees that surrounded the clubhouse, and lined the fairways. It was a green-green landscape. Squirrels were scurrying

Pittsburgh Penguins

FIRST PENGUINS TEAM (1967-68) — Back row (left to right): Gene Ubriaco, Val Fonteyne, Ken Schinkel, Bob Dillabough, Keith McCreary, Billy Dea, Ken Carson — trainer. Second row: Hank Bassen, Dick Mattiussi, George Konik, Andy Bathgate, Art Stratton, Noel Price, Bill Speer, Paul Andrea, Les Binkley. Front row: Jack Riley — general manager, Leo Boivin, Earl Ingarfield, Jack McGregor — President, Red Sullivan — coach, Ab McDonald, Al MacNeil, Joe Gordon — director of public relations.

about, chasing after each other, shooting up and down trees, and across the tee placements and the greens. The squirrels stood at attention, I swear, as if they were trained, whenever anybody would line up a putt. The squirrels were storing away chestnuts for the winter. Binkley had plenty of chestnuts of his own from so many winters working his trade over the mainroads and backroads of this continent.

"Ol' Number 3-0 is talking about the way it used to be," said Peter Taglianetti, one of the Penguins' present-day defensemen. Taglianetti was teasing an old-timer. Binkley smiled back.

Binkley was always good for a beer and a laugh. "We were both playing in Toronto at the same time," offered George Ferguson, a former Penguins' performer (1978-83). "I was with the Maple Leafs in the National Hockey League, and Bink was with the Toronto Toros of the World Hockey Association. He'd come over to my house all the time with one of his buddies, and we'd drink beer late into the night. He nearly caused me a divorce."

There were not many towns or leagues in North America where Binkley didn't do time during his days as a gritty goal-tender. He played for teams in cities like Charlotte, Cleveland, Baltimore and Toledo. Mario Lemieux, Tom Barrasso and Jaromir Jagr have no idea what it was like to work your way up through the minor leagues, or what it was like to be young and talented and frustrated because there was no room in the inner sanctum that was the NHL when it was comprised of only six teams.

The Penguins were one of six new franchises that were added to the NHL when the league expanded by doubling its size in 1967.

"There were only six goalies' jobs in the National Hockey League, and you couldn't get them out of the nets," recalled Binkley. "They were in there every night. Now those goalies are all in the Hockey Hall of Fame."

Binkley never played with a strong lineup when he played for the Penguins, but there were magic nights, now and then, when he played as good as anybody who ever guarded the goal nets.

Binkley had six shutouts that first season for the Penguins, which is incredible, especially for those who were witness to many of the games that year, and remember how bad the Penguins played in those days.

He had 11 shutouts altogether in parts of five seasons he played for the Penguins, leaving for greener pastures in the World Hockey Association after the 1971-72 season. Those 11 shutouts were still a team record as the Penguins were preparing for the 1993-94 season, but Binkley expected that Tom Barrasso would break it before long.

"It's harder to get shutouts these days," allowed Binkley. "The game is more wide-open. The scores are higher. But Barrasso is one of the best."

Mention of Barrasso prompted me to ask Binkley about the Penguins' present top goalie. Why was he so good?

"He plays the same way I did," offered Binkley, for beginners. "He's a big man, and he's really quick, and he's got a good glove hand.

That helps your balance. He handles the puck as well as a defenseman does. He helps the team get started the other way, and the opposing teams know that."

There were some nights when nobody was better at tending goal than Binkley.

No night was better than the one in Boston on January 28, 1968, during the Penguins' premier season. Binkley turned back 33 shots by the Bruins at Boston Garden to get a 1-0 shutout, his fourth of the season. He drew a rare standing ovation from a crowd of 13,909. "It was one of those nights you couldn't do anything wrong," he said. Binkley recalled that the Bruins back then included Bobby Orr, Phil Esposito, Fred Stanfield, Johnny Bucyk. "There were some shifts we never got out of our end of the rink. And Gerry Cheevers was playing great in goal for them," said Binkley.

Binkley harkened back to other starring performances by those Penguins pioneers. "In our first week, we beat Chicago, 4-2. We were the first expansion team to beat an established team. And they had Bobby and Dennis Hull, and both had among the hardest shots in the league, and they had Stan Mikita. We set a few records that year."

"Every trip you could write a book."
—Les Binkley

Binkley had quite a medical history in his hockey career. Before long, he may need more than a hip replacement. "I remember early in my career," Binkley related, "I was having my knee done at Divine Providence Hospital on the North Side. Dr. John Best looked after our players as well as the Pittsburgh Steelers. Dr. Paul Steele also worked with both teams. Terry Bradshaw was in the next room at the hospital. He had some kind of injury. He was a teetotaler. I was not and my teammates kept bringing me beer and such to make sure I was OK. Talk about contrasting rooms and contrasting patients. Dr. Best was a grumpy guy, given to coming into the room and twisting my leg when I wasn't looking, just to see my reaction. He'd be in there, checking me out, and nurses would be sticking their heads in the room and asking me, 'Mr. Binkley, do you need any more ice?' I think Dr. Best knew what that was all about.

"I never gave much thought to those knee operations back then. They cut it and fixed it, and let you go back to play. Now I'm at the point in my life where I am getting the results of all those old injuries and medical treatment. Here I am still plugging away in hockey, but I wouldn't do it any different.

"Every trip you could write a book. We played in all the old rinks. The conditions were different wherever you went. They had old rinks in New Haven and Providence. They had small locker rooms, small ice surfaces. There was no regulation rink; there still isn't today. Nobody made any money. We were closer then; you had to be. You had to share rooms on the road and at home. You had to share expenses."

When Binkley was talking about the old rinks, I recalled going to games as a kid at the old Duquesne Gardens in Oakland, just across the street from St. Paul's Cathedral. I still have an autograph from Gil Mayer, who was the goalie on the Hornets in the mid-50s, and came to a sports banquet — along with Frankie Gustine of the Pirates and Jim "Popcorn" Brandt of the Steelers and Pete Dimperio, the City League's top football coach — at St. Stephen's Grade School in my hometown of Hazelwood.

When I mentioned Gil Mayer to Binkley, it brought a knowing gleam to his blue eyes. "Mayer was the guy I replaced in Cleveland," said Binkley. "He got hurt, and I was brought in to fill the void. Then they traded him to Providence. I think he still lives there.

"The GM's name in Cleveland was Jim Hendy. He had a goalie coming in to take Mayer's place, but the goalie got fogged in, and I was within driving distance in Toledo. I went and filled in against the Buffalo Bisons. They invited me back the following year to be the spare goalie and team trainer. I told Hendy I had no knowledge whatsoever to qualify as a trainer. He sent me a home-study course.

"I thought I might get a chance that way," said Binkley. "They couldn't afford two goalies.

"That gives you a clue as to how important they considered having good trainers in those days. I had to get all the equipment ready, too. That was good and bad. I didn't have to skate as much as the other guys because I'd be in the clubhouse getting things ready. It was the same way at practice. You know what it's like at the outset of practice. That's where they really work the hell outta the guys. At the end of the first year I played the last eight games and gave up about 11 goals. I was the regular goalie the next year. I was the Rookie of the Year."

The star of the Barons back then was Freddie Glover, one of the greatest scorers in the American Hockey League. The Hornets had a great goal-getter in Willie Marshall. Neither Glover nor Marshall could stick long in the NHL, however, when they would get called up each year. Glover and Marshall were both in the NHL for four seasons, Glover for only 92 games and Marshall for 33 games.

"Cleveland was a great city to play in, though. It was a lot like Pittsburgh. The fans followed the Browns, the Indians and us," said Binkley. "When they move into a new rink in Cleveland, I think they'll have a great franchise. Nobody can find that place where they've been playing.

"I played that one year in San Diego before the Penguins started play. Max McNab was the general manager and coach in San Diego. We ended up in the cellar, but I was the team's MVP."

"There's no way anybody could be like Les Binkley."
—Red Sullivan

Red Sullivan was the first coach of the Penguins. He was a redheaded, square-jawed, tough-talking individual who tossed hockey sticks in angry spells, but was a good guy. The team's record that first year was 27-34-13 and the team missed by four points of making the playoffs.

"Red Sullivan just retired from working in the NHL; he had been scouting for the Flyers in Philadelphia up until this year," said Binkley. "He was great for our team. Talk about fiery redheads. When he was fired up, or upset, he'd kick garbage pails all over the place. He was such a competitor."

Sullivan liked to say of Binkley, "Most goalies are like the original Mr. Grump. There's no way anybody could be like Les Binkley. He gets upset, but he doesn't tie himself up in knots."

I asked Binkley how much money he made that first year in the National Hockey League. "I'm embarrassed to tell you," he said. "I signed to make $12,500. I wasn't supposed to be the regular goal-tender. I had no NHL experience, and they had Hank Bassen. But I played 55 games that year, and then I think they were embarrassed. So they paid me $15,000.

"I was hurt a lot in the last couple of years. I played only 196 games in the National Hockey League.

"The ice surface at the Civic Arena was bigger then. It was more difficult for the defense and goalies. Guys had more room to skate around you. The rink was wider and longer. They brought it in mostly because it opened up more room for the most expensive seats.

"We didn't draw well during the week in those early years with the Penguins, but we had good crowds on weekends. It's great to see how this franchise has grown, and how the fan interest has picked up, after the signing of Mario, and to see how great it is today. Just to be involved with this team, even as a scout, is an exciting and rewarding situation. This is the best team to be associated with in the league nowadays.

"I remember my first game in goal for the Penguins. We tied Minnesota, 4-4, at the Arena. I was a backup to Hank Bassen, who'd come from Detroit, at the beginning of that season. We were behind, and I didn't feel I played as well as I could. I was very nervous. The players came to my rescue, and backed me up. They played so hard just to get us even. I had tears in my eyes; I thought I was going to lose my contact lenses.

"I played bare-faced those first two years in Pittsburgh. I have teeth missing to prove it. One time we were playing St. Louis, and I saw Bill McCreary winding up to take a slap shot. There was a defenseman in front of me. I didn't see the puck until the last second, and it was only a few inches from my face when I picked it up. It was coming 100 mph and it hit me in the mouth. My mouth was really chewed up. The doctor shoved my teeth back into the bottom of my mouth in the locker

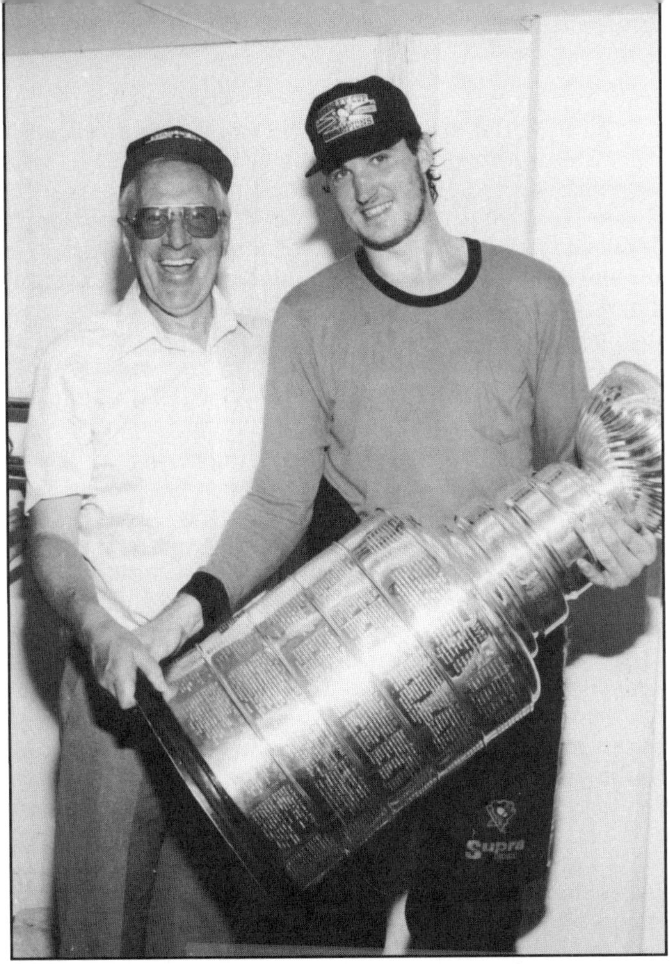

Dennis Cavanaugh

Les Binkley helps Mario Lemieux hold first Stanley Cup.

Detroit Red Wings

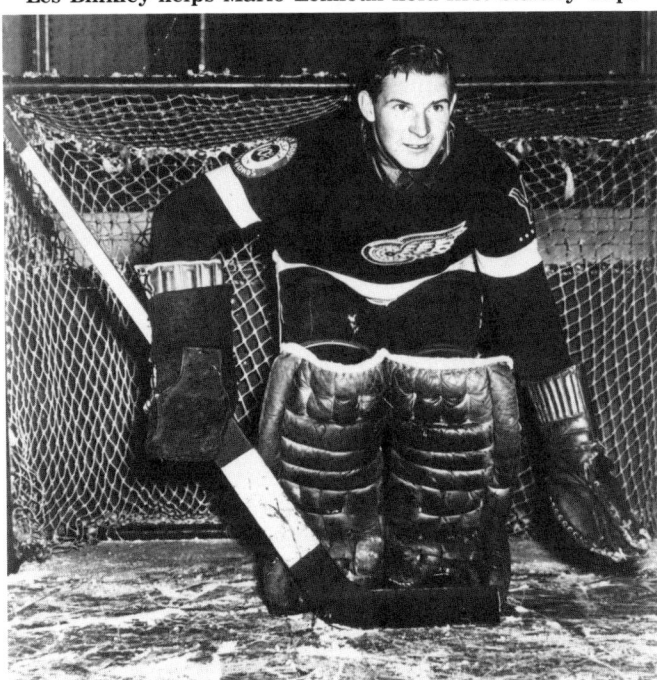

Binkley's boyhood idol Harry Lumley of Detroit Red Wings.

room, and the next day he put a plastic cap on them to hold them in place. I was able to keep them for a few years.

"I was nicked around the eyes a lot. I remember getting hit in the face by Bryan Hextall. It was an accident. I had my mask on, but I still got cut. It drove my mask into my nose. One day in practice, I was talking to our coach, and I wasn't even in goal yet. A guy hit me right in the temple with a shot, and nearly killed me."

I recalled how I was hit in the head by a hockey puck one night while standing alongside the rink during the pre-game warmup of the New York Islanders at Nassau Coliseum. My first thought was that I had been shot in the side of the head. I stumbled forward and grabbed onto a fellow sports writer standing opposite me. It left dried blood under the scalp, and the team doctor told me I was lucky, that I could have been killed if it had hit me about an inch away. Another time I was sitting in a pressbox just above one of the goals at Madison Square Garden, covering one of the New York Rangers games. The puck was shot into the seats, about a dozen seats to the right over from where I was sitting. But I kept my eye in that direction for awhile, and sure enough, I spotted that puck ricocheting right toward me like a heat-seeking missile. It just missed hitting me.

I was drafted out of gym class to play goalie for a few games for the freshman soccer team at the University of Pittsburgh, and I know what a tough position it is to play. I couldn't ice skate too well in my youth, and usually ended up standing in a snowpile in front of a goal cage.

"I can't believe how easy you could get cut," said Binkley. "Back in those days they'd put a butterfly on a cut, and they'd stitch it later. They didn't want you coming off the ice too long.

"I've had several procedures on my knees. They took out cartilage in my left knee, then I had my left kneecap planed and, finally, they removed my knee cap. And yet my left knee is better than my right knee. And I had only one operation on my right knee, to have cartilage removed. And now I've had my right hip replaced. I had the same doctor who did my knee twice.

"I went to some specialists in Canada because it's free up there. But it would take me a two-year wait. There have been so many cutbacks in the Canadian health system that there are long waits to get the doctor you want. Their system is not the answer to our health care problems in the U.S.A."

"Lugging all that equipment across town was a real chore."

It didn't take much prodding to get Binkley to go back to the beginning. "When you're young, you listen to the NHL games on the radio, and then on TV," said Binkley. "When I started playing junior hockey, the Toronto Maple Leafs sponsored a team called the Marlies. But our team was sponsored by the Blackhawks, so I wanted to see the Blackhawks do better than the Maple Leafs.

"When I first started out playing hockey as a kid, when I was seven or eight, I played a lot of road hockey, or what they call street hockey today. I started out as a right winger. Our goalie got hurt, and someone said, 'You play goalie in road hockey; how about trying it here?'

"Harry Lumley was from my neighborhood. He still lives there. He played in Detroit with the Red Wings as an 18-year-old. He played for Detroit, Boston and Toronto. He played about 16 years in the NHL altogether. He's in the Hall of Fame today.

"When I was playing, it was hard for him to teach me, because he was usually away from home during the season. You didn't get much positional coaching in those days. You didn't have the luxury of individual coaching. Back in our era, we didn't have that. We'd watch the goalie at the other end of the ice, and see what he was doing, then try to do the same thing in practice the next day.

"Today, you have hockey schools. You can really learn and improve, and you don't pick up bad habits in the beginning."

Binkley grew up in Owen Sound, Ontario. "It was a small town that had a couple of factories, and it was right on the water," he recalled. "There were a lot of freighters, and a lot of grain was sent out from there.

"The only thing I hated about being a goalie back then was that a bay and a river divided the town, and lugging all that equipment across town was a real chore. I went to public school, and we'd practice hockey early in the morning. I'd be up at 6 in the morning, and out the door. It was more important to practice than to eat breakfast. My mother would be screaming at me as I ran out of the house.

"I had an older brother, but he didn't play hockey. His name is Wade, and he's 5 1/2 years older. He played baseball. But hockey was our national sport. That's what I wanted to play. I became a rink rat. I'd be scraping ice between periods when I was 14 and 15. That was our job. We had a senior A team, and after the game we'd get free ice for an hour.

"Hockey was my whole life. I lived and died hockey. I played golf, because it helped my reflexes, and helped me stay in shape."

I asked Binkley when he first met Harry Lumley, the NHL goalie from his hometown.

"We met at a banquet, and we were introduced," said Binkley. "His parents lived next door to me. I'd already been playing hockey, but he was definitely an influence on me to want to play at a higher level."

I wondered how many neighbors made it to the NHL through the years.

"He played in Chicago when I was in Gault, and he'd slip me goalie sticks on occasion. They were over-sized and wider than what I was used to. He told me not to mind, that no one would notice the difference, and it would give me an edge. He'd come through town in a train — that's how the NHL teams traveled then — and he'd drop off some sticks for me.

"That first year (1951) in organized hockey was hard. To leave home at 16 is difficult. You're leaving all your friends and your family, and the school you went to. I remember my first two months I was calling home every night. I'd be crying, 'Get me outta here.' My parents told me to hold on, and give it a chance.

"I got to like it, though," said Binkley, "and, in time, my family would call me, and ask, 'Where are you? How come you don't call?'"

Binkley played for the Cleveland Barons in the American Hockey League for six seasons prior to playing for the Penguins, with one year in between with the San Diego Gulls of the Western Hockey League.

"As much as I wanted to play in the National Hockey League, I could've lived with staying longer in San Diego. San Diego was a great place. The weather was great, and you'd be on the golf course at 12:30 or 1 every day. There was a swimming pool no more than 20 feet from my front door. I lived in Pacific Beach, near Sea World. It was just beautiful."

As much as Binkley loved playing in the National Hockey League, he jumped to the World Hockey Association (WHA) with the Ottawa Nationals, and played with them for a year, then he went to the Toronto Toros for three years.

"When I was 16, I left my home in Owen Sound, Ontario, a little town about 150 miles north of Toronto, and went off to play junior hockey. I jumped from midget hockey to the juniors, which was a quite a feat at that time. I went to Gault, and played for the Gault Black Hawks. All the teams were sponsored, and we were sponsored by the Chicago Blackhawks.

"They wouldn't give me a chance with the big team, though, because I wore contact lenses. They said I couldn't see well enough. What a fallacy, when you consider how many guys there are today who play goalie while wearing contact lenses.

"I was in the minors for 12 years. But I persevered. I went to Baltimore in the Eastern Hockey League for the 1955-56 season. John Muckler and John Brophy, who both made it to the National Hockey League, were teammates of mine in Baltimore.

"One day, in January or February, we were having coffee, as was our custom, at a White Tower at the bottom of hill, below where the arena where we played was located. The arena sat on a knoll. I said to the guys at one point, 'We better hurry up, or we'll be late for practice.' And, just then, somebody in the restaurant said, 'Take your time. You've got no place to go. There's no arena anymore.'

"The rink had blown up. These ammonia tanks were set off somehow. All that was left were the girders. The Hershey (Pa.) Bears gave us some extra equipment, and we played all our games on the road the rest of the season.

"We shifted to Charlotte the next year. We were still in the Eastern Hockey League. Then I went to Toledo of the International Hockey League, and played there for two years. Then I went to Cleveland of the American Hockey League, and stayed six seasons.

"I don't think players today have the fun we had. When we played in Charlotte, the club didn't have a lot of money, like most new franchises. We'd travel to road games in four cars. I'd go with Muckler and Brophy and somebody else. I swear the cops in North Carolina had our club schedule. They were forever stopping us. They didn't just give you a ticket; they took the driver to jail until they got their fine. They wouldn't release you until they had their money. We'd go to the jail. The trooper would bring you in, and then change his hat and become the judge. It was usually a tiny building, with a small cell. You'd have to get someone to wire you money to get out. We'd drive from Charlotte to Johnstown, Pa., and Utica, N.Y. We played the New York Rovers at Madison Square Garden in New York. There weren't many people in the stands in some of those places, but most of them did OK on the weekends.

"We didn't make an awful lot of money, but you made a lot of friends, and it was great to play hockey for a living. The NHL had six goalies. They had guys like Terry Sawchuck, Jacques Plante, Gump Worsley, Glenn Hall and Johnny Bower. So who were you going to beat out? They never got hurt enough to sit down.

"There's more opportunity for young players today. We have more teams, and I think more are yet to come as hockey grabs hold in more cities. It's an exciting growth that is taking place.

"I have a grandson playing hockey now. He's my son's child. He's just starting; he's seven. He just loves it. I bought him a Penguins' shirt with his name on it. Just BINKLEY. Skates cost today what all my goalie's equipment cost me. I get a kick out of seeing him in his jersey."

Letter to the Editor in the Pittsburgh Press on March 20, 1970

Penguins Fans Melt Ice With Language

Having attended a Penguin game recently, I would like to comment about the vile language used by some spectators. Many immoral words were spoken by people of high social standing. I feel that these people are giving Pittsburgh a bad name.

—Judith Holt
Greenfield

1970-71 — THE PITTSBURGH PENGUINS: First row: L to R Bryan Watson, Jim Morrison, Keith McCreary, Red Kelly, Duane Rupp, Bob Woytowich, Dunc McCallum, Les Binkley; Second row: Glen Sather, Dean Prentice, Ron Schock, Bryan Hextall, Nick Harbaruk, Ken Schinkel, Lowell MacDonald; Third row: Trainer Ken Carson, Bob Blackburn, Val Fonteyne, Jean Pronovost, Greg Polis, Wally Boyer, Al Smith, John Stewart, John Doolan, Assistant Trainer.

Brian Spencer
How "Spinner" was shot to death

*"He puts a little life
into the team."*
—Phil Goyette,
Islanders' coach

Brian Spencer was nicknamed "Spinner" because he was a whirling dervish on the ice. Spencer liked to mix it up in the corners, and crash into people, and get into mischief. There were a few magic nights in his life, and some tragic nights that ended his life and that of his father.

This is the flip side of life in the National Hockey League, in professional sports for that matter, the messier side. There are lessons to be learned, however, from the players who take the wrong turn in the road, too, the ones who lead ruinous lives, who dance with danger and lose. Cocaine and crazy behavior are a bad combination. They can kill you, one way or another, as Spencer learned the hard way.

It's a shame. Spencer was a fun guy. One of his former teammates in Buffalo, Mike Robitaille, a former NHLer turned broadcaster for the Sabres, remembered Spencer as "full of life."

So how did Spencer end up dying of a gunshot wound to the chest in a friend's truck in Florida? What was he doing buying crack cocaine that fateful night? Only the year before, Spencer had been acquitted of murdering a restaurant owner, and been fingered as the prime suspect by his own girl friend. What went wrong in his life? How did he end up keeping company with such nefarious folks?

Should people have been keeping a closer eye on Spencer to start with? Wasn't he kind of crazy, moreso than being a character, during his NHL days?

Spencer was never more than a solid competitor during his 11-year career in the NHL, playing for the Toronto Maple Leafs, New York Islanders, Sabres and Pittsburgh Penguins. He played for the Penguins from 1977 through 1979. A left winger, who wore No. 22, he saw action in 86 games for the Pens and totaled 9 goals and 11 assists and 81 penalty minutes over two seasons. He was obtained from Buffalo for Ron Schock in September of 1977.

There was one night when all the stars were aligned right, a night when Spencer's stick had magic in it. He was only the 15th opposing player to score a hat trick against the Penguins in team history, putting the puck past goalie Al Smith three times while playing for the Maple Leafs in Toronto on January 9, 1971.

By doing so, he joined the likes of Stan Mikita and Phil Esposito, who had both done it twice, Dick Duff, Jean Beliveau, Bobby Hull, Gordie Howe, Dave Keon and Bobby Rousseau, some of the top players of that period, who had also recorded hat tricks against the Penguins prior to Spencer's big game. That's keeping the kind of company a hockey player dreams about.

In 553 NHL games, he scored 80 goals and added 143 assists. But he was known as a scrapper more than a scorer — collecting 634 penalty minutes — and his pugnacious play made him a popular player with fans.

The writers who covered the NHL liked him, too, because you never knew what Spencer would say next. Spencer liked to shock people. I first met Spencer when he was playing for the New York Islanders, and I was reporting on the team for *The New York Post*.

He told me a story that caught my attention in a hurry. He related a tale about how his his father, Roy Edward Spencer, was killed by the Royal Canadian Mounted Police in 1970, the same week Brian broke into the NHL with the Leafs. The young Spencer was scheduled to be interviewed between periods of a televised Maple Leafs game, but the local station instead decided to telecast a Vancouver Canucks contest. Roy Spencer was incensed, and he drove two hours from Fort James, and forced the station off the air at gunpoint. He was killed in a subsequent shootout.

Furious because the CBC station at Prince George was not carrying the Leafs' game, after it had been announced that it would be televised, Spencer Sr., 59 years old, held the station staff at gunpoint and was shot and killed.

Brian played the next night in Buffalo. Leafs' captain Dave Keon recalled Brian saying, "My father would have wanted me to play." Keon said Spencer played a great game.

"Brian, he's always been a survivor," said Byron Spencer, a twin brother. "But I don't know if he ever accepted it and put it to rest. He carried it with him every day. It had a direct bearing on everything that happened to him in his life since 1970."

Cool-headedness was never a trait of the younger Spencer, either. He flared quickly. It was part of his role in the NHL. I always suspected Spencer wasn't wrapped too tightly.

This feeling was reinforced when I visited him in the summer of 1978 in Freeport, Long Island, not far from my home on the south shore. He was playing for the Penguins at the time, and I was interviewing him and taking photographs of him for a feature story for *GOAL*, the official magazine of the National Hockey League back then.

Spencer spent his summer — wasted his summer, I thought — building the most bizarre and ugly looking motor vehicle that you never saw. It would have been something to see the expressions on the faces of people in Pittsburgh when Spinner spun into town for the 1978-79 season.

His pals tabbed it "The Incredible Hulk." Spencer preferred to call his creation "a dream come true." His wife at the time had to think it was a nightmare.

Bruce Sherman, one of the many mechanics who lent Spencer an experienced hand on his demanding engineering project, said of

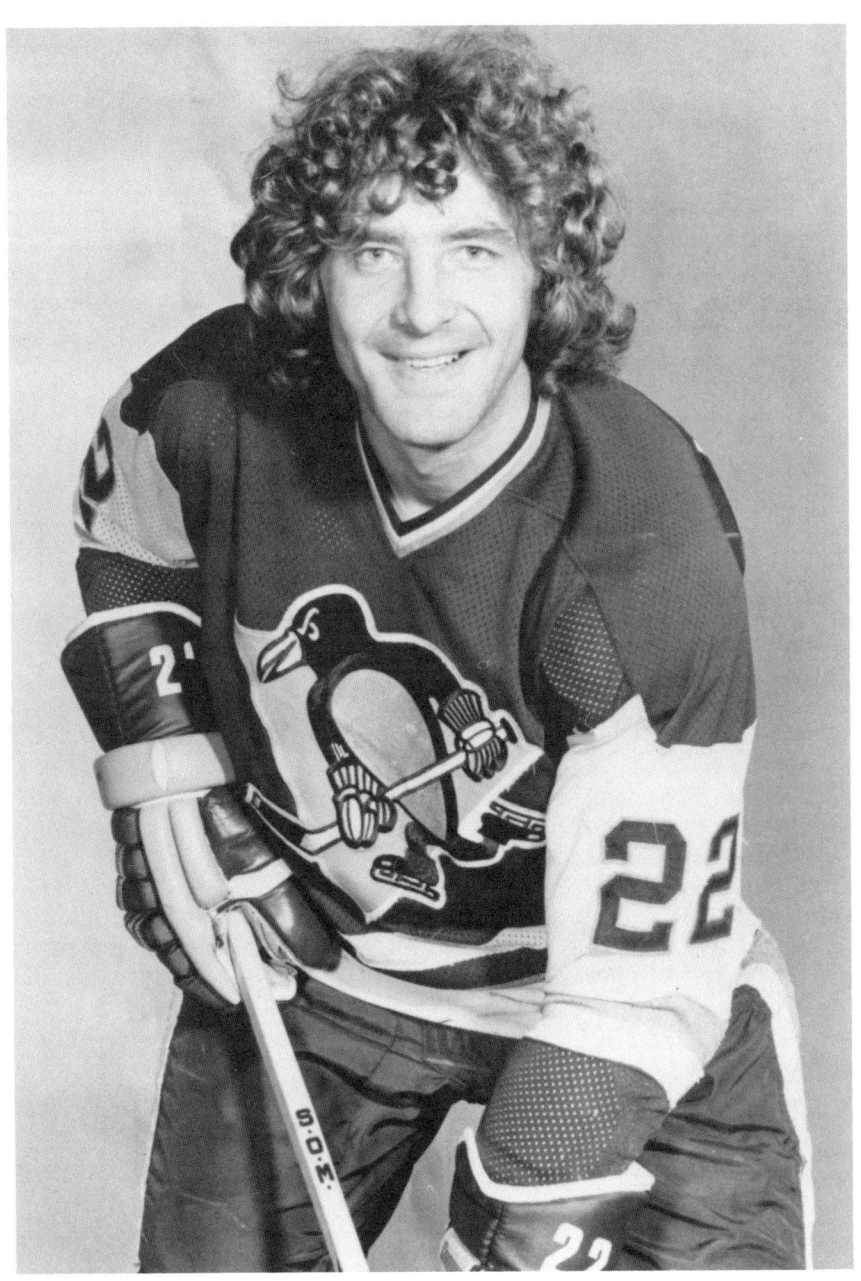
Brian Spencer

Spencer's effort: "It's crazy, yeah, but imagine how dull the world would be without guys like him. He's got great ideas."

What Spencer did, in the crowded backlot of an auto body shop — about five miles from Nassau Coliseum where he once played for the Islanders — was assemble a veritable tank of a van.

It seemed more suited for war than recreation, but maybe that was on Brian's brain, too. "I'm going back to Pittsburgh," he boasted with a mischievous smile, "and drive right over Dave Schultz's van."

No one doubted he couldn't or wouldn't do just that. Danny Hansen, a local garage mechanic and auto racing enthusiast who watched the progress of Spencer's summer project from start to finish, observed, "He can go any place he wants with that truck."

Pointing to a nearby cinder-block wall, Hansen added, "Even through that wall!"

Spencer started off with a 2 1/2 ton Army convoy truck, and took the body off it. He then installed a 651 Cummins diesel engine, the sort you'd normally find powering the biggest of tractor trailers on the highway. Atop that, he put the shell of a 1972 Dodge van, and the hood, or nose, of a Mack Truck, with the familiar bulldog ornament riding high out front.

Spencer stuffed it, with special assistance from Sherman, with all sorts of goodies — 24 volt batteries, endless wires and mechanical mishmash, a power-steering unit (Brian should have been able to handle a puck as smoothly as this van) and whatever else could be dredged up from auto wreckers round Long Island, and perhaps the nearby canals of Freeport. The cab looked like an airplane cockpit, and wherever there wasn't an instrument panel there was soft blue shag carpeting. It provided quite a contrast to Spencer's constantly black face and hands.

"Nothing just bolted in," said Spencer, "because everything was from different kinds of trucks and cars." So Spencer had to drill holes here, and cut holes there with an acetylene torch. Some things were welded together, others were held fast by brackets and so forth.

For 40 days, nearly non-stop, Spencer worked at his creation. Dr. Frankenstein didn't work any more feverishly than Spencer in assembling a monster. He would arrive at Cromwell's Auto Body each day at 8 a.m. and wouldn't leave until 10 or 10:30 p.m.

He was always covered with grease, from his blond eyebrows down to his black boots, every time we visited. You could have lubricated your car by driving over Spencer's body. He reminded me of "Dr. Dirt" from engine oil TV commercials of that period.

"He's a worker, that's for sure," said Frankie Conway, who owned and operated Cromwell's Auto Body. "We get a couple of guys like him in the shop and we'd be rich."

Such talk about Spencer's intensity did not surprise Don Luce, one of his former teammates with the Buffalo Sabres. Told about Spencer's summer-long project, Luce allowed, "When Spinner takes on something like that, no one takes it on quite the way he does."

I have never been mechanically inclined, or to crawl under a car unless I was looking for a baseball or football or coins. I think all cars and trucks that sit high off the ground should be outlawed. To me, they are a danger to the rest of society. What would happen if one of those high-flying heaps hit you? None of them ever looked attractive to me.

Spencer's summer efforts would not surprise his supporters in any of the NHL cities he called home during his pro hockey career, starting with Toronto in 1970. He alternated between Toronto and the Maple Leafs' farm team in Tulsa for three years. Then Spinner spent 1 1/2 seasons with the expansion Islanders at Nassau Coliseum — his name was on the first banners that went up in the building — and then 3 1/2 seasons in Buffalo, before he was traded to the Penguins in 1977.

He was popular wherever he went because of his hell-bent style of play, his willingness to work hard and hustle and hit. "All-out is the only way Brian Spencer knows how to play," read a line in his brief bio in the Buffalo Sabres' yearbook. "He gives 100 per cent" was the description in one of the Islanders' press guides.

His durability and intensity were cited in other booklets published by previous employers. "He's usually the only one who really hits," said Phil Goyette, his first coach with the Islanders. "He puts a little life into the team."

People always talked about Spencer in the same manner, ever since he came out of Fort St. James, British Columbia — a backwood settlement in western Canada that's as backwoods as you can get.

"I've worked around heavy equipment all my life," said Spencer. "Where I'm from, you're working against the elements all the time. You don't have a Midas Muffler shop or a garage just around the corner. You learn to handle such things yourself."

He knew he had sacrificed most of his summer on this truck/van project, and was poorer for it. He estimated there was at least $30,000 worth of equipment in it. The inside of the cab and the back of the van had more gadgets to startle the eye and boggle the brain than a "Star Wars" setting.

He had spend most of the summer in the home of Don and Penny Langton — she was in promotion and sales with the Islanders and the vice-president of the team's fan club — and away from his family in Bradford Woods, a suburban community in Pittsburgh.

He had been away from his wife, Janet, and their two children, Jason, 2 1/2, and Jared, 1. "My wife's been so good about it," said Spencer. "She's been understanding about my engineering fetishes."

That, too, hit me the wrong way. Why would a guy leave his wife and young children during the off-season to spend his time working on a truck? It struck me as irresponsible.

He got back home in time to celebrate his 29th birthday just before training camp commenced. "I don't have to worry about being in shape," he said. "I'm eight pounds under my normal weight, I've been working so hard."

That tells you something about Spencer, too, that he would confuse working on a truck to serious off-season conditioning, or getting in shape for a hockey season.

His project still wasn't completed and it certainly wasn't pretty.

Some finishing touches still had to be applied, as well as a couple coats of paint. Frankie Conway had painted the cars of several Rangers and ex-Rangers who resided in nearby Long Beach — like Walt Tkaczuk, Greg Polis, Danny Newman and Mark Heaslip — and Spencer was planning on returning the following summer to have it finished.

"I'm still just as happy as when I started," said Spencer. "I'm very impressed with it. I'll use it for recreational driving. I can go through snowstorms and never get stuck. I can pack food and supplies in it and go hunting. There's a TV set in it, too, and it's damn near indestructible."

There was a time in his life that people would have said the same of Spencer.

In 1980, after bouncing from Binghamton to Springfield to Hershey, he quit before the playoffs began that year. With 11 seasons, two marriages and five children behind him, he packed his belongings and headed for Florida.

Then one fateful night he took a ride in a pickup truck with a friend named Gregory Scott Cook. It was Cook who told police that Spencer was shot during a robbery attempt that followed a crack cocaine buy in a place called Riviera Beach, Florida at the outset of June, 1988. It seemed ironic that Spencer was shot to death in a pickup truck. He was 38. He had been working on the car for Cook.

Cook, who was 38, and had been previously arrested for possession of marijuana, told police that an unidentified robber gunned down Spencer shortly after a cocaine deal nearby. Spencer had been seen buying drugs in that area before, and that he had been seen stopping at several bars throughout the evening.

Cook and Spencer had pulled over to the roadside. A black male poked a .357 pistol into Cook's open window and demanded money. Cook turned over $2 or $3, but Spencer refused to comply. According to Cook, the man then shot Spencer.

Spencer was pronounced dead later that night at St. Mary's Hospital. The autopsy showed the bullet pierced his left arm, the left side of his chest and his heart before coming to rest in his abdomen.

His brother Byron said, "He gave everything of himself. That's the way he was. He loved life. He loved people. Maybe he was a little too outgoing."

"I hit hard and trouble seems to come to me."
—Russ Anderson

"We're constantly looking for symbolic people. They may symbolize goodness, badness, mediocrity, whatever it is. In part, it's a way to make sense of the world."
—Leo Braudy
Literary historian

When beer made its debut at Arena
Imagine a game without any brew
There was no beer in first season

Here's an article that appeared in October 11, 1968 issue of **Pittsburgh Weekly Sports:**

The Public Auditorium Authority has voted to permit the sale of beer in soft containers at the Civic Arena beginning October 12 (1968) when the Pittsburgh Penguins open their National Hockey League season against the Montreal Canadiens.

Iron City and Duquesne beer will be dispensed at concession stands, but vendors will not be selling it in the stands, it has been learned by *Pittsburgh Weekly Sports.*

The Penguins had appealed to the Authority board in recent months, urging them to permit the sale of beer. Every other NHL arena, except for the one in Oakland, California, has beer sold at concession stands.

It was prohibited by law, until an amendment to existing legislation in Harrisburg was made two years ago, to sell beer at public arenas in this state. Last year, beer was sold at the Spectrum in Philadelphia.

The Authority studied the matter and learned that there had been no special problems at the arenas that sell beer, other than those which might occur whenever a crowd is assembled at a sports event.

Beer and other alcoholic beverages have always been banned from Forbes Field and Pitt Stadium, but fans still sneak in a few bottles. It has never been sold at either sports facility. This may have caused the problems which have existed.

Fans brought bottled beer, some as much as a case or more, and drank to excess and became obnoxious in their behavior at the ballpark. Other fans complained, and rightfully so, about the drunken orgies in some cases.

The Arena will permit the sale on a seasonal trial basis. The Igloo, a private club for season ticket holders who care to come up with an extra $100 for membership, will also make its debut on October 12. Beer and whiskey and mixed drinks will be available there.

Welcoming Back The Penguins
Checking out practice

"I'm teaching all the time."
—Eddie Johnston

The Penguins were practicing at the Civic Arena prior to attending a luncheon where they would be honored by the Greater Pittsburgh Chamber of Commerce.

It was one of the annual rituals suffered by the players. They were not always comfortable at getting that close to the fans, or to the city's dark business suits over grilled chicken and fettucini alfredo. They weren't always as deft with a knife and fork as they were with hockey sticks, and conversation with strangers didn't always come easy. Most of them were too young to understand why management asked them to do things like this. It is not so bad once you get by the political proclamations that always find their way for whatever reason into such programs, with the "wherefore" and "whereas" repetitiveness, and you realize that the dark business suits won't smack your hands with the butter knife.

It was officially called the Pittsburgh Penguins 1993 Face-Off Luncheon. The site was the 17th floor ballroom of the Westin William Penn Hotel, about four blocks from the Arena where Centre Avenue runs into Grant Street. It's a refurbished old-fashioned sort of ballroom, the kind they don't build anymore, and there's a grand, opulent look to it.

But that task of meeting their public was still ahead of them as they went about the business of getting ready for the 1993-94 National Hockey League season, which was just a week away. September would soon be over, and October and the real stuff, or regular season scrimmages, would soon be starting. Some critics insist that the real stuff doesn't start until the Stanley Cup playoffs commence, but most fans don't feel that way.

The Civic Arena was a noisy workshop. Construction was still going on to get the Arena ready for the opener, and the workers about the building were attacking their assignments with as much intensity as the Penguins at practice.

Sparks were flying here and there as welders sealed joints on the bars that separated various seating sections. Power saws were buzzing. Something was screeching. Sounds of spinning steel cutting into cement created a sound every so often that was harsh to the ear, and gave one shivvers.

Fifteen hundred more seats had been added to the Arena during the summer months, boosting capacity to 17,537 for hockey, 18,500 for concerts. More skyboxes had been added to boost attendance and revenues. There were more orange-red seats in the building than ever before, and only a half dozen of them were occupied for the practice session. Some office staffers and some construction workers were taking a break to catch the Penguins at practice. There were now seats in the uppermost ceiling of the Civic Arena. They would have to open the roof, which is still possible, if they wanted to squeeze in any more fans. The Arena still boasts of having the largest retractable steel roof for such a building. The new press box was as high in the sky as they could go. It was as close to heaven as most of the media would ever get. A guy could get a nosebleed in that lofty atmosphere. The Penguins couldn't possibly appear to be the biggest team in the NHL from up there.

I was sitting in a seat, about 15 rows off center ice, or where the press seats used to be when the building first opened back in early 1961. I was sitting in on a practice that was off limits to the public, one of those situations that sports writers take for granted, not always realizing how the average fan would love to be in their place. There wasn't an actual press box to begin with in this facility, which was originally called the Civic Auditorium because the Civic Light Opera was the prime tenant. Somebody forgot to include a press box in the plans, which shows that the press was never a prime consideration in the Civic Arena. But the same thing happened at Madison Square Garden and Nassau Coliseum, which the Rangers and Islanders call home, respectively. I know this from working in those buildings when they originally opened.

Eddie Johnston waved from mid-ice when he spotted me in the stands, and that made me feel more at home. After all, I had not attended a hockey practice at the Arena, or anywhere else for that matter, for probably 20 years. I was still a stranger among the Penguins, and feeling a little uneasy in strange halls. But Johnston would soon change that, as he would introduce me to everybody who passed us the remainder of the day. And he would do the same for weeks to come.

I wanted to catch up, to get into hockey again in a hurry-up manner, the way the Penguins were practicing.

That may account for why I was as interested or fascinated with the choreography of the skaters on the ice before me. Most of the media were elsewhere in the building, entertaining each other with the latest gossip, and waiting for the coach and players to come off the ice so they could stick a tape recorder or camera in their faces for their latest words of wisdom, or sound bites. They passed on practice. It was boring, they thought. Covering every game of the regular season, and maintaining an interest and enthusiasm, can be demanding enough. They had watched earlier practices and it is not something you would want to do on a daily basis. Though you never know when someone will get hurt or pull up lame in practice. I always found it worthwhile to watch practice, as often as possible, when covering a club in any sport. Something always happened that you could use in a report on that day's news. There was always a scene, or some activity or exchange, that could be woven into a story.

It brought a story to mind. I remember that Chester L. Smith, the late sports editor of the late *Pittsburgh Press*, was once asked back in the '60s by Jim Tarman, the sports information director at Penn State University back then, what time he wanted picked up at his hotel to attend a Penn State football practice on the eve of a game at University Park.

"Are they going to be doing something they haven't done at every other football practice that's ever been held?" Smith shot back at Tarman, as Smith ate his breakfast at the Nittany Lion Inn on the central Pennsylvania campus. Penn State's SID looked perplexed by Smith's inquiry.

"I'll pass," said Smith with a smile. "I don't watch practices. If you can guarantee me they'll surprise me, I might consider going."

Of course, Smith also said if they played the national college basketball championship outside his bedroom window, he would pull down the window shades. College football was his true passion, but not college football practices.

I was intrigued, however, as I studied the skating drills. Cindy Himes, the Penguins' public relations director, joined me in the seats briefly, sitting in the row behind me, and identifying some new players. "You can tell a lot about a player by the way he practices," offered Himes, who has been checking out such practices since she first joined the Penguins as a student intern from nearby Duquesne University in 1977. The last time Himes had sat near me, exactly a month earlier, she was a few rows ahead of me in great seats to see *Phantom of the Opera* at the Benedum Center in Downtown Pittsburgh. We both were still raving about that stirring performance as she filled me in on some recent club activity.

The Penguins had pared the practice squad by six players the day before, and were close to the regular season squad of 23 or 25 players. They would be signing several players to new contracts the following day, and that would include Bryan Trottier.

He had been hired on June 22 by Craig Patrick to serve as an assistant to Johnston, but had indicated that he also wanted to attempt a comeback as a player after a year's layoff. Management really wanted him just to coach, but were convinced that he could still help the cause. Continued expansion had thinned the ranks of legitimate NHL players. An old-timer like Trottier could still hold his own in spot duty. It appeared that his training camp and pre-season game performances had been satisfactory enough to continue the experiment. Trottier's intensity, face-off dominance, skills, skating ability, leadership and Stanley Cup experience were tough to ignore. He knew what he was doing out there and, most of all, he knew how to win.

> *"Even without Mario, that team has great players. In my opinion, the only thing missing last season was someone to crack the whip."*
> —Rick Tocchet,
> LA Kings
> September, 1994

> *"You can cut the ribbons*
> *out of a guy hitting*
> *a rolling puck."*
> —Eddie Johnston

The Penguins were wearing different colored jerseys during the practice session, and there was a significance to the color scheme. Just like *A Chorus Line*. Everyone had a role to play and the different-colored costumes helped to identify everyone. The defensemen all wore black — the bad guys, of course — and they were all at one end of the ice, working with assistant coach Rick Kehoe. Tom Barrasso was the goalie for their drills.

Johnston was skating here and there at the other end, still nimble as he moved about the ice, wielding a stick, and moving the puck to this player and that player, and hollering out so he could be heard over the workers' din, offering instruction when necessary, telling the players where they should be and what they should do. Ken Wregget was their goalie.

Johnston was working with four offensive lines. One wore white, another wore teal blue — that dark greenish blue popularized by the Charlotte Hornets of the National Basketball Association — another wore light gray and the other gold-yellow. Kehoe had ten players, plus a goalie, and Johnston had 12 players, plus a goalie. There were 28 people on the ice altogether.

The white line consisted of Trottier, Rick Tocchet and Kevin Stevens, the teal line was Joey Mullen, Ron Francis and Jaromir Jagr, the gray line was Markus Naslund, Leonid Toropchenko and one of the other players would fill in, and the yellow line was Jeff Daniels, Doug Brown and Martin Straka.

Mario Lemieux was missing from the activity. He would come onto the ice after the other players departed, and he skated for about ten minutes, his first skating session of the pre-season camp. He was under doctor's orders to give his balky back more rest. He was not expected to rejoin the team until the end of October. Lemieux was the man most responsible for all those extra orange-red seats — this was the second expansion since he joined the team in 1984. The original capacity of the Civic Arena was just under 13,000.

The defensemen in black formed what Johnston described as a horse shoe alignment — a semi-circle about 30 feet from Barrasso — and began to fire pucks at him in machine-gun fashion. One player after another would take a swipe at a puck. It was like a black wave, each player in turn from right to left unleasing a shot. One stick after another was swung high in the air and then swept downward like they were cutting wheat with a vengeance. The movement was similar to the high-stepping of legs of the Rockettes at Radio City Music Hall, or any Las Vegas or Atlantic City chorus line. Barrasso knew where each shot would come from. The players knew the rules: don't shoot out of turn, keep the shots low, and never, never strike a rolling puck.

"You can't control where it's going," Johnston said afterward in his office. "You can cut the ribbons out of a guy hitting a rolling puck. I've seen it happen. If you hear a guy cursing on the ice, it's usually the goalie getting after somebody for taking a dangerous shot. The goalies won't stand still for it. You can't afford to lose a goalie like that in practice."

The target practice has a rhythm to it. The pucks are fired from right to left, or Barrasso's left to right, and then it goes back in the opposite direction. Non-stop. The victims in the St. Valentine's Day Massacre didn't catch as much flak. At one point, Barrasso put aside his wide stick, and stood there trying to stop pucks with his pads and glove. He fielded the hardest shots with the glove on his right hand, blocked some shots with his leg pads, kicked at others. Some skimmed off his pads into the nets, others eluded him altogether. He thwarted the majority of shots that came his way. The action was fast and furious.

The part I liked best was when the players mixed, and in fivesomes or, in two cases, sixsomes, would skate in line about the rink. A lead-off skater would set the pace and the direction, and they would head this way, and then turn harshly, cutting the ice and sending a spray off their skates, as they swerved and went back where they came from. It was like roller derby on ice skates, something hockey has been called by its harshest critics, when they would come around a curve one after another, so close on each other's steel-plated heels. The hockey players weren't holding onto each other's hips, but they were skating close in formation, like the Flying Angels aero show teams. Occasionally, they'd elbow each other, like schoolchildren in a cafeteria line, just for the hell of it. It was fun to watch. Too often, the skating skills of hockey players are taken for granted. The majority of hockey fans have no way to appreciate that particular ability. Most hockey fans have never been on ice skates.

The goalies were skating around solo, not as swiftly, and not taking the turns quite as sharply as the other skaters. Those bulky leg-pads make it difficult to look too smooth in skate-arounds. Goalies are hockey's answer to the kickers in football. They are different. They are always apart from the pack. They are often isolated like lepers at practice and workouts. They have different psyches and sensitivities. They are under more pressure than most of the players.

The swift skating, with the quick turns, was demanding on the legs. It's a conditioning drill. When they stopped and took a break, and removed their helmets, the players' hair was wet and standing up in shocks. Everybody was sweating, rivulets running down their cheeks. Some leaned on the sideboards. Some squeezed green Gatorade bottles and shot a stream into their wide-open mouths for refreshment.

The practice lasted less than two hours.

"Players don't want to stand around."

There was a yellow sign with a black printed message in Johnston's Arena office that read: **YOU MAKE THE DIFFERENCE**. Johnston could read it as he changed his attire after practice. There was a method to the madness I had watched from my seat on the sidelines. Johnston showed me some large yellow legal pads on which he had scrawled in large letters what he wanted to accomplish at practice that day. He transcribed his notes onto a small white index card that he carried in a pocket with him during practice.

The practice had started, for instance, with ten minutes of stretching and warm-up skating. Another session followed in which the defensemen and wings worked at getting the puck out of the defensive end of the ice. Drills were designed to improve the way the Penguins would come out of their own end of the rink. Johnston took the centers and goalies to the other end to work on something different.

This was followed by shooting drills. Johnston said he changed this part at every practice. They worked on four-corner drills, and there were maneuvers when one man and then two men in tandem would assault the goalie.

Then they worked on back-checking, and sometimes it was two on two, sometimes three on two, and then four on three, recreating the kinds of situations the skaters were sure to find themselves in during a game. They worked on some plays, moving about in a thought-out maneuver. Then there were shifts in which the skaters went full tilt. There was constant motion. There were what Johnston calls reaction drills. Players were tested to see if they knew what their options are under certain circumstances, what their outlets were, where their teammates were supposed to be stationed in different situations. Hockey players, as well as football players and basketball players and baseball, must have a sense of where they are at all times. They must have a "feel" for where their teammates are, where the side boards or corners are, where the goal is located. Without always looking.

"You want to have flow all the time," Johnston explained afterward. "There's more of an onus on skating today than there was when I was playing. We have very up-tempo practices. You don't stand around; players don't want to stand around. You want to get everyone going, and work like hell. You have a purpose to your practice."

I noticed Johnston saying things to players as he pushed the puck their way on a particular play. He'd holler out something on some occasions, skate up to a player and get close for a quick conversation.

I mentioned that Chuck Noll, the former coach of the Steelers, enjoyed the one-on-one instruction as much as any aspect of practice sessions. "I'm teaching all the time; you have to work with them, some more than others, of course," Johnston said.

"I was showing them how to set picks and screens to help set up shots. You have to be careful how you do it so you don't get whistled

Eddie Johnston joins Joe DiMaggio on golf course and Teddy Green and Bobby Orr at Bruins 20th year Stanley Cup reunion.

Eddie, Diane and Joseph at Penguins' 1993 Christmas party.

Johnston Family Album

for it, just like in football and basketball. There are illegal picks and you have to know what you're doing."

I asked Johnston which players practiced the hardest and had the best attitude about it.

"Kevin and Ulfie and Tochett come very enthused. Both Samuelssons. Ronnie Francis hates to miss any days.

"We have a good work ethic here. Guys appreciate a good practice. If the guys know you're going to go like hell they'll give you a good effort."

The team travels in a no-nonsense manner, too. "We have our own plane now, and we just go in and out," Johnston told someone on the telephone.

Johnston's critics insist he's not really in charge of the team, that the stars, starting with Lemieux on down, do pretty much as they choose to do. That they humor Johnston. He gets along with them, contend the critics, because he doesn't demand anything of them. Everyone likes Johnston, but some question his hockey coaching ability.

"Francis was the fans' favorite player."

I live around the corner from Johnston in Upper St. Clair and I had seen his youngest son, Joseph, 12, playing street hockey in front of their home. Joseph Johnston is a combination of Mario Lemieux and Mike Lange, handling the puck and shooting like Lemieux — in his mind, anyhow — and accompanying his movement to his own excited play-by-play call like Lange. Sometimes he's Ronnie Francis, too.

"He never skated, and he came to a Christmas party during our second year at Hartford, and Ronnie Francis bought him a pair of skates, and started him playing hockey," recalled Johnston. "When I traded Ronnie Francis to Pittsburgh all kind of chaos broke out in my home. Ronnie was his favorite player with the Whalers. He was so mad at me for ten days. He wouldn't talk to me. He couldn't understand how I could do it. There were a lot of fans in Hartford who were mad at me, too. Francis was the fans' favorite player. But I was under orders from the owner to do it. He thought Hartford had become a country club, and he wanted changes. Joseph started playing hockey last year. He just turned 12; he was 10 when Ronnie got him the skates. His team was the state Squirt B championship team. My older son, E.J., is at Penn State, and my daughter, Michele, is in her last year at the University of Hartford. Joseph made the AA team and the freshman team at Upper St. Clair High School. He plays left wing. He plays street hockey and rollerdeck hockey. He's really got the bug now. I have cautioned him about his approach. I tell him to have fun."

"How about E.J.?" I asked Johnston.

"He played for a few years when I was in Chicago, but when he came here his buddies were playing soccer and skiing, so he turned to that. Soccer became his sport."

I asked Johnston what age most of the Penguins began playing hockey. "They started at five or six, for the most part," said Johnston.

It was difficult for me to determine what kind of skater Johnston was as I watched him at practice. To me, he skated like most of the men his age that I've seen striding around gingerly at the Mt. Lebanon Recreation Ice Rink. Nothing special.

"You have to be a good skater to play goal," Johnston said.

"I always thought they put the poorest skater in goal," I said to Johnston.

"It used to be that way," Johnston said. "Because nobody wanted to go in there. Especially when you were playing hockey outside. You'd freeze your butt off, just standing there. Smart guys didn't want to be in there. But you have to be a good skater now. You have to be a good skater to keep your balance, to go up and down, to move from here to there as quickly as you need to in order to stop shots."

"Who were the starting goalies in the league when you were playing?" I asked Johnston.

"Terry Sawchuck was in Detroit, Glenn Hall in Chicago, Jacques Plante in Montreal, Gump Worsley in New York, Johnny Bower in Toronto and myself in Boston."

"And nobody sat down, is that right?" I asked.

"Nobody wanted to lose his job, so they stayed in there," Johnston said. "One year I broke my nose three times in ten days. It happened Wednesday night, again on Thursday and Saturday night the following week."

"I guess they all heard about Wally Pipp," I said.

"I know I've heard that name, but I'm not sure who he was," Johnston said.

Rick Kehoe had come into Johnston's office as we were talking. I asked Kehoe if he had ever heard of Wally Pipp. Kehoe shook his head negatively.

Wally Pipp, I explained, had been the regular first baseman for the New York Yankees. He took a day off once and was replaced by Lou Gehrig. Gehrig went on to play the next 2,130 consecutive games.

Johnston may not have been familiar with Wally Pipp, but he was not going to provide a job opening for anybody. "I came off the airplane in Boston after I broke my nose for the third time in ten days," Johnston recalled, "and my eyes were closed shut. I went right to Mass General (Hospital) and I laid on a table for an hour. They stuck leeches on my eyes to draw the blood out. That's what they did in those days. I went home and got up the next day and played that night. It was all out of fear. Fear was a big factor back then. There simply weren't that many jobs in the NHL. The competition for spots was fierce. I loved playing in the National Hockey League and I didn't want to lose it.

"I got hit by a puck in the ear that year, and it tore my ear lobe. It was just dangling. Just hanging there. It was bleeding. They sewed it back on between periods. The only guy who was wearing a mask then was Jacques Plante. He was the first one to wear one in the NHL. That's the answer to a hockey trivia question. I was the last goalie to play every game in a season.

"That's because I had no brains. Plante was the only guy with brains.

"In Boston, I replaced Bobby Perreault in 1962. He started the season and I was hurt. He played about five games, then I took over. I later played one year in Toronto, then I was in St. Louis for four years, and I finished up as a player in Chicago."

Johnston does not need much in the way of a cue to provide a good story.

"The trainer was your backup goalie. We had a guy in Boston named John Aitken, who was a fireman. He became the chief fireman in Boston. He was a great guy. I got hurt in this one game, and John had to go in for me. They were putting the pads on him, and his legs were shaking so bad. He was like a man who'd been put in an electric chair. They had to hold his legs just to tie the pads on. That's how nervous he was. He had to go in for me at Boston Garden and he had a bad case of the nerves. They scored on the first shot from center ice. After that, he was OK."

Johnston had to laugh at his own story. I told him he was a storehouse of such stories.

"When we get together at a golf outing, or have some kind of reunion," Johnston said. "We'd bring up stuff and what we got away with. We'd laugh till six in the morning.

"We had a great team when I was in Boston. We had a club very similar to the one we have here now. We had Bobby Orr, Phil Esposito, Johnny Bucyk, Ken Hodge, Derek Sanderson, Wayne Cashman, Teddy Green and Gerry Cheevers. Orr was the big guy, like we have Mario here. There are a lot of similarities. Cheevers was a good goalie. He could win 1-0 or 8-7. One year, 1967-68, we alternated at goalie, taking our turn every other game.

"I got hit in the head one year (1969-70 season) at practice. I got hurt in late October and I didn't go back until February. I went from weighing 205 to 160 in 48 hours. Nothing was functioning right. I got hurt during a warm-up in Detroit. There were two or three pucks on the ice. I knew Orr was going to take a shot, but I took my eye off him to peek at Eddie Shack. He was always joking around, and I looked at him because I thought he might hit a puck at me.

"Orr caught me in the side of a head with a slap shot. It knocked me down. They took me to the hospital that night, and brought me back on the airplane after the game that same night. No way they'd do that today.

"I spent six or seven weeks in the hospital. Actually, I ended up staying in the hospital longer than I should have. The guys came to the hospital one night and got me all excited and carrying on. I was on medication, and it screwed me up. I got all messed up again. I had to stay two weeks longer. I had a blood clot in my head. They wanted to operate, but the doctors all had different opinions about what should be done. I think I stayed in the hospital for eight weeks altogether."

"Pittsburgh has really changed for the better since I came here."
—Rick Kehoe

I told Johnston I needed to go to the bathroom, and asked him where I might find one. He directed me through two doors, and the next thing I knew I was in the players' locker room. Most of them had just showered and were walking about with towels wrapped around their middles. Some were shaving. Others were combing their hair. Some were standing at the nearby urinals. I was wearing a business suit. None of them knew me. I felt so out of place. I figured they must have been wondering, "Who the hell is this guy? What's he doing in here?" It was a wasted trip. I was too ill at ease to do what I'd come to the urinal to do in the first place. Maybe Eddie was rushing things, a little, I thought.

There was some interesting activity about me. Jaromir Jagr, the 20-year-old wunderkind who was the favorite of so many young women who followed the Penguins, was wearing black sweatpants. He was barechested and barefooted. He was posing in front of a mirror, playfully, flexing his muscles, striking some sexy poses — pulling his towel down a little to expose some more skin — having fun. His fans would have fainted if they had seen him up close and personal like this.

Trottier, the oldest player on the team at 37, was lying on the floor, doing sit-ups. He looked like an old boxer. In fact, most of the hockey players looked like boxers, with the nicks and scratches about their faces, and muscular frames. "You getting ready for a fight tonight?" I asked Trottier. He smiled. He had a shiner over his right eye. "I don't know about tonight, but I'm sure I'll have a few this season," he said. Ulf Samuelsson came by. He smiled and said hello. He was shorter than I expected, handsomer than I expected, and was impressive the way his wide shoulders contrasted with his narrow waist. He was a tough-looking customer. I introduced myself and spoke briefly with Barrasso and Mullen.

Several media types were in the room, interviewing Johnston and several players, like Tom McMillan, who doubled as a contributing writer for *Penguins Report* as well as a sports talk show host and hockey analyst for WTAE Radio. McMillan had covered the Penguins for the *Post-Gazette* for several seasons, and had a real passion for the sport. He had left the *Post-Gazette* two years earlier in favor of free-lance activity. Eric Hagman of KQV and John Duffy, who filed radio reports for UPI and several area stations, were there as well.

Lemieux declined to talk to the news reporters. He had a club spokesman tell them he felt fine after his short skate.

I walked from the Arena to the Westin William Penn Hotel with Johnston and Kehoe as company. We chatted as we strolled down Centre Avenue on a pleasant fall day. It was a bit brisk, with temperatures in the mid-50s, but you didn't need a topcoat for the four-block sojourn.

Most of the players walked the distance, while some drove there in cars. They didn't look much different from the young businessmen who work in the nearby USX Tower. But there probably haven't been as many millionaires making the stroll since the days when Richard W. Mellon and Henry Clay Frick moved about in that same area.

"Pittsburgh has really changed for the better since I first came here," commented Kehoe, checking out the landscape ahead of us.

"Mayor Caliguiri deserves credit for much of that," Johnston said. "Geez, he was good for this town. Geez, the city misses him."

Caliguiri had been the mayor of Pittsburgh from 1977 to 1988 and was considered the catalyst for Renaissance II. Mayor David L. Lawrence filled a similar role in Renaissance I, when Pittsburgh cleaned up considerably and took on a new and impressive Downtown skyline.

Both were big sports fans and champions of the city. Indeed, Pittsburgh was labeled "The City of Champions" during Caliguiri's reign. The Steelers, Pirates and Pitt, to name a few of the city's representatives, all won championships in the '70s.

"I knew Caliguiri when I was a kid," I told Johnston and Kehoe. "I was the sports editor of the bi-weekly newspaper in our section of Pittsburgh, and I used to visit a local bowling alley each week to get scores, and Caligiuri looked after the place for his dad. I was 14 and he was only a few years older. He always helped me when he could when he became the mayor."

Johnston said, "Caliguiri had a way with people. He was a popular and effective leader."

Johnston had to hope that people in Pittsburgh would be saying the same about him some day.

"I remember walking just a block from here one day when I spotted Tim Horton when he was playing with the Maple Leafs," I said. "Here Horton was one of the great defensemen in the National Hockey League, and he was walking in front of the Carlton House Hotel with several of his teammates, and they didn't turn a single head."

"Horton played here for the Penguins, and before that, early in his career, with the Pittsburgh Hornets," said Kehoe. "He met his wife here. He married a Pittsburgh girl."

"Where's Horton nowadays," I asked. "Is he still in hockey?"

"Horton is dead," Johnston said. "He was killed in an auto accident. He was the third star in a hockey game that same night, and he was in an auto accident on the way home that night."

"It's good to see Mario doing something for the Penguins."
—Wise-cracking sportswriter

At the William Penn, Johnston and Kehoe were among those who sat at the dais. Kehoe sat next to Mayor Sophie Masloff. Also seated on the dais were Allegheny County Commissioner Larry Dunn and hockey broadcasters Mike Lange, Paul Steigerwald and Stan Savran. Mario Lemieux and Bryan Trottier were seated there, too.

"It's good to see Mario doing something for the Penguins," said a sports writer at the table where I was sitting. There were several young women at our table. Two of them were so thrilled at being in the same room with all those Penguins. They made pests of themselves, however, seeking signatures from the players while they were eating, and were publicly chastised by a Chamber of Commerce leader over the microphone.

Except for Lemieux and Trottier, the rest of the players were spread around the room, each of them representing the team at a table with seven or eight fans.

Nearly two years earlier, at a celebration at Three Rivers Stadium marking a second straight Stanley Cup triumph, Mayor Masloff had mimicked one of Lange's signature hockey calls, by screeching into a microphone, "Well, scratch my back with a hacksaw!" Her cry raised the hair on many people's necks, as most of her boisterous cries at such celebrations normally did. She is a graduate of the Myron Cope School of Broadcasting.

So this time Lange presented Mayor Masloff with a hacksaw, just to have some fun. The Mayor, who is a good sport, went along with the gag. She didn't say much, which was smart on her part.

"I'm here to deny the rumor that I've been hired as Mike Lange's colorman," said Mayor Masloff. Not bad. "When the Penguins won back-to-back Stanley Cups, that was one of the highlights of my tenure as mayor."

But she couldn't resist employing another Lange line, "Get in the fast lane, Grandma, the bingo game is about to start!" Then she returned to her seat.

All the others offered a few pre-season remarks.

Lange alluded to Johnston's return to Pittsburgh, by saying, "Once a 'burger, always a 'burger."

Johnston said, "I don't think you know how great it is to be back in Pittsburgh."

In his remarks, he said he was happy "to coach these wonderful bunch of guys" and "this tremendous bunch of young players."

He also said, "My No. 1 goal is to bring the Stanley Cup back to the City of Champions."

Soon after the remarks were concluded, several of the Penguins made a fastbreak from the room, trying to beat the traffic.

"Is it easier to stop pucks than to do this?" I asked Tom Barrasso, the Penguins' gritty goalie, as he moved swiftly past me in a hallway.

"Yes, and it pays much better," Barrasso shot back.

He was hurrying to catch an elevator before the crowd departed the luncheon. There were not that many elevators and the luncheon was held in a ballroom on the 17th floor, so he didn't want to end up standing around waiting for an elevator.

Suddenly, someone shouted, "Hold that elevator! Mario's coming!"

The young staffer in the Penguins office made this cry as if he were sounding an alarm, such as "The British are coming!"

Barrasso shouted. "Big deal! To hell with Mario! Let him wait!" Then he smiled as Mario moved into the elevator. The elevator got a lot smaller in a hurry. Mario looks big enough on the ice. In an elevator, he is even bigger.

Red Fisher
The Dean of Hockey Writers

"Without Lemieux, Pittsburgh wouldn't be in the NHL today."

Red Fisher is the foremost hockey writer in North America. He is a respected newspaper reporter who has covered the Montreal Canadiens beat and written a sports column for Montreal newspapers for over 40 years.

This surely makes him the dean of hockey writers on the National Hockey League scene. "The guy would have to be a hundred years old to top me," offered Fisher when I asked him about his status in the ice sport. He was 67 and looked terrific when he took in the game between the Canadiens and the Pittsburgh Penguins in the home opener at the Civic Arena on Thursday, October 7, 1993. He had no plans to retire. "I'm going to do it until I get it right," he said with a wink.

Fisher sat at the end of a lineup of five members of the Montreal media contingent in the new press box at the Arena, high in the sky, but still offering a fine view of the action below. Fisher held to old-fashioned standards, as he wore a muted green sportcoat, a white button-down dress shirt, a contemporary multi-colored tie that had some green in there somewhere, and gray glen plaid slacks and dark shoes. Some sportswriters these days dress as if they are planning to change tires on a tractor, so Fisher was a reminder of a more refined era. When the fourth estate looked the part. Fisher reminded me of George Burns as he talked easily and authoritatively about his favorite game, peppering his comments with a jibe or flippant remark. All he needed was a cigar to complete the act.

Jack Riley, the original general manager of the Penguins, was in the press box working for the league office, reviewing instant replays on controversial calls. When he spotted me speaking to Fisher, he said, "Red told me hockey would never go in Pittsburgh. I wonder what he thinks now."

Riley was referring to the fact that there were more people in the seats for this 1993-94 season opener than for any previous home game in the franchise history. The Penguins had added 1,100 seats during the summer, expanding the capacity at the Civic Arena to 17,537 compared to 12,800 when Riley ruled the team back in its maiden season of 1967-68. Fisher and Riley, both redheads, exchanged smiles.

I approached Fisher and sat down next to him because I felt he could offer an intelligent, outsider's view of what has transpired during the previous 26 years with the Penguins, and how the team and its star performer, Mario Lemieux, stacked up with other franchises during Fisher's tenure at the typewriter and, more recently, a laptop computer. After all, no one had watched better hockey for a longer period of time than Fisher. The Canadiens had long set the standard for excellence in the NHL. We spoke while the game was going on, and Fisher took notes on the hockey activity while he fielded my questions. He was in mid-season form.

Lemieux was missing from the Penguins' lineup, resting a bad back which had caused him to miss the team's training camp and pre-season schedule. He was scheduled to return at the end of October, but some suspected he might be out much longer. Lemieux had made light of missing the pre-season games, and early schedule, which did not sit well with season ticket holders, especially at the recently-inflated ticket prices, or with some sportswriters.

Like Lemieux, Fisher is a legendary figure in the business, and takes pride in his enduring reign as one of the most knowledgeable and respected writers around the league.

Fisher has a good sense of humor. That has helped him to keep company and travel with the same hockey club for so many years. "It's easier to do it with a club like the Canadiens," said Fisher, firmly, the way he says everything. "I couldn't have done it with a team like the Pittsburgh Penguins during the same period. You couldn't do it with a shit team. It's easier when you're with a winner. Some of these people who are here tonight may not realize it, but the Penguins have just started to win.

"The Canadiens won their 24th Stanley Cup last season," he continued. "I've covered this team during 17 of those championships. Do you know anyone who's won 24 Super Bowls, or 24 World Series, or 24 NBA championships? No, the Yankees and Celtics come the closest, but no one's really that close. The Canadiens are in a class by themselves."

The Yankees have won 22 World Series. The Celtics have won 16 NBA titles.

Fisher was on hand, of course, the night before in Montreal when the club hoisted its 24th Stanley Cup banner into the rafters before the season opener at the fabled Montreal Forum on St. Catherine Street. He mentioned that Jean Beliveau, the Hall of Famer who once graced the ice for the red-and-blue shirted Canadiens, took part in the ceremonies. Beliveau remains one of the classiest athletes ever to compete in any sport. The Canadiens had displaced the Penguins as league playoff champions after the Penguins had put two consecutive banners into the ceiling of their own building. So, interestingly enough, it was the third year in a row that a defending Stanley Cup champion was skating in the opener at the Civic Arena.

Lemieux led the Penguins to their two titles. Regarded as the greatest player in the game, and the successor to Wayne Gretzky in that respect, Lemieux grew up a few blocks away from the Montreal Forum. He is French-Canadian, and would have been an enormously popular player in his hometown. Even more than he is wearing the black and gold of Pittsburgh.

"There was no outpouring of great disappointment in Montreal when they didn't get him," said Fisher. "They knew the team with the poorest record gets the best player in the draft — though it doesn't always work out that way — so nobody marched on the Forum. Nobody wanted them to change the rules so the Canadiens could get Mario Lemieux. They dealt with it the same way they did when Gil Perreault was drafted (from the Junior Canadiens) by Buffalo (in 1970).

"Everybody in the Montreal Forum is a Mario Lemieux fan. If he scores a goal in the Forum, he'll get a bigger ovation than anyone on the Canadiens. Everybody in Montreal is aware that he's the best in the game."

"What kind of commotion would Mario Lemieux create if he were seen walking down the main street of Montreal?" I asked Fisher. "Here in Pittsburgh, most hockey players go unrecognized when they're out of uniform and crossing a Downtown street."

"Paul DiPietro can walk down the street and create a traffic jam in Montreal," said Fisher, referring to a rookie starting what could be his first full season with the Canadiens. "and he's scored just five NHL goals so far. That's the difference. That's just the way it is. We've missed out on having some great players, but these guys have won 24 Stanley Cups, so they've hardly had any complaints.

"They wished they had Mike Bossy here, too — even though he wasn't a true French-Canadian — because he grew up in Montreal. We had to wait a long time to get Denny Savard, and they would have liked to have had him from the start, too. Hey, it's natural that every team would like to have the best players. But the fans in Montreal have had more than their share of star players."

I had not seen Fisher for 20 years, or since I traveled to Montreal with the New York Islanders after their inception in the early '70s. I mentioned that it was a thrill to meet Beliveau and Rocket Richard in the media room prior to the game, and how impressive they were. I remembered those two and that they had red-checkered tablecloths. I mentioned that Beliveau, in particular, struck me as a class act, causing the same sort of stir in a press room as I remembered Joe DiMaggio might when he came into the midst of those in the media room at Yankee Stadium.

"Beliveau retired from a front office position with the Canadiens on his 62nd birthday," said Fisher. "But he was there last night to raise the 24th Stanley Cup banner."

"Is he the most popular of the ex-Canadiens?" I asked.

"If the Rocket and Beliveau walked into the Forum one after the other, within a minute of each other, Rocket would get the bigger ovation," replied Fisher. "It's just that Rocket Richard always did that to people. He just lifted them out of their seats more often than anyone else, with the possible exception of Guy Lafleur.

"Beliveau is the best possible example of what an athlete should be in any city, anywhere. He's always been the biggest guy in any room he walked into."

People in Pittsburgh, of course, figure there has never been anyone better than Lemieux, and Fisher would not argue about that. But Lemieux is not Fisher's all-time favorite.

"Over the 40-year period that you have covered the NHL," I asked, "who was the best player you ever saw?"

"The guy who pulled me out of my seat more than anyone was Bobby Orr," Fisher responded. "Lemieux is pretty close, with some of the things he's done, especially the last few years. What he did last year: coming back so strong after being diagnosed with Hodgkins disease, was just mind-boggling. Lemieux is right in the ballpark.

"But they had different kinds of skills. The thing that made Orr so special was that he could do everything skating at full speed. Some can shoot when they're going full speed. Bobby Orr did everything at full speed. Even Lemieux doesn't do that.

"You don't get a more exciting team than the Boston team that had Orr, Esposito, Cashman, Hodge, Bucyk, Stanfield. They had six guys who were absolutely dynamite. They had good goal-tending with Gerry Cheevers and Eddie Johnston.

"But they didn't win as many Stanley Cups as other great teams (they won it twice, in 1970 and 1972). Some of it probably came down to coaching. The Bruins, even with Orr, never had a dynasty. The Canadiens had a dynasty. The Islanders had a dynasty. The Oilers had a dynasty. The Pittsburgh Penguins could've made a run at it, but now they'll have to bounce back and hope that Lemieux gets healthy and stays healthy. There are no guarantees that he will.

"Media people in Pittsburgh and around the league were calling me for my thoughts after the Penguins had won two in a row to ask me if I thought the Penguins had put together a dynasty. I told them to call me back when they've won four in a row, or five in a row, the way the Canadiens did."

The Canadiens, indeed, won four in a row from 1976 to 1979, and five in a row from 1956 to 1960.

"The team I'm watching tonight is not a dynasty," he said. "Without Mario, this is no dynasty."

I asked Fisher how he felt about the coaching change on the Penguins, going with Eddie Johnston again, after Scotty Bowman had coached the team a year earlier to a Stanley Cup championship. Could Johnston coach this team to a Stanley Cup?

"The team of the last few years didn't need a coach," said Fisher. "I don't think Scotty meant that much. Hell, he never attended a practice. They didn't want him around. Last year they had an outstanding team, even with Mario out.

"But Bowman will mean a lot to Detroit. He meant a lot to the Montreal team when he coached there. His talent as a coach, or of any coach who is successful, is getting the most out of what you've got. No matter the talent. He's done this. Bowman had to get something special out of a team when they lost only eight games all season (1976-77)."

I mentioned that Johnston said that Bowman usually accepted coaching jobs where he had a chance to win, and would not be interested in coaching an expansion team. Johnston said there was no way Bowman would coach the San Jose team, which was a rumor making the rounds during the off-season.

"Eddie's wrong," offered Fisher. "Bowman would go where he could get the money. He has nothing more to prove. He's won six Stanley Cups coaching, with one in Pittsburgh. He's won more games than any other coach in the history of the game. So he can afford to go for the money. You have to remember that hockey coaches don't have the integrity of hockey writers."

Fisher laughed at his own line.

"When Bowman started out, he coached the St. Louis Blues when they came into being during the 1967 expansion, and they were a terrible team," said Fisher, further making the point that Johnston was not on the mark with his observation that Bowman only took coaching assignments where he knew he could win. "Bowman referred to them more than once as 'dogs.' But he got to the Stanley Cup final with St. Louis that first year and again the second year."

"How do you think Johnston will fare here this second time around?" I asked Fisher.

"He's a great guy; I like him a lot," said Fisher. "I knew him when he was a backup goalie with the Canadiens. He wasn't really with the Canadiens, officially, but he came to camp with them one year. He was the best goalie in camp in 1960 by a country mile, but he wasn't going to beat out Jacques Plante. They did him a favor by trading him to Boston.

"I'd like to see him do well. He had so many shit teams here. Now he's got the players. Lemieux makes every coach look a little better."

I mentioned to Fisher that Johnston had told me he had played with Bowman on the same junior hockey team in his youth in Montreal. "Scotty had to get a steel plate in his head back then," recalled Fisher. "He got whacked over the head by Jean-Guy Talbot. I think the plate rusted after awhile. Scotty was a great coach, but the players hated him. He knew how to do it, and he had his own way. He learned from Toe Blake. There wasn't anybody any better, as far as I'm concerned. Blake could have been the best coach in any sport. He won eight Cups in 13 seasons, including five in a row. No one else ever did that."

Once more, Fisher's attention returned to the ice. "Lemieux makes a difference, no doubt about it," he offered.

"They (the Penguins) had 13 shots on goal in the first period, and they came out of it with only one goal," said Fisher. "Do you think if Lemieux had been playing that he might have scored one or two goals?

"If this team has Mario Lemieux, anybody — make that a lot of people — can win the Stanley Cup, including Eddie Johnston. Mario makes everybody better. It's nothing complicated. Whenever he's playing, he makes everybody play better.

"His big weakness is his off-the-ice conduct. There's no reason Mario Lemieux shouldn't have been here tonight. For the money he's making, he could have at least participated in pre-game ceremonies. He could take a bow."

I told Fisher that Lemieux had also skipped a golf outing with the club's top corporate sponsors. In the past, Lemieux was the star player in the event, but his back ailment sidelined him this time around. Maybe he didn't come, I volunteered, because he would have wanted to play.

"He should have been there," snapped Fisher. "That's ridiculous.

Jim Cunningham

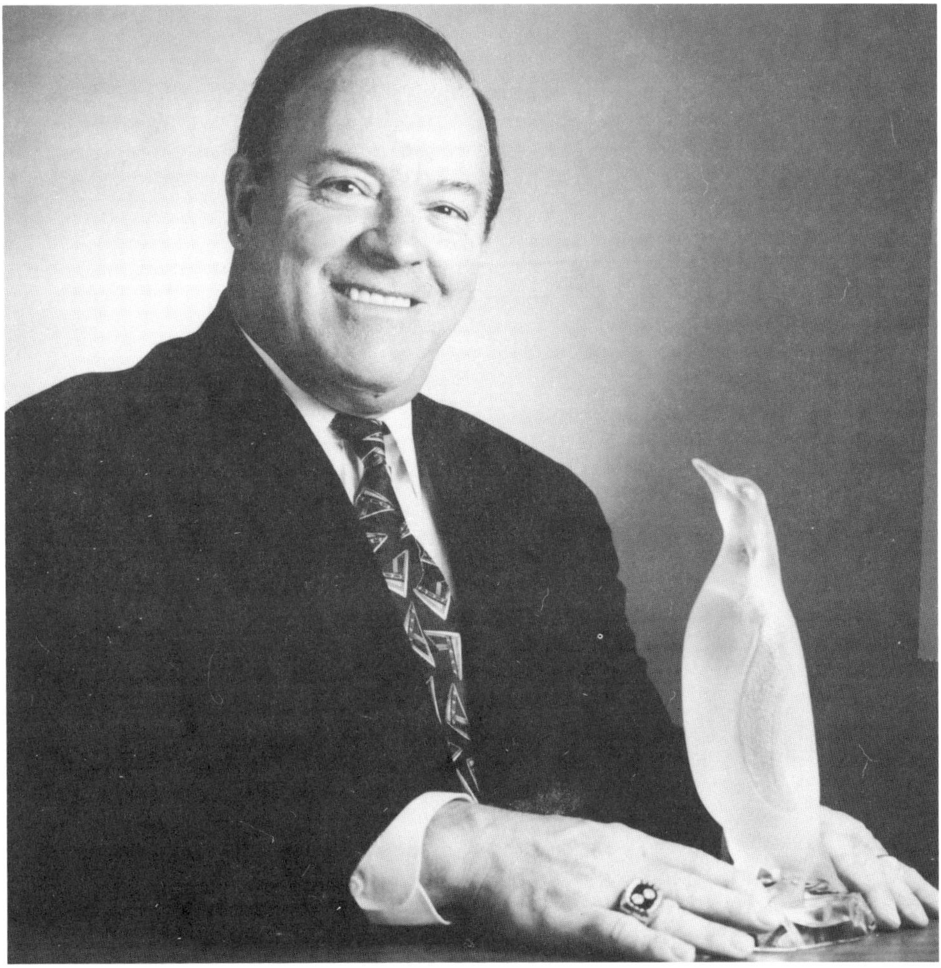

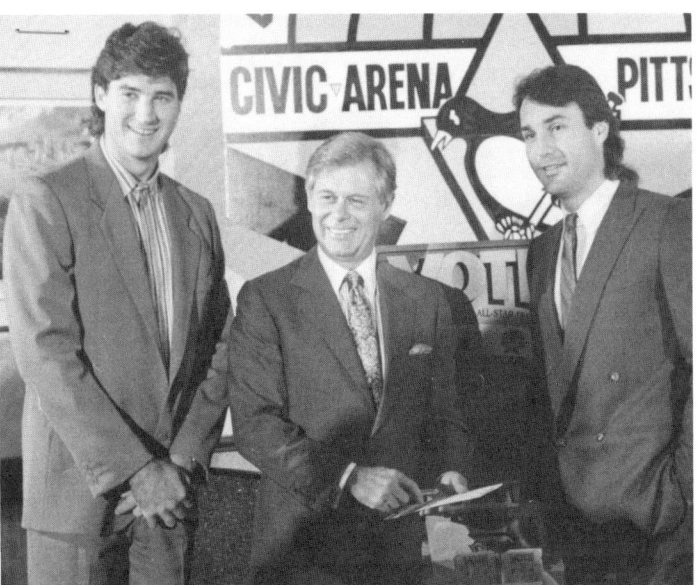

Scotty Bowman coached Penguins to second Stanley Cup title.

Elmer C. Brewer, McKeesport Daily News

Penguins Mario Lemieux and Paul Coffey flank NHL president John Ziegler at league's All-Star Game promotion in Pittsburgh on December 12, 1989.

He's going to kill himself with the fans. I hear he's not cooperative with the press anymore, that he doesn't want to do interviews. You can't be a recluse in this business. This guy is marvelous in an interview situation. It's not like he can't do it. He's good at it. Taking a bow tonight is just part of the game.

"If Jean Beliveau can do it, Mario Lemieux can do it. That's what I'm saying. He doesn't appear to understand what his role is all about, and he couldn't care less. I've been watching him as a hockey player, and nobody can handle him one-on-one. I haven't had a whole lot to do with him, otherwise.

"I'm the kind of guy . . . I don't chase people. I don't talk to rookies. I don't see any point in wasting their time or me wasting my time. I didn't talk to Guy Lafleur for three years."

"Who knows how long the miracle can last?"
—Red Fisher

Fisher worked for the *Montreal Star*, the city's leading newspaper, for 26 years and then, when it went out of business, he joined the *Gazette*, and has been there since 1976.

He won the National Newspaper Award in 1992 for the second time in his career — "that's the Canadians' answer to the Pulitzer Prize," offered Fisher — and he attributes his ability to stay on the beat so long to "a great and understanding wife."

Hockey has been his passion, but he has covered other sports. "I used to cover a lot of boxing," he said. "I've covered some great ones from Sugar Ray Robinson to Muhammad Ali. I loved to cover boxing. You meet some great people. I never found finer athletes to work with than you find in boxing. People in boxing need to promote themselves, so they give you all the time you want and then some.

"I spent some time with some outstanding sports writers, real giants in the business, when Archie Moore came to Montreal to fight Yvon Durelle."

Moore KOd Durelle, a hometown contender, in 1958 and again in 1959, in 11 and three rounds, respectively.

Fisher mentioned Milton Gross, Frank Graham, Ring Lardner and Red Smith as some of the famed sportswriters he had in his home for dinner during the pre-fight buildup for the Durelle-Moore fights.

One of the early thrills in my career back in 1970, two weeks after joining *The New York Post*, was covering a baseball game at Yankee Stadium, and being seated between Gross and Smith. It was like playing centerfield as a rookie for the Yankees between two Hall of Famers.

I remember riding with Gross, who was the lead columnist at *The Post* when I worked there (1969-1978) and hearing him tell me, "I don't envy you. It's not as good as it used to be on the sports beat. The guys aren't as pleasant to be around as they used to be, especially when we

traveled with the teams on trains. They're more difficult, and it's become more of an adversarial situation. And it's going to get worse."
There have always been difficult or recalcitrant performers in sports, but they were few and far between at one time, and now they are more populous in the clubhouses of every big-time sport. They are no longer the exception.

Fisher had seen a lot of them come and go, and had held his own with most of them. Lemieux's star was sinking with the sportswriters in Pittsburgh because he didn't seem to have time for them anymore, and was guarded when he did speak to them.

"When did you first hear about Lemieux?" I asked Fisher.

"When he was playing junior hockey," said Fisher. "I didn't see him then. I had enough of junior games when I was starting out."

That remark points up an interesting facet of Fisher. He feels he has paid his dues, and he does not even talk to new players until they have been on the team at least three years. "I don't talk to rookies," he said, with more than a hint of regality and arrogance.

"I might've made an exception for Orr and Lemieux," allowed Fisher, flashing a smile. The man may be proud, but he is not stupid.

At that point, some action on the ice caught Fisher's attention. He observed some chippy competition between Patrice Brisebois, a rookie defenseman for the Canadiens, and Marty McSorley, a multi-millionaire enforcer recently re-acquired by the Penguins. McSorley was imported to put some punch in the lineup, and some protection for Lemieux whenever he returned to action. They do not come much tougher, or richer, in the NHL, though his stay with the Penguins proved a short one the second time around.

"Brisebois wants to die young," offered Fisher, "picking on McSorley like that."

Then Fisher reflected on the young Lemieux once more. "I never saw him play until he got to the NHL," he said.

"Lemieux might have been as talented a junior player as there was, with the possible exception of Lafleur. Lafleur might have gotten more attention. Lemieux had a rap that he was lazy when he was a junior. But it might have been a matter of style. Lafleur was short, and always looked to be working hard. Lafleur was a blur, a very exciting guy, pure speed. Lemieux was so big, and he didn't look like he was pushing himself. He made it look that way.

"Lemieux has to learn to be responsible to the game which has been just as good to him as he's been to it. I've seen him in gang-bang interviews when he's done well. He doesn't think that's one of his responsibilities, but it is. Wayne Gretzky did it, and does it. Jean Beliveau did it. Bobby Orr hid in the clinic (training room) quite a bit, but he was a very shy guy, and didn't want any credit for what he did. But I sat down with Orr many times, and though he was a shy guy, he gave me some great interviews. He tried.

"Time and money has changed things. If a guy is making $42 million for six years, he doesn't give a shit what the writers think. That doesn't make it right, but I can understand it."

"That said," I said, "what has Mario Lemieux meant to this franchise?"

"Everything," said Fisher. "They wouldn't be here if it weren't for Mario Lemieux. If anything happens to Lemieux, they're hurting. As we speak, we don't know how much he can play. The guy was part of a memorable story last year. Who knows how long the miracle can last?"

Guy Lafleur

Jean Beliveau

Montreal's Henri and Maurice Richard lace on skates.

Eddie Johnston's Christmas Tree
Rooting for a neighbor in the New Year

*"I'm an old-fashioned
guy, I guess."*
—Eddie Johnston

A Christmas tree with tinsel on it is rare these days. How about one with real candy canes hanging from the boughs? How about one with Christmas balls with the emblems of the Boston Bruins, Chicago Blackhawks, Toronto Maple Leafs, St. Louis Blues, Hartford Whalers and the Pittsburgh Penguins?

How about one with two balls with the Penguins emblems — the old one and the new one — front and center?

If you haven't guessed by now, this Christmas tree belonged to Diane and Eddie Johnston.

This was Christmas Eve, 1993, and no one in the National Hockey League was enjoying the two-day holiday break any more than Eddie Johnston, the coach of the Penguins.

He and his wife were hosting a Christmas party for close friends and neighbors, and Eddie was enjoying pointing out the different decorations he had picked up wherever he worked as a player, coach and administrator in the NHL.

There was even a decoration from Moncton, New Brunswick, a minor league hockey town where Johnston had his first job as a coach back in 1978.

Eddie said he and Diane and their youngest child, Joseph, 12, had decorated the tree. They let their oldest, Michelle, 22, and E.J., 20, put the tinsel on when they returned home from college. "We left the finishing touches for them," said Eddie.

The tree was beautiful, tall and shaped perfectly. "It's an old-fashioned tree," I ventured.

"I'm an old-fashioned guy, I guess," said Johnston.

I first met the Johnstons when they attended a block party in our neighborhood soon after they came to Pittsburgh in 1980. "We participate in anything going on here," he said, proudly. "We've got great neighbors."

The Johnstons are fun people, and they would be popular in any neighborhood. He's the kind of down-to-earth guy you'd like to see succeed, to have him win a Stanley Cup this year. Diane is a delight, often saying the first thing that comes to her pretty mind. She was an airline stewardess at Eastern Airlines when she and Eddie met, and that was during the days when "airline stewardess" and "attractive" were synonymous.

Johnston, who turned 58 in November of 1993, has been around the NHL circuit, but he says he was never happier than when he had a chance to come back to Pittsburgh in the summer of 1993.

He had said that day that he came back because he wanted to be the guy who was coaching the club when it won another Stanley Cup championship banner. "I want to be the guy here when they hoist it," he said.

I rode to work with him on his first day on the job at the Civic Arena, back on June 22 when the Penguins announced that Johnston would succeed Scotty Bowman as the bench coach. Johnston hadn't coached in ten years, and that was a cause for concern as far as the media were concerned.

But Johnston was confident he could get the job done. In a way, back then at least, it seemed like a no-win situation for Johnston. The Penguins, led by Mario Lemieux, were thought to be the most talented team in the NHL, and no one thought they would slip and slide in the playoffs as they had done the previous spring.

In short, if the Penguins won the Stanley Cup for the third time in four years Johnston would get little credit. If they didn't win it all, Johnston would surely bear the brunt of the blame for coming up short.

That was before Lemieux was sidelined with a bum back, and goalie Tom Barrasso missed a month's action with a bum hip, and Marty McSorley missed a month, and Rick Tocchet, Kjell Samuelsson and Ulf Samuelsson were shelved for several games with one ailment or another.

"One time we had close to $13 million in salaries sitting in the stands," recalled Johnston.

Despite all these setbacks, as Johnston toasted his friends and neighbors at his Christmas Eve party, his Penguins were spending Christmas alone atop the NHL's Northeast Division. Ken Wregget had been a wall in goal, and the rest of the Penguins had put forth a pretty consistent effort.

They'd gone to Boston the night before and beaten the Bruins, 4-3, to hold off the division's second-place team. It has always been particularly satisfying for Johnston to come away from Boston a winner.

He was a goal-tender there for two Stanley Cup championship teams. While working there, he was the last goalie in the NHL to play every minute of a season (1963-64).

Johnston had a right to feel proud. "This has been good for me," Johnston said, sitting at a table in his family room. "It's been great for my family, for my mind. I feel good about myself again."

"Eddie loves that painting.
It reminds him of his boyhood street."
—Diane Johnston

There is an L-shaped gameroom in the Johnston home that contains some classic photos that Diane had just had framed and put up on the walls. It was Eddie Johnston's own Wall of Fame. There are some great shots of him when he was a fearless goalie for the Boston Bruins, shots

Diane Johnston sits atop Stanley Cup

showing him in action against the likes of Phil Esposito and Bobby Hull of the Chicago Blackhawks when he didn't wear a mask and at ease in his dressing cubicle afterward, one showing a goodly supply of beer cans in front of him after a particularly demanding day of work. One showing Eddie sitting in his goal-keeper's gear on the bench in a series in Russia.

Even though he was born in Montreal, Johnston looks so Boston. He looks like a character right out of one of Robert B. Parker's "Spencer for Hire" series of books. Johnston had the perfect mug and disposition to be a Bruin. There were photos showing him at reunions of the Bruins teams that won the Stanley Cup in 1970 and 1972. There was a beautiful color photo showing three of Boston's all-time greats all holding their uniforms overhead, Bobby Orr, Ted Williams and Larry Bird, with accompanying large signatures. "Bobby sent that to Eddie," said Diane.

Orr remains a close friend. There is a classic photo showing Orr flying through the air after scoring a goal that won the Stanley Cup for the Bruins in 1970. Orr is airborne, like Peter Pan.

"That game was on Mother's Day at Boston Garden," said Eddie. "It was the fourth goal of the game. Everything about this was the number four. It was the fourth and final game of the playoffs. It was scored by No. 4 at 44 seconds of the fourth period of sudden death overtime. All the numbers on the scoreboard were 4, except for the score after St. Louis. We swept them in four games. Bobby was tripped as he scored by Noel Picard, No. 4 of the Blues, which is why he was flying."

That Boston team had gotten together for a 20th year reunion in 1990 and was planning a 25th year reunion in 1995. "Most of the guys are still around Boston," said Johnston.

There are pictures showing Eddie with his five brothers and their mother, and of Eddie with his wife and children. The Johnstons are big on pictures, big on memories. In the foyer as you enter their home there's a painting depicting the same kind of row houses on the street where Johnston grew up in the West End of Montreal, just a ten-minute walk from the Montreal Forum. "Eddie loves that," said Diane. Some of the homes have wooden stairways from the sidewalks in front of them leading up to the second floor.

"That's exactly the way the houses were on my street," explained Eddie. "One family lived on the first floor, and another family on the second floor."

There's a large photo showing Eddie with Mario Lemieux, who later grew up in a neighborhood called St. Henri, about ten minutes away from Eddie's early digs. Lemieux signed the photo. Eddie drafted Lemieux when he was the general manager of the Penguins, and they have remained good friends.

Diane showed me a framed photo that a friend had sent Eddie. It was a stark black and white scene. "This is supposed to be the first outdoor hockey rink in Montreal," she said.

There's a white piano in the living room. "We've all taken a stab at learning to play it," said Diane.

"I'm doing something I enjoy."

After he left Pittsburgh, Johnston had been working for three seasons as the general manager of the Hartford Whalers. "I feel like I'm doing what I'm supposed to be doing," he said of his comeback as a coach. "I'm doing something I enjoy."

When he first returned to his home in Upper St. Clair, a home he had tried unsuccessfully to sell after he parted with the Penguins, he expressed a desire to sit down someday with Chuck Noll, the former Steelers coach, who lived nearby.

"I just wanted to talk to him about how he dealt with different situations," Johnston said. "I know I could learn something from him."

Noll moved to Sewickley soon after the Johnstons returned, and Eddie had not been able to hook up with him.

I mentioned to Johnston that Noll never talked about players who weren't around. Once, in an attempt at wry humor in dismissing the media's constant questions about Franco Harris, then a holdout, Noll responded with his infamous retort: "Franco Who?"

I suggested to Johnston that he shouldn't say anything like that regarding Lemieux. "Oh, no, never," Johnston said. "So far, so good. Our guys are working like hell, and the veterans are pushing the young guys in practice.

"But we want to get Lemieux back. It'll be a shot in the arm for everyone, for the players and the fans. When he's playing, everybody else's game moves up a notch. We've got 50 games left, and we need everybody out there."

Eddie Johnston's 93-year-old mother, Brigit, is surrounded by her six sons, left to right, Steve, Mike, Billy, David, Eddie and Tom. Eddie says his mother's first love is playing bingo.

Bobby Orr and Eddie Johnston ride in parade celebrating Boston Bruins' Stanley Cup championship in 1970. Check out their attire.

Eddie Johnston (at right) was playing goal for St. Louis Blues in 1976-76 when Bobby Orr (4 at left) and Tony Esposito (30) were with the Chicago Blackhawks.

Here's a dream for Pittsburgh hockey fans: Bobby Orr as the property of the Penguins. He came to Pittsburgh to help his buddy Eddie Johnston and worked with the Penguins on their power play tactics in the early '80s.

Kevin Stevens
Saving face

"I didn't know if I'd ever be able to play again."

When Kevin Stevens smiles he can light up a room. Playing left wing for the Pittsburgh Penguins, he can also turn on the lights behind the goal nets with his blazing shots. The more he scores the more he smiles. His smile and handsome face are a testimonial to his parents and to the surgeons who put his face back together again after a scary fall he took in the final playoff game of the 1993 season. He was knocked unconscious in a collision, and fell face-first to the ice. He fell like a Murphy bed. It was a terrible sequence. It is a miracle that he can now look in the mirror and still smile at what he sees, and that he was able to perform at the level he did during the 1993-94 National Hockey League campaign. More on that later. Let's go back to the beginning to learn how Stevens started his sports career, and how he became a big-time hockey player.

Stevens was born in Brockton, Massachusetts on April 15, 1965 — which made the income tax filing deadline more of a joyful event in the Stevens home than it might ordinarily have been. I interviewed Stevens on April 14, 1994, following a practice session at the Civic Arena. "I'll be 29 tomorrow," said Stevens.

Brockton is also the birthplace of Rocky Marciano and Marvelous Marvin Hagler, two tough guys in boxing lore, and Stevens comes from the same fiber. "I think that's why they still list Brockton as my hometown in the Penguins' press guide, even though I never lived there," said Stevens. "So it builds up the tough guy image." A nice guy off the ice, he has a short fuse and a mean streak once he is out there competing for the puck. He's big — 6-3, 220 pounds — and he can bang with the best of them. He always thinks every loose puck belongs to him. He needs to improve on his defense, and get back up ice to check his man. He gets into more than his share of fights. He's a left-handed shooter, but he punches with both hands. Yeah, he's a tough guy, all right.

He is quick to point out, however, that Brockton is not really his hometown. He grew up in nearby Pembroke, in a community called Vryantville, which Stevens says was "a small town, a great place to grow up."

His coal-dark eyes positively gleam when he goes back to his boyhood days in Vryantville.

"We lived on a dead-end street with lots of kids around who enjoyed playing all sorts of games," said Stevens. "There were cranberry bogs and lakes around us. That's where cranberry juice comes from. The water in those bogs is only about five or six inches deep. It froze faster because it wasn't that deep, and our parents didn't have to worry about us falling through the ice.

"My mother and father both worked. My mother is called Pat and my dad is Art. That's why I still get called Artie, even by some of my teammates, though that's not my name. I have two older sisters, Kelly, who's 32, and Kim, 31. Kelly and I went to Boston College, and Kim went to the University of Maine. We have a very close family. I was always close to my sisters, and I still am.

"My mother ran a snackbar in a supermarket, and my father sold life insurance for 30 years. Now he works for the post office. My dad was a catcher in the Cincinnati Reds organization; I think he got as high as Double A. He had hurt his knee playing football in junior college, and he hurt it again in baseball, in a collision at home plate, and that was the end of his ballplaying days. He was always a big athletic guy growing up, playing basketball and baseball. I knew he was a good basketball player. He couldn't skate, but he played street hockey with me.

"He loved sports, and we used to go to the Boston Garden a lot. We'd see Saturday afternoon games with the Bruins, and we went there to see the Celtics play, and he took me to Fenway Park to see the Red Sox play."

I asked Kevin if he ever heard of Jim Piersall, and he had, but he was not familiar with the book or movie about Piersall, a real flake who was an outfielder for the Red Sox. Piersall's story was called *Fear Strikes Out*, and Tony Perkins played the part of Jim Piersall, and Karl Malden played his father, who was obsessed with the idea of breeding his son to be a big league baseball player. The father overdid it, causing his son to have real emotional problems. "It was never like that," said Stevens, picking up the story line, and where I was heading. "My dad didn't drive me to do anything. He was just always there, always eager to share in my sports experiences. And I played whatever sports I wanted to, depending on what season it was."

He inherited a deep love for sports from his father, but he also learned from his dad's experience that dreams do not always come true.

"My father worked with Babe Ruth League teams in our town before I was born," said Kevin. "Later on, I was the bat boy for his teams. He was involved in that 15 years before I played. He had great teams, and won a lot of titles. That's probably why I played so much baseball. I loved Carl Yastrzemski. But my dad never told me if he was still disappointed that he didn't make it to the big leagues. If he was, he kept it from me.

"The Bruins had a great team then, back in the '70s. They were the 'Big Bad Bruins.' They had Bobby Orr, and Phil Esposito, Wayne Cashman, Johnny Bucyk, Ken Hodge, Gerry Cheevers and Derek Sanderson. E.J. (Eddie Johnston) was on that team. They were quick to fight. Everybody loved them.

"It was a thrill to be there and watch Orr, the things he could do with the puck. Orr definitely had an influence on me and a lot of other kids growing up in Boston in those days. After watching Orr, we all wanted to play hockey.

"I was also into the Celtics. They had John Havlicek when I first started following them. My favorite athlete was Larry Bird. He was there when I was in college. He was such a dedicated athlete. He wasn't that quick, and he couldn't jump that high, but it was just amazing what he accomplished. He worked so hard during the off-season to constantly improve his game. He was my idol in sports. Bobby Orr was my favorite hockey player. Math was my favorite subject in school. I liked reading *Inside Sports* magazine. I loved *The Boston Globe*; it had a great sports section.

"I was just caught up with the way Larry Bird prepared himself, the way he handled himself. How he met the challenge every night. I read in the sports magazines and newspapers about how hard he worked in the off-season. I loved the way he led that team. I tried to pattern myself after him. He had more talent than I had, but I knew I had to work hard."

Kevin Stevens never dreamed of playing in the National Hockey League when he was a youngster. Baseball was his favorite sport back then, and he thought he might like to be a baseball player someday. He might have been a handsome hero in the tradition of Tony Conigliaro, Fred Lynn or Jim Rice. He didn't know if he was good enough to make it in any sport.

"I was a late bloomer," said Stevens. "In high school, I was one of the top three or four players on our hockey team. I was the captain of the team in three sports. Baseball was my love, until I got to the level where someone could throw 20 curve balls in a row and put them all over the plate. It was the *bender* that took me out of baseball. I went to a few tryout camps, and I did well until they kept throwing that *bender* at me."

When Stevens said "bender," he said "ben-dah" with his strongest Boston accent, which is pretty strong no matter what he is saying.

There is no denying he is Boston bred. "I loved the atmosphere at Boston Garden," he said. "It always brought a special light to my eyes. It was so loud in there. Sometimes it was real hot in that building, too. It had the greatest atmosphere.

"Playing at the Boston Garden in the Bean Pot hockey tournament when I was at B.C., after going there as a kid to watch the Bruins, was the biggest thrill in my life at that time," said Stevens. "To step out on the ice and look up at the rafters and to see all the pennants for the Bruins and the Celtics and feel the atmosphere. It was great."

With that in mind, I asked Stevens how he was able to resist the temptation to become a Bruin when he had the chance after the 1990-91 season, after the Penguins had won their first Stanley Cup championship. The Bruins signed him to an offer sheet as a free agent in the summer of 1991 for better than a million dollars a year. The Bruins offered him a reported $5.375 million over five years. The Penguins matched it.

"It was tough," said Stevens. "I thought I was in a no-lose situation. I had just come off a Stanley Cup year. There was a chance to go

Stevens Family Album

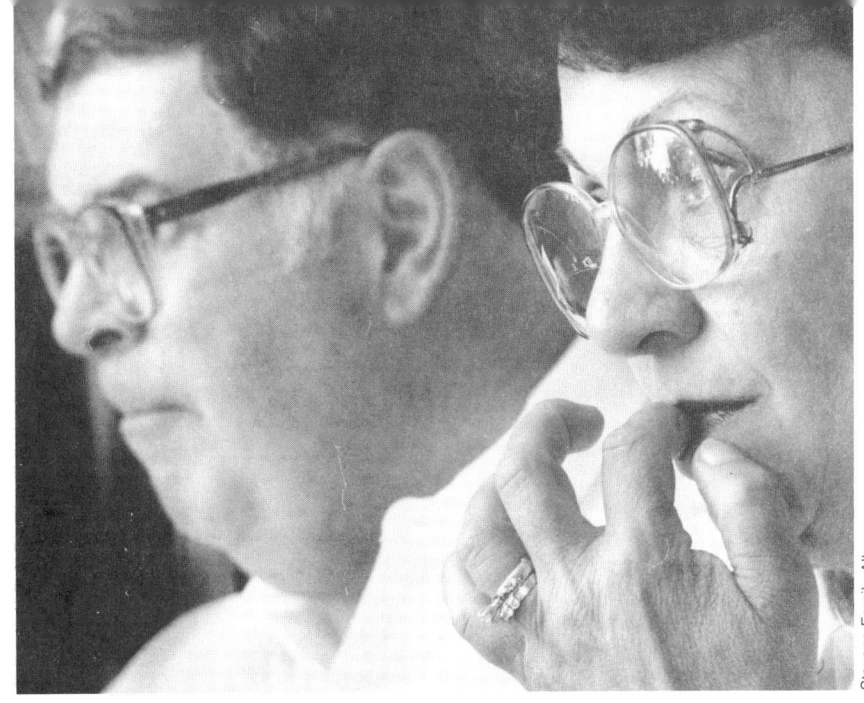

Art and Pat Stevens watched son Kevin compete in first Stanley Cup final in May 1991, and stood tall (below) when he was presented MVP award in high school in 1983. Art had been a minor league baseball player.

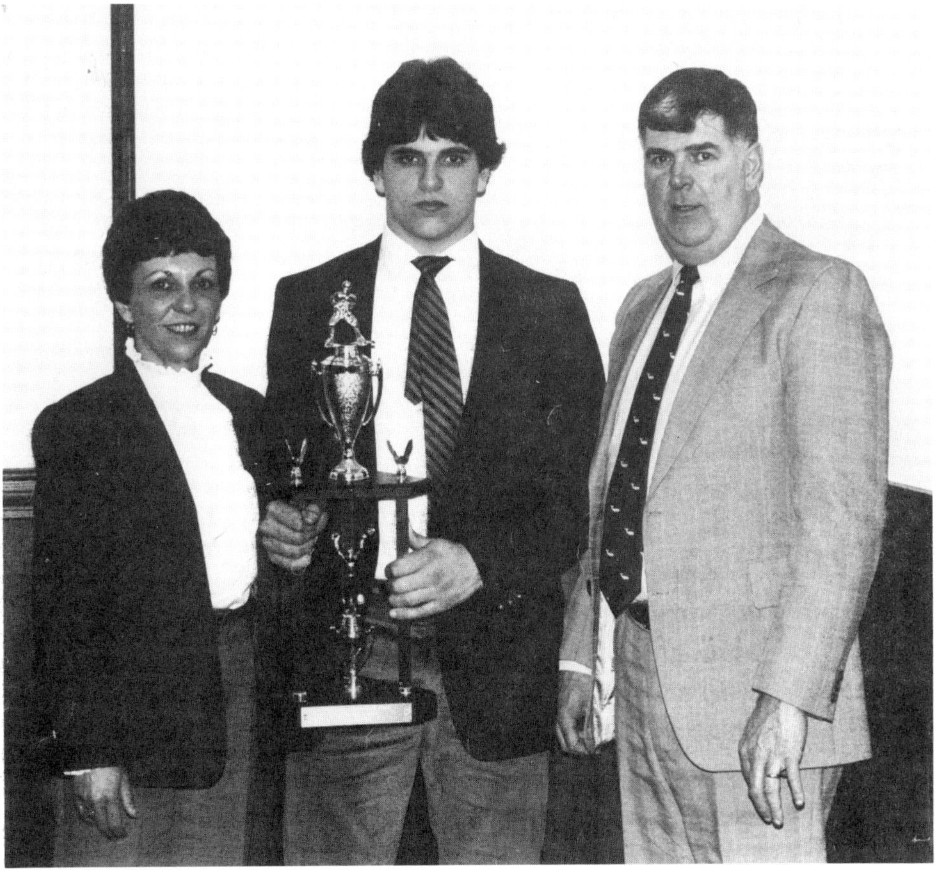

home and play for the Bruins of my boyhood, or I could stay put. How can you leave a team that's got the greatest player in the world? I was happy to stay here for that kind of money. I was upset, however, when the Penguins were sold by the DeBartolos soon after I signed a new contract. At first, it appeared that the new owners might sell off some of the high-priced players to raise some operating money."

After he chose to stay with the Penguins, he had one of his greatest games in the playoffs at Boston Garden. It came on May 22, 1992. He had a hat trick in five minutes and 55 seconds of the first period and four goals altogether as the Penguins beat the Bruins, 5-1, to take a 3-0 lead in the Wales Conference playoff finals. Stevens was skating on the same line as Mario Lemieux and Jaromir Jagr. It doesn't get any better than that.

"That was one of my exciting times in the Garden; I was struggling at the time, and it turned out to be one of the highlights of my career. My parents were both there, and I had bought 50 or 60 tickets for friends. A lot of people saw that game on TV, too. When I went home in the summer, I bumped into so many people who had seen that game."

Stevens won't soon forget where he came from. "I go back to Boston every summer," said Stevens. "It is so beautiful, and I love the ocean."

Stevens was an accomplished high school athlete and he accepted a scholarship to play hockey at Boston College. He was inducted into his high school's Hall of Fame in 1994.

He was drafted by the Los Angeles Kings when he graduated from high school. He chose to stay in school. His NHL rights were traded by the Kings to the Penguins, when Eddie Johnston was serving as general manager, for Anders Hakansson on September 9, 1983. It was a lopsided swap, as it turned out. Hakansson finished his NHL career with 98 points in 330 games.

I asked Stevens if he knew Doug Flutie when he was a student at Boston College. "I was a freshman or sophomore when he was the star of the football team," said Stevens. "I'd see him on campus. He never said anything to me when I was in school, because he was at least two years ahead of me. He brought excitement to my life. He was a gutsy quarterback, and that had been my position in high school. So I identified with him. I met him a couple of times after we got out of school. He was a big play guy, even though he wasn't a very big guy."

Stevens is still a big football fan, following the New England Patriots and the Pittsburgh Steelers. "I love to go to the Steelers games," he said. "I go to Patriot exhibition games before I get here each season."

Stevens played hockey all four years he was at Boston College, getting better and boosting his statistics each season. He kept his nose to the books and was graduated with a degree in economics.

He scored only six goals as a freshman, and boosted that to 13 as a sophomore, 17 as a junior and 35 goals and 70 points in 39 games his senior season at B.C. He was a second team NCAA All-American. He made the U.S. National team and the 1988 Olympics team, and delayed joining the Penguins. He played in the 1987 World Championships in Vienna and the 1988 Olympic Games in Calgary.

Jim Cunningham

Stevens Family Album

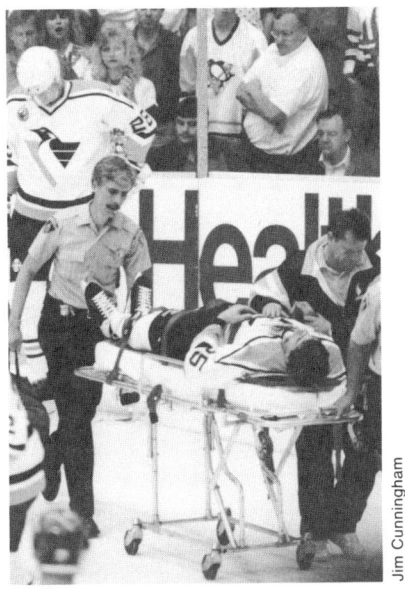

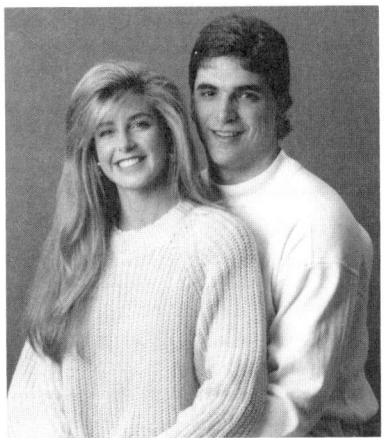

Kevin Stevens (at left) is taken from Arena after crashing face-first. He's favorite of wife Suzanne and young Penguin fans.

Jim Cunningham

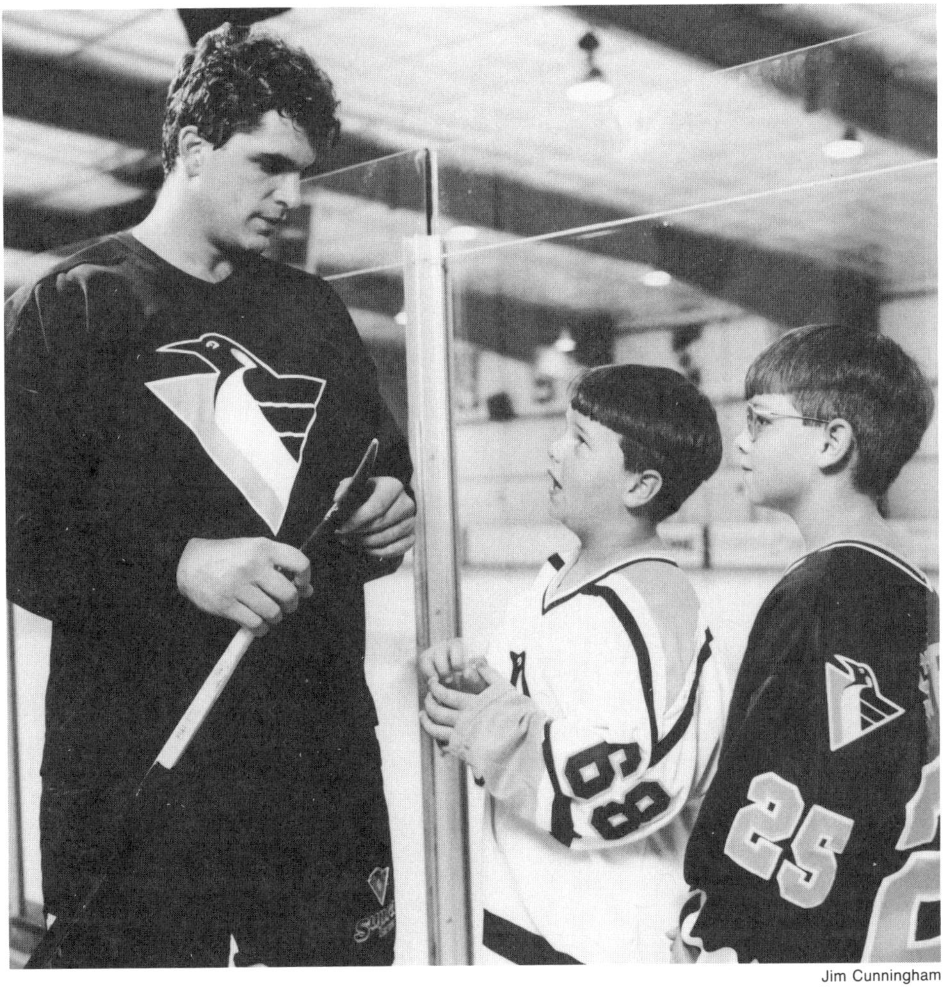

When he returns home each summer, he spends a lot of time skating with old friends and former teammates as well as former opponents at Boston University's Walter Brown Arena, named after the late owner of the Boston Celtics.

"Kevin is so hard on himself."
—Suzanne Stevens

The 1993-94 schedule was a tremendous challenge for Stevens. He was not having a season that was up to his own standards. His plus-minus rating was the worst on the team. He had been booed at home, which really hurt, and he made the mistake of saying he would prefer to play on the road.

"People don't realize what I had to go through," said Stevens. "I didn't know if I'd be able to ever play again. It was something that happened. I wish it hadn't. But I was unable to work out the way I usually do during the off-season. That is important to my performance. My doctors told me to avoid activity for six weeks. I never had my legs this year as I have in the past. I need the summer to work out. You can work out all year long, but you can never work as hard as you can during the summer. I haven't been the way I would have liked to have been. This isn't the season I wanted to have. I'm looking forward to the summer, to getting ready, so I can be the way I want to be. I'm not looking past the playoffs, but I am excited about what I will be able to do during the off-season. It's not so much my face that's a problem; it's what I couldn't do last summer."

When he got off to a slow start, he worried about what was going on in his life. In October, the Penguins checked into the Don DeSar Beach Resort in St. Petersburg, Florida. "It's a nice place," Stevens said when a local reporter asked him how he liked the posh resort. "But right now it means I just get to lie awake on better sheets."

His wife, Suzanne, could understand what was going on. "I can just imagine him staring at the ceiling," she said. "It really gets to him. Kevin is so hard on himself."

When he wasn't, the fans were hard on him.

"The people aren't just picking on me," said Stevens, trying to make sense of it all. "In Mario's situation, I've heard a lot of nonsense, too. People overlook some things. It's scary what happened to him, first with his back and then with his Hodgkins disease. To have done what he's done as a hockey player since all that came to the surface is simply unbelievable. I hear some of the criticism about him on the sports talk shows, and they say the stupidest things. He's still a big hero here, but there are a handful of people who are so stupid with their comments about him. And about me. It's hard to understand. And it bothers me."

Back in mid-March, Stevens had said, "I wish I didn't pay any attention to it, but I hear everything. It bothers me, it bothers me a lot. I'd rather play the games on the road sometimes. I hate to say that, but that's how I feel."

But if he thought about it enough he would have realized how lucky he was to be able to hear those fans. Back in 1989, he was on the staff at the Stan Mikita School for the Deaf, teaching hearing-impaired youngsters how to play hockey. "It makes you think what life is all about," he said.

"There's only one way I can play."

Here's how Stevens came this close to a career-ending injury. It was five minutes into the final game of the 1993 playoffs for the Penguins when Stevens was seriously injured. This was back on May 14. He crashed face-first to the ice after a violent collision which he had instigated with Rich Pilon of the New York Islanders. Stevens was trying to wipe out Pilon when his head struck the face shield of Pilon's helmet, and Stevens was knocked out in the collision. He was unable to break his fall.

It took 4 1/2 hours of surgery to reconstruct Stevens' face. Surgeons made an ear-to-ear incision and peeled his skin back to do their work.

Stevens' nose was flattened and had to be rebuilt.

Doctors said they normally saw something like this after head-on car collisions. Stevens splattered his nose, crushed his sinus cavities, and smashed every bone in his forehead.

Doctors likened his forehead, which had been reconstructed with metal plates, to a trampled potato chip. They told him if he hadn't been so big his neck likely would have been snapped when he hit the ice.

Soon after his surgery, Stevens was discussing a comeback. "There's only one way I can play," he said. "I have to play hard and I have to play physical and I feel I can do that. If I can't play that way, I might as well not play."

By coincidence, I sat next to Stevens at a dinner following an annual fund-raising golf outing for the Penguins and some business bigwigs on September 13, 1993, at the Fox Chapel Golf Club. Earlier in the day, Stevens had undergone a CAT scan, and was given the green light to play during the 1993-94 schedule. He was so elated, understandably enough.

He was among those who thought the Penguins might put Stanley Cup banners up in the ceiling of the Civic Arena to rival the banners at Boston Garden. Stevens proclaimed in 1992, "The dynasty is here in Pittsburgh." That was before the Penguins slipped in the playoffs, before he got hurt, before Lemieux learned his back was going to continue to keep him out of the lineup, before Lemieux learned he had cancer.

After the Islanders knocked the Penguins out of the playoffs, and the Montreal Canadiens claimed the Stanley Cup, Stevens would say, "It was really tough seeing Montreal skating around with *our* Cup."

Stevens was told to wear a face shield upon his return to action, but he hated it, and he shed his face shield in mid-February of 1994, during a 3-0 victory in Philadelphia. He also signed a lucrative new contract in February.

It put him in the million dollar-a-year category of players, and he could end up making as much as three millon dollars a year with all the production-linked compensation clauses in the contract.

All that showed on his face from his accident was a scar that runs over his right eyebrow. He had broken every bone in his forehead. He had 140 stitches, most of them about a quarter-inch into his hairline. The doctors would not let him look into the mirror for quite a while after his operation because they did not think it would be very therapeutic. Stevens seemed to have more furrows in his brow during the 1993-94 season, perhaps because he was frowning more than usual. All things considered, Stevens should have been smiling more. He was a very lucky young man. And Penguins' fans were fortunate to have him playing for their favorite team. Doctors at Mercy Hospital saved my life after I had suffered severe head injuries when I fell from a moving taxicab when I was three, so I could appreciate his experience.

It was amazing that he didn't break any teeth in the collision and the subsequent fall to the ice. There was blood on the ice after he was removed and taken to a hospital. He was able to listen to a radio in his room, but he couldn't watch TV because his eyes were swollen shut. Observers say his head was swollen to the size of a basketball. He was wheeled into surgery the next morning.

"What the surgeon did was absolutely amazing," said Stevens. "Basically, they built me a new face."

Surgeons removed most of the bone fragments, reconstructed his forehead with metal plates. They put his nose back together again. Then they pulled the skin back on his face and stitched it in place.

His face swelled up again after the surgery. "When the swelling was up, he had no profile," said his wife Suzanne. "His nose had disappeared. His eyes were about up to his ears."

Kevin hardly resembled the man she had met during their college days. "Those first few days, he was Elephant Man," said teammate Peter Taglianetti. Suzanne kept the photos from the hospital, and checks them out every now and then, and just shakes her head. Kevin counts his blessings. "I probably should be in a wheelchair now," he conceded during his recovery period. "If I wasn't so big, my neck would have snapped when I hit the ice."

"I just had so much fun, no matter what level I was playing."
—Kevin Stevens

When things are going well for Stevens, he says his parents enjoy it so much. "My father is living my dream. You'd think he was a Pittsburgher the way he dresses. He wears the hats, the shirts, the coats. He has one of my Stanley Cup rings. He wears it all the time. That's his pride and joy. He grew up and lived for 44 years in Pembroke, before he moved to Sagamore Beach by the cape (Cape Cod). He knows that territory well. As a kid, we'd go fishing together. We'd go to a lake.

Kevin Stevens is shown at several stages of his young hockey life, in his poster-filled bedroom and with teams he played for as a kid in suburban Boston.

Stevens Family Album

Anything I did, he was always there. We'd play catch every night in the backyard. We had a hoop in the backyard and we'd shoot out there all night. We played hockey in the basement, using a tennis ball. He was always the goalie, and I was always trying get the ball by him. Now I can't fit in that basement. I was never forced to do anything, but he was always there if I wanted to play a game. I just loved to do it; it wasn't winning or losing. I just had so much fun, no matter what level I was playing.

"I never zeroed in on hockey as a kid. A lot of Canadian players had a lot more ice time than I did by the time I got to the NHL. Some of them . . . all they did was play hockey. I played whatever the season was.

"I don't like coaches telling kids to concentrate on this sport or that sport. How do you know what they'll be like when they're ten? I was great in hockey when I was seven, eight and nine. Nobody could touch me. Then the guys caught up to me, and it was awhile before I moved out of the pack again. I'm glad I never gave up baseball, even though it turned out it wasn't going to be my sport. I had a great time playing baseball and softball. I played everything, and I'm glad I did. I think that's the best way. You'll have plenty of time to concentrate on one sport later on."

Stevens sure made believers out of anybody back in Pembroke who believed he was chasing an unrealistic dream. He set a team record for left wingers with 55 goals in the 1992-93 season, and tied Jimmy Carson's NHL record for most goals in a season by a U.S.A.-born player.

Stevens was the first player in NHL history to exceed 50 goals, 100 points and 200 penalty minutes in a season.

Rick Tocchet, a former power forward for the Penguins, is a big fan of Stevens. "Kevin's probably the purest power forward in the league," said Tocchet. "He reminds me of a big running back in the NFL who just wears you down."

"The game's all confidence," said Stevens. "If you don't have confidence, you're second-guessing yourself, second-guessing what you're doing, and you wind up a step behind everybody."

Stevens started playing organized hockey at the Hobomock Arena in Pembroke back on March 6, 1972.

John Lane, his coach, who is still coaching in the league, told sports writer Bill Utterback, "We had 165 youngsters on the ice and 150 of them looked like Bobby Orr. Same haircut. Same black and gold Bruins jersey, No. 4. Kevin just came in an ordinary sweatshirt."

Kevin's dad, Art Stevens, told Utterback, "Even when he was small, Kevin could never see himself as Orr or Phil Esposito or anybody who played in the NHL."

He never thought he was a big deal in high school, no matter the success he enjoyed. "He never took credit for anything good that happened to him," said Pat Stevens, his mother.

Scott McKee, Kevin's linemate at Silver Lake High School, told Utterback, "Every kid who ever laces on a pair of skates dreams about playing in the pros. But Kevin was different. The only thing he ever talked about was playing for Boston College. I think he thought that's as far as he could go."

Friends said Kevin didn't get excited when he was drafted by the Kings, or when the Kings traded his rights to the Penguins. "He didn't make a big deal about it," said one of his friends, "because he didn't think anything would come of it."

Kevin's wife Suzanne said, "I think playing in the NHL was a dream for Kevin, but I don't think he thought it could come true."

Then again, it was Kevin's modest manner that made him even more appealing to Suzanne.

His dad thought Kevin had the physical attributes to be an athlete at an early age. "Ever look at his hands?" Art Stevens asked Utterback during a lengthy interview. "He has large hands. Even when he was little he had huge hands. He could throw a football 40 yards when he was ten. And he could handle a hockey stick when he was six or seven."

Art Stevens would be the goalie in the basement of their home, and Kevin would wield his hockey stick and slap a tennis ball at his dad till it was time to go to bed. "I wonder if some of that pop he's showing now came from all those nights with the tennis balls," Art said.

Kevin caught the fever for hockey in February of 1980, at age 14, when he watched the underdog U.S. hockey team win a gold medal at the Olympic Games. "You got all caught up with what happened," he said of that miracle win. "You wanted to out there and play. If anything was going to lean you toward hockey, the 1980 gold medal would do it."

As a high school sophomore, Kevin quarterbacked the team to a league title. As a high school baseball player, he attracted the attention of the Baltimore Orioles and Toronto Blue Jays, but they backed off when they heard he accepted a hockey scholarship to Boston College.

It wasn't until he got to college that Kevin concentrated on hockey for the first time in his life. He felt he needed to learn how to skate better if he was ever going to become a good hockey player.

Stevens says it's different today for young prospects. "What's amazing is how many American kids are out there playing hockey in the youth programs," said Stevens. "No wonder there are more and more Americans in the National Hockey League."

He told sports writer Tom McMillan, "There are so many programs run for 16-17-18 year olds around the country, even all summer long. I know I never played hockey in the summer. I played football in the fall, hockey in the winter, and baseball in the spring and summer. It's different now.

"Of course, maybe they had all that stuff back when I was a kid, and I just didn't know about it. Or maybe they didn't tell me. Maybe they didn't want me out there."

Stevens still has many interests. He loves to play golf. He used to be into cycling, but he has gotten away from that, not willing to risk getting hurt and blowing his hockey career. He made that choice before Ron Gant of the Atlanta Braves busted himself up on a bike and blew millions of dollars when he was unable to play ball for the start of the 1994 season.

"I can still see him in the hospital."
—Suzanne Stevens

Kevin and Suzanne Stevens live in a lovely two-bedroom condominium in Mt. Lebanon, and they have a summer place in Cape Cod, close to their Boston origins. In Mt. Lebanon, they live next door to former neighbors of mine, Al and Sue Marthinsen, who have season tickets to the Penguins, and are huge fans. Other Penguins and their families live in the same condominium complex. Susan has helped several Penguins, including Mario Lemieux, handle their fan mail.

This was a Wednesday, May 4, 1994, a week away from the season-ending setback to the Washington Capitals in the first round of the Stanley Cup playoffs. We had an early morning meeting in their family room to talk about the past season, and for me to pick up some photographs for this book. Suzanne was going to a luncheon later on to say goodbye for the summer to the wives of several Penguins players, notably Nathalie Lemieux, Megan Barrasso, Mary Lou Francis and Linda Mullen. Kevin had some chores and stops to make so the couple could depart Pittsburgh the following evening.

They would be taking more baggage with them than they would have wished. It hadn't been the best of seasons for Kevin or the Penguins. Many NHL players would have loved to have the statistics Stevens recorded, but they were not up to his own standards, or everyone else's expectations for him. On the one hand, he was fortunate to have been able to return to play hockey. All things considered, whatever he did on the ice during the 1993-94 campaign should have been regarded as a bonus. But fans are fickle. They forget fast.

"It was difficult," said Suzanne Stevens, a beautiful, bright-faced woman who has that Kathy Lee Gifford gee-whiz in her makeup, and makes one feel comfortable in her presence. "It was the first season when everything wasn't going their way.

"It was frustrating. People were booing Kevin for the first time. It's hard to hear negative things said or written about him. It was hard for me. I'm a fan, and I know how fans think, but he's my husband. Unless you're married to one, you don't know how these players feel. He's a human being. We have feelings. And it hurts. I felt like saying to people, 'It's not his fault.' I can still see him in the hospital. I remember how badly he was hurt in that last game a year ago. We still look at the pictures of how his face looked then. Three of the doctors said if he were their son they wouldn't let him play hockey again. That was hanging over us all season.

"He wasn't able to do anything too physical all summer long. He couldn't work out. This is a man who never missed a day of conditioning work. He worked out on his conditioning routine for two hours on the day of our honeymoon. That's how dedicated he was."

Suzanne had been showing me photographs she had gotten from Kevin's parents, and some that she had in her own scrapbooks and frames. There were photos from happier days: when they got married

— they were a stunning couple, Kevin in his black tuxedo, she in her white wedding gown, all smiles — and when they posed with the Stanley Cup at a celebration party. There were lots of photos of Kevin as a kid, with his first hockey teams, as an NHL All-Star, receiving awards in high school with his parents at his side, stuff like that. Happier times.

I had spoken only two days earlier to Jack Riley, the former general manager of the Penguins, and a close observer of the scene at the Arena. Riley had a view from directly above when Stevens smashed face-forward to the ice in the game in which the New York Islanders eliminatated the Penguins from the playoffs in 1993.

Riley doesn't buy the excuse about Stevens missing off-season conditioning. "The off-season stuff is mainly for your upper body," said Riley. "You get your legs at training camp and during the season. He never skated well all season. I watched him, and Kevin wasn't coming back on defense like he should. He loafs back. He doesn't go into the corners the way he did. Maybe I can't blame him, after what happened to him. But he has to be honest with himself. He has to work harder when he's out there. He's a helluva hockey player. Maybe he'll rebound next season."

There were reports in the newspapers the day after the loss to the Capitals that Penguins owner Howard Baldwin would have to break up the team, that he could not afford to have the highest payroll in the NHL and get eliminated early two years running.

Stevens said he had spoken only the day before to Craig Patrick, the team's general manager, visiting him in his office at the Civic Arena. "He cares about the guys," Stevens said of Patrick. "He wants to know how you feel. He's a great general manager. He's a great hockey man.

"If I get traded it will be for the good of the team. He won't give any of the guys away. The same is true of Howard Baldwin. They both want to win so bad. He's been the best owner anybody could ever play for. They have to make some adjustments, there's no doubt about that. As a players' owner, I haven't heard of too many better."

There was also some post-playoff talk that Lemieux might call it quits, if he decided during the summer that he simply didn't want to continue playing with a bad back.

"I see him in the locker room, and you can tell he's hurting," said Stevens. "There are times he can't bend over to tie his shoes, or lace his skates. His back is worse than people think."

I suggested that even when he's not a hundred percent that Lemieux can accomplish more than 75 percent of the players in the NHL, and that he should not retire. Retire to what? Financially, he can afford to retire. But, spiritually, he might find little satisfaction in life without hockey. Where's the Rocky Bleier in him?

"He wants to be the best," Kevin came back. "He doesn't want to be half of what he's been. Sure, he's still better than 75 percent of the guys, but that doesn't fulfill him. I hope he comes back. He's the best there is.

"We did OK when we were able to put our team on the ice in the regular season. Winning the division was a great accomplishment of the coaches and the guys and the organization. I had two great years before this one. I have no excuses. You're kinda remembered by your last game. We all have to take a long look at what happened this season.

"We didn't skate. We need some youth, some spark, some life."

There was a far-off look in his dark eyes. He wanted to change the subject. Checking out the photos brought smiles from both Kevin and Suzanne. I asked them how they had met. She was Suzanne Pannuto back then.

"It was at a country fair right before college," said Suzanne. "We went to Boston College together. It was during the summer of 1983. I had an early decision to go to B.C., and once he found out I was going there he wanted to go there, too."

I wasn't sure whether she was just teasing Kevin or whether that was true. Kevin offered a lopsided grin in response to his wife's remarks. "I was working in the stands at the horse races, and he was there every day with his friends to bet on the horses," said Suzanne.

"I had seen her before," conceded Kevin. "I saw her watching our baseball games. She was dating one of the guys on my team, the Duxbury Legion team."

"I never noticed him before," came back Suzanne, smiling. "We have different versions of every story." Looking toward Kevin, she continued, "It wasn't until you came to the fair the tenth straight day, and stood next to me for a long time, that I noticed you."

She said she studied journalism at Boston College, and worked at a local ABC-TV affiliate. What did she like about Kevin Stevens?

"His sense of humor, his modesty," she began. "It was refreshing to meet a guy who is modest about his achievements. He was also very polite."

You don't get many scouting reports like that on Kevin Stevens.

Kevin and Suzanne Stevens skate at Penguins' 1993 Christmas Party.

Bryan Trottier
He collects Stanley Cups

*"I kept telling myself
I had something left."*

It seemed strange bumping into Bryan Trottier and his wife, Nickie, in the hallway at an open house at Upper St. Clair High School in February of 1994. My wife Kathie and I were there to meet the teachers of our daughter, Rebecca, who was a junior at the school, and the Trottiers were there for their son, Bryan Jr., a 15-year-old freshman who was playing forward for the school's club hockey team. The Trottiers had two other children, Lindsay Ann, 12, and Tayler, 4.

I had first met Bryan Trottier when he broke in with the New York Islanders in 1975. He was 19 then, not long out of high school himself, and I was 33 and in my fifth year as a sports reporter for *The New York Post*. Now he was 37. Now he was a player/coach with the Pittsburgh Penguins. He had been on four Stanley Cup championship teams with the Islanders, and two with the Penguins. He had gone back to Long Island to work for a year in the front-office of the Islanders, but found little joy or satisfaction at selling tickets. He jumped at the opportunity to come back to Pittsburgh and be a real part of an NHL team, and bought a beautiful new home in Upper St. Clair. Now the oldest of his three children was of high school age. It made me feel older.

I could remember when my oldest daughter, Sarah, 21, was four years old and had dressed up at Halloween as an Islander hockey player. The photo of her in that costume in our family album comes to mind.

The Trottiers had resisted a recruiting effort by administrators at Sewickley Academy, out in Mario Lemieux's neighborhood, and were happy with their decision to have their son go to the local public school, one which had gained national recognition for its academic achievements, and where its sports teams routinely won western Pennsylvania (WPIAL) championships, state-wide honors and always fielded first-rate teams in boys' and girls' competition.

"Bryan started playing hockey when he was nine," said his father. "His skating was somewhat limited before that. He had done a little skating and stick-handling, but nothing serious. He was a big fan of Kelly Hrudey, so he played three years as a goal-tender. Bryan came down to Washington with me once, and the two top stars of the game were goal-tenders. That was it for Bryan. We put him in a hockey school as a goal-tender. He was a goal-tender the first three years he played the game. And he went to my hockey camp on Long Island.

"When he was 12, we had eight or nine goalies at my camp. We didn't have the equipment for him to play a regular position, but we scrambled and came up with some stuff. He played defense for that week, and liked it. Last year, he played forward for the first time. He had a healthy attitude toward different positions. He had a really good year.

He was third or fourth in scoring on the team. He's very unselfish. He knows a lot of little tricks, and he plays a heady game. He's probably the hardest worker on the team. He has a short fuse and limited patience. He's like a Kevin Stevens out there. He loses his cool very quickly. He plays a high-test hockey game."

I asked Trottier how he deals with the idea of his son playing hockey, and what is the extent of his son's ambitions in that area, or his own ambitions for his son. I had seen a hockey net in the driveway of their home.

"I'm not sure how far he wants to take this," said Trottier. "I'm just a dad, and I'm enjoying the hell out of it." His son didn't get started with the sport as early as he did. That's the case with the kids of most Canadians who have come to live in the U.S.A. while playing for state-side teams in the National Hockey League.

"At this level," said Trottier, "I was playing midget hockey and getting some exposure to junior hockey. Last year, he was playing against kids anywhere from 11 to 18. Some were bigger and more mature, but he did extremely well. I didn't have to cringe when I saw him out there. He took some real shots, but he came back for more.

"He didn't have the same opportunity I had to play hockey every day. He didn't think he did very well. But I can see a change in him. He's feeling more confident, and his self-esteem is good. His high school classroom work has gotten better. He coordinates his own time well. He's more motivated. He's doing just fine."

> *"He's like the little*
> *boy in all of us."*
> —Rick Tocchet

Bryan Trottier had fashioned one of the most distinguished careers in hockey history. He has been a winner wherever he has played. The 1993-94 campaign was his 18th year in the National Hockey League.

A 5-11, 195 pound left-handed shooting center, he ranks among the league leaders in goals and assists. He played in eight NHL All-Star Games, seven with the Islanders and the last, in 1992, as a special honor for a veteran player when he was with the Penguins.

He was the most valuable player in the Western Hockey League (WHL) with Lethbridge in 1975, his last season in junior hockey before being drafted on the second round, 22nd choice overall, by the Islanders. He won the Calder Memorial Trophy in 1976 as the league's top rookie. He won the Art Ross Trophy in 1979 as the NHL's leading scorer (47 goals and 134 points). He was honored with the Hart Trophy as the league's MVP the same season. He earned the Conn Smythe Trophy in 1980 as the playoff MVP. He was named to the NHL First All-Star Team in 1978 and 1979 and the Second All-Star Team in 1982 and 1984. He was honored for his leadership and community service with the NHL Man of the Year Award in 1988 and King Clancy Memorial Trophy in 1989.

He was the president of the National Hockey League Players Association for eight years, which points up the high regard players throughout the league have had for him.

Trottier averaged 106 points per season in the Islanders' championship seasons from 1979 to 1983.

In a memorable game on February 13, 1982, Trottier set a team record for the Islanders with five goals and two assists in an 8-2 victory over the Philadelphia Flyers. He entered the 1993-94 campaign ranked 15th on the all-time list of goal-scorers, fifth in assists and sixth in points.

He has a home in Manhasset, Long Island. He owns and operates the Bryan Trottier Skating Academy in Port Washington, Long Island.

No one was more jubilant than Trottier when the Penguins won their Stanley Cup championships. No one who follows the Penguins will soon forget the sight of Trottier skating around the Met Center in Bloomington, Minnesota after the Penguins beat the Stars to win their first NHL title. Trottier was pumping his fist and bear-hugging anyone who was near him. When I saw him and his teammates at Point State Park at a celebration following the first championship, it reminded me of seeing him at similar festivities at Eisenhower Park on Long Island when I went back to my old neighborhood to visit friends, and joined them at the Islanders' victory celebration. It was more of the same when I attended the Stanley Cup celebration a year later at Three Rivers Stadium. Trottier was hugging the Stanley Cup and sliding across the rain-dampened tarpaulin that covered the infield. Trottier acted like a kid at every one of those events.

Teammate Rick Tocchet, eight years his junior, remembered as a boy watching Trottier on TV. "And now he's the little boy in all of us," said Tocchet. "He's got six (rings) and he acts like this is the first."

> *"Isn't it wonderful when people achieve their dreams?"*
> —Bryan's wife, Nickie

Trottier was wearing only a white towel, wrapped around his waist. He sat down on a huge cream-colored couch in the center of the Penguins' clubhouse. The couch faces a huge TV screen which, at mid-day, normally is carrying one of the soap operas or talk shows. Eddie Johnston sneaks by, and asks one of the players to fill him in on what's going on, or what the subject is that has brought the latest off-the-wall guests or twilight zone citizens to the show. We talked on Friday, April 15, 1994. The day before, players were milling around in the same area when NBC interrupted its regular programming to carry a breaking tragic story about how two American F-15 fighter jet airplanes shot down two of our own helicopters over northern Iraq, mistaking them for enemy aircraft in a "no-fly" zone, killing 26 people, 15 of whom were Americans. Some of the reporters in the room had paid scant attention to the report, but none of the Penguins paid any mind to it. Athletes tend to have tunnel vision, and limited interests.

Up close, Trottier resembled an old boxer. Someone like Carmen Basilio or Fritzie Zivic. There were bumps and scars about Trottier's face. A dark mustache covered up some of the mischief about his mouth from high sticks and skirmishes. There was a wicked scar on his chin, to the right side. There was a war story for every scar. He had more combat souvenirs than any of the younger Penguins in the room. Jaromir Jagr was jumping about the room, singing aloud, doing a little dancing, as he often does, his long brown hair flying, and smiling broadly. It's a smile that melts many young women fans. I wondered if Jagr made Trottier feel as old as he made me feel. Trottier smiled thinly, and winked in response. "No, Jaromir and these guys help me stay young," said Trottier. "He's got great enthusiasm, and he loves to play this game. He's good, too."

Trottier had not suited up for the Penguins in seven weeks when we talked. He had been sidelined at the outset of the season, and again at the end of the regular schedule. He had strained the muscle behind his right knee in the third period of an October 9 game against the New York Rangers, and missed six of the next seven games. Then he was sidelined the last 27 games because of back spasms. He was eager to return to play, and hoped to see action in the playoffs. He wanted once more to be a part of a Stanley Cup championship team. He had played against the best of them as a young NHLer — "I went up against Bobby Orr four times," he volunteered — and he wanted one last skate around the ice, holding the Stanley Cup high overhead. He was no longer a kid, but he could still have kid's dreams.

Trottier said he played a lot of sports when he was a youngster, starting with hockey, baseball, softball and soccer. He grew up in a small community called Val Marie, once described in an article about Trottier as "a high-prairie whistlestop in Saskatchewan." Trottier said there were just a few hundred people there, maybe 500 in the entire municipality. How small is Val Marie? Well, when I asked Trottier to place it on the map, he said, "It's about 70 miles south of Swift Current, and about ten miles north of the U.S. border."

His father had gotten involved in some road construction work in the U.S. when Trottier was a child, and the family relocated to the States. They moved back to Canada when Bryan was about six. "I started playing hockey when I was 7 or 8," he said. "But I didn't play much. I stood around a lot, looking lost. I just watched for the most part. I scrambled for a year just to get the equipment to play. I bought a pair of skates for two dollars. My dad gave me a hockey sweater he'd once worn; it was a moth-eaten sweater from the 1920s.

"I fashioned some home-made pads, and I wore winter mittens. I had no real pads, no cup. When I was nine, I played in three games. I played against teams in Bracken, Climax and Cadillac, all communities in Saskatchewan about 20 to 30 miles from our town. I didn't get my first coach until I was ten. My dad helped organize a local hockey league.

"My dad ran a ranch in Val Marie. I remember it wasn't that big. But we had a lot of bills. Lots of loans. We had cows, horses. We didn't

Trottier Family Album

Jim Cunningham

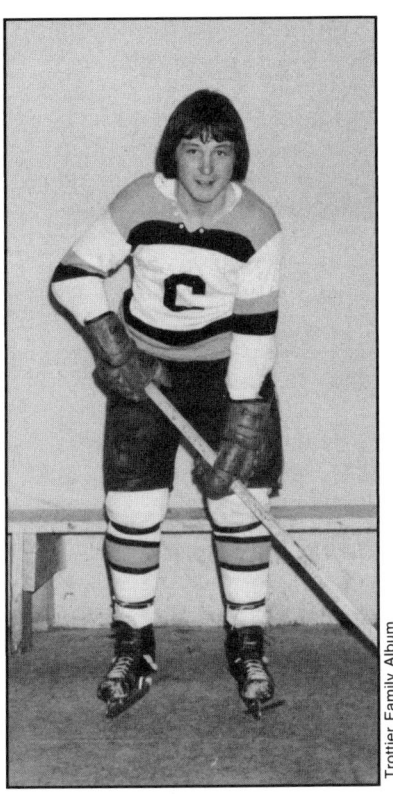

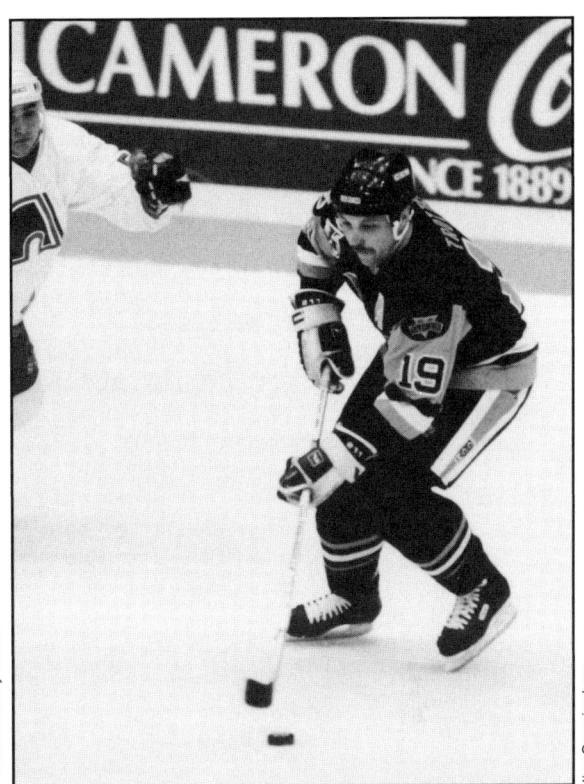

Bryan Trottier, at left, as a 15-year-old hockey aspirant, and, at right, at age 37, playing for the Pittsburgh Penguins during the 1993-94 campaign.

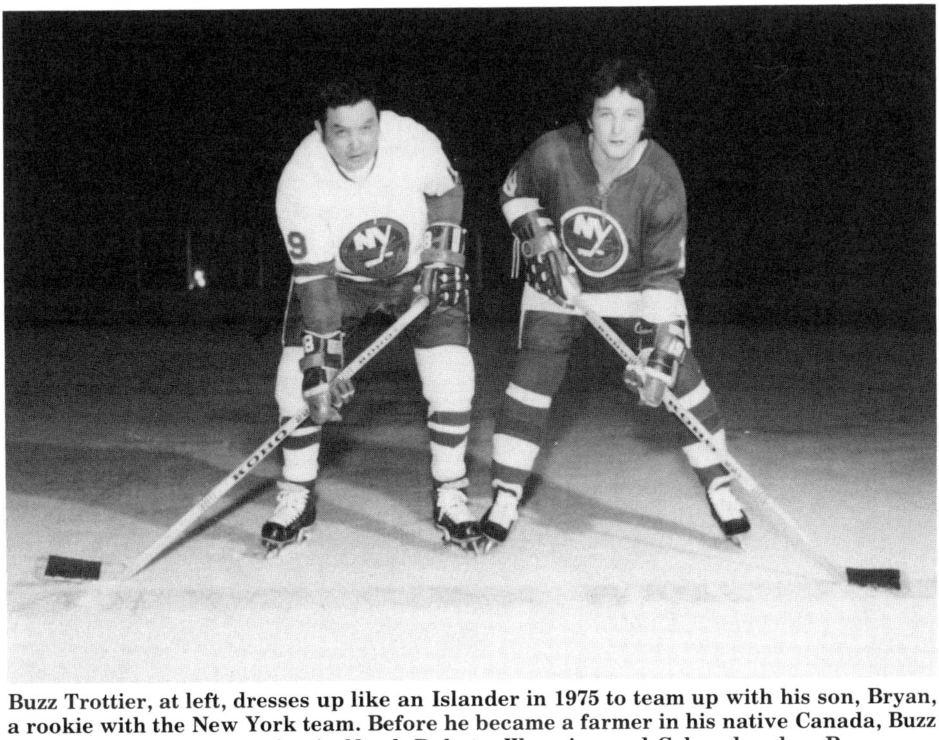

Trottier Family Album

Buzz Trottier, at left, dresses up like an Islander in 1975 to team up with his son, Bryan, a rookie with the New York team. Before he became a farmer in his native Canada, Buzz worked in road construction in North Dakota, Wyoming and Colorado when Bryan was a little boy.

have a lot of acres. I did chores morning and night. I started off just helping my dad doing whatever he wanted me to do. Everybody did chores. My mother would make sure we did what we were supposed to do. We had to milk the cows in the morning and again at night. We had to water and feed all the animals, clear their stalls and yards, and look after the chickens and round up the eggs every day, twice a day. I always had to do my share. I liked to work; I had all kinds of odd jobs. It was great for self-esteem."

Bryan was the middle child in a family of five children. He has two older sisters, Carol and Kathy, and two younger brothers, Monty and Rocky.

"I was always short for my age, even in junior hockey," he said. "I was really naive. I didn't know how anything worked. My dad might have known, but he didn't tell me. We had some pretty good hockey players come out of our area, like Tiger Williams and Terry Ruskowski (who was a winger with the Penguins from 1985 to 1987). They were pretty motivated guys. I liked the way they worked, the way they took care of themselves.

"In my rookie year in junior hockey, when I was 16, I only got 45 points. The following year, I got a lot more ice time (and points, 112 to be exact)." Then he had 144 points, with 46 goals and 98 assists, at Lethbridge, in his third and final year of junior hockey.

Cincinnati of the new World Hockey Association sent a scout to see him play, and they wanted to sign him. "Somebody advised us that we better get an agent to represent me," recalled Trottier. "We were all farmers and ranchers and we had no idea what we were supposed to do.

"When I came to the Islanders I was pretty naive. I was like a big sponge, trying to soak it all up. I was scared out of my wits. I wouldn't leave my room except to play a hockey game or to go to practice. I roomed with Billy MacMillan on the road, and he said all of about five words to me. The team held its practice sessions at a rink in Farmingdale. I had come down to see the Islanders in the playoffs the previous year. I got to see them against the Rangers. I saw them come back after losing the first three games to the Penguins to win the next four in the playoffs. That was something special. I had met everybody. Gerry Hart had taken me for a boat ride. Bert Marshall took me out. I got to know Clark Gillies and Lorne Henning and Chico Resch. Ralph Stewart took me to the Salty Dog a few times."

The Salty Dog was a popular bar-restaurant near Nassau Coliseum. Billy Paultz, a playful 6-11, 250 pound pivotman for the Nets who had played his college ball at St. John's, was a part owner. It was a lively night spot, a great meeting place for young people. After the Penguins won the first three playoff games over the Islanders in 1975, they stayed on Long Island rather than return home during a three-day break. Some observers say the Penguins spent too much time at the Salty Dog at the break, celebrating their success prematurely, and it cost them dearly. Trottier remembers the Salty Dog for other reasons.

"Stewart would hand me $20 and say, 'Here, Kid, have a good time.' The next day, he'd ask me for his $50 back. He'd do that with all the rookies. He figured you'd get a few drinks and forget where you got the money, and how much he'd given you. I was just growing up, and they were all great guys. Billy Harris, their first draft choice, was my roommate for awhile. We had Jean and Denis Potvin, Dave Fortier, J.P. Parise and Andre St. Laurent, and I was always paired off with them because my name was French. But I had not grown up in a French-Canadian environment. I didn't know any French. They'd be talking French all night. They took me to a stripper bar, I remember that. We ended up somehow in a gay bar. I was so naive; I had no idea what was going on. Some of the regulars were looking at us in a loving way. Those guys were always trying to set me up with girls, and relatives of theirs. Most of the crew that won the Stanley Cup had been together for five years. Then Mike Bossy came to the club, and that's when we really started moving. He and I became good friends. He stayed at our house when he first came to the Islanders. We were close. We were a group of young guys and we were used to being in the middle of the pack, and all of a sudden we could play with anybody, and beat them. We started playing with more confidence. Butch Goring used to say, 'We have to play with a little fear.' He told us not to be cocky, yet he was the cockiest guy on the team. But we knew what he meant."

The Islanders went into decline after they won four Stanley Cup championships. They lost out in the finals in the fifth year, and were out of the playoffs by the 1988-89 season. They didn't make the playoffs the following year, either, and Trottier's point total was down to 24 (13 goals and 11 assists). The Islanders bought up his contract and called it quits.

"I was pretty scared," said Trottier. "The two people I thought the most of in my hockey career, Bill Torrey and Al Arbour (the Islanders' general manager and coach, respectively), didn't want me anymore. They were telling me I was through. I kept telling myself I had something left, but I looked upon these two men as being so wise. I respected them so much. But things weren't working, and they made a change.

"They were saying, 'We don't think you have anything left.' It made me look at myself. It really made me angry. And, of course, I'm asking myself, 'What if they're right?' I had to prove to myself that I could still contribute. I thought I had something to give and I was looking for a team that wanted to win as badly as I did."

The Penguins turned out to be the team Trottier was looking for, and they signed him as a free agent, and paid him $400,000 on a one-year contract.

"I knew right off the bat that I'd come to the right place when I talked to Craig Patrick in Pittsburgh," said Trottier. "He said simply, 'Why do you want to keep on playing?' And I said, 'I want to win.' And Patrick said, 'If you're committed to winning, we'll do it' And I said, 'If you want to win, I want to win. I'm ready to win.' I liked the way he thinks, the way he approaches things. It was a great opportunity to leave Long Island and see what another part of the world looked like.

It's not that different for me, really. Once you get to the locker room, it's all the same.

"People sometimes think of the team as being made up of a bunch of selfish guys because of the money that's being made here, but that's not the case at all. I'm always amazed at how close this team is. To me, that's a pretty healthy situation."

Mario Lemieux's back was acting up at the outset of Trottier's first tour of duty with the Penguins. So Trottier took Lemieux's place on the Penguins' No. 1 line, playing between Kevin Stevens and Mark Recchi. "He's playing like a 20-year-old," allowed Lemieux at the time. In truth, Trottier was no longer hockey's best two-way center, but he had the savvy and skills to remain an effective player, much like Joey Mullen, one of his new teammates.

Stevens remembered how Trottier once centered for Mike Bossy and Clark Gillies on the greatest power play line in the league. "He was unbelievable then," said Stevens. "And I still can't believe I'm playing with him. He brings out the best in everybody."

Trottier's point totals in two seasons with the Penguins weren't any more impressive on paper than they had been in his last two seasons with the Islanders. But the Penguins pointed to him as helping to show the way, with his skills and leadership ability, for all the intangibles he brought to the team. They thought, and so did the team's fans, that Trottier made an impact on the Penguins, and was an important cog in two championship efforts. But after that second season, the Penguins thought they had gotten everything out of Trottier that was there to tap.

Trottier saw a different Penguins team when they lost in the playoffs to the Islanders in 1993. "When you watched them play, they didn't look like they were ready to win. It just looked like they were ready to get knocked off," he said.

His presence on the team might have helped the third time around. Who knows? "When I got here, a lot of guys had respect for me," Trottier said of his first tour of duty with the Penguins. "When I said something, they seemed to buy it. They liked my work ethic. They said, 'You really want to do something.' I brought a lot of intangibles, I believe. When I was with the Islanders, I worked extra hard in the off-season to help young kids. I tried to help bring them along. But that didn't seem to be appreciated. I like working with young players. That's why I want to continue as a coach in this sport.

"Last year proved to me that you can do anything you want to do, and you can do a good job. But if it's not something that turns you on then you're not going to be happy. I thought I was doing something I wanted to do, as far as sales were concerned. I wasn't with a hockey team. I wasn't working with young players. When the opportunity came to do it here, I was so happy. When I talked to Craig Patrick about coming back to Pittsburgh as a coach, I said to him, 'I'll throw one more at you. I want to play.' And Craig Patrick said, 'Do you think you can still play?' And I said, 'I know I can.' And he just nodded."

Eddie Johnston was willing to give Trottier the opportunity to resume playing. Johnston was glad to be back, with a chance to win another Stanley Cup. He'd been a member of the Boston Bruins team when it won two Stanley Cups. "They say the Cup follows him around," said Johnston.

When members of media asked him if he thought he had lost a step, Trottier's retort showed he was as quick as ever on his feet: "I lost a step ten years ago," he said.

Nickie Trottier thought it was great. "Isn't it wonderful when people achieve their dreams?" she said in early September of 1993. "This is a good chance for Bryan. It's made him a very happy man. Look at him. You can see the twinkle in his eye when he talks about playing again. That was missing last year. It's definitely back."

"This year was a good transition year," Trottier told me during our lengthy interview in the Penguins' clubhouse. "It was another good bonus year for me. When we won the two Stanley Cups here, I wasn't the engine leading the charge. I was the caboose, making sure no one fell off the track. I was leading from the back; I like that."

I asked him if he thought he might play in the playoffs. "I feel confident I can help," he said. "Absolutely. I want to be a hundred percent before I get out there again. I want to play hard. It's the only way I'll be useful."

Or, as he told Dave Molinari of the *Post-Gazette*, "I'll get an opportunity to slide back in there. It will be when I'm good and healthy and the team really needs me. I'm not looking to be a Moses, but I can slide in there and help out."

At that time, only Wayne Gretzky, Gordie Howe, Marcel Dionne, Phil Esposito and Stan Mikita had scored more points than Trottier. But he wasn't concerned about his statistics. "My challenge is to help this team win again," he said.

"The whole object is to have fun and make the most of your time in the game. You have hockey now, then you have something else later. Believe me, the hockey is more fun."

New York, New York

Talking to Trottier brought back many memories of my nine years in New York. I had been the beat reporter on *The New York Post* for the New York Islanders in their infancy. I covered them in their first season when they were known as the "hapless Islanders." They won only 12 games in their first season of 1972-73. I was still covering them, and the Rangers on occasion, when Trottier came to the team in 1975-76.

I may have named the Islanders. Before the team had chosen its nickname, I wondered aloud one day in a column in *The Post*, "How about the Islanders?" Who knows?

I was living on Long Island at the time. My wife Kathie and I left Miami, where I had covered the Miami Dolphins for a year (3-10-1 in George Wilson's last season) and moved to New York in 1970.

My beat was going to be Long Island. We moved to an apartment in East Rockaway, New York, about 15 minutes from where Nassau Coliseum would soon be built. It was already on the drawing board. I would be covering the New York Nets of the American Basketball Association, and an expansion team in the National Hockey League, which would be the main tenants of the Coliseum in Uniondale. In 1972, when the Islanders came into being, we bought a home in Baldwin, just ten minutes from the Coliseum. Our daughters, Sarah and Rebecca, were both born at Mercy Hospital in Rockville Centre, in 1973 and 1977, respectively. So the neighborhood near the south shore of Long Island is quite important in our lives.

1970 was a great year to move to New York. Joe Namath and the Jets upset the Baltimore Colts to win the Super Bowl the year before, and Tom Seaver and the Amazin' Mets won the World Series, and New York was still on a real sports high. I got there in April of 1970 and was immediately put on a four-man team to cover the Knicks in the NBA playoffs. The Knicks, with a starting five of Willis Reed, Dave DeBusschere, Bill Bradley, Walt Frazier and Dick Barnett, won the first NBA championship in the club's history. They would do it again two years later, with Earl Monroe and Jerry Lucas joining the cast.

Madison Square Garden was a great place to be in those days. I even had a ringside seat for the first of the Muhammad Ali-Joe Frazier heavyweight championship fights, and the electricity for that and the Knicks' games was unreal.

I covered the Nets on a full-time basis beginning with the 1970-71 season, and was with them for two seasons when Rick Barry was the star of the team and Lou Carnesecca was the coach. Carnesecca returned to St. John's University the next season and Barry went back to the NBA's Golden State Warriors. Both are now in the Basketball Hall of Fame. The Nets obtained a local lad in a deal with the Virginia Squires, for the following season. His name was Julius Erving, but he was better known as Dr. J. He was the Michael Jordan of his day. He became one of the top scorers in pro basketball history and is also in the Hall of Fame. The Nets won the ABA title that year and did it again two years later. Kevin Loughery and Rod Thorn were the coaches and both were good guys. Covering the Nets was a lot of fun. You couldn't ask for more cooperative people. Both teams were owned by a Yale-educated businessman named Roy Boe. Barney Kremenko, who had covered the New York Giants baseball team and given Willie Mays his nickname of "Say Hey," was the team's publicist. He was born to a Jewish family in Russia and emigrated to America as a child. He taught me a lot about journalism and even more about being the father of two daughters. Once I was complaining to him about something one of the editors on the desk had done with my story. He said, "Jimmela, when you go home tonight, reach into your daughter's crib and take her hand. Just hold it for awhile. And none of that other stuff will seem to matter." He was right, of course.

There were some familiar faces on that first Islanders team. Bill Torrey, the general manager, had gotten his start in sports management and marketing as a young aide to John Harris with the Hornets and *Ice Capades* in Pittsburgh. Bert Marshall, a veteran defenseman, had played for the Hornets and we had some mutual acquaintances. He knew some of the people I knew at a hockey hangout on Liberty Avenue in Bloomfield known as the Pleasure Bar. In fact, he had once roomed upstairs of the popular Italian restaurant as a rookie with the Hornets.

It took time, but Torrey put together a team that would win four Stanley Cup championships. Some of the pieces of that championship club came to the team when I was still writing about the Islanders: Denis Potvin, Bryan Trottier, Billy Smith, Chico Resch, Garry Howatt, Lorne Henning and Bobby Nystrom. They added people like Duane Sutter, Mike Bossy, Butch Goring and John Tonelli. I used to play tennis with Marshall, Henning and Nystrom, as well as some of the early Islanders like Billy MacMillan and Gerry Hart. It's hard to believe that Smith, Potvin and Bossy are now in the Hockey Hall of Fame in Toronto, and Trottier will be in there as soon as he stops skating and becomes eligible. These guys were easy to work with. I had them conduct clinics a couple of times at my local tennis club in Baldwin, and for the kids in my neighborhood in the cul-de-sac where my home was located. I had no idea then that they would eventually win four Stanley Cups. It was as improbable back then as anybody in Pittsburgh in the '70s or '80s thinking that the Penguins would win the NHL title some day. Trottier told me he remembers me writing a "scathing article" about him when he had a bad playoff series with the Buffalo Sabres. It didn't ring a bell with me. I didn't remember doing it, and it was best forgotten.

Brian Trottier has "one for the thumb" — the Penguins' first Stanley Cup ring.

Rick Kehoe
Always a smoothie

"I couldn't get enough of it."

As a youngster growing up in Windsor, Ontario, Rick Kehoe discovered hockey at his doorstep. His home on Edinborough Street was directly across the road from an outdoor hockey rink. All he had to do was cross the street and he was in a game.

It was called Remington Park and, in truth, it was a recreation park. Each winter they would flood part of a ballfield and it would freeze over, forming a skating surface. "The best thing was when they put up the lights," recalled Kehoe. "Then we could play all night. My mother would scream out the door for me to come home at night. I couldn't get enough of it."

Kehoe thinks he was three or four years old when he received his first pair of skates. It started a lifelong love affair with hockey.

"In Canada, the schools go from first to eighth grade, and then you go to high school," he said. "When I was in eighth grade, the teachers asked me what my interests were, so they could determine where to place me in high school. 'What do you want to be when you grow up?' they asked me. I said, 'I'm going to be a hockey player.' And they'd just smile."

Kehoe can smile back now. At 43 in the summer of 1994, he was still making his living doing what he liked best, working in the National Hockey League. He was serving as an assistant coach to Eddie Johnston with the Pittsburgh Penguins. Before that, he assisted Scotty Bowman and Bob Johnson, and contributed to two Stanley Cup championship efforts. Before that, he was an assistant to Pierre Creamer, Gene Ubriaco and Craig Patrick when the Penguins didn't qualify for the playoffs.

In June of 1992, Kehoe joined Johnson and former teammate Jean Pronovost as charter members of the Pittsburgh Penguins Hall of Fame. Kehoe had also distinguished himself in ten seasons (1974-1984) as a sparkling right winger with the Penguins. His name is often found in the Penguins record book, right behind Mario Lemieux and above or below Pronovost. Kehoe claimed the Lady Byng Trophy in 1981. This is an annual award "to the player adjudged to have exhibited the best type of sportsmanship and gentlemanly conduct combined with a high standard of playing ability."

It all began in Windsor. I said, "Isn't that right across the river, just north of Detroit?" Kehoe came back, "A little geography lesson: Windsor is south of Detroit, southeast really. Most Americans think it's north of Detroit because they think of Canada being north of the U.S.A."

Detroit had Gordie Howe and the Red Wings, but Kehoe was Canadian to the core, so he followed the Maple Leafs of Toronto, 220 miles away. As a kid, Kehoe never went to Detroit or Toronto to see any NHL games.

"It was about a 20-minute drive from where I lived to Detroit. It would be like going from Mt. Lebanon to the Civic Arena," said Kehoe.

"Some of the people in Windsor were Red Wings fans, but the majority were Maple Leafs fans. When I was playing midget hockey, which was for 13-year-olds up to 16-year-olds, we used to practice Monday mornings from 5 to 6 at the Windsor Arena. After practice, these guys from Detroit used to come out on the ice, and one of them was Ted Lindsay, who had been a great hockey player with the Red Wings (he was a tough high-scoring forward known as 'Terrible Ted' Lindsay). He was just one of a bunch of guys who rented the rink to play hockey. We'd stand around and watch them for awhile, before we had to go to school. He may have been the first NHL player I ever saw in person.

"I didn't see an NHL game until I was playing junior hockey. We went to London, Ontario once, and played an exhibition game against the Boston Bruins. Eddie Johnston was playing for the Bruins back then. That was 1969. Bobby Orr was the star of the Bruins. I was 18 at the time."

I asked Kehoe if Johnston played goalie in that game. "I didn't score, so I don't remember who was in goal," he said.

"I got traded to the Hamilton Red Wings, and ended up playing against the Red Wings. We were their junior team. Howe was there. That was all during my first year of junior A hockey."

Was Howe or Orr one of his heroes during his early hockey-playing days?

"No, Dave Keon was my favorite. And I got to play with him in Toronto. I played a half season in Tulsa in the old Central League, and then I went to Toronto. I had a good time in Tulsa. I was the third-leading scorer in the league when I left, and I was the third-leading scorer on my team. So we were loaded, and winning. Marcel Pronovost, the older brother of Jean Pronovost, was our coach at Tulsa. He had been an All-Star player in the National Hockey League.

"Johnny McLelland was the coach at Toronto when I got there that first year, but he got sick. King Clancy took over. He was a legend in Toronto."

King Clancy had coached the Pittsburgh Hornets back in the '50s, when the Hornets were a farm team of Toronto in the American Hockey League. When I mentioned some of the magic names of that team to Kehoe, players like Gil Mayer, Bobby Solinger, Marc Reaume, Frank Mathers, Willie Marshall, Tim Horton, George Armstrong, he interjected, "Marc Reaume was from just outside of Windsor; I remember him."

This reminded Kehoe of his childhood in Windsor. "Hockey Night in Canada was on the radio on Saturday night," said Kehoe, "and you couldn't get me away from it. My mother thought I had a hearing problem. She couldn't get my attention.

"My parents divorced when I was 13. I had a brother who was eight years younger. I have a step-brother and a step-sister, and a half-sister. I was the oldest of five; they were just sisters and brothers to me."

Kehoe's father worked for the public works department of the city of Windsor as a backhoe operator. He was not a hockey fan. Rick's grandfather on his mother's side of the family, Russ Hillman, was a big sports fan, however, and so were his sons. "My uncles were all into sports," said Kehoe.

So was Rick. While he wanted to grow up to be a hockey player, he also wanted to be a baseball player. He started out as an infielder, then switched to the outfield, before giving up the game when he got involved in junior hockey.

"When I turned pro in hockey, I played in a slow-pitch softball league in the summer that was pretty competitive," said Kehoe.

"Neither Kehoe nor Maz are Madison Avenue guys."

Kehoe and I had this conversation at The Korner, a subterranean neighborhood hangout located at 4 Bower Hill Road, just off Washington Road, catty-corner from St. Bernard's Church in Mt. Lebanon. It was called the Korner Bar before Kehoe and a couple of partners purchased the place six years earlier. "And we just kept the name," said Kehoe, with a no-big-deal shrug.

It would seem that it would make more sense, and even sound OK, if it were called "Rick Kehoe's Korner Bar." That would capitalize more on Kehoe's popularity in Pittsburgh, especially with the hockey crowd. Then again, Bill Mazeroski, the hero of the Pirates' 1960 World Series triumph, calls his place in Ohio simply "Bill's Bar." Neither Kehoe nor Maz are Madison Avenue guys.

I was fifteen minutes early for our meeting, and had a chance to check out The Korner. The only indicator that the bar belonged to Kehoe was that his Penguins jersey — No. 17 — is displayed in a large glass case at the end of the bar.

The Korner is cut into a steep hillside, and doesn't have what real estate agents refer to as "curb appeal." Inside, however, its appearance improves considerably. It's clean and comfortable, looked after by Kehoe's partners, Mary Ann and Madonna Crouse, two sisters-in-law.

There were a half dozen men seated on stools at the 20-foot long bar. They were silent when I arrived and their conversations were somewhat muted. There were beer-sponsored signs and logos on all the walls. There were two dining rooms, sort of a split level situation.

There's a dart board that gets a lot of action in a league on evenings and weekends. The tables have backgammon playing surfaces, but no one plays backgammon, according to Kehoe, not since he took over the place, anyhow.

At the end of the bar opposite Kehoe's jersey-under-glass are three 8 x 10 black-and-white photos, showing an overhead view of Forbes Field, one showing several Pirates, including Willie Stargell and Roberto Clemente in a dugout scene, and one of Mazeroski's game-winning home run in the seventh game of the 1960 World Series.

There was a baseball game on the TV, from WWOR-TV in New York. The Mets were playing the Cubs at Wrigley Field in Chicago on the third day of the 1994 Major League Baseball season, and the familiar voice in the room belonged to Ralph Kiner, a Hall of Famer and former Pirates home run hitting hero of the '40s and '50s. Kiner was now 70 and in his 32nd season as a Mets' announcer.

Then Kehoe came through the screened-door, at 3 p.m., as scheduled. He looked terrific, as usual. He had just come from a practice session on a day between NHL games at the Civic Arena, a day before the regular-season finale for the 1993-94 campaign.

He was wearing an over-sized windbreaker, with patches of violet, teal and orange, but mostly white. The sleeves had the fullness of those blouses once worn in the movies by the swashbuckling likes of Douglas Fairbanks and Errol Flynn. Kehoe has that look. You can easily picture him on a ship with a sword in hand. He and Duane Rupp, who once operated a hockey equipment store next door, have the same look. Kehoe's once jet-black hair has a gray dusting on it now, but it always looks like he just got out of a hair stylist's chair, just right, swept back with the kind of fullness and body that makes most of us envious. He wore white sneakers, light blue slacks, and a two-toned blue plaid shirt. He had coordinated his colors well.

There was a smile under his meticulously-cut mustache, as coal-dark as his gleaming eyes. In short, Kehoe has kept his boyish looks, and remains a handsome devil. He knows it. Kehoe was called "Chico" during his playing days, after a mustachioed Puerto Rican played by Freddie Prinze in a TV sitcom called "Chico And The Man."

Kehoe checked out the surroundings in his saloon, when I asked about The Korner. "We had the Stanley Cup on display here both times that we won it, and we had a thousand people go through here in a short time," said Kehoe. "We did a Sportsbeat Show for KBL right here with Guy Junker.

"It's a neighborhood bar. We have a lot of apartment buildings nearby. There's no parking, so everybody walks here. It's not a big money-maker, but it takes care of itself. We have PennVision, and we get a good crowd to watch the games.

"We have friendly competition in softball games with some of the other sports bars in Mt. Lebanon, like The Saloon and Atria's. Jimmy Sheppard and Nick Atria, who own those places, come to my place, and I go to their places, even though we're in the same business. We've played softball games against their teams. Whichever team loses, the owner has to bartend the other team's bar. Nick Atria has tended bar here. We play at a field up in Scott Township."

Kehoe was divorced in 1983, after ten years of marriage. His 17-year-old daughter Karrie was a senior at Mt. Lebanon High School during the 1993-94 season, and is a frequent visitor to his condominium at the Timbercreek Apartment complex near The Galleria.

Interestingly enough, Rick, who has been married and divorced twice, said he had been dating his first wife, Peg, in recent years. "Maybe we both matured a little; but I'm glad we got together again," he said.

Kehoe has come a long way since he first arrived in Pittsburgh. He was acquired from the Toronto Maple Leafs on September 13, 1974. He was one of the first Penguins to win an NHL post-season award, winning the Lady Byng Memorial Trophy in 1981.

Kehoe's credentials are impressive. He scored a career-high 55 goals in the 1980-81 season, which is the third highest total in club history. Only Lemieux has more goals in a season with the Penguins. During his playing days in Pittsburgh, Kehoe led the team in goals and points on three occasions. He scored 25 or more goals in nine of his ten seasons with the Penguins, while passing the 30-goal mark five times. His eight hat tricks were second only to Lemieux.

His 636 points with the Penguins ranked Kehoe runner-up to Lemieux and, at the time of his induction into the Penguins Hall of Fame, he was second in games played (722), third in goals (312), fourth in assists (324) and second in power play goals (95). He played in two NHL All-Star Games.

He retired after the 1984-85 season due to a pinched nerve in his neck. It still bothers him from time to time.

"When I first came here, the Steelers were so dominant back in the '70s, and the Pirates were always in contention. Hockey was kinda in between. The football season had already started when we began to play, and then the Pirates would start up before we finished. We were like the third sport in town.

"I was happy to come here, though. At the time, I was ready to make a move. It was a nice change for me. In Toronto, I couldn't go anywhere without being recognized. We were on TV twice a week. Hardly anyone wore a helmet back then. Everybody knew you when you walked down the street. I lived in downtown Toronto for two years, and it was really hectic. In Pittsburgh, you could go out and not be bothered. In Toronto, people would come up to you no matter what you were doing and ask for an autograph. That's fine sometimes, but it got out of control. You couldn't have a life of your own."

Hockey was a dress-up affair for many years in Toronto. Men in the best seats at rink-side sometimes showed up in tuxedos. Dark suits were in the majority in the most expensive seats.

When I mentioned this to Kehoe, he came back with this item: "We had a dress code for the team. We had to wear a shirt and tie to practice. They figured people would see you coming and going and they wanted you to look like professional businessmen. A lot of times the shirts and ties didn't match; guys grabbed whatever they could come up with on the way out of their homes and apartments."

I also recalled that Maple Leaf Gardens had the steepest incline for seats in the NHL. "You can't see the faces of the players, just the numbers, from the grays — that's what they call the seats in the rafters."

Kehoe didn't care where he was playing, as long as it was in the National Hockey League.

"I'd always dreamed of playing in the NHL; and I was doing it and doing it well," he recalled. "I was just thinking of playing the game,

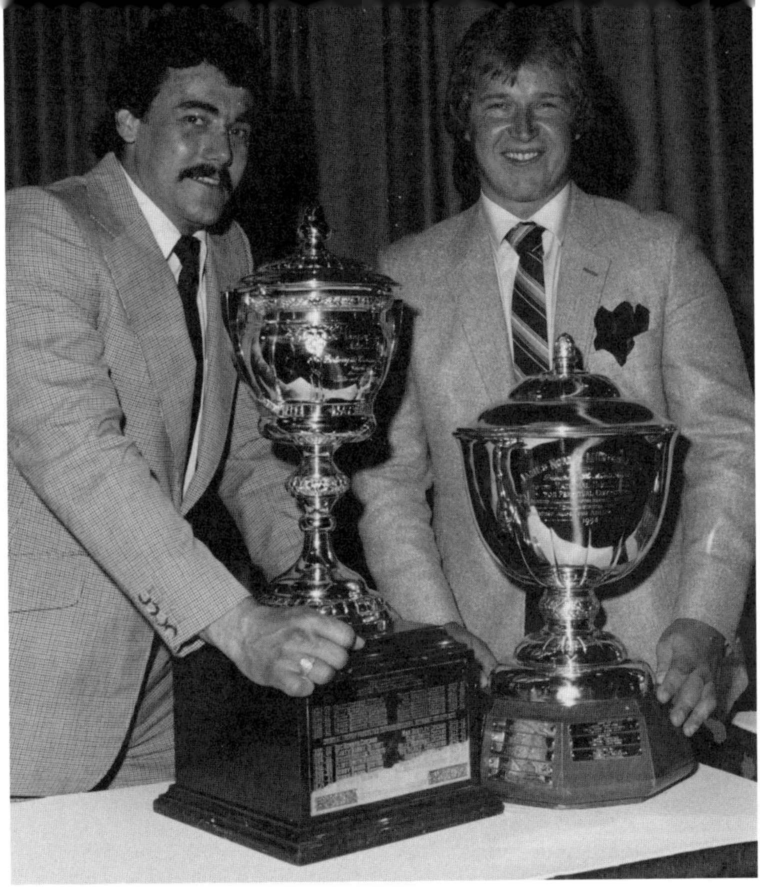

Pittsburgh Penguins

Two Penguins distinguished themselves during the 1980-81 season. Rick Kehoe captured the Lady Byng Trophy for sportsmanship and Randy Carlyle won the James Norris Trophy as the league's top defenseman.

Jim Cunningham

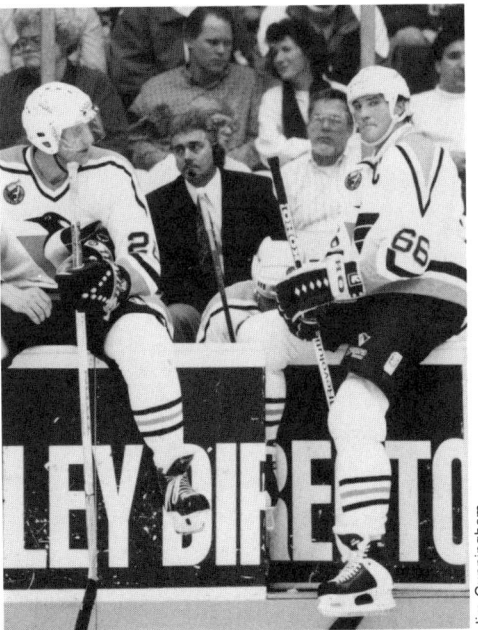

Kehoe gets information from above at Arena as assistant coach to Eddie Johnston.

Jim Cunningham

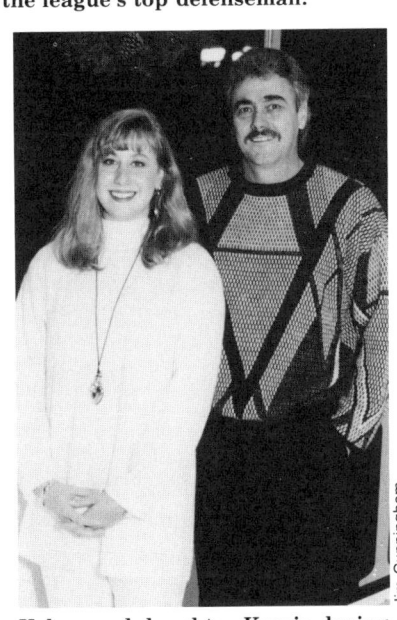

Kehoe and daughter Karrie during her school days at Mt. Lebanon High School.

at the highest level. It came down to how you handled it. It all comes down to how you were brought up.

"My grandfather had the biggest influence on me. We used to compete against each other. If we were playing pool, my grandmother always knew who lost. Whoever lost would be the first one up the stairs into the kitchen. Whoever lost would be upset. Whoever won stayed behind and put everything away.

"My grandfather, when he was younger, had been a professional boxer. He could handle himself. We lived in the same neighborhood as my grandparents, and my parents both worked. I'd get dropped off at my grandparents, so I spent a lot of time with them."

"I had played with E.J. my last year in Toronto."

When Kehoe recalled the good times and bad times with the Penguins, he cautioned me, "There are a lot of great stories that I can't tell you."

When Kehoe came to the Penguins, the general manager was Jack Button and the coach was Marc Boileau, who had replaced Ken Schinkel behind the bench the year before. Schinkel would bump Boileau the following season, and would be followed during Kehoe's playing tenure by Johnny Wilson, Eddie Johnston, Lou Angotti and Bob Berry.

After he retired, Kehoe was chosen by Johnston, then the general manager, to head up the team's professional league scouting. He did that for two years, then became an assistant coach for the 1987-88 campaign, working under Pierre Creamer. In subsequent seasons, he helped Gene Ubriaco, Craig Patrick and Bob Johnson, and that's when the Penguins couldn't get into the playoffs without tickets.

"We had a good team my first year here as a player," said Kehoe. "We set a club record with a 20-game unbeaten streak (by beating St. Louis, 3-2, on February 22, 1975)."

During Kehoe's playing career with the Penguins, some other important things happened. Tad Potter and his group gave up the ghost and sold the team to Wren Blair and his group who, in turn, dealt the team to Edward J. DeBartolo. Three years later, DeBartolo would take over the Civic Arena.

Baz Bastien became the club's general manager in December of 1976. In 1976, Jean Pronovost became the first Penguin to score 50 goals and Pierre Larouche became the first Penguin to record 100 points in one season. Bob Prince became the Penguins' television play-by-play man. Unreal.

Eddie Johnston became the coach and was later kicked upstairs to be the general manager after Bastien was killed in an automobile accident. The team switched uniforms, going from dark and light blue and white to black and gold. And Johnston staved off the buzzards and held onto the Penguins' first pick in the 1984 draft. That's when the Penguins picked Mario Lemieux.

Rick Kehoe was a playboy back in Windsor, Ontario.

Kehoe Family Album

"That turned things around for this franchise," said Kehoe. "At the time, we were drawing 6,000 to 8,000. A lot of fans had lost interest. But he was 18 and became an idol. The kids wanted to go watch him and that meant their parents had to take them. Before long, you couldn't get a ticket."

Kehoe's recollection of Johnston goes back even farther.

"I had played with E.J. my last year in Toronto; that's when we got to know each other," said Kehoe. "He went to St. Louis the next year and I went to Pittsburgh."

Lemieux was not the first great young player Kehoe saw up close. "Larouche was 19 when he came here," said Kehoe. "I was on a line with him and Bob 'Battleship' Kelly when Larouche got 53 goals our second year with the team. Kelly was the guy who took care of everybody. He was our enforcer. Larouche had so much talent. Give him the puck around the net, and he could put it past anybody. He scored 30 or 31 his first year and then 53 the second year.

"He just got around the wrong crowd. It happens when you're young. He could have probably been like Mario is now. He got sidetracked, which is easy to do when you're young. The best thing that happened to him was to get traded to Montreal. He went there and scored 50 goals and he went to Hartford and then New York with the Rangers, and he nearly had 50 goals there. He almost became the first player to score 50 goals for three teams in the National Hockey League."

Then Kehoe came up with a story that points up a major difference in what life was like for professional athletes in those days, and what it's like now, when most players tend to go their own way, and seldom socialize together when the team is at home.

"With that team, many of the guys lived in the Chatham Park Apartments in Green Tree," said Kehoe. "Some of the Steelers live there, and so did some of the Pirates. We had a pretty good time back then. A lot of the guys liked to go to a bar and restaurant near the apartments called the Jamestown Inn. Lots of sports guys went there.

"We were pretty close. There were a few guys who owned homes, and they were close by, too. I was out in the parking lot one day, after it had snowed, and I was cleaning off my car. I started making some snowballs and I threw them at the windows of the apartment where Gary Inness, our goalie, was living. He came out of his apartment, wondering who the hell was hitting his windows with snowballs, and we started throwing snowballs at each other. Ron Schock really got upset because he didn't know who was tossing snowballs at his windows. He came racing out in a fury, and we all ambushed him. He still didn't know who was out there, and he ran back into his apartment, wondering what was going on.

"Then we went to Jean Pronovost's place and got him all riled up, before he realized it was us who were throwing the snowballs at his house. By the end, we had about eight players from Chatham Park in a snowball fight. We went to Kelly's place, then to Lowell MacDonald's place. We ended up having a party, with guys and their wives, and we ended up at the Brookside where Vic Hadfield and Dave Burrows lived.

We ended up with three-quarters of the team. What started out as a snowball fight ended up as a great party. We did some crazy things in those days. But we had fun."

Nobody had any more fun than Hadfield. I knew Hadfield from his days with the Rangers in New York. We had the same agent, Steve Arnold, and Arnold succeeded in getting then record contracts for Hadfield and three of his teammates, Brad Park, Jean Ratelle and Rod Gilbert. Hadfield had a reputation as a real practical joker.

"He was always playing tricks on the maintenance crew at the Civic Arena," said Kehoe. "There was a guy there named Obiecunas..."

I interrupted Kehoe because Jerry "Obie" Obiecunas had been a left-handed pitcher on the men's baseball team in our hometown of Hazelwood. There were people who called me "Obie" at the same time, much to my chagrin. Obiecunas was one of several people from our community who got jobs on the maintenance staff at the Arena, including an infielder named Buddy Martine.

"He was in on this, too," recalled Kehoe. "Hadfield had this Mercedes-Benz 240, a beautiful sports model, and he was the only one on the team who had a car like that back then. He parked it on the ramp outside Gate 5. So one day Obiecunas and his buddies jacked up the car and put it on blocks so that the wheels were just slightly off the ground, by an inch maybe. Hadfield got in the car, pressed on the gas, and the car went nowhere. All he was doing was spinning the wheels. That's how they got back at him for what he was always doing to them. You didn't want to mess with those guys. They'd get even."

There were other light moments:

"I remember once when we got paid when the team was having a lot of financial problems. I went and put my check in my account right away. I told the other guys, 'Did you put your checks in the bank yet? I hear the team's going bankrupt.' And they all took off for their banks.

"Tad Potter was operating the team then. He told Jack Button to get the players, and he did. But they couldn't afford it. And the bottom fell out eventually. They ended up padlocking the doors of the Penguins' offices at the Arena."

What about the worst of times?

"The lowpoint was the year I got hurt. It was a neck injury and it eventually forced me to retire. I had a herniated disc. There are some days when I still feel it. When the weather changes, I know about it in my neck. It'll bother me. Back then, they weren't sure you could have an operation and correct it. It would come and go. They can correct it now with an operation. The doctor said as long as you can live with it, let's not mess with it."

"We keep learning every day."
—Rick Kehoe

Kehoe keeps tapes on file of every NHL team's power play, and how they set up for penalty-killing. He likes to review it with players who want to study what the opposition is doing. One of his tasks is to break down tapes that are made of each game. Kehoe believes players should always be trying to improve their skills and their overall approach to the game.

"You have a dream, and that's where you want to end up," he explained. "You have to do the things in between, to try and get better. There are so many things that you can improve on, if you want to be better. We keep learning every day."

When Scotty Bowman was coaching the team, he only conducted a few practices the entire campaign. The players told Craig Patrick they preferred not having him at practice, if you can believe that, and so Bowman left his assistants in charge of practice. Kehoe and Barry Smith set up the practice drills. The players preferred communicating their thoughts through the assistants. Bowman gave them the chills.

"They generally talk to us and then we talk to Scotty," Kehoe said at the time. "But we organize practice, and decide what drills we want to do." Neither Johnston nor Bowman did as much individual coaching or teaching as did Bob Johnson, who had been a college coach, but both know their hockey, according to Kehoe.

"I know what the players can do. I know when they're at the top of their game. It's not so much you have to teach then, you just have to offer reminders now and then about what they're doing. Guys know what to do, but they get away from it now and then.

"They know, for instance, that when you get the puck along the board in the defensive end of the ice, you have to get it out of there, and there's a way to do it. But they don't always do it the way you're supposed to; they don't work at it in practice, that's why.

"Nobody likes to practice back-checking or checking. You don't have to knock players down in practice, but you have to work at back-checking. Players prefer to shoot the puck."

Kehoe's comment reminded me of something Chuck Noll used to say when he was coaching the Steelers. "People tend to practice what they do well, not what they don't do well," noted Noll. "It feels better. But people should work at their weaknesses, not their strengths."

Kehoe nodded at that comment.

"Badger (Bob Johnson) was a little different. He taught us all. He was such a salesman for the game. We'd be in a slump, and he'd come in for a morning skating session. Maybe we'd lost four or five in a row, and some guys were sulking. He'd come in, 'We have a lot of work to do today. C'mon, it's a great day for hockey.' He'd always find something good in every situation.

"Bowman was more of a strategist. He would watch films all night at the Arena. And he had a satellite dish at his home in Buffalo, and he'd spend a lot of time watching other teams. He was always trying to figure out match-ups. He wanted certain lines against certain lines. And he'd be patient, waiting to get the chance to get the match-up he wanted.

"He'd ask you all kinds of questions, and seek your thoughts on every subject. But he offered little in return. He didn't give away much of what he was thinking. What he wanted was an edge; he always wanted that edge.

"People ask me about Eddie Johnston. The best way to describe E.J. is that he's in the middle of Bowman and Badger Bob. He's always talking hockey. We're coming off the ice together after a game, and he's still talking hockey. Bob Johnson would say, 'You've got to be like a salesman. You go to work today and you've got to hope they're buying.' That was one of his sayings.

"I'm always finding quotes in books that I can bring to the players. I'll be reading a book, and I see a quote I can use, and I write it down. Everything Bob talked about related to the team. The team comes first; you have to sacrifice for the team. With Bob, he believed you won as a team and you lost as a team. Scotty would come in the locker room after a loss, and he'd be bitching about this guy didn't do this, or that guy didn't do that. Scotty would yell at everybody. He'd get personal. But nobody likes to lose. Everybody takes losing hard."

Kehoe said he wanted to tell a story about Bowman he thought was funny. "We're playing a game in Cleveland, and our Penguin mascot came up for the game," he said. "He was hot, and took off his head and put it down on the floor. Our trainer comes along, and picks up the head and puts it on. He jumps out in front of Bowman as he's coming out of the locker room. Bowman just drilled him. And he went down. A cop was standing nearby, and he hollered out, 'I can't believe he hit the mascot!' We were still laughing about that on the bench the whole next period."

Kehoe can appreciate the change in fortunes for the Penguins better than just about anybody in the organization. "I've seen Mario from Day One," he said, "and it all changed because of him. It didn't happen overnight, for sure, but he was the key to the turnaround in this team's fortunes."

He credits Craig Patrick for putting together the missing pieces of the puzzle, and building a winning team. "It didn't just happen; it was a process," he said. He believes the players are eager to extend their success.

"They've had a taste of what it takes to win," he said. "They know what it takes to win. All of a sudden, the level of play moves up. When we played Boston, I knew we'd be ready to play them. Last night, when we played Tampa Bay at home, I was scared. I didn't know if they'd be ready to play Tampa Bay."

He believed that Johnston's strength was his ability to keep the communication lines open with the players.

"His door's always open," he said. "He's always talking to them about the game. E.J. is just easy to be around."

Where Are They Now?

Ken Schinkel, left, as a player for the Penguins in 1971-72 season, and, right, as chief scout for Hartford Whalers in 1993-94 season.

No one was associated with the Penguins as long as Ken Schinkel. He was a player on the team when it came into the NHL in 1967-68. He stayed with the franchise for 21 years before he joined GM Eddie Johnston at Hartford in 1989. He was named the Whalers' chief scout in 1993 when Johnston returned to Pittsburgh.

Schinkel played right wing in the NHL for 11 seasons, starting his career in 1959-60 with the New York Rangers. He ended his playing career on January 13, 1973 to become head coach of the Penguins. He held that post twice over a four-year span before becoming a front office official. Schinkel, 62, and his wife Shirley are the proud parents of three children: Kenneth, Karen and Steven.

Glen Sather was a journeyman left winger who played for six teams during his nine-year playing career, including the Penguins from 1969 to 1971. He became one of the league's most successful coaches, directing the Edmonton Oilers to four Stanley Cup championships. He has most recently served that club as its president and general manager.

Earl Ingarfield was the first Penguin taken in the 1967 expansion draft. He has been a scout for the New York Islanders. Billy Dea, also a forward for the Penguins in their first two seasons, is the Red Wings' U.S. Scouting Director.

Among other original Penguins still in the NHL, Al MacNeil is the director of hockey operations for the Calgary Flames, and Noel Price is a scout for the Vancouver Canucks.

Glen Sather   **Earl Ingarfield**   **Billy Dea**

Jack Riley
He put the Penguins on ice

*"It was a thrill to put
a team together from scratch."*

Jack Riley was the original general manager of the Penguins. He put the team together and, in some respects, he has never let go. It is still his team, in his heart, anyhow. That helps explain why he was still stewing five days after the Penguins had disappointed their fans by getting eliminated from the 1994 Stanley Cup playoffs by the Washington Capitals in six games in the first round. The Penguins had won their divisional title during the regular season, had their team intact just in time for the post-season competition, and were thought to have a real shot at winning their third Stanley Cup in four years.

"Where'd our hunger go?" Craig Patrick, the general manager of record, was asking. "Why didn't we have it?"

Patrick was not the only one asking those kind of questions in the wake of the abrupt end to the season. Riley was ruminating about what went wrong with the Penguins the past season, and choosing his words as carefully as he chose what he was going to spear next in the lemon chicken salad he was eating. He had his own feelings, but he did not want to speak out of turn. The Penguins were not his responsibility anymore, hard as that was to accept. He was in good humor, but I had the feeling there was molten lava bubbling in his belly. Maybe it was just the limp French fries in his salad.

"They missed guys like Bob Errey, Phil Bourque and Troy Loney, guys who would go into the corners and get the puck," said Riley. "They had four guys who ran out of gas by the time the playoffs came along: Larry Murphy, Ron Francis, Joey Mullen and Kevin Stevens. Stevens couldn't skate a lick by the time the playoffs began. You could see that coming."

It was Monday, May 2, and I was having lunch with Riley at Chicago's Pizzeria & Ice Creamery at the Gallery Shoppes in Mt. Lebanon, across the way from St. Clair Hospital, and near Riley's residence in Scott Township. Riley has had a home in Scott since he was hired as general manager of the Penguins back in 1967. He looked good, fresh-faced and healthy looking, little more than a month away from his 75th birthday (June 14). There was still some red in his hair. An affable fellow, Riley looks like the sort of guy you would expect to be the grand marshal of a St. Patrick's Day Parade.

It was not a particularly good day to be the general manager of the Penguins, or a past general manager who still cared about the club. Not only were the scars still fresh from the team's second straight disappointing playoff performance, but to worsen the situation there was negative news on the radio that morning involving the Penguins. Stories were coming to light about a fight involving three members of the Penguins organization at a Downtown restaurant/saloon just three days earlier.

Penguins defenseman Peter Taglianetti had tagged one of the customers — a student at the nearby Art Institute — at Froggy's, a popular three-story sports hangout on Market Street, and John Welday, the strength and conditioning coach of the Penguins, head-butted the young man and broke his nose, according to police reports. Goalie Tom Barrasso was accused of making some menacing remarks, or what were later termed "terroristic threats." Kevin Stevens was there, but stayed his distance. Steve "Froggy" Morris told the news media it was no big deal, just a few punches, usual saloon stuff.

"It isn't something you'd want to put in your season ticket brochure," club owner Howard Baldwin would concede two days later at a team state-of-the-Penguins press conference. "I'm disappointed and frustrated."

The Penguins and Froggy's have a dark history. Back on March 15, 1983, general manager Baz Bastien died in an auto accident while driving to his home in Upper St. Clair after drinking at Froggy's. Bastien had been a good friend of Riley. Bastien brought back some memories for Riley.

"I played against Baz when I was about 20 or 21 years old," recalled Riley. "We were in the same outfit in the Canadian Army; we were stationed together in Cornwall, Ontario.

"He was a helluva goal-keeper. The NHL teams carried only one goalie in those days. That's something that always amazed me about hockey. You have the most important position in the game, and they had no one in reserve. They usually had someone sitting in the stands who could suit up, just in case.

"Speaking of Baz, people are always telling me, 'I was at the game at Duquesne Gardens when he lost his eye.' That's not where he got hit with the puck. It was a training camp miscue at Welland, Ontario, just north of the border, near Niagara Falls. That's where it happened. Speaking of Duquesne Gardens, I'm always reading about crowds of 6,000 being there for this and that sports event. They must have included the rats in that attendance count. I played there, and that place didn't hold more than 4,500 people. History has a way of making everything bigger as time goes on. Frank Mathers, who was such a great player for the Hornets, just retired from hockey. He could have been a great expansion player."

There is not much that Riley does not know about the hockey history of Pittsburgh. He knows where all the skeletons are stored.

Even though Riley has been involved in hockey in Pittsburgh in one capacity or another longer than Bastien, his old friend remains "Mr. Hockey" in Pittsburgh sports lore.

"I remember Baz won the Dapper Dan Man of the Year after guiding the Hornets to the American Hockey League championship in 1967," said Riley, who was the commissioner of the AHL prior to joining the Penguins. "I didn't think I'd see that honor go to a hockey person here.

"To me, he was just a great friend. I was talking on the telephone to him one day, and he told me he was playing in a celebrity golf outing here called the Ham-Am Tournament. I said, 'Who's the celebrity in your foursome?' He said, 'I am! I am!' And I was serious. To me, I just never saw him as a celebrity."

That tells you a lot about Baz Bastien, but even more about Jack Riley. He has always been an approachable fellow, a down-to-earth gentleman, a class act, easy to talk to and quick to smile, quick to smirk, and usually pretty candid. The media have often sought him to check out stories and items relating to the history of the Penguins.

Riley had been serving as video replay judge at the Civic Arena for two years, but gave up the post late in the 1993-94 campaign. Riley said he made the move "just to get away from the pressure of the game. I want to just sit and enjoy the game."

Riley revealed that he had developed an ulcer during the previous season, and thought about retiring then.

"There wasn't one kid in Canada who didn't want to play hockey."
—Jack Riley

I remember a night with Riley back in December of 1967, walking briskly into Maple Leaf Gardens, moving past the hockey fans shouting for tickets outside the entrance, "Who's got a pair of blues?"

The Penguins were in Toronto on December 13 to take on the Maple Leafs for the first time in the team's history. Riley would be rooting against the Maple Leafs for the first time in his life. Jack was born in Toronto, lived there until he was 20, and worked in their organization as general manager of their Rochester farm team prior to the Penguins' beginning.

Riley rushed through the hallowed hallways of the Maple Leaf Gardens. It was kind of a contagious pace in Toronto in those days where excitement was generated before the puck was ever dropped for the first face-off.

The Penguins' executive was moving past the long line-up of life-size photographs of the great Toronto stars of the past which adorned the walls. He looked up at the face of Charlie Conacher, and smiled as he thought back to his boyhood when Charlie Conacher was his idol. Charlie Conacher was one of the all-time great players in the National Hockey League, the leading goal-getter for the Maple Leafs in the '30s.

Jack Riley was 11 years old in 1930, and playing hockey for a midget team in Toronto. "Every kid was Maple Leaf conscious," Riley recalled. "There wasn't one kid in Canada who didn't want to play hockey."

Riley remembered that when he was 13 when Conn Smythe had the present Maple Leaf Gardens built. "It was during the Depression," said Riley, "and Smythe went to all the builders and offered them stock in the team in exchange for their labor. Somehow he did it, and everyone had thought in the beginning that he couldn't pull it off."

Riley played on a team called the Maple Leaf Junior Bantams, which practiced at 6 a.m. on Saturdays in the Gardens. It was a thrill of a lifetime just to glide about on the same ice on which the NHL stars also played.

"We played with their cutdown sticks," recalled Riley, "and I guess Charlie Conacher was my favorite because he played right wing and so did I then. I also admired their defenseman, King Clancy, because of his gutsy play."

Clancy would later coach the Pittsburgh Hornets when they were a Maple Leaf farm team at Duquesne Gardens in the '50s. He is in the Hockey Hall of Fame, along with Conacher.

The Maple Leafs played on Saturday nights and Riley and some of his teammates used to talk the trainer of the team into locking them in the dressing room until the night's game, and then they'd slip out and watch their heroes in action. "I guess I used to bring a bag lunch in case I got hungry in there," Riley said with a smile.

One of Jack's teammates didn't have to sneak in. That was Stafford Smythe, the son of Conn Smythe, the general manager of the Maple Leafs.

"They didn't have sellouts right from the start," Riley reminded us in explaining the madness that was Maple Leaf Gardens at the time of our visit. "They gave their discounts on tickets, and had promotions like we have to have now in Pittsburgh."

Riley credited Foster Hewitt for making the Maple Leafs a major attraction in Canada. "I believe the intense interest stemmed from his broadcasts. He did a heckuva job selling the sport. He made the Maple Leaf players household names in Toronto."

When Toronto started selling out the Gardens with regularity, Riley recalled that Smythe sent letters to season ticket holders and told them to start dressing up for hockey games. "They used to come in old clothes and working boots," said Riley. "But he built it up as a showplace. But he didn't demand the dress-up until every seat was being sold."

People started outdoing one another. Men wore tuxedos and dark suits and women wore gowns and furs.

Maple Leaf Gardens had a seating capacity of 15,591 in 1967 (15,642 today) and had not had a seat unsold since 1946. Some seats were empty for hockey games — not many — but all the seats were paid for. Over 12,000 season tickets were sold then, and there were over 8,000 on a waiting list ready to secure season tickets. They were often passed along in family wills.

Capacity, including standees, was 16,291, and you could bet that the Toronto house was packed with that many people and then some when the hated rival, the Montreal Canadiens, came to play.

2nd Lt. Jack Riley of the Canadian Army and his wife Jeanne on their wedding day Oct. 30, 1943.

Riley, at 26, as a player-coach with the Baltimore Clippers of the Eastern Hockey League in 1945-46 season.

Riley, as commissioner of the AHL, checks schedule with public relations aide Jack Button back in 1964-65 season. Button would later serve as general manager of the Penguins in mid-'70s.

Penguin fans who listened to Ed Conway's play-by-play broadcast of the game in Toronto were startled to hear cheering when Pittsburgh goalie Les Binkley would make a great save, or when Pittsburgh put the puck in the nets for the winning score.

"Toronto fans are very knowledgeable," Riley related then. "They know and appreciate a great rush, or a goal save. They'll applaud good play, even if it's done by Montreal. They appreciate a good play the way you appreciate a good song.

"But then there are Maple Leaf-haters, too. They're just like the Yankees in Canada. Folks who live 20 miles or more outside of Toronto call it Hog Town because they think Toronto tries to grab all the attention and action. So they come and root against Toronto. It's a good situation."

I recall something else about that trip to Toronto. As I was walking one afternoon toward the entrance to our hotel, the heralded Royal York, I spotted jazz great Erroll Garner coming out. The internationally-renowned pianist orginally came from Pittsburgh.

I stopped him and introduced myself, telling him I was a sportswriter from Pittsburgh. I asked him a question, "Mr. Garner, how do you explain that so many jazz greats — like you and Earl 'Fatha' Hines and Dakota Staton and Billy Eckstine — all come from Pittsburgh?"

Garner gave that some thought, and replied, "I guess because we were all born there."

Not the insight I was seeking, but not a bad retort.

"It was hard to improve the team."
—Jack Riley

Riley was officially the general manager of the Penguins on two occasions in the team's early years. He served initially from June 6, 1967 to May, 1970. Penguins owner Donald Parsons replaced him in favor of Red Kelly, who was also coaching the team, but Kelly insisted that Riley remain in the organization or they would both have to go. So Riley shifted into the scouting department during much of Kelly's tenure. When the owners changed, Riley returned and served as general manager once again, from January 29, 1972 to January 13, 1974.

It was a struggle from the start. As owners came and went, demands on Riley were different from month to month, and there was never enough money to work with. "For a lot of reasons, it was hard to improve the team," recalled Riley.

Riley hired Red Sullivan to coach the team. Sullivan was also a redhead, which seemed a requisite for people in the Penguins' organization in those days. Red Kelly, of course, fit the bill, as did Earl Ingarfield, the first-ever Penguins' draft pick. The team colors were light blue and dark blue and white, but Riley and Sullivan saw red a lot in those early campaigns.

"There were a lot of banners and signs around the Arena in those days," said Riley. "I remember one that said RILEY AND RUPP AND

NO STANLEY CUP. There was another one that said SULLY MUST GO, AND RILEY, TOO. They must have run out of paint on that one because it started out with red letters and finished up with green letters.

"Red was really ticked off because a fan had match books made up, and was passing them out in the stands that said SULLY MUST GO."

Riley remembers all the details of those difficult days. He remembers how his sanity was questioned when he asked the league office to schedule the Montreal Canadiens for the Penguins' home opener at the Civic Arena that first year. The Canadiens were the class of the NHL, having won back-to-back Stanley Cups coming into that expansion season.

"I wanted an attraction," explained Riley, "and I thought we might sneak up on them. I figured they might not take us too seriously right out of the gate."

Riley was right. Montreal managed to hold off the Penguins for a 2-1 victory on October 11, 1967, but the Penguins pushed the Canadiens all the way. Andy Bathgate scored the first goal in Penguins' history at 7:06 of the third period to make it close. There were 9,307 in the stands at the Arena.

"Some of our fans got carried away, and figured we had a shot at the Stanley Cup," said Riley, chuckling over the recollection. "I think we disappointed them."

Riley discussed the differences between those days and the more recent history of the Penguins.

"No one has coached the Penguins in four years," he said. "They think they can coach themselves. They have a real attitude. I've seen them for a lot of years, and they think they can handle it all by themselves now."

I mentioned that I was under the impression that Bob Johnson was the last coach to really coach the team. "He did for awhile," said Riley, "and then he threw his hands up, too. They got the best of him, too, and he got frustrated. The players should appreciate the situation that's been created for them, but they don't."

Even so, Riley would not be reluctant to run a hockey team again, even in the current climate of the NHL, and major league sports in general.

"I didn't say I wouldn't want to be a general manager," he said. "The money is so good today; it would be hard to turn down. I was getting $25,000 when I first came here. Nowadays a good GM makes $500,000. Craig Patrick must make that much, maybe better after winning two Stanley Cups.

"Sullivan's salary as coach was $17,000 the first year and $20,000 the second year. Now there are at least three coaches making $700,000 to $800,000, like Scotty Bowman in Detroit, Jacques Lemaire in New Jersey, and Mike Keenan with the Rangers in New York.

"Our whole payroll for 20 players that first season was $315,000. Andy Bathgate was our highest paid player at $25,000. He had won the Hart Trophy as the league's MVP when he was with the Rangers (in

1959)." Mario Lemieux won that award in 1993, the only time a Penguin has won it.

"Guys like Kenny Schinkel and Billy Dea and Art Stratton were making $15,000, and the average salary was about $13,000," continued Riley.

I felt good when I heard this. I had always assumed that pro hockey players were paid more money than that in those years. I left Pittsburgh in 1969 to write sports for *The Miami News*. I would be covering the Miami Dolphins. I was told by sports editor John Crittenden that I would be the highest paid sportswriter on the staff — making $10,400 a year, or $200 a week. I was not to let anyone know what I was making as it would cause internal strife. No wonder. The horse racing writer, for instance, had been on the staff for 17 years and was making $170 a week, apparently $10 for each year of service. To show you how money doesn't go as far as it once did, consider this:

Including my free-lance work for magazines and radio work, I was probably making about $15,000 total in 1969. When we moved, I told my wife Kathie she did not have to get a job in Miami. We leased a great two-bedroom apartment in an attractive cream-colored stucco garden apartment in southwest Miami. Our apartment overlooked a swimming pool and a lake. It took me twenty minutes to get to the office in Downtown Miami. It was a terrific set-up. My rent was $200 a month. That kind of apartment today would probably cost about $1,000 a month. Then again, that apartment today is probably in the middle of a ghetto.

The top sportswriters today at major city newspapers are making about five times what I made back then, or about $50,000 a year. The star hockey players are now routinely making more than a million dollars a year. In short, when I was writing, the top hockey players were making twice as much money as I was. Nowadays they would be making twenty times what I would be making. Doesn't seem fair, does it?

Riley remembered that I did a sports commentary each morning for two years, including my year in Miami, for WEEP Radio in Pittsburgh. "Yeah, I remember you were cutting us up pretty good on a frequent basis, and I asked our people, 'Why the hell are we sponsoring his show if he's coming down on us so much?' " Riley has always asked good questions.

Doing a sports show on Pittsburgh subjects was quite a challenge when you are living in Miami. On Sunday nights, I would often take my wife out to see a movie. After we were sitting in the theater awhile, Kathie would say to me, "You've got perspiration on your forehead. It's not that hot in here." It was if you were worried about what you were going to talk about the next day for a Pittsburgh sports audience.

Jack Riley ran the International Hockey League as its commissioner from 1979 to 1983, but maintained his Pittsburgh residence. He took an apartment in Windsor, Ontario because it was in the center of many of the league's franchises. He still does consultant work and draws up the schedule for the IHL, as well as the East Coast Hockey League, and does trouble-shooting assignments for the presidents of both leagues. The ECHL has teams in Johnstown and Wheeling and the winner gets the Jack Riley Cup. How's that for prestige?

He was living in 1994 in Scott Township with his daughter, Barbara, a single parent with a son Patrick, six years old. "I spend five times as much time with my grandson, as I did with my own two sons," confessed Riley. "Early on, you're just so busy with your job. Patrick is a big hockey fan." Barbara is a legal secretary in Downtown Pittsburgh. Jack's wife, Jeanne, had died five years earlier. They were married for 46 years. They also had two sons, John and Tom. John died two months after his mother. Tom is in business in Stratford, Ontario.

"I met her when I was playing hockey in Baltimore, many years ago," said Riley, when I asked him about his late wife. "I was born and bred in Toronto, and was a big fan of the Maple Leafs. I played in streets and on ponds as a kid. I played with my high school team, Humber Side Collegiate, and we won the city championship."

Riley played for a team sponsored by the Maple Leafs. The owner of the Leafs, Conn Smythe, built Maple Leaf Gardens in 1932. The Leafs won the Stanley Cup that same year. "Our team had all the sticks cut down that some of the great Maple Leafs like Charlie Conacher, King Clancy and Joe Primeau," related Riley, repeating a story he had told me 26 years earlier. "Stafford Smythe, the owner's son, was on our team. I was from the other side of the tracks. The other players came from affluent families. I don't know how I got involved with those guys in the first place. Maybe I played football with a few of them, or something like that.

"I played Junior A hockey with a team called the Toronto Lions. I played center or right wing. I later played with the Hershey Bears (1941-42) and then I went into the military service. I was a lieutenant in the Canadian Army. I played again at Hershey (1944-45).

"You know the Pittsburgh Hornets — that's when they played at Duquesne Gardens — were the farm team of the Toronto Maple Leafs. I played with Billy Taylor, who later played with the Hornets. I played against the Hornets at Duquesne Gardens.

"They changed the rules while I was in the service, and it was the end for me, in a way, as far as pro hockey was concerned. I was a good stick-handler, but I wasn't a very good skater. When I first started playing, you had to make a pass in the third of the ice in which you were skating. You couldn't pass the puck over any blue line. So you had to advance the puck one-third of the ice at a time. Then they put in the red line at mid-rink. You could pass across two lines. It was a good rule change; it speeded up the game and reduced offside calls. I knew it would make a big difference, not in my favor, though, and I knew then I wasn't going anywhere."

Riley regards himself as a purist, and takes exception with those who would like to see more rule changes. The most radical proposal these days relating to the NHL is to decide contests that end in a tie after overtime by having a shoot-out. "They say it packs the buildings in the minor leagues, but I don't see it," said Riley. "It's not what hockey is all about. It would be like having Gary Anderson of the Steelers come out and have a field goal kicking contest to decide who wins. If they do bring in the shoot-out, I hope each team gets at least a point, and the team that wins would get an extra point. But, basically, I don't like it at all."

I asked Riley to name some of the Penguins he enjoyed the most. "Jean Pronovost is one of my all-time favorites," responded Riley. "So is Davey Burrows. I loved Les Binkley. He was probably the funniest guy. He was different. You never knew whether he won or lost. He would shed it with his uniform. Some guys couldn't. He turned in the greatest goaltending job I've ever seen in that first year. We won by 1-0 at Boston. I never saw a Boston crowd give an opposing player a standing ovation, but they did that day. They never even had to use the Zamboni to clean the ice at the Boston end. All the action took place in our end of the rink. George Konik on our team hit a shot off the skate of their goaltender, Gerry Cheevers, for the only goal in that game. Binkley and Burrows belong in that Penguins Hall of Fame. Syl Apps is the only one going in this year. That was a good deal, getting Apps. We sent the Rangers Glen Sather, a defensive forward and shit-disturber, to get Apps. Kelly was the GM then."

Riley is less enthusiastic when you mention the string of owners who employed and annoyed him.

"The original 20 owners just didn't have any staying power," he said. "When I saw that they couldn't pay to put in lines for the soccer games at Forbes Field I knew we were in trouble. They wanted out in a hurry, and they headed south as soon as the bills started stacking up on their desks. The toughest part of the early years was dealing with the owners. They weren't bad guys; they just didn't have much hockey know-how or enough money. But they became experts in a hurry.

"It was fun, though. I enjoyed working with Red Sullivan, for starters. We're still great friends. I talk to him once a month. He retired last year, and built a home north of Peterborough.

"It was a thrill to put a team together from scratch. Starting a hockey team is an interesting challenge. You know you're going to get leftovers. There was no amateur draft as such for the first two years after expansion. That was part of the deal. The new teams couldn't take away any of the players from the NHL-sponsored junior teams. There were six new teams and there were about 400 juniors they couldn't touch. It wasn't until the third year that we had a real draft. We had traded our first pick to Boston for Pronovost. We took Rick Kessell on the second round and Michel Briere on the third round. He was the 26th player picked in the draft. We made a mistake there.

"People said you should never give away a top draft pick, but I'd do it again and again, if I could get a young player like Jean Pronovost. Boston ended up drafting a player named Frank Spring, and he was never heard from again. They'd have lost Pronovost anyhow in the intraleague draft. They could protect only so many players."

The mention of Michel Briere always brings a pained expression to the face of people like Riley who remember him well. Briere was injured in an auto accident after his rookie season, and was in a coma for 11 months before dying.

"That was really tough," remarked Riley. "He had such a great playoff, and he offered so much promise. He was absolutely dedicated to being a great hockey player.

"Briere was hospitalized nearly a year. I'd go in, I'd grab a doctor, and they'd tell me, 'He's not going to come out of it.' I'd grab Michel's hand. I'd say, 'C'mon, Michel, we're gonna play St. Louis tonight.' That was our top rival. I'd feel a tightening of the hand. Later on, when I did the same thing, I'd hold his hand and there'd be nothing.

"They had an impressive ceremony when he died. They closed down his hometown that day. I remember kids standing on the roofs of buildings as the funeral cortege was going by. There was a strange feeling about the whole thing. Nurses and people who looked after him at the hospital were taking pictures of him in the casket. The nurses would be talking to him, saying stuff like, 'Ah, Michel, you look good.' It gave me a strange feeling. He was getting married that same month when he had the accident. His girl friend was pregnant. She had a son, Martin, while Michel was in the hospital. He never saw his child. His girl friend wrote me a lovely letter, and told me how much Michel loved Pittsburgh.

"When I signed him in Brantford, I told him I'd give him $4,000 to sign and $12,000 for the season. He came back and said he wanted $5,000 and $13,000. I said, 'Why? You haven't even played a game yet. How do I know you're worth it?' He said, 'I'm going to play for Pittsburgh for 20 years.' He insisted we sign the contract that day. I wanted to get the papers properly prepared. He said, 'We have to sign it today.' And I said, 'Why?' He said, 'It's my father's birthday. He worked in the mines all his life, and he never made this kind of money. He'd be so proud.' Michel had what it takes to be a special player. He wouldn't have been Lemieux, but he'd have been a damn good hockey player. A lot of people compared him to Davey Keon, and that was quite a compliment. Keon played for Stanley Cup winners in Toronto."

There was no rhyme or reason to the sequence of Riley's recollections. He just started tossing off some stories.

"I remember one night against Chicago we put Kenny Schinkel on Bobby Hull, and told him to shadow him wherever he went," said Riley. "Schink ended up scoring three goals. We were the first expansion team to beat one of the old teams. Red Kelly was the second to pull that off, when he was at LA.

"Philadelphia and LA bought entire teams out of the American Hockey League and that really helped them. They finished 1-2 in the Western Division. Philadelphia bought the Quebec Aces and LA bought Springfield. They were independent teams, whereas the others were sponsored by NHL teams. That gave them a big edge. We bought a few players, like Binkley and Dick Mattiusi."

There have been reports that the Penguins wanted to buy the Hornets and keep them intact. "Detroit owned the Hornets, and their players were subject to the NHL draft. The rosters were wide open for the established clubs. They protected 11 players before the expansion draft. As soon as they lost a player in the draft, they could recall one of the players they had on their available list. They'd fill their roster with the 13th player. There were side deals, complicated drafts. We took Larry Jeffrey from Detroit in the expansion draft and sent him to the Rangers in exchange for Dunc McCallum, George Konik and Paul Andrea.

"We needed players. It's uncanny how many defensemen from those early Penguin teams have died. Dunc McCallum died of a brain tumor; Bob Woytowich died of a heart attack, driving a truck home after working at a liquor store, and Billy Speer died in a snowmobile accident. He was driving across the ice near his home in Lindsay, Ontario, and he went through the ice. Then Brian Spencer was killed after he got involved in drug trafficking in Florida. He came from a wild family. When Brian was playing for Toronto, their game was supposed to be on TV one night. But they canceled the telecast. His dad went to the television station in Vancouver and shot someone in the studio because he wasn't going to be able to watch his son play hockey.

"It must have run in the family; they both had too long of a lead off first base.

"I remember one night that Syl Apps and Jim Rutherford were on a radio show here one night. The announcer asked Apps: 'Do the fans around here really know you when they see you in public?' Apps answered: 'No, not really.' So they asked Rutherford, who was a goalie, the same question. And he answered, 'Only when I wear my mask around.'

"Greg Polis won the MVP Award in the All-Star Game in New York (scoring two goals on January 30, 1973). He had a lot of promise, too. But he never really grew up; he was never mature enough. I remember he took us to arbitration. He was making $13,000 and he wanted $30,000. I remember he kept pointing out all his stats and, finally, he says, 'I checked with the people at the concession stands and they said they sell more photos of me than anyone else.' And Polis won the arbitration case.

"I remember another arbitration case. Keith McCreary took us to arbitration. Red Kelly wanted to go to arbitration. I didn't. I thought Red was too hard on McCreary. We walked into the room at the arbitration and the arbitrator hugged McCreary. It turns out the arbitrator had been the commissioner of the league where McCreary had played. I said to our guys, 'This is one we're not going to win.' And we didn't. I didn't mind because I thought McCreary deserved what he was after."

I asked Riley what he recalled about Pierre Larouche, another of the Penguins' most gifted performers.

"He was a good hockey player, very talented," said Riley. "He was one of the best passers I've ever seen. He scored a lot of goals just like Lemieux. He'd be to the goal-keeper's right, or on our left side as we were attacking. He was a right-handed shot, and he had a long reach. He could make that shot. Pierre was a very intelligent hockey player.

He almost scored 50 goals (in a season) with three different clubs. A lot of people didn't think he was serious enough. He got mixed up with a bad crowd for awhile here.

"That reminds me. I don't hear as many drug stories relating to the hockey team as I once did. I'm not trying to whitewash them — the right combination is there: young with lots of money — but you just don't hear much talk about that these days. And that's good."

Jack Riley remains a big Penguins' booster.

Penguins' power play
E.J. drew credit back in 1982

"We never really had a power play until Eddie came here."
—Rick Kehoe

It was the summer of 1982, and sports fans in Pittsburgh were eager to see the Penguins become full-fledged citizens of "The City of Champions," a label Pittsburgh came by in the late '70s when the Steelers won four Super Bowls, the Pirates won two World Series, and the Pitt football team won the national championship in 1976.

I interviewed Eddie Johnston, who was getting set for his third season as coach of the Penguins, for a feature story in GOAL, the official National Hockey League magazine. It was entitled "Are You Ready, Eddie?"

Coach Eddie Johnston of the Pittsburgh Penguins believes a coach should pattern his hockey team around the type of players the fans in his city will respond to and appreciate. "The fans in Pittsburgh want hard workers who do their jobs game after game," he said.

A more fitting description could not be found for Johnston himself. For 16 seasons he was a tireless goalie in the NHL, 11 with the Bruins, with shorter stays in St. Louis, Toronto and Chicago. Indeed, he was the last NHL goalie to play every game in a season (1963-64) when he was the Bruins' backstop for all 70 contests.

Last season (1981-82), Johnston was credited with providing the rhyme and reason for the resurgence of the Pens in the Stanley Cup playoffs. One of the main reasons for their success was their superior power play, which produced 92 goals during the regular season, only one less than the champion New York Islanders who set an NHL record in that department.

Winger Rick Kehoe had 20 power play goals among the 53 goals he scored last season. He had 88 points altogether, and just six penalty minutes, while winning the Lady Byng Trophy which goes to "the player adjudged to have exhibited the best type of sportsmanship and gentlemanly conduct combined with a high standard of playing ability."

Kehoe credited Johnston for much of what he and the Penguins accomplished. "We never really had a power play until Eddie came here," said Kehoe, a one-time teammate of Johnston in Toronto.

Randy Carlyle, who won the Norris Memorial Trophy as the league's outstanding defenseman, was the point man on the Pens' power play. He was on the ice for 75 of those 92 power play goals, and was credited with seven goals and 39 assists when the Pens had a manpower advantage. "E.J. made it all possible," said Carlyle. "He came in and gave us the leadership and direction."

Johnston said he got many of his ideas for his power play from his days at Boston Garden, watching the Celtics of the NBA in their games and practices.

"When I was with the Bruins, I'd have a few beers with Tommy Heinsohn, their coach, at an oyster bar on the north shore, and we'd get talking about 'picks' and how to set and use them," said Johnston.

"You can pick up a lot of things from basketball, how to screen for a guy to shoot, and so forth," he said. "When I was at Boston, we had one of the best power plays in the league, and we used lots of picks to free people. We had Bobby Orr and Phil Esposito, Ken Hodge, Johnny Bucyk and Wayne Cashman and they did so much picking. You're going over the blue line, and crossing over; it's really a basketball play, only at a different speed. It makes the opposition think more.

"I was a big fan of the Celtics," Johnston said. "I was there when they had the greatest basketball team. They'd lose maybe 20 games a year and we'd be lucky to win that many. They'd put 4,000 to 5,000 fans in the Garden to see them back then, and we'd get 13,909 and we were dead last. Now it's the opposite. You can't buy a ticket to the Celtics. But the Bruins will come back."

In Pittsburgh, the Penguins are gaining the popularity, recognition and rewards enjoyed by the Steelers, Pirates and the University of Pittsburgh football team. Two years ago, when the Steelers won their second straight Super Bowl and fourth in six seasons, and the Pirates won the World Series, and Pitt's football team was high in the national rankings, Pittsburgh was tabbed "The City of Champions."

But at that time, the Pens were still on the outside looking in. Club owner Edward J. DeBartolo was determined to turn things around, however. His organization took over control of the Civic Arena, where the Pens play, and embarked on an ambitious program to boost the winter sports schedule in town. The Penguins, at long last, developed a farm system, and seemed willing to pay the price necessary to build a championship team. While Johnston succeeded in improving the Pens' power play and overall attack, he was aware that some tightening up was needed on the team's defense. As a former goalie, he recognized the need for improved play in the Pens' end of the ice.

The Penguins' penalty-killing unit left a lot to be desired last season. Whenever a power play situation emerged, the fans could count on someone scoring a goal — one way or the other. The Penguins gave up 99 goals on power plays by the opposition, the worst mark in that respect in league history.

The Penguins gained a lot of new fans, and restored the faith of some old ones, with their performance in the playoffs last season. They pushed the St. Louis Blues into the second overtime of their fifth game before succumbing, and captured the town by doing so. It was something to build on for the 1981-82 season.

"All you have to do in Pittsburgh is win," said Randy Carlyle. "It's the City of Champions, right? The people here seem to enjoy hockey as a rough-and-tumble, rock-'em, sock-'em sport. I think the decision to stay in Pittsburgh, and bringing in E.J. has turned things around.

"We were always up there with Colorado on the list of endangered species in the National Hockey League. Now we're buying homes here because we believe we're here to stay."

Johnston believes the stability of the franchise is a key to future improvement. Since the club's inception, the Penguins were plagued with financial problems, and ownership shifted hands too often to get anything solid established.

"You never knew if the team was going to be here," said Johnston.

That's different now. Johnston has received a new contract to continue as coach — even though the Montreal Canadiens came calling on him after last season — and his front office responsibilities have been expanded.

"Mr. DeBartolo has given us stability and direction, and when he calls, you know he wants answers to questions and solutions to problems," Johnston said.

"There were always rumors that the Penguins were going bankrupt, and that they weren't going to meet the payroll. That was very unsettling. It made it tough for people to buy homes here. Nobody stayed around in the off-season. Now the Penguins are staying in Pittsburgh. We want to be the same as the Steelers."

In Johnston, the Penguins might have gotten lucky and come up with their own version of Chuck Noll, the outstanding coach of the Steelers' championship teams. "He prides himself on being a teacher and so do I," Johnston said. "Now if we can just win consistently."

That will be the ultimate measuring stick.

Eddie Johnston behind Penguins' bench

Mike Lange
The Voice of the Penguins

"It was like God said, 'this is the place where you should work.'"

Mike Lange looked across the table from his favorite booth in the back of Elby's Restaurant near his home in Mt. Lebanon. Lange looked through wisps of smoke over the second ashtray he had filled with cigarette butts during a three hour conversation. To say he is a chain-smoker is like saying Mario Lemieux is a hockey player. "He can really fire 'em up," says a good friend of Lange. He was drinking Diet Coke and dashing out cigarettes, and reflecting on his days with the Penguins. Lange's ice-blue eyes looked back to a day in November of 1991, which he said was the highlight of his 19 years as the prime broadcaster of Penguins games on radio and TV.

"It was probably the greatest moment in my time here," allowed Lange, loafing in early May, 1994, wondering why the Penguins weren't still alive in the playoffs for the Stanley Cup. He had turned 46 just two months earlier, and was one of the most successful and best-paid sports announcers in the city's history. Mike and his wife Chrissie and their 12-year-old son Tanner lived in a lovely suburban home. Mike had arrived for our meeting in a well-polished ruby red Cadillac. His face was fresh-scrubbed — there's always a pink glow to his cheeks — and beaming.

"The greatest thrill for me was when Edward DeBartolo Sr. wanted me to come to Youngstown with Paul Steigerwald. He brought us into a room in his office complex, and literally threw two Stanley Cup rings at us. He said, 'I just appreciated all that you've done.' It made all the work and time spent doing it so worthwhile. It was so rewarding."

The Penguins had won their first Stanley Cup the previous season, and DeBartolo had just sold the team that same month to Howard Baldwin, Morris Belzberg and Thomas Ruta. The challenging national economy had created some financial problems for DeBartolo in his shopping mall empire, and he felt pressed to unload the Penguins just when his investment was paying off. The Penguins had the best team in the National Hockey League, and were in the midst of a second consecutive Stanley Cup championship season. It was fun to own the Penguins, the way it had been fun for the DeBartolos, with Eddie Jr. calling the shots, to bankroll the 49ers when they were winning four Super Bowls.

"Young Eddie was there, and so was his sister Marie," said Lange. "I never realized how big of hockey fans they were until they started talking about different games. They watched every game. They may not have been at all the games at the Civic Arena, but they were watching or listening. They were so much a part of it."

I asked Lange if he was a little leary when he first heard that DeBartolo wanted to see him. DeBartolo was a demanding boss. Getting called to Youngstown was the beginning of the end of other employees in the Penguins' organization. Lange laughed, waved away some smoke and shook his head.

"No, I wasn't worried. His secretary had called me and she had said, 'He wants to give you something.' So I knew it was going to be a positive meeting. I wasn't expecting him to give me a pink slip."

Lange was wearing a Stanley Cup ring he had purchased on his own after the team repeated in 1992. He said his first ring, the one DeBartolo gave him, was at the jewelers getting cleaned. He was planning on giving one of the rings to his son, Tanner.

Ownership has always been walking on a tight wire ever since the Penguins came into being in 1967. Lange looks at DeBartolo and Baldwin as the two best in the history of the once-beleaguered franchise.

"Without DeBartolo, there is no Stanley Cup championship here," said Lange. "He's the guy who footed the bill. Without him, there is no hockey in Pittsburgh. And Howard Baldwin has put up the money to maintain excellence here, and that's why it hurts what's happened the last two years. Baldwin has made a big commitment to having a first-class franchise, and he's still investing in hockey in this city by building a practice facility that will be great for the Penguins and for young players in this area out at Southpointe."

DeBartolo shied away from the spotlight in Pittsburgh, unusual for an owner in today's professional sports world. So he has always been a man of mystique, an intriguing individual.

"He was like I was when I was 20," said Lange. "He didn't know what the red line or blue line were all about, in the beginning. It's interesting how he came to buy the Penguins in the first place.

"After the Penguins went bankrupt (in 1975), when a Pittsburgh group headed by Tad Potter went belly up, the club was purchased by Al Savill, Otto Frenzel and Wren Blair. Savill asked DeBartolo to lend him a million dollars so he could buy the team. And then he came back and asked him for another million. DeBartolo figured he better find out what this was all about. He started out lending money as a friend, and ended up owning the hockey club.

"I never knew how much he appreciated me until he called me to his office that day in Youngstown. To him, I was part of the team."

I asked Lange to reflect on several key figures, in addition to DeBartolo, who called the shots for the franchise in recent years, and he provided the following observations:

Bob Johnson — "He's the man most responsible for turning the whole thing around. He established an attitude here that we'll never lose. He brought a whole new meaning to the word Penguin. Finally, it meant something to be a Penguin. The players became a direct reflection of the coach."

Craig Patrick — "His stamp on this team? The greatest move he ever made was hiring Bob Johnson. With all the outstanding deals he made, his greatest legacy will be that he hired Bob Johnson."

Mike Lange relaxes at his Mt. Lebanon home with wife Chrissie and their 12-year-old son Tanner, and can be coaxed into a game of catch in the backyard.

Jim Cunningham

Scotty Bowman — "He is a brilliant, brilliant hockey mind. Maybe the best I've been around. He was not appreciated by people who weren't around him enough to understand what he was all about. His attitude is, 'If you do your job and do it well, I have the ultimate respect for you. If you don't, I don't have any time for you.' He demands excellence. He's one of the most fascinating people. If you want to talk hockey, he's the guy to talk hockey with."

Eddie Johnston — "If you can't get along with E.J., you can't get along with anybody. He's been a big part of the Pittsburgh scene for many years. He has a tremendous amount of pride. I feel for him in a way. I think he deserves more than he's gotten. Everything comes to the top after he departs Pittsburgh. He returns and they get zapped. I want to see him do well. He deserves to win it again."

Paul Martha — "I have a lot of respect for J.P. He kept things together here. They were losing a lot of money for a lot of years. He kept telling the DeBartolos to hang in there. He kept telling the boss 'We'll be all right.' He was taking those calls from Youngstown. He got his ass kicked. He survived it. He had great negotiating ability, and he negotiated some great deals for the organization."

Some of Mike Lange's patented lines have become so familiar to hockey fans who follow the Penguins. Phrases like "Buy Sam a drink and get his dog one, too," and "Ladies and gentlemen, Elvis has just left the building" and "Look out, Loretta..." have become part of Penguins hockey.

He can appreciate how DeBartolo came into hockey through the back door, so to speak, because it was similar to his own experience in the sports broadcasting business. Lange was born (March 3, 1948) and bred in Sacramento, California. As a kid, baseball was his favorite game. He wanted to become a baseball broadcaster. He listened with great interest to baseball broadcasts in northern California, and also basketball and football broadcasts as well. He was not into hockey at all.

Lange graduated from Sacramento State University with a degree in broadcasting and started his career with the Phoenix Roadrunners of the Western Hockey League (WHL) in 1970. During the 1973-74 season, he called play-by-play for the San Diego Gulls of the WHL before joining the Penguins in 1974.

He began broadcasting Penguins games on radio in 1974-75. He left after one season, after the team had gone bankrupt and the club offices had been padlocked by IRS agents, but returned as the team's radio voice in 1976-77 until the 1979-80 season when games were simulcast on radio and television.

In addition to his responsibilities with the Penguins, Lange handled play-by-play for the Pittsburgh Pirates in 1986 and 1987 on the KBL Sports Network.

"I went back to San Diego after that first year in Pittsburgh. But I've been here ever since. I enjoyed doing the Pirates games as well.

That's what I wanted to do early on. When I was ten years old, I knew I wanted to be involved in sports. I was a big baseball fan. Hockey certainly wasn't in my mind at the time. The Giants had just moved to San Francisco, and I became intrigued by it all. I played organized baseball as a kid. We also had the San Francisco 49ers and the San Francisco Warriors and the Oakland Raiders.

"A fellow named Bill King was doing the Warriors and Raiders games. I loved listening to him. He got me hooked on sports broadcasting. I wanted to be like him."

I knew Bill King. He had a very theatrical mustache and goatee, a devilish-looking gentleman. He had a Vincent Price quality about him. I had guested with King on several occasions when I was covering the NBA and NFL beats. "I've never met him, strangely enough," said Lange. "I'd dearly love to meet him because he had such a positive influence on my life. I listened to Lon Simmons and Russ Hodges who were doing the Giants, but I liked King's style the most. I always had a dream to be a broadcaster like that."

Mike's father, Jim Lange, was a telephone repairman, and a big sports enthusiast. Mike's mother, Ramona, was a housewife. Mike was the oldest of four children, with a brother and two sisters.

"My dad was a big NFL fan," said Lange. "If I tried to talk to him when he was watching a game on TV, he'd say, 'Watch the game! Listen . . . you'll learn.' I remember him saying that. We were big fans of Kenny Stabler and George Blanda and that bunch."

Lange started out at Sacramento City College, a junior college in his hometown. Then he matriculated to Sacramento State.

"My interest in being a radio broadcaster sort of faded away when I first went to college," related Lange. "Computers were coming along, and it was a field that really came out of California. I thought about exploring that. I thought about economics as a major. Then I came back to sports broadcasting. You search for what you want to do. That's what college is all about.

"The guy who got me going was a classmate named Len Shapiro. He was majoring in broadcasting, too. By the way, he did OK for himself eventually. A year or so ago, he sold 35 pizza places he owned, and retired. Back when we were in school, he did some p.r. work on a part-time basis. Len got involved with amateur hockey. I went down with him and watched a couple of games when the California Seals came to Oakland. I was 20 at the time that the NHL expanded into six new cities, including Pittsburgh. That was my first exposure to hockey. I was doing football, basketball and baseball for the college radio station at the time. Shapiro scolded me, saying I had to learn how hockey was played, and what the rules were. He said, 'If you're going to be involved with sports, you should know all sports.'"

I agreed. I told Lange that I had purposely covered as many sports as possible during my college days, and even more so when I worked at daily newspapers in Miami, New York and Pittsburgh. Versatility is important. It is something Chuck Noll preached when he coached the

Steelers during their Super Bowl days. It certainly paid off for Mike Lange.

"When I was getting ready to graduate, I started writing to people all over the country, looking for an opening, a way to get started," said Lange. "Most of them ignored my letters. Al McCoy in Phoenix answered my letter and was encouraging to me. He sent me one of the few positive responses. I learned so much from Al McCoy. He was like a father to me. He had the most influence on me of all the people in the professional sports broadcasting world. What I admired about him was that he knew what was going on. And he was willing to share and help a youngster trying to break into the business.

"There was no job or position in Phoenix, but I just packed my bags when school was out, and moved to Phoenix. I got a place for $85 a month. McCoy got the Phoenix Suns and the Phoenix Roadrunners to give me a press pass. He lent me a tape recorder from his radio station. He was the general manager of the station. He'd listen and critique my work. He was helping me. I don't know why, but he took a liking to me. I was 21. I'd go to the games, and pester him, and drive him crazy.

"Midway through the first season, I was hired to do p.r. for the Phoenix Roadrunners in the Western Hockey League. I was the p.r. director, doing game notes and stuff like that. The guy who hired me also let me do color on the radio. Al was doing the play-by-play. I got to Phoenix in September of 1970, and I got hired in January, 1971 to be the p.r. man. I replaced a man named Moon Mullins at mid-season.

"The Western Hockey League was a great minor league. There were teams in Phoenix, Portland, Seattle, San Diego, Salt Lake and Denver. Guys loved the league. If they couldn't play in the NHL, they wanted to be in the WHL. You'd fly to all the games and you stayed in first-class hotels.

"I had a pretty good idea what was going on in when I first got into hockey, but it was a learning process. There's nothing like being around it day-by-day to learn what it's all about. I'm pretty proud of what I've accomplished in my career. There was a lot of hard work and determination involved. There was a determination on my part to be in the big leagues someday. It's ironic that it turned out to be hockey. I've exceeded what I thought I'd do."

> **"Bob Prince was the most recognizable person I've ever been with in my life."**
> —Mike Lange

Pittsburgh and Mike Lange have been a good match. Lange says it was love at first sight. "I never knew the uniqueness of the city till I got here," said Lange. "My timing was excellent. I was fortunate to have arrived here when I did. My first year in town, the Steelers won their first Super Bowl.

"It was 1974 and the reaction of the city overwhelmed me. The unity of the people . . . the black and gold . . . the signs in the windows. You don't see it on the same scale in other cities I've been in. What stood out in my mind was the parade they had Downtown after they won the Super Bowl. The atmosphere, the small-town excitement. It made me a Pittsburgher very quickly. I didn't go to any games in the beginning, but I definitely followed the Steelers."

The Steelers were a rival of the Raiders during the heyday of both teams, and they were supplanted as the dominant team in pro football by the 49ers. If the Steelers were, indeed, the team of the '70s, the 49ers were the team of the '80s. Al Davis might dispute those claims, as would some Cowboy and Dolphin fans, but the Steelers and Lange's favorite boyhood teams certainly came to the fore following his arrival in Pittsburgh.

"I had lived with the 49ers and Raiders all my life, so to have that come about when I came here had great meaning; to see that develop the next few years. The Pirates were strong. Pitt won a national championship in football in 1976. I was coming to a place where I fit in well. The way I broadcast games was more Pittsburgh than anything else. I didn't know Bob Prince, and I didn't know Rosey Rowswell, or Myron Cope. But they were all unique. And I came here. It was like God said, 'this is the place where you should work.'

"I had my own style, and you're not sure how you'll be accepted. But I felt right away that I could accomplish what I wanted to do right here in Pittsburgh.

"I met Prince that first year. I learned an awful lot from Bob. He taught me what the people would like. He was unbelievable. He had the respect of everybody in the business. He was one of those guys who went out of their way to help young people find their way in the business.

"He'd see me, and he'd say, 'Hey, laddie, welcome to Pittsburgh. What's your wife's name?' And, you know, he never forgot it. He'd see her, and he'd say, 'Hi, Chrissie!' I'd go to baseball games and get to talking to Bob. He'd tell me, 'The ladies are very important here. You have to pay attention to them when you're broadcasting a ballgame. You have to get out and see the people. You have to do this and do that.' Now I do what he did: I go to bars and sit down with people, buy them a drink, and talk to them.

"Bob Prince was the most recognizable person I've ever been with in my life. Wherever we went, at the airports, in hotels or restaurants, inevitably someone would holler out, 'Hey, Gunner, howya doin'?' I've been with Mario Lemieux, and I'm telling you more people recognized Prince, no doubt about it.

"He knew a lot of people. He could go into a restaurant where he'd never been before, and tell the manager or owner, 'Send me the bill.' He was always picking up the tab. He'd feed six to eight guys. He taught me how to deal with the waiters and waitresses and bartenders, the greeter. The maitre'd. He always took care of people. He'd fuss over busboys. It's not that difficult when you think about it. You'd like to be treated the same way.

"On my first day in Pittsburgh, there was a strong sulphur smell in the air. I wondered what it was, as I had never smelled anything quite like it before. I got picked up at the airport by Terry Schiffhauer, the team's p.r. man, and some team officials. They took me into town and checked me in at the Hyatt. I met the people I was going to work for at KDKA. He took me out to dinner, and then we went from one joint to another, including a few after-hours clubs. I didn't get back to my room until 4:30 a.m. That's when I realized what Pittsburgh was all about. When we were moving through Market Square at one point in the evening, I said to myself, 'I am in the right place. This is my kind of city.' I had never stayed out at any other city past 2.

"I had to be at the zoo at 9 the next morning for some promotion involving the Penguins and the radio station. I had left my luggage in different cars. So I had to wear one of Terry's shirts. It was twice my size. That's how I made my debut representing the team and the radio station."

"He's been given a rap as a guy who didn't want to play."
—Lange on Lemieux

Mike Lange looked at the Penguins of the past season — the 1993-94 campaign — and wondered what would become of them. Would Mario Lemieux return? Would the Penguins bounce back after two straight playoff disappointments? What would Baldwin and GM Craig Patrick do to turn things around?

"To me, it's more a mental thing than anything else," he said. "They've had a taste of defeat again. And they won't be any younger. It will be interesting to see how the young people will react to it. They certainly have a lot of character people.

"The Penguins, as a franchise, have given you a chance to experience everything. There's been mediocrity, and there have been great times — the full roller-coaster ride. I've been kinda glad to have worked with the kind of teams I've worked with since I've been here, the way things happened. I got my feet wet with a fair club, then they went all the way down to the bottom, during the dog days. Then the rise back up and, finally, hitting the peak."

I asked him to talk more about Lemieux.

"You don't realize how great he is until he's not able to play up to his own standard. This time Mario just couldn't do it. And he was the difference. He was the reason they won it. Ask anybody who played against you in the series, and they'll tell you.

"It's like taking Willie Mays out of your lineup. This year, whether he dressed or not, and certainly in the playoffs, Mario wasn't there. He just wasn't there this year. Mario will do everything he can to play again. He is still searching for the miracle cure: what will make him well. Because he wants to play.

Dennis Cavanaugh

Mike Lange checks his notebook during broadcast high above Civic Arena and celebrates Stanley Cup championship in clubhouse with Mario Lemieux.

Bruce Bennett Studios

"He's been given a rap as a guy who doesn't want to play. That's not true. It couldn't be farther from the truth. I saw him score in 46 straight games. I saw him get on the plane and he couldn't even sit down. He couldn't put his own things in the bins above the seats. And he never, never complained. He could hardly move.

"But he kept at it and he kept the scoring streak alive. He wanted to play. Even the last game in New York, you knew he couldn't play. But he had to come out on the ice and try it.

"He proved to me, without question, he had the courage and he had the inner strength to be the best. And that's why he was. We all take his talent for granted. If you don't use that talent, you waste it. There are a lot of guys with talent who never played in the big leagues. Mario can play on any level and be the best. He was like that as a kid, and he was like that against Gretzky, or in All-Star Games and Stanley Cup games. It was like he always wanted to show who was the best. He'll dominate showcase games. I've seen him do it.

"He's like Superman on some nights, when he can play. People don't appreciate what the playoffs are like. The wear and tear on the body in the playoffs is unreal. You must play in four series to win the Stanley Cup. It's one of the most grueling competitions in sports. It's so physical. It beats up the body."

I mentioned that several teams that were expected to do well in the 1994 playoffs were eliminated early. The Red Wings, under Bowman, were thought to be the class of the west. They were upset by the San Jose Sharks in the first round. The Montreal Canadiens, defending Stanley Cup champions, were knocked off in the first round. And, of course, the Penguins.

"Three of the four divisional winners were knocked out in the first round," said Lange. "Only the Rangers survived. That's proof that it is a different season.

"When the regular season ends, the players get so locked in mentally. They're more emotional and more physical, and it rises to the top in the first series. That's where most of the upsets happen. There's a history to it.

"That's the beauty of sports. That's what the fans forget. Or overlook. It does happen. Teams that are supposed to win get knocked off. If it didn't happen, sports would not be that interesting. When the Penguins won in '91, nobody expected them to win. That year Chicago was everybody's pick. Ninety-eight percent of the people picked Chicago, and they got whacked early."

"I can't think of a better place to work."
—Mike Lange

Life has been good for Mike Lange. Does he ever pinch himself to be sure his good fortune has been real? Does he realize how lucky he has been that things have turned out so much in his favor?

"I have no complaints," he said. "I can't think of a better place to work or to raise a family. I like working in hockey. Every game is different. It presents a lot of different scenarios. I feel most comfortable doing games. I just turn the mike on and let 'er go. That's where I get a real enjoyment. I'm really not working. I'm having fun.

"We're pretty blessed here, and no one should overlook that. Look at the number of teams in this city that have won championships. Name me another city that has had so many champions. We've experienced a great time since I've been here. In some other cities, you could live a lifetime and never experience what we have experienced here in just the past 20 years."

Lange realizes ticket prices are too high. They need the revenues to pay the players' salaries. But he also realizes that he is making more money than he ever dreamed possible, so everybody connected with the club is doing well. He fears that professional sports could be heading for problems, though. Something has to change to get things sane again.

"Somebody is going to have to go bankrupt," he offered. "It's headed that way. There are teams in difficulty in every pro sport. In hockey, you don't have that national TV revenue."

He expects the Penguins to stay in Pittsburgh, and for the club to bounce back and be a top contender.

"We have lots of character people. The club is blessed in that respect. You have guys like Ronnie Francis. You can go through the lineup and find those type of guys. I don't want to name them all because I'll leave somebody out. Even the little guys; I don't think anyone could question their character. Guys like Jock Callander and Dave Michayluk and Mike Needham came up and played in '92 and when we beat the Rangers, those guys were unbelievable.

"I'm sure we missed guys this past season like Troy Loney, Bob Errey, Jim Paek and Paul Stanton, and Bryan Trottier, or the Bryan Trottier we had the two terrific years when he could play center on that third line and get the job done. With all the character we have among our stars here, you can't win a Stanley Cup without 25 or 27 guys. They all have to come in and play. I had admiration for all the guys, down to the last guy on the roster, when we won the Cup. But Mario was the difference. Never forget that."

Joe Mullen
From Hell's Kitchen to the NHL

*"My parents showed us
the way to go."*

Joe Mullen was sitting in the left field bleachers at a baseball park for young players in Upper St. Clair, a suburb 12 miles south of Pittsburgh. He was one of a dozen parents sitting in the sun, watching their boys play ball in an early morning contest on Saturday, June 18, 1994. He was wearing a white T-shirt and beige shorts, white socks and sneakers, and he blended in with the other parents. He was an urban cowboy in a suburban setting. Joe Mullen moves unobtrusively through this community. Only a fervent Penguins' fan could pick him out of the crowd. Mullen likes it that way.

He is on the small side, as athletes go, at 5-9, 175 pounds. He was the shortest and the second oldest, at 37, of the Penguins during the 1993-94 season. Only Bryan Trottier was older and not much taller.

He is hockey's answer to "The Little Engine That Could" story, someone who was too small, skated funny and came from the wrong neighborhood to ever dream of playing in the National Hockey League. No American-born player has ever produced more points in the NHL than Joe Mullen. No one with his numbers has ever been denied entry into the Hockey Hall of Fame.

He is a New York Irishman and he looks the part. He was wearing a Jets T-shirt for our meeting. "I have a Yankees' T-shirt, too, an authentic one from their clubhouse," he told me. He said he often wears a Yankees baseball cap. "I root for the Celtics, but that's the only Boston team I root for." He has curly and thinning light brown hair, a high brow, a bumpy boxer's brow, with small blue eyes, made even smaller this Saturday morning by the rising sun. There's a glint of mischief in those narrow blue eyes.

On a similar sultry day once upon a time, Wellington Mara, the owner of the New York Giants football team, and I were both squinting through blue eyes into a noonday sun as his team practiced at Pleasantville, New York, on the campus of Pace University.

"The Irish were not meant to be out in the sun," observed Mara. "They were born to live in peat bogs and caves, which may account for why they spend so much time in dark places like bars and churches."

Mullen just smiled when I told him of Mara's remark. Mullen is also a man of few words, not exactly an Irish trait.

It was hot and humid and temperatures would be soaring to a record 95 degrees. Record-setting temperatures had been the norm all week in Pittsburgh. It made the U.S. Open Golf Tournament at Oakmont even more of an ominous test for the best golfers in the world. The Open would be concluded this same weekend at the storied golf layout just to the north of Pittsburgh. As Arnold Palmer approached the 18th green the day before in his final go-round at an Open in his home area, the crowd roared in an extended and heart-warming show of affection, appreciation and admiration. It was a moment for Palmer to remember, for the fans to cherish.

There was much sports activity that was fodder for conversation. The NBA finals were coming down to a seventh game between the New York Knicks and the Houston Rockets, in which the Rockets would prevail. The New York Rangers had just won the Stanley Cup over the Vancouver Canucks. Mullen found it difficult to root for either team from his hometown. He didn't care for the Knicks' street gang mentality, their attitude, constant Bogart-ing, and the Rangers . . . well, they remained arch-rivals of the Penguins, that's all. "There are some guys on that team I've gotten to know, and I can root for them," admitted Mullen. "As a long-time Rangers fan, I'm for them. There was something about this year that made it hard for me to pull for them, though. I was and I wasn't."

Mullen had watched the first six Stanley Cup championship series on TV, but missed the finale. "I was at the Samurai Steak House with Linda celebrating our 14th wedding anniversary," he said with a smile, "so I didn't see it. If I'd been home, I would've watched it."

I asked him how he felt about someone else winning the Stanley Cup again, after the Penguins were the pick to do so. "I felt like this year we didn't deserve it," admitted Mullen, a much-valued member of the Penguins' Stanley Cup champions in 1991 and 1992. "The Rangers had a great season; they came in first overall. They deserved to win."

It was one day away from Father's Day, and the Major League Baseball All-Star Game would be played in Pittsburgh in a few weeks, and was already getting a lot of attention in the city's newspapers and airwaves.

But everyone in the stands that morning, as well as at a nearby basketball court, was talking about O.J. Simpson. The former college and pro football star, network TV personality and movie actor, was believed to have brutally murdered his wife and a male friend of hers that week. Mullen was among the millions who had watched on TV the night before as Simpson and his buddy, Al Cowlings, led police on a spooky 60-mile freeway chase to Simpson's home, where he finally surrendered. A cameraman in a helicopter had captured Simpson's home run from start to finish. The TV ratings were unreal. Everyone was watching. My daughter Sarah was with friends at Bowling City in Mt. Lebanon that night, and the monitors over the lanes that normally show the scoresheets were instead showing Simpson's flight. It was like a made-for-TV movie, even stranger than fiction. I had interviewed Simpson several times when I was covering the pro football beat in the early '70s, when he was the star running back for the Buffalo Bills, and I felt badly about the entire mess.

Being at a ballpark and watching young boys playing a game was a pleasant respite from the negative news, and the apparent fall from grace by another American sports hero. O.J. wasn't that big in Mullen's mind. "Sure I remember him as a ballplayer, but we weren't into football much in our neighborhood," said Mullen. He was more into his sons' game on this Saturday morning. It was an opportunity for Joe Mullen to play catch-up with his kids, after being busy for so long with the demands of the Penguins' schedule. School would be out at week's end for the kids, but Joe had been on vacation earlier than he had planned, and he had been able to attend some year-ending activities at their school. The Penguins were knocked out of the Stanley Cup playoffs in the first round by the Washington Capitals. Mullen was struggling at season's end. It had been a relatively good season, but it came to a disappointing finish. This had happened to Mullen and the Penguins two straight campaigns, and it was getting stale.

Mullen did not know where he stood with the Penguins. A few days after our meeting, the Penguins would announce that they had signed Mullen to a one-year contract for 1994-95. Again, he and his agent were disappointed. They had hoped for a multi-year contract. The Penguins were playing it close to the belt. After all, they knew Mullen was among the Penguins who had no legs left in the playoffs. Then, too, he would be 38 midway through the next season.

Two of Mullen's sons were playing with a kids' team called the White Sox. Ryan, 12, was playing third base, and Michael, who would be 11 in a month, was playing catcher. Ryan is a runt, just like his dad at the same age. But a gamer. Michael is more muscular, which may account for his being a catcher.

Michael bent down at one point to pick up his catcher's mask, and the pitcher failed to note what he was doing, and delivered another pitch. The baseball struck Michael on the head, and he fell down and rolled over, holding his head. It hurt.

His dad jumped off his bleacher seat, like he was coming out of the penalty box to get back in action at the Civic Arena, and moved swiftly down the sideline to see if his son was OK. "It looked worse than it was," said a woman leaning against the fence near third base. "It was scary the way he was lying there."

Michael Mullen is made of the same stuff as his dad and his uncles, and he was back on his feet, and resumed playing after a brief play stoppage. Joe returned to his seat in the bleachers. "He'll be OK," he told everyone around him who asked.

The next time I saw Michael, a few days later, he was playing catch with his mother, Linda Mullen, on the lawn in front of their beautiful two-story Colonial brick home in Upper St. Clair, in the same neighborhood where Chuck Noll lived during the 23 years he served as the Steelers' head coach. It is a rare sight in the suburbs to see a father and son playing catch, and even rarer to see a mother and son, or mother and daughter doing the same. Joe was filling up a small blue plastic swimming pool for his daughter, Erin. Ask Erin how old she is, and she will show you three extended fingers. Her dad turned the plastic pool sideways first, spraying it to clean it out, and then he filled it. Unlike her dad, Erin is an enthusiastic non-stop talker. She sat atop the kitchen table in her wet bathing suit and talked to me at length.

Joe Mullen has Hall of Fame numbers to his credit.

Veteran center sets for faceoff.

"He's just a scoring machine."
—Ron Francis

Joe with wife Linda and daughter Erin at Penguins' 1992 Christmas party.

Joe hoists Lady Byng Trophy at ceremonies in Toronto in June of 1987. He won it twice.

When I asked her what her dad did for a living, Erin explained, "He plays and he paints walls. He makes things." The Mullens are a typical suburban mini-van family, with Linda usually at the wheel taking the children to all their various activities. They have a black dog named Benson, part Labrador retriever, part springer spaniel. "All mutt," said Mullen. Linda was looking in the rearview mirror, trying not to run over Benson as she backed out of the driveway. "I have to take two of them out, and bring one back," she said of her chauffeur duties. She had Patrick, 8, at her side. Altogether, there are four young Mullens.

"I'm really relaxed when I'm at home," said Joe. "I enjoy playing with the kids. We have some great games. And I enjoy watching them develop. I like seeing the changes in them."

While Ryan and Michael play baseball and hockey — Ryan says he wants to be a goalie — Patrick may be the most like his father. "He loves hockey," said Linda. "He comes home from school and goes right down to the basement and starts shooting the ball against the wall or shooting it against the net. He'll be down there for hours. And when they play, he really hates to lose."

They were back at the ballpark a few nights later. The White Sox were in the playoffs, and they kept on winning, which delayed the Mullens' plans to travel to their home in Cape Cod, Massachusetts for the summer.

Mullen was making a lot of money, but trying to live on a lot less. He wanted to be conservative, and not spoil his kids. "Whatever success I've had, I try to be level-headed about it," he said. "I don't overdo anything. I like to see the kids play as much as they can. I try to get them on ice whenever they want to. I've told my kids to play other sports, too, so they don't get bored with one sport. Some parents push their kids to concentrate on one sport, and they're burned out by the time they're 14. The idea is to have some fun."

The ballpark for kids in Upper St. Clair is something to behold. It is a miniature Field of Dreams. It is on McLaughlin Run Road, named after a creek that runs by the ballfield. The outfield is all grass, watered and cut regularly and well-maintained. The infield is frequently rolled and brushed. The white lines are bright, easily visible and straight. The fence around the field is fairly new. There are no holes in the fence. There are spacious dugouts and even an announcer's booth above the dugout on the first base side. There is an electronic scoreboard in center field. There is a large refreshment stand that was being expanded that same weekend, and a large paved parking lot. To top it off, the third base coach had a camcorder balanced on his shoulder as he shouted out base-running instructions and video-taped the action at the same time. I mentioned to Joe Mullen that this recreation area was quite a contrast to what he knew as a child in his neighborhood in New York City, and Mullen just smiled in response.

"Everyone in the neighborhood knew my dad. He was just a regular guy."

Joe Mullen and his younger brother Brian both made it in the NHL, rare for kids from Manhattan. They grew up on West 49th Street on the city's West Side — popularized by Leonard Bernstein's Broadway show *West Side Story* — in a section called "Hell's Kitchen." It's a tough area that once produced a lot of boxers and tough guys.

Joe and Brian Mullen started out playing street hockey, on roller skates on asphalt streets and playgrounds, as their father, Thomas, had done before them. Thomas and Marion Mullen had five children, and they all turned out to be model citizens. "We lived a half-block from the old Madison Square Garden," said Mullen during a breakfast meeting at the Eat'n Park Restaurant at South Hills Village. He pointed out the window across Fort Couch Road to the St. Thomas More Catholic Church about a hundred yards away. "It was closer than from here to the church over there," he said.

Joe's dad also progressed from playing roller hockey to skating in the big league. Tom Mullen's ice time, however, came *between* periods at the "old" Garden. Prior to the advent of the Zamboni ice-cleaning machine, Tom was one of the men who skated the resurfacing water barrels around the ice. When the Rangers and Knicks moved downtown to a more modern Garden on 33rd Street in 1968, Tom remained on the service staff to help set up facilities for whatever events were staged. He worked at one Garden or another for four decades.

"Everyone in the neighborhood knew my dad," said Joe. "He was just a regular guy. He'd play street hockey with us. We'd have a father-son game every so often. The Irish Christian Brothers would come and play with us, too.

"My dad had a good time. He was popular. He'd stop on the way home and have a few beers with his buddies. He liked Schlitz, Pabst, and he knew all the watering holes. My dad was quiet. He worked a lot. I can't tell you how many times he worked around the clock. He spent nights at the 'old' Garden. He could get better sleep.

"He never gave us compliments. He'd come to watch us play. We'd beat a team, 22-1, and you could have six goals, and you'd feel real proud of yourself, and he'd say, 'You're a bunch of lemons.' He called everybody in the neighborhood a lemon. He never gave any kid in the neighborhood a compliment, not in front of them.

"Our neighborhood was called Hell's Kitchen, but it was no big deal to us. We were near a schoolyard. The New York School of Printing was across the street from our home. We lived in a five story apartment building. We lived on the top floor in what they call a railroad flat. All the rooms are in a row, like cars in a train, that's why they're called railroad flats. There were two adults, my parents, and five of us kids. We had a kitchen, bathroom, three bedrooms and a living room. There were no doors, no privacy. The only door was to the bathroom. The rooms were about fifteen feet wide, from the front of the building to the back."

That was also the width of our rowhouse in Pittsburgh when I was growing up. But our house had three floors, two rooms on each floor. And we played ball on the street in front of our house, and in a field a few doors up the street.

"We also used to go to a playground at East 42nd Street," said Mullen. "We participated in CYO activity there. It used to get cold over there, as the wind came in off the East River."

That was just up the street from *The Daily News* building, near the entrance to a tunnel that takes you from Manhattan to Long Island. I worked in that area during my nine years in New York, and knew the neighborhood well that Mullen was describing.

"There was a sense of excitement when we went there," said Mullen. "We traveled everywhere as kids on subways and buses. We knew our way around the city. Today, these kids around here don't take public transportation. Someone has to drive them wherever they want to go.

"The trouble today is that kids don't want to do anything on their own when it comes to sports. Everything has to be organized, with umpires and referees."

I asked Mullen if that was our fault, for the way we make sure they have such organized activity, and perhaps because we are overly-protective. "I'm not sure," said Mullen. "I just never hear any of my kids saying, 'Hey, Dad, a bunch of kids are going to get together and play some ball.'

"We played roller hockey after school every day. Everyone knew me and my brothers would be there. If they wanted us, they'd stand on the sidewalk in front of our home and holler up through the windows. The windows were always open in the summer. You could yell up through the stairways. Or ring somebody's doorbell and yell up the hall to them.

"We knew where to go and where not to go. We knew what streets to stay away from. When you grow up in New York, you become cautious. At the time, it was like growing up anyplace else. That's all we knew. I never got to see the other side of life, like the nice suburban neighborhoods, until I went to college.

"There were boundaries our parents imposed on us, as to where we were allowed to roam. At first, when we were real young, we could go out from corner to corner, unless you told my mother where you were going.

"It was great for my mother. She could walk to the window, and look down from the fifth floor, and count heads. If one was missing, she'd holler, 'Where's Brian?' Brian was the youngest. The oldest was Kenny, then Tom, then me. And I had a younger sister. Debbie.

"It was a fifth floor walk-up, of course. We'd go up and down with our rollerskates on. We'd make a lot of noise. The neighbors complained once in awhile, but their kids were doing the same thing. It's scary when I yell at my kids for doing things I did routinely."

His education was Catholic all the way. From the fourth grade through high school, he was taught by Irish Christian Brothers at Sacred

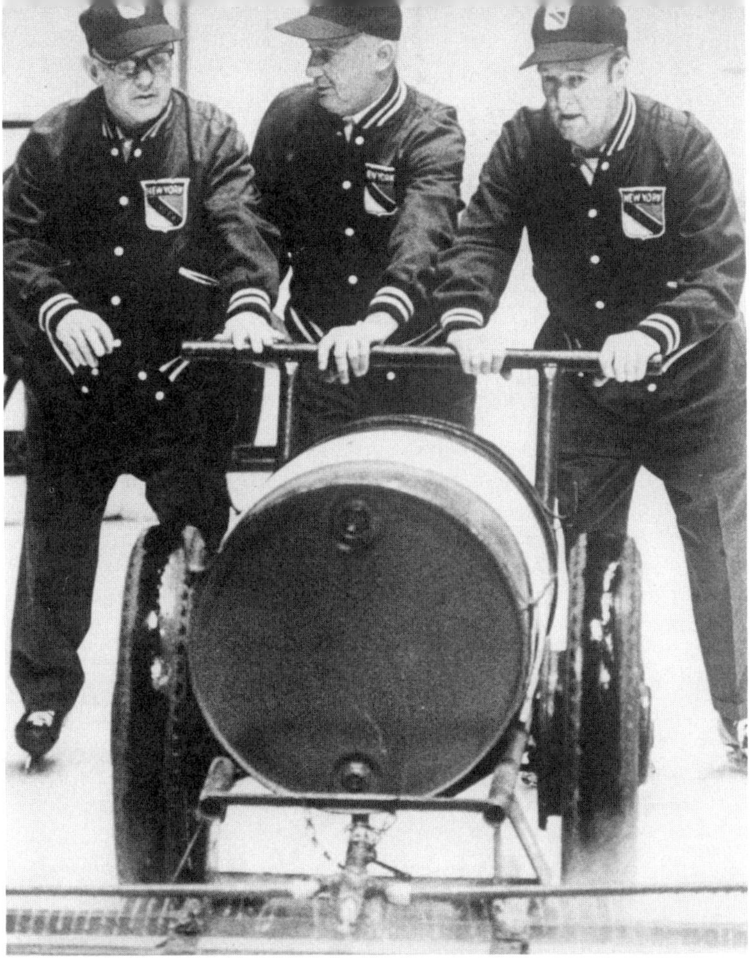

Joe's dad, Tom Mullen, center above and at lower right below, worked on ice maintenance crew at Madison Square Garden and played street hockey with neighborhood team. His uncle, John "Hoppy" Grasso, is to the left of Joe's dad in team photo.

Mullen Family Album

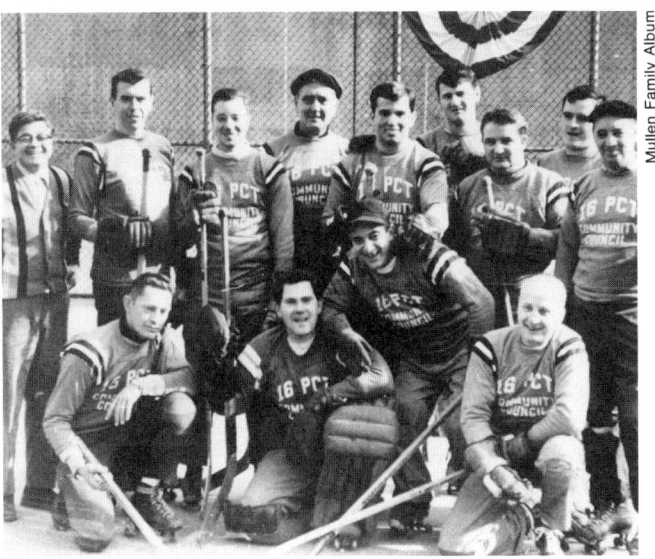

Heart Grade School and Power Memorial Academy, just three blocks from their apartment.

As a youngster, Mullen followed the Rangers, the Yankees, the Knicks — "Walt Frazier was my favorite" — and the Giants, but admits "we never paid much attention to football."

When I asked him who his heroes were on the Rangers, he responded, "Rod Gilbert, Jean Ratelle, Vic Hadfield and Brad Park, guys like that. I'd try to copy their moves. It was something I loved to do."

Boy, Mullen sure knew how to make a guy feel old. At 51, I knew I was 15 years older than Mullen, but this made it seem like a greater age difference. I was writing for *The New York Post* during that same period, and interviewed all those guys when I would take an occasional turn on the Rangers' beat. I reported on more Islanders games in those days, the early to mid-70s. The Islanders were my beat when they came into being in 1972. I lived near Nassau Coliseum and covered the Islanders and Nets who played there.

Mullen mentioned that he and his brother Brian weren't the only local kids to click as big-time hockey players. "Nick Fotiu came out of New York City to be the enforcer for the Rangers," recalled Mullen. "He had won a Gold Gloves title before that. He was pretty tough."

I asked Mullen if Hell's Kitchen was more myth than fact, as far as being a tough neighborhood. "We might have seen more than the normal kid," said Mullen, "but I wouldn't give it up for anything in the world. I loved living there. We might not have had the nice houses you have out here, but it was a great place to grow up.

"There aren't many kids in the cul-de-sac where we live for my kids to play with; I never lacked for kids to play with where I grew up. You just went out in the street and there was a game.

"It might be more dangerous in Pittsburgh these days than it was in New York when I was growing up. Things have changed. You can't even drive by and give a guy a finger. He might shoot you."

"We didn't deserve to be there."
—Joe Mullen

The Rangers won the Stanley Cup, but Mullen wouldn't say they were the best team in the NHL. "I still feel like if we were there, we'd have given them a hard time," he said. "But we didn't deserve to be there the way we played."

Soon after the Penguins' disappointing finish, the local media called for a shake-up in the roster, and suggested some of the older players had to be replaced with younger players.

"I wonder every day about what kind of plans they have for me," said Mullen, who was a week away from signing a contract to continue to play for the Penguins. "If I get a one year contract . . . is that all they want me to play? I try to think about what I want to do after hockey. I know I'm not going into business.

"Hockey has been such a big part of my life. I never showed any interest in anything but hockey. I'll probably get into coaching, I guess."

I asked him if there was any chance he might do what Bryan Trottier was doing, play roller hockey. Trottier was extending his hockey-playing year and career by cavorting for the Pittsburgh Phantoms of Roller Hockey International. "I tried that for the first time on Tuesday at the Arena, just to try it out," Mullen admitted. "I skated after the Phantoms finished practicing. They've asked me and my boys to drop the first puck at an upcoming game. You have to adjust your skating to play that game; you can't stop as well. I haven't played a game yet, but I think it would be fun."

I mentioned to Mullen that Jack Riley, the former general manager of the Penguins, had ventured the opinion that Mullen was one of four Penguins who didn't have their legs for the playoffs. Riley also mentioned Ron Francis, Larry Murphy and Kevin Stevens. "He's correct on all of those," said Mullen, "but there were more than that. I lost mine with a month and a half to go in season.

"I struggled for the last month and a half. Everything I tried didn't work for me. I tried working through it; I tried to rest. Nothing worked."

Mullen had overcome more than his share of disabling injuries in the past, career-threatening injuries, and came back to resume playing. "Hockey players get used to playing with pain." As for his ability to make comebacks, he knocked on the dining table. "A lot of doctors have said I am a quick healer. I've been able to come back from some major injuries."

"Joey, I'm really scared."
—Brian Mullen

I asked Joe about an incident that occurred the past season that had to take him back to West 49th Street, sitting on the stoop at the bottom of their apartment with his brothers and buddies. It had to scare him. It had to shake him. He thought his brother Brian might die in his arms.

His brother Brian was attempting a comeback with the Islanders. In July of 1993, Brian, at age 31, had suffered a stroke. Joe was with his family vacationing in New Hampshire when it happened. "I didn't find out until a day later," he said. "I called my sister-in-law; she was baby-sitting Erin for us in Massachusetts. They had taken Brian to the Huntington County Hospital on the North Shore of Long Island." Brian had bounced back from that, gone through rehabilitation, and was about to resume playing in the NHL.

"Back then, I was just hoping he'd be OK and safe," said Joe. "I knew he was worried about his hockey career; so were we. 'Can he play again?' I asked myself. 'Can he play?' That's what makes him happy. I want him to be as happy as possible."

This was eight months after Brian had suffered that stroke. He was back skating, eager to rejoin the Islanders and don his uniform in NHL action again.

The Penguins were flying from Pittsburgh to New York to play the Islanders the following day, on Sunday, March 20. Joe and Brian were looking forward to a family reunion. "We got in late at night and I called Brian on the phone," related Joe. "I said, 'I'll see you tomorrow at the Coliseum.' We had played that afternoon, and I was tired, and I thought I'd see him after the game the following night.

Joe passed up an optional skating session on the day of the game. "I slept in," said Joe. "I needed my sleep, so I didn't go down to the rink. I got a phone call in my room from our goalie, Kenny Wregget. He said I better come down to the rink, that Brian got hurt. I got dressed and ran across the street from the hotel to the Coliseum. It's not that far from the hotel. Kenny didn't want to worry me, so he hadn't told me the truth.

"Brian had collapsed on the ice during the skating session. There was an ambulance on the ice when I showed up. Brian was already in the ambulance. I jumped in the ambulance. They took him outside the Coliseum where they were going to life-flight him by helicopter to a nearby hospital. We were asking him questions, and he couldn't answer them. 'Brian, what day is it?' And he'd say, 'I'm thinking . . . I'm thinking! Wait a minute!' When he saw the helicopter, he grabbed my hand. He said, 'Joey, I'm really scared.' I was scared, too, but I said, 'Brian, do what they say. You'll be fine.' They wouldn't let me in the helicopter. They took him to a hospital about eight miles away. The cops drove me there. I was worried. I thought I might lose him.

"Everyone said he'd had a seizure. They said it was caused by fatigue. His wife had a baby the week before. So they were not getting much sleep at night. And he was pushing himself to get back to play.

"That morning he had talked to his coach, Al Arbour, and he had asked to go down to the minors to play some games, so he could play for the Islanders in the playoffs. He had worked hard to get in great shape. He'd been practicing. He had been confined the whole year to skating on his own."

Brian recovered, but his hockey career was put on hold again.

"Joe Mullen is a champion."
—Frank Brown

Joe Mullen was the first American-born player to record 900 career points in the NHL when he recorded three points on February 27, 1993 in a 3-3 tie with the Tampa Bay Lightning. The third point, a goal, was his 900th point.

"Joe Mullen is a champion," wrote sportswriter Frank Brown.

Mullen was a piece of Bob Johnson's coaching legacy. Johnson coached him for two seasons in Calgary and admired Mullen's dependability and work ethic as much as his skills as a natural scorer.

On draft day, in June of 1990 — in one of his first official acts as a Penguins employee — Johnson advised general manager Craig Patrick

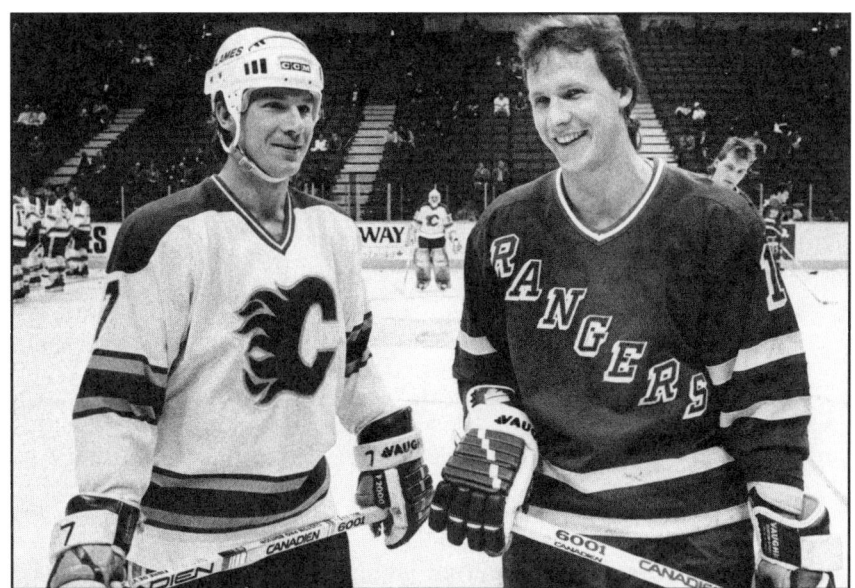

Joe Mullen, during his days with the Calgary Flames, poses with his kid brother Brian when he was with the New York Rangers.

Mullen Family Album

Joe Mullen is third from the right in the back row with his peewee team, the New York Greenleafs, for 10 and 11 year-olds. "He's the one with the big ears," says wife Linda.

to trade a second round draft pick to Calgary for Mullen and Patrick complied. The deal drew some criticism because Mullen was thought to be too old, and the draft class was considered a deep one.

During the 1986-87 season at Calgary, he was the first American-born player to win the Lady Byng Trophy since 1936. In 1988-89, he became only the 13th player to win the Lady Byng Trophy more than once. He scored a career-high 51 goals and 110 points for the Flames that season. He became the second-oldest player to record 50 goals in NHL history.

In the 1989 playoffs, he led all players with 16 goals, while helping Calgary win the Stanley Cup championship.

Mullen recalls a telephone call from Cliff Fletcher, the general manager of the Flames, during the summer of 1990.

"When I heard who was on the phone, I said, 'Oh, oh.' I knew it was draft day," said Mullen. "Fletcher said, 'I have some good news and some bad news for you. We decided to trade you, but you're going to a team that's up and coming and can use you. You'll have a chance to play with Mario Lemieux and work for Bob Johnson again. And he and Craig Patrick will look after you.'

"Bob had been the reason they got me in Calgary, in the first place. I was excited to come back to the States, and be closer to home. There were so many positives to playing in Pittsburgh. I always felt Pittsburgh had a good team; they needed some direction. Bob and Craig provided that.

"I never saw a guy as positive as Bob Johnson. He loved the game of hockey. We had that in common. Before I got to Calgary, they were on an 11-game winless streak. They beat Edmonton the night before I arrived. One of the players told me, 'You won't believe this, but he (Johnson) found something positive in every game in that stretch.'"

Mullen underwent surgery in early 1991 to remove a herniated disk from his neck. Dr. Peter Sheptak performed surgery between the fifth and sixth cervical vertebrae. Some thought Mullen was finished, but they did not know Joe very well.

He missed the final 31 games of the regular season. He returned for the playoffs and scored an astonishing eight goals and 17 points in 22 playoff games. He tied teammate Larry Murphy for the NHL playoff lead in plus-minus rating with a plus 17 rating.

His two goals helped lift the Penguins to an 8-0 victory over the Minnesota North Stars in the decisive game of the Cup finals.

During the 1991-92 season, he ranked third on the team with 42 goals, his seventh season with 40 or more goals. He recorded back-to-back four goal games on December 23 against the Islanders in New York and on December 26 against Toronto to become the first player in Penguins' history to do that.

He suffered a strained knee ligament on May 5 in Game Two of the Patrick Division finals against the Rangers in New York and missed the remainder of the playoffs. He had surgery to correct that a week later. As he sat in shorts that Saturday morning watching his boys play baseball, I noticed the stitchmark scars on his knees.

Johnson felt Mullen made a difference, wherever he played. "He goes through traffic, he takes a check to make a play," Johnson said. "He gets knocked down, and that's when he's dangerous. He's a guy who's a game-breaker. He does other things, too. Plays well defensively. But no matter what, he'll get his goals."

Even so, he was thought to be past his prime when he came to the Penguins. He is what they call a sniper. He sneaks into a crowd and comes away with the puck, and can put it past a goalie before they can say Joe Mullen.

Craig Patrick was a former teammate on the U.S. National Team. "He was a funny-looking skater at the time (1979)," recalls Patrick. "Now he's more polished. He was kind of herky-jerky; he had good speed, but a real funny style."

"I know I've got a choppy stride," said Mullen, "and it is definitely from the roller hockey."

He did not grow up planning a career in the NHL, so it never occurred to him that he had no chance to make it. He played hockey in the street, dodging cabs.

"We played all different sports," said Mullen. "And it kept us out of trouble. Some of the kids I grew up with, they played a little bit of sports and hung out a little bit. Then they hung out a little bit more. And they took the other direction. I played sports more. Anything to keep me out of trouble."

Larry Rauch, Mullen's long-time agent, attorney and friend, once observed, "I remember him saying that he wasn't scared on the ice because he'd seen so many people die in the streets."

To which Mullen says, "You did see a lot of that stuff, not so much gang wars or people being shot, but people just taking drugs and taking overdoses in the street. Sometimes they were people you knew. The thing that kept me alive was sports."

Mullen said he did not start ice skating until he was about nine or ten. His father, Thomas, was on the ice-maintenance staff at Madison Square Garden, but that didn't help Joe or his brothers get any ice time because of the glut of events at the Garden.

"The building was booked solid every minute of the day, so we really didn't get a chance to skate there."

He and brother Brian played on every rink they could find.

Joe joined the St. Louis Blues as a free agent in 1979. He was signed by Emile Francis, who had been the coach of the Rangers that Mullen had rooted for as a youngster.

He turned pro late, at age 22. He had played a rather limited schedule at Boston College compared to what he would have experienced in minor league hockey. The fact that there was less wear and tear on his body early in his career than some NHL vets may account for his longevity.

Mullen credits Francis for being a man who made a difference in his hockey life. "He's the first one who gave me a chance, an opportunity," Mullen said. "He showed me a different side of hockey."

I remembered Francis well from my experience of covering the Rangers on occcasion when he was the team's coach. He was a bantam rooster of sorts, a little guy who could command the attention of big guys and little guys.

I was covering the team when two of the team's players, Ron Stewart and Terry Sawchuck, got into a drunken brawl one night on a beachfront home on Long Island. No one ever determined just what happened, but Stewart stomped on Sawchuck, and Sawchuck died from the resulting internal injuries.

I stopped Stewart on the way out of the locker room one day shortly thereafter, attempting to talk to him about the incident. Francis spotted me and came after me, ordering Stewart to keep going, and chastising me in front of some fellow reporters. He was hot.

A few nights later at the Garden, I was among a group of reporters talking to Francis following the game. "How can you talk to him after the treatment he gave you the other day?" asked Jerry Eskenazi of *The New York Times*. I told him I didn't think my readers cared whether or not Emile Francis had snapped at me. I still had a job to do.

I liked Emile Francis. So did Joe Mullen. "He showed me that a man in his position can care," said Mullen. "He flew my dad out to St. Louis to see me play. My dad had never flown before. My dad wanted to say no, but he couldn't. He had too much respect for Mr. Francis, having worked at the Garden so long. But my dad was scared out of his wits. He took a couple of belts in the morning in order to get on the plane. Mr. Francis showed me he had a soft spot. He knew my dad worked at the Garden. He knew I was from New York. He may have thought that maybe I was a kid who could help. He gave me a great opportunity."

Francis once said of Mullen: "He's just a scoring machine and always has been. He's unselfish and a good team guy, but he's one of those guys who just has the knack."

Actually, Francis and Mullen made a connection earlier in their lives. When Francis was running the Rangers, he started the Metropolitan Junior Hockey League. Francis saw kids playing street hockey — thought it was dangerous — and decided to do something about it. "Geez, these kids should get a chance to play real hockey," he said then.

Joe and his brothers went to the Port Authority bus station on the West Side and took a bus across the river to New Jersey to skate on ice. Joe was just 10. Kenny was in high school and Tommy was two years older than Joe. They went together.

Marion Mullen, his mother, remembers it was tough to get Joe up in the morning. He loved to sleep. And when he wasn't sleeping in the summer, he was playing sports.

"Joey was always a very aggressive player," Marion Mullen told Tom Wheatley for *GOAL* magazine. "I've seen him do things on roller skates that made me put my hand over my eyes — like flip over somebody's back and land on his feet."

Most of the time, anyhow.

"Talk about wearing out pants," Joe's mother continued. "You were always in the store buying clothes for them because the concrete just ate through them."

> *"He's my kind of player.
> I'd go to war with him."*
> —Bob Johnson

I asked him how Badger Bob Johnson, who coached him at Calgary and with the Penguins, had helped him.

"I can't say enough about that man," Mullen said. "He cut me from the first Canada Cup team I tried out for, but I deserved to be cut. I didn't get in good enough shape."

Johnson coached Mullen for two seasons in Calgary and admired Mullen's dependability and work ethic as much as his skills as a natural scorer.

I mentioned to Mullen that Johnson had once said of him, "He's a winner. He's my kind of player. I'd go to war with him." Mullen responded, "That's the best compliment I ever got in sports."

"He's a player, who, if you only see him three times a year, you don't realize how important he is to a hockey team," said Brad McCrimmon, a former teammate in Calgary.

Mullen passed up the opportunity to play for the U.S. hockey team in the 1980 Olympics, the one that captured the heart of the world with their upset victory in the finals to capture the gold medal. "I had met a lot of the guys and it was great to see them win; I felt good for the guys," said Mullen. "I had no regrets. I was out at Salt Lake City getting started in the minors. We won two championships in Salt Lake. I enjoyed playing hockey there. It was a good decision for me. It was a great learning experience. A lot of those players on the U.S. team had short professional careers. I learned a lot in the minors that helped me to make it in the NHL."

> *"Once we put on our uniforms,
> we're all the same age.
> Everyone's a kid."*
> —Joe Mullen

After Johnson obtained Mullen from the Flames, he said, "I think he'll score 40-plus goals for the next two years." And he did just that.

Mullen was only the fourth player to record a 40-goal season at age 35 or later. The first three were Hall of Famers Gordie Howe, Phil Esposito and Johnny Bucyk, who did it twice.

Mullen once told Bill Utterback of *The Pittsburgh Press*, "I know this is late in life for a hockey player, but I try not to think about it. Once we put on our uniforms, we're all the same age. Everyone's a kid."

Utterback discovered doing some research that The Hall of Fame has never denied a player with 400 goals and two championship rings, and Mullen now had three championship rings.

Mullen told Utterback: "I think my enthusiasm is what keeps me going. I think if I ever lost that I might slow down a little. But I still love to play the game. I love to go out and do the best I can every night. I have the same enthusiasm as when I started and I can't see myself ever giving it up, even though I know that someday I'll have to."

His wife Linda has known him since they met as students in 1978, during his third year at Boston College. She was from Brookline, Massachusetts. "Nobody loves the game more than he does," she said. "Joey is hockey and hockey is Joey."

Craig Patrick, his present general manager, served as assistant coach and assistant manager for that 1980 Olympic team. "Besides being a great goal-scorer," offered Patrick, "he's got great character."

Former Flames head coach Terry Crisp said, "Joey's got an unbelievably quick release. He's one of the greatest scorers in the game."

His teammates think the world of him.

"You don't really realize how good a player he is until you actually play with him," offered Ron Francis. "He does all the little things right, defensively as well as offensively. He's so easy to play with because he is always in the right spot at the right time."

Former teammate Bob Errey once said, "He's a great example for this team."

Larry Murphy said, "He's got the attitude of a 15-year-old and the body of a 25-year-old."

Mario Lemieux said, "Like a good wine, he gets better with age."

Even so, Mullen may have wondered what was in stock for him when yet another coach came on the scene at the Civic Arena, namely Eddie Johnston. "Eddie Johnston has been good for me," said Mullen. "With a new coach coming in, who hadn't been with the organization when I came here, I wasn't sure what my status would be. He let me do the same things I'd been doing. He shows a lot of confidence in me. He'll put me in the last minute of a game, to hold a one-goal lead. He'll go with me at clutch times."

The year before Mullen moved to Pittsburgh, the 1989-90 season, was an emotional roller coaster for him. He played for the Campbell Conference in the All-Star Game January 21, 1990 at the Civic Arena. His dad died during that season.

His dad had raised money so his kids could play hockey in New Jersey and other distant outposts.

"I loved this game so much that I played with other kids after midnight at a hockey rink in West New York, just to get to play on ice," remembered Mullen. "We were determined to do whatever we had to do to get playing time on ice instead of the streets. Those were the conditions we grew up in.

"I saw a lot of trouble growing up in New York. A lot of kids that I grew up with died because of drugs or guns or loan-sharking. But I knew where I shouldn't go, who I shouldn't know. My parents showed us the way to go."

Mullen told Tom Capezzuto in the February, 1991 issue of *Hockey Digest*: "Acrobatics have always been a big part of my game since I was young. Roller-skating helped me to learn how to handle the puck, pass and, most all, to stay on my feet. I don't go out there on the ice trying to be acrobatic or cute, but I am a lot smaller than most players in the league and I'm not as strong. But I'm able to use my quickness and balance to overcome my small size. I learned how to play on cement, remember?"

"Would you sign an autograph for my daughter?"

During our interview at the Eat'n Park Restaurant at South Hills Village, an attractive blonde-haired woman who was wearing gray shorts with a Penguins logo on the left thigh approached our table, a child about three-years-old at her side.

"Would you sign your autograph for my daughter?" the woman asked Joe. She offered no pen or pencil. "I don't have a piece of paper," she said with a smile. "Could you sign your name to this?"

She presented Joe with a bag that contained what is called a Smiley cookie. Unreal. Joe just smiled and signed it, and handed it back to her. Maybe he was pleased she recognized him.

Erin stretches in front of her three brothers, left to right, Ryan, Patrick and Michael at Mullen's Upper St. Clair home during 1993 holiday season.

Greg Malone
Sweet smell of success

"It boils down to how badly they want to succeed."

Penguins were passing elephants and horses in the hallway at Gate 2 of the Civic Arena. It was quite a menagerie. The Shrine Circus had taken over the building for four days in early April of 1994, chasing the Penguins who had to practice at the Harmarville Bladerunners Rink. Some of the players were returning after an optional skate, and they were careful not to get too close to the pachydermal parade, a half dozen elephants linked by trunk and tail, while dodging what the elephants and horses had left behind in their trail.

There were brightly-costumed show girls, animal handlers who looked as bored as the animals, and all kinds of clowns moving about. It was a toss-up as to whether the show girls or the clowns wore more make-up on their faces. The show girls had glitter on their hair and even their eyelashes. A blacksmith was shoeing an anxious horse, and the clinking was echoing through nearby hallways. I was also careful — big animals make me nervous — and kept my distance from the horses and llamas that were being temporarily housed in the straw-strewn area outside the doors of the Penguins administrative offices on the floor level of the Arena. I had to dance out of the way of a long-horned steer that resembled the University of Texas mascot.

I was there to see Greg Malone, a former Penguins star and the head of the club's scouting staff in recent seasons. He had been a solid two-way center from 1976 to 1983, and his name remains in many of the Penguins top ten listings. He had played seven seasons with the Penguins — remember his distinctive Prince Valiant haircut? — and was in his fifth year in the scouting department. He was hired by Tony Esposito the second time around. The NHL regular season was fast coming to a close at the time of our meeting. Malone was getting ready for a trip to Europe to check out the talent over there.

For a fleeting moment, though, I thought I was visiting Del Miller, the dean of harness racing, whose offices are in a barn at the Meadowlands in Washington County. Yes, a real barn. Miller is used to the fragrance in his workplace. To Miller, it's the smell of money. The scene also reminded me of the days when I worked in New York, and how Madison Square Garden would stink for weeks after the circus had occupied the building for a few days. Malone didn't seem to mind.

That was understandable when I quickly learned that he had grown up in a community called Chatham in New Brunswick, located along the Miramichi River, just off the Miramichi Bay in the Gulf of St. Lawrence on the eastern seaboard of Canada. "Ted Williams has a fishing camp there, salmon fishing is big," Malone mentioned. It is a fishing community, but the major industry in Chatham is a pulp mill or paper mill. Anybody who has ever passed a paper mill in their travels — in Tyrone, Pennsylvania, for instance — knows that nothing smells worse than a paper mill. It can make you ill.

"When the wind blew a certain way," recalled Malone, "it was especially bad. Here, it's the elephants that smell the most. The smell hasn't gotten into our offices yet."

Malone's father worked in the paper mill back in Chatham. "He'd come in the house and take his work clothes off, and leave them in the basement," said Malone. "His clothes were so full of soot and smell. It was tough to get rid of it."

Malone's memories reminded me of my own youth. I grew up in Glenwood, between Hazelwood and Hays, at the southeastern end of Pittsburgh proper. There was a meat packing company or slaughterhouse, as well as two junkyards, in Hays, on the other side of the Glenwood Bridge that spans the Monongahela River. When there was a westward wind the breeze blowing through my third-floor bedroom window was enough to turn your stomach. Then, too, there was a sulphur plant at the western end of town where Hazelwood bumped into Greenfield. It always smelled like rotten eggs or worse. When we took the street car to Downtown Pittsburgh we always knew when we were entering Greenfield because of the bad odor. As kids, whenever someone would pass gas in our company, usually on purpose in crude child's play, someone was sure to signal the event by calling out, "Greeeeenfield!" Green was nearly stretched into a two-syllable word. Ah, the sweet memories of youth.

"I was a real rink rat."
—Greg Malone

Malone has more pleasant memories of his hometown of Chatham. "It was a small town, with about six thousand people," he said. "They had an excellent sports program, in baseball and hockey, in all sports for that matter. Once you made a team, you played with the same kids every year as you grew up."

Greg's father, Bill Malone, was an electrician by trade at the paper mill, but he was a hockey player at heart. He had played University hockey, and he continued to play senior hockey. He liked hockey and he liked to drink, and sometimes he mixed the two pastimes. Bill was a scrapper, and Greg remembers that many people called his dad "Wild Bill," and that he was known throughout the province.

"As I got into peewee and bantam hockey," said Malone, "I traveled throughout the area, playing in tournaments. A father of some player on the other team would always come over and say, 'I know your dad.' Then he'd roll his eyes to emphasize that statement. They have a peewee tournament in Quebec City, and some great players passed through there in their youth. Wayne Gretzky was among them. But they also remembered my dad.

"Senior hockey was a big thing when I was growing up. I never saw my dad play. He lost his eye the year I was born, and that was the end of his playing days. It happened playing hockey. He got hit with a puck in the eye and he lost most of his sight in that eye. As a result, my mom was always petrified of me playing. She was always worried about me getting injured.

"She wasn't opposed to me playing, but she worried about me getting hurt. I had skates when I was two or three years old; ever since I can remember I was walking around on skates. I used to go up to the rink and play in the early morning. I used to walk to school, walk to church, walk to the rink, walk to the ballfields.

"My mother's name was Natalie. She was a nurse at the local hospital. She was worried about my welfare. I was always one of the smallest guys on our team. I never grew up until I got to high school. I was playing in a playoff game once, and I got speared, and was stretched on the ice. When I looked up, my mother was leaning over me. I felt embarrassed. After that, I told her never to leave the seats again to come out on the ice, no matter what happened to me.

"After he finished playing, my dad would referee some games. I'd carry his skates to the rink, and I'd get in free. I made the mistake once of playing in a game he was refereeing for the kids. He kept calling penalties on me. My mother was so mad at him; she thought he was picking on me. She really raked him over the coals when he came home from that game. He never did another of my games after that.

"Sometimes I'd go up and play with any team that would take me. I'd even play goalie if it would get me in a game. My Saturdays were non-stop hockey. I'd go up and play and stay and watch all the other games. I'd go home for supper. I'd get some homemade beans and bread. Then I'd watch Hockey Night in Canada on TV the rest of the night. Foster Hewitt and Danny Gallivan described the action. It was usually a game with the Montreal Canadiens or the Toronto Maple Leafs. On Sunday nights, I could pick up the Boston Bruins station on the radio. That's when there were only six teams in the National Hockey League.

"I was a real rink rat. As I got older, I started refereeing to get more ice time. We'd scrape the ice ourselves. This was before the Zamboni machines. We'd scrape the ice and someone would drag a barrel of water behind us to smooth out the ice and put a shine on it. If you helped out like that, they'd give you an hour or two of free ice time.

"When it got cold out, our friends and dads would help us make outdoor rinks. You'd put up boards, and pack the snow, put a base down and build it up as the winter progressed. We'd keep it all winter. Your feet would freeze from being out there so long. You had no feeling in your toes. It was so cold you had to wear a tuke — like a tassel cap — or your ears would freeze. When you came home for dinner you'd keep your skates on, and spread some newspapers under your chair to catch the drippings from your skates and pants. We used to get a lot of snow in Chatham, even more in those days than they do now.

Malone Family Album

Malone clan includes, left to right, Jim, Dot, Greg, Kelly and Sue. Below, Greg enjoys participating in Penguins' annual golf outing that helps fund local amateur hockey leagues.

Jim Cunningham

"We used to get this Beehive honey, and if you collected the lids and sent them in, you'd get pictures of the Maple Leafs. I had an aunt who worked in the local grocery store, and she'd get me lids I was missing. So I had the whole set. It would probably be worth a fortune today. I put them on the wall of my bedroom, the way kids hang posters today.

"Another connection to the NHL was that we had a hockey banquet at the end of the year. We had a house league all-star team that traveled to play similar teams throughout the region. Someone from the NHL would come down every year and speak at our banquet. It's something that had a great influence on me in my youth."

I mentioned to Malone that it's rare that an NHL player would appear today at a similar get-together. He nodded in agreement. He shrugged his shoulders. He had some thoughts on the subject, I could tell. But it was better to be silent. "Everyone's missing something today," he said.

"I had an opportunity to meet Bobby Orr and Gordie Howe at that banquet," recalled Malone. "Howe was making appearances on behalf of Sears back then. I remember meeting Bobby Rousseau, Floyd Smith and Danny Grant. It was great. I have fond memories of my early days in New Brunswick. I'm a firm believer in not forgetting where you come from."

"I still have the values I learned from my dad."
—Greg Malone

It would be difficult for Malone to forget where he came from. As a teenager, his family moved to Fredericton, where he played his high school hockey. Federicton later had a franchise in the American Hockey League, and Malone finished up his professional career there. Malone had come directly from junior hockey to the Penguins of the NHL, so he initially bypassed minor league hockey. "I'm glad I went there at the end of my career, though, so I have a better appreciation for what it's like for a young prospect to play there," he said. "At first, though, I'll admit I was asking myself, 'Why am I back in Fredericton?' But I knew everyone, and I enjoyed my stay there."

There is a painting on the wall alongside Malone's desk at the Penguins' office complex at the Civic Arena. One of his sisters sent him the painting, which depicts a kids' hockey game at Fredericton High School. The painting is called "The Battle of Waterloo," as Waterloo Drive was the name of the street alongside the outdoor rink. The painting is understandably a precious one in Malone's eyes. It also reminds him of his sisters and brothers: Dot, Sue, Jim and Kelly. He remembers his boyhood coaches, Doug Cain, Gus Bondar and Harold Flieger.

Malone possesses even more from his early days. "I still have the values I learned from my dad in those days," said Malone. "When I was little, I started having a lot of success. I could skate well, better than anybody else I was playing with. I used to get the puck and nobody could take it away from me. I could go through everyone. I could score ten or eleven goals. I started getting ink in the local papers. This one year, Bobby Hull was going for the record of 50 goals in a season, and he broke Rocket Richard's record. At the same time, I was closing in on a similar record in our league. I ended up with 52 goals, and had my picture in the local paper.

"In the spring, when the snow was melting away, we'd all be paying attention to the Stanley Cup playoffs. We'd make wooden goalie cages, and fill them in with potato sacks for netting to catch the pucks, and we'd play street hockey. We'd start out with regulation-size sticks, but after a few weeks of scraping them along the street surface the blades would be pencil-thin, and we couldn't use them again."

Malone has some hockey prints adorning the other walls in his office, two of them picturing goalies. Some of his pals have signed their signatures with Magic Marker pens right on the glass. "It's my Hall of Shame," he said. "Look at some of those signatures."

They included Les Binkley, a former Penguins goalie who now works for Malone on the Penguins' scouting staff, and Charlie Hodge, who replaced Jacques Plante as a net-minder with the Montreal Canadiens. Then, too, there's Wendell Young and Eddie Johnston, and Brendan Rupp, the son of former Penguins' defensman, Duane Rupp. He also has the signatures of his friends on the Civic Arena maintenance crew right next to those NHLers. Malone keeps things in their proper perspective.

> *"I guess in order to get someplace you have to be prepared to put your nose to the grindstone."*
> —Greg Malone

Malone's marriage ended in divorce and he lives by himself in Bridgeville, in an apartment complex called Hickory on the Green, built around an 18-hole golf course. His former wife, Dianna Smith of Pittsburgh, was living in the neighboring community of Upper St. Clair with their two children, Ryan, 14, and Mark, 11, at the time of my visit with Malone. Greg and Diane used to make a lot of appearances together at fund-raising programs in Pittsburgh, and they were a popular pair. "She's good about letting me have the boys," said Greg. "I get to see them a lot." The boys are frequent visitors to his apartment, and he takes them fishing in Canada each summer. "They both play in the Mt. Lebanon Hockey Association," said Malone. "Ryan was a first year bantam this season, and Mark was in his last year as a squirt. He moves up to peewee next season. When we go back to Canada, they go through my scrapbooks. My mother kept them from the time I was little till I turned pro. Now I appreciate that more, especially when my sons look at it."

His mother is still looking after him. A few weeks after our interview, I bumped into Malone on Community Day in Upper St. Clair. "When I told my mother about our interview," he began, "she asked me if I told you about how I used to go to bed some nights wearing my hockey equipment so I could jump out of bed in the morning and go right to the rink. I told her I forgot about that. She said to tell you. She said writers like stuff like that."

Malone admits he sometimes looks over his sons' shoulders at the clippings in the scrapbook his mother maintained for him, and recalls his hockey-playing days.

"As a player, the camaraderie was what I enjoyed the most, the characters I played with," said Malone. "At first, it was a thrill just to get an opportunity to play in the NHL. Just the chance. It never dawned on me as a kid that I could go that far in hockey. To me, it was just a game I enjoyed playing."

Malone was born March 8, 1956, one of five children in the Malone family. Twenty years later, in 1976, he was drafted in the second round by the Penguins, the 19th player picked overall. He had been playing junior hockey in Oshawa for three seasons. He went there for his 12th grade in high school, and played for the Oshawa Generals in the Ontario Major Junior Hockey League.

"Even after I was drafted, the idea of playing in the NHL was still like a dream kind of thing for me. I thought I'd get a sniff, and go play in the minors for two or three years and then go home and be a school teacher.

"A few days before training camp opened, I got a telephone call from the coach, Kenny Schinkel. He told me 'if you have a good camp, you can make the team.' I was sorta going through the motions before Schinkel spoke to me. After that, I was determined to make that team."

Malone remembers the camp was held at the Rostraver Gardens, just off Route 51 out by Belle Vernon and West Newton in Westmoreland County. Malone mentioned that the 1994 state high school hockey championships were being held there.

"I stuck with the Penguins at age 20, and I didn't hit the minors until my last year, when I was playing for the Nordiques, and they sent me down to Fredericton.

"Things were different when I first broke into pro hockey. When we'd be playing on the road, for instance, someone would say we were going to meet and eat at a certain restaurant, and everyone would show up. We had all kinds of parties, like Halloween parties and '50s parties. Everybody came. As I got older, some guys wouldn't come anymore."

The Penguins had a lot of financial problems when Malone made the team. The club had declared bankruptcy two years earlier. Albert Savill, Otto Frenzel and Wren Blair bought the team on July 11, 1975. Blair was the team's general manager.

During that 1975-76 season, Jean Pronovost became the first Penguin to score 50 goals in a season and Pierre Larouche became the

Greg Malone scored record 52 goals as a 10-year-old in 1966.

Malone played his junior hockey for Oshawa Generals.

George Gojkovich

Malone skates and shows off Prince Valiant haircut back in 1976-77 season.

first Penguin to score 100 points. Both reached those milestones in the same game against Boston.

Malone joined the team for the following season, 1976-77. Malone says Baz Bastien came back to Pittsburgh half-way through that season to run the front-office.

"Baz was a sincere guy," said Malone. "The players felt sorry that the team was going under. But Baz kept the money problems away from the players. Baz never brought up the problems to us. We had a pretty good hard core of players, and we were always respectable. We were always in the middle of the standings."

When Malone was an amateur the scouting report on him was that he was "hard-working, rugged, good attitude." That was the book on him as an 18-year-old prospect. He wasn't thought to be a particularly fast skater and he didn't show a propensity for scoring goals. The Penguins thought the book was incomplete.

At first, he was reluctant to shoot. Penguins coach Johnny Wilson asked him one day at a team meeting, "Greg, what's the easiest thing to do in hockey?" Malone was stumped for a moment. Then Malone said, "Shoot." So Wilson said, "How come you don't shoot more?"

After that, he did. Malone remembers scoring a hat trick in a 7-1 win over the New York Rangers at the Civic Arena. Fans actually threw hats onto the ice. His best season was the 1978-79 campaign when he scored 65 points in 80 games. He led the Penguins in goals that year with 35.

"I don't consider myself to be anything more than an average hockey player," he said back then. "Anything I get, I generally have to work for. But I guess in order to get someplace you have to be prepared to put your nose to the grindstone."

He certainly had a fan in Johnny Wilson. "Malone really works his tail off," said the Penguins' coach. "He's a strong, tough kid who'll go into the corners and get the puck for you. And he's got a heck of a shot. He's a hard guy to knock off the puck. And he has a good, quick shot. He does the very most with the talent he's got."

Edward J. DeBartolo bought a piece of the Penguins in 1977, and took over control of the franchise in 1978. Things changed after that, according to Malone, and for the best. Eddie Johnston came in as coach in 1980. "He traded away the older players, and went with youth," said Malone. "Our record dropped off, but it put us in a position to draft better players. Eventually (in 1984) we had the first pick for the first time, and that's how we got Mario Lemieux."

Malone was one of the players Johnston traded away ("I made the deal for the future," Johnston said at the time). "At the time, I was very upset," said Malone. "I didn't want to leave Pittsburgh. Once I got to Hartford, however, it was a better situation for me. It prolonged my career."

I asked Malone to tell me about Larouche, a very gifted goal-scorer who was on the Penguins when he joined the team.

"I think a lot of that guy," said Malone. "It was tough for him. Everyone else was married and he was single. It created a lot of problems. I came in with two other rookies, Russ Anderson and Blair Chapman. Wren Blair put us in an apartment he had leased originally for himself at the Washington Plaza apartments, right across the street from the Civic Arena. He probably figured they'd be sending us down to Hershey, which was our affiliate then.

"We had some good players. Davey Burrows was a very strong defensive player. We had Ron Stackhouse — he got into trouble with management by complaining about the potholes in Pittsburgh — and Syl Apps, Rick Kehoe and Bob 'Battleship' Kelly.

"Jean Pronovost was a real talkative guy, a leader. He was always trying to get the guys up. He was very serious, very competitive. He hated to lose, and he'd be ranting and raving in the clubhouse after a loss. Apps was a leader, too, but in a different way. He was not as vocal as Pronny was."

During his prime, Malone was a tough left-handed shooter, who was hard to stop once he got rolling. "When Greg Malone gets up a head of steam," wrote Dan Donovan, who covered the Penguins' beat for *The Pittsburgh Press*, "he is a locomotive on the rampage, impossible to stop."

Malone was a hard-worker who could hang onto the puck, just like when he was a kid, and wait for his wingers to get free. During the 1979-80 season, Malone had 51 points, including 19 goals, in 51 games before he wrecked his right knee in a collision in Toronto in mid-February. He had ripped a tendon and had a couple of torn ligaments that were repaired at Allegheny General Hospital. He missed the remainder of the season, 29 games altogether, yet still led the team in assists. Malone was the Penguins' best player when he got hurt, struck down by a blind-side check. He provided one of the season's highlights when he recorded six assists vs. Quebec on November 28. He tied the club record for most assists in a game held by his buddy Ron Stackhouse. Lemieux later tied that record.

Malone also topped the Penguins in assists with 32 in 1979-80 and again with 44 in 1982-83.

Malone said his role with the Penguins changed as he went from rookie to veteran performer. "All of a sudden you look around and you're one of the senior guys," he said with a smile. "All of a sudden I was helping guys break in like Bob Errey, Jimmy Hamilton, Kevin McClelland, Marty McSorley and Mark Johnson, the Olympic kid. The first year I was here, I had guys like Don Awrey and Eddie Van Impe helping me. Awrey had played with Bobby Orr on a Stanley Cup championship team in Boston (and on a Stanley Cup winner at Montreal), and Van Impe had played with a Stanley Cup championship team in Philadelphia. They knew the ropes. They took me and Anderson and Chapman — the three rookies — out for a couple of beers one night after practice at Rostraver. We had a team meeting later that night and they had to prop the three of us up together, so we wouldn't pass out on the floor.

"It was unusual for veterans to help rookies in those days. Back then, when a new kid came in, everybody got after him. There was a lot of animosity toward young kids. They didn't want them bumping their buddies off the team. These guys told us, though, that from now on when rookies came in, you were to treat them right and look after them. It would help them adjust to the pros and, in the end, it would help the team. It would help the young players develop."

I asked Malone about his job as head of the scouting department, and how he determined who had what it takes to play in the NHL.

"I don't like to get too close to the kids," he said. "Besides their size and skills, I am interested in their attitude and character. I want to see what their work habits are. Does he want to sacrifice? Does he want to be an NHLer? Some kids don't want the life."

How often does he see a prospect that makes his heart skip a beat?

"It happens a few times a year," he responded. "I see a kid who has something exceptional. He starts doing things you can't teach, or he has special poise. That's impressive. A lot of times you sit there and you wonder. 'Does he skate well enough? Can he improve?' There are so many intangibles. You wish you could get a system that's a hundred percent, or foolproof. But there is no such thing. You're always searching for answers. It boils down to the individual, and how well they can play the game, and how badly they want to succeed."

Though he didn't think he was good enough to ever play in the NHL when he was a young man, Malone believes he wanted it badly once he saw that it was possible to play in the big time. "It became a big part of my life," he said. "The one year I was out of hockey, nothing came up that made me want to get away from the game. It's always been important in my life. It's always paid the bills."

Greg Malone is flanked by sons, Mark, 11, and Ryan, 14.

"Arrogance? It's not arrogance. Mentally, you have to believe that you can stop every shot taken. Physically, you may not have the skill to do that, but if you doubt yourself, in my mind you've really lost the battle before you ever go out there."
—Tom Barrasso
on goaltending

Tom Barrasso
Demon Goalie

"If I make a mistake a red light goes on, and everyone knows it."

The view from the first tee at the Sewickley Heights Golf Club is spectacular. On a clear day you can see green forever. Or so it seems. The initial drive is a downhill one, a steep slope with a dogleg to the right. It's a hilly course, one of those up and down layouts familiar to golfers in western Pennsylvania, the kind that produced Arnold Palmer and Rocco Mediate. It lacks the reputation and tradition of the Oakmont Country Club, where the U.S. Open was played in the summer of 1994, but it is rated "the toughest golf course from the white tees" in the area. It is a PGA championship-caliber course, and regarded as a stern test of anyone's golf skills.

Tom Barrasso likes it that way. He has always enjoyed a good challenge. The bigger the challenge the better. That's his history. The Penguins' goalie loves to play golf, and spends much of the off-season indulging himself, and has even gone to Europe to play one of his favorite games. But Barrasso likes to be successful, he likes to win, in the worst way. And that's the way he often plays golf, to hear one fellow member talk about Barrasso in the most unflattering terms.

According to this member I stumbled upon while touring Sewickley Heights and the golf club layout, Tom Barrasso sounds like a modern day Tommy Bolt, a former pro golfer who was known as "Terrible Tommy" Bolt in his heyday. Like Tommy Bolt, Tommy Barrasso has been known to toss golf clubs and expletives about the fairways and greens of the Sewickley Heights Golf Club with equal abandon. Tom is intense, whether he is wielding his goaltender's stick or a 7-iron.

"If he weren't Tom Barrasso, he'd have been fined a few times by now," said the fellow club member, who asked to remain anonymous. "He has a terrible temper. Sometimes he plays by himself, sometimes he brings Mario Lemieux along. He has some friends he plays with regularly. I think some of them are former teammates. When he's by himself, we've let him play through a couple of times. But he never nods or says thank you or hello or even acknowledges anyone as he goes by. He thinks he's better than everybody else. That's the impression he gives, anyhow.

"You know, there are a lot of people around here who have a helluva lot more money than he makes. Some people around here . . . all they do is manage their family's money . . . and they could care less that he's a goalie making a million a year in the National Hockey League. They're not impressed."

In short, wherever he's been, Tom Barrasso has never been mistaken for Mr. Congeniality. It's difficult to understand why someone so successful, from such an early age, and someone who has so much going for him, is such an angry young man. What's bothering Barrasso? Why doesn't he stop and smell the flowers at the Sewickley Heights Golf Club?

Former Steelers Lynn Swann and Jack Ham both belong to the Sewickley Heights Golf Club. Their coach, Chuck Noll, moved to Sewickley in 1993 after living 24 years in the same home in Upper St. Clair, a suburb to the south of Pittsburgh. He, too, likes to play in golf outings on the local layouts.

"Those guys are all gentlemen on the golf course, and are pleasant with everybody," said our man about town. "Franco Harris is that way, too. They say hello to people, and talk to everyone. They don't have their heads in the clouds. I remember meeting Art Rooney once. It was the first time I was ever at the Allegheny Club at Three Rivers Stadium. I must have looked lost. Mr. Rooney came up to me and said, 'Do you need some help?' He showed me where to go. That's the way people in sports ought to be. I think Barrasso ought to lighten up a little, and treat people better. In the long run, he'll be better off."

The man, who has his own business, said he lives in the same neighborhood in Sewickley as Lemieux. From the Sewickley Heights Golf Club, you have to drive down a long, winding road, with treacherous curves, called Camp Meeting Road, to get to the neighborhood where Lemieux lives in a grand old red brick mansion he bought for a reported $1.2 million.

Lemieux lives on the flatlands of Sewickley, just above Ohio River Boulevard, near the Sewickley Academy, a highly-regarded private school, and the Edgeworth Country Club, where his wife, Nathalie, plays on tennis and platform tennis traveling teams.

I have played platform tennis at Edgeworth on several occasions. On my last visit, my partner and I played two men with the first names of Ham and Gunter. It's that kind of place. I have also played in a mixed tournament against Nathalie, before she was married to Mario. She's quite good at the game.

"She's very active in the community, and you see Mario around town," the man went on. "You never see Barrasso. He keeps to himself. He doesn't seem like a very sociable sort. I see kids, about eight to ten years old, camped on the curb outside Mario's home in the morning. They're waiting for autographs. And I have seen him stop on the way out of his driveway to accommodate those kids on several occasions. He has a gate at the driveway, so you can't just go in."

The gate is a huge black iron one. Where there isn't a gate there's a wall around Lemieux's property, and plenty of security system signs. There are lots of gates and walls wherever you drive around Sewickley or Sewickley Heights. Greta Garbo ("I vant to be left alone.") would have loved this community. Sewickley is known as a bastion of the wealthy, but there are middle class and even poor people living in the community.

Chuck Knox, the coach of the Los Angeles Rams, grew up over a saloon in Sewickley. It's all a matter of location.

There are sections, though, where you know the rich people dominate the landscape. There are estates with never-ending green landscapes behind those gates and walls, and they all seem to have long, private driveways. There are lots of signs that say DO NOT ENTER or PRIVATE DRIVE and NO TRESPASSING. The small lots are two and three acres, and they go up from there.

There are deep, dense, dark woods, preserves and sanctuaries. One sees boarding kennels and equestrian layouts on horse farms. There are fields where they play rugby, and there are polo enthusiasts there, too.

This was in late July of 1994. I had interviewed Barrasso in the morning at the Civic Arena and later on that day, by coincidence, attended a golf outing hosted by Integra Bank/Pittsburgh at the Allegheny Country Club in Sewickley Heights, a 100-year-old club with a proud tradition. "I live just a few minutes from there," Barrasso had told me. I took advantage of a break before dinner to tour the area in my car.

I was curious about where Barrasso and Lemieux were living and wanted to see their respective homes. Mario moved to Sewickley from Mt. Lebanon two years earlier because he sought a more private, more secure setting for his home. He had married Nathalie, his one-and-only girl friend from their teenage days, and they had a baby daughter. They had a swimming pool of their own now, and were close to a club where Nathalie could go and be one of the girls.

It's a great location because its inhabitants claim that it's less than a half hour to the Civic Arena and to the Pittsburgh International Airport, a perfect triangle for a hockey player.

Barrasso had built his own home a year earlier, a "too-big-house," as Barrasso described it, somewhere between the Sewickley Heights Golf Club and the Allegheny Country Club. He and his wife, Megan, had three daughters, ages 2 to 6. They previously lived just off the No. 2 fairway of the Sewickley Heights Golf Club.

"Do you know the difference between a golf club and a country club?" our resident expert asked me. "A golf club doesn't have a swimming pool. That's about it." Some golf clubs aren't open year round, either, tending to be spring-to-fall retreats.

It is not all green at the Sewickley Heights Golf Club. There are flower beds here and there, breaking up the green landscape with lilac and red and yellow floral arrangements. Crows were cawing and breaking the silence on this particular day, a Monday when the club was closed and only a couple of the caddies were playing. It was empty otherwise. It was the kind of day Barrasso would have enjoyed being out there, alone, just him and the ball and his clubs. Barrasso is a fine golfer, playing to a five handicap at Sewickley Heights.

Asked how good his golf game was, Barrasso said, "Never good enough. I get it down to a 3 or 4 handicap. I just can't get it any better. I think it's this hockey thing that's killing me. If I could play golf 12 months a year it would be interesting."

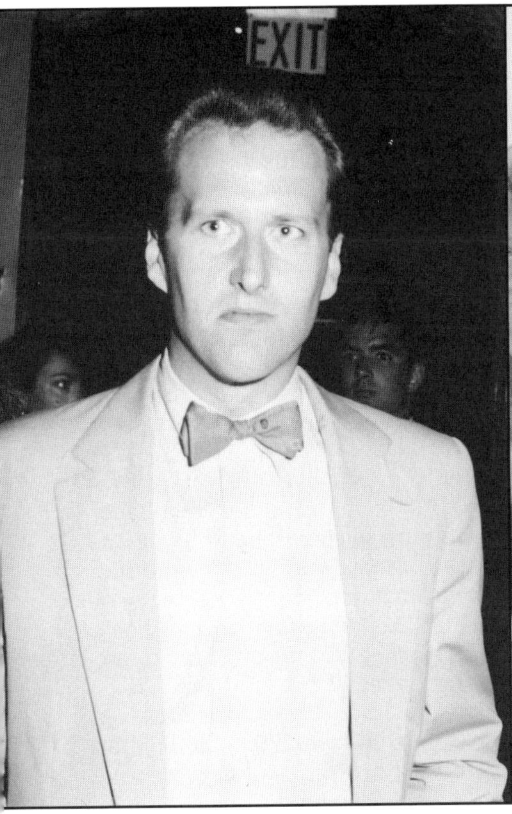

Dennis Cavanaugh

Tommy "Bowtie" Barrasso at formal outing, Bob Johnson and Mario Lemieux move in to congratulate Barrasso after his sparkling shutout performance in 1991 Stanley Cup clincher and, below, Barrasso dives to thwart Toronto Maple Leafs at Civic Arena.

Jim Cunningham

People have always talked behind Barrasso's back, whether it was in Boston, where he grew up, or in Buffalo, where he first played professional hockey as a precocious 18-year-old, and certainly in Pittsburgh.

I have heard daytime radio talk shows where people have called in with stories of marital discord regarding Barrasso. He was accused of threatening to break the legs of a customer who got into an altercation with a couple of his teammates at a season-ending party at Froggy's Saloon in Market Place. He told me he never made any such threat. It is all trash talk, as far as Barrasso is concerned. His face turned crimson when I mentioned the rumors to him during an hour-and-a-half interview, and he angrily dismissed them as nonsense. He cooled off quickly and continued talking. He could not have been more cordial or cooperative.

Even though he went directly from high school to the NHL, Barrasso seems bright, and is well spoken. In fact, he is one of the deeper thinkers on the team — that, too, is annoying to some — and has some interesting outlooks on life. He expresses himself well, though he confounds some with his candor and observations. He suffers most sportswriters when approached after a game, but he often provides good copy. He got burned early in his career by the media, and is reluctant to forgive or move on in that respect. He gets enraged by small slights.

Barrasso reminds me of another pro athlete I have encountered in my career. He seems a lot like Rick Barry, the Hall of Fame basketball player. He's handsome, well-paid, sure of himself, self-deprecating, seeking proper acknowledgment, openly disturbed by the shortcomings or mistakes of teammates, feels superior to the press and most people, for that matter, and is not much of a politician or popularity contest vote-getter in the clubhouse.

"I don't give a damn what people think of me, or what they say about me," said Barrasso late in our interview. "I care for my wife and family, that's all. Most of it is a bunch of nonsense, anyhow. I don't know where people come up with some of the stuff they say about me, or why they do it."

I don't believe Barrasso when he says he doesn't care what people say about him. Everybody cares. We want people to be fair with us. We want to be liked. It's human nature. Barrasso has the ability, the physical appearance, and the brains to be an attractive athlete, an admired athlete. Just like Barry Bonds.

The bottom line is that Barrasso is probably the Penguins' second most important player, second only to Lemieux. They were the key factors in the team winning successive Stanley Cups in 1991 and 1992.

There may be more about Barrasso than meets the eye. There's got to be another side of him that is more redeeming. He has been to hell and back, and has something to offer, if he'd just shake that huge chip off his shoulder.

*"I thought it was the greatest
place in the world."*
—Barrasso on Boston Garden
when he was a boy

This was late July, 1994. Mario Lemieux was away in Scotland, playing golf with some of his buddies. Craig Patrick was in his office at the Civic Arena, making plans for the Penguins' summer training camp. Barrasso came to the Civic Arena earlier than usual, so we could talk, and then he did some conditioning work, lifting weights, stretching, staying in shape for the challenges that awaited him sooner than he would have liked.

Barrasso wore a long-sleeved black jersey snug at the neck, stonewashed blue jeans and black boots. His hair was cut close, and he had worked styling gel through it, so it stood spiked and shiny. He looked lean and mean without all that goalie paraphernalia. He sat on a couch and talked freely.

His face brightened as I urged him to go back to his boyhood in suburban Boston, to talk about his beginnings as a skater and then a hockey player. They were the best of times, and the worst of times, as Charles Dickens would put it.

We are talking about the early '70s, when the Bruins won the Stanley Cup twice in a three-year period. "Hockey was booming in the Boston area," said Barrasso. "Back in the early '70s, when I was 5 or 6 years old, hockey took off in Boston like it did here in Pittsburgh when we were successful. Bobby Orr, Phil Esposito, all the great players of that era, were there."

Barrasso was three years old when he first put on skates, and he wasn't too happy about it. It was at a rink in Boston. "I cried and cried," recalled Barrasso. He had a sister, Lynne, who was seven years older who wanted to go skating. "I hated it and I was cold and just wanted to go home," said Barrasso.

"About a year after that I really got interested in doing it again. That's when I got into hockey. I was four years old. Most of the kids in our neighborhood were closer in age to my sister than they were to me.

"They played street hockey at the end of the cul-de-sac where we lived. The only way for me to play hockey with those older kids was to play goalie. No one wanted to play goalie. I didn't realize, at first, that the ball hurt when it hit you in the head, or in your face, or chest. That it left you with sore spots and bruises. I was rather naive.

"But I was pretty good at stopping shots, even when I was four. When I played against the older kids — they were eight to eleven — they'd get so aggravated at me. When I made a save on them they really got mad about it. I liked the idea that those kids — who were always excluding me from their group and aggravating me — were so frustrated by what I was doing to them. I thought it was terrific, since they had always been giving me a bad time. Here were these kids who were always beating down the little guy and I was annoying them for a change.

"My parents went along with the idea of me playing hockey, but they weren't too thrilled with the idea of me playing goalie. I wanted to play goal from the start, but my parents insisted that I play defense and learn how to skate and get a better understanding of the game.

"I did that for the first year. I'd play defense on Saturday morning and then we'd drive from one arena to another on Saturday afternoon and I'd put on the goalie equipment. I went to a goalie school all through the winter and the following winter I played goal all the time. That's how I got started. It's a strange story but it's true."

He also took figure skating lessons as a youngster. It reminded me of how Lynn Swann had been forced by his mother to take dancing lessons in his youth. "If you think I'm fast now," Swann once said when he was a top receiver for the Super Bowl champion Steelers, "you should have seen me running home from dancing school when I was a kid."

Just as Swann didn't want the other kids to know he went to dancing school, Barrasso was a little embarrassed about taking figure skating lessons. Both said they benefited from the forced lessons.

"I took figure skating lessons every day during the summer," said Barrasso. "It was like going to a sports camp. I was on the ice for two hours, at a rink in the suburbs just outside of Boston. They taught you how to stroke your strides, and they made me so much better of a skater. My mom and dad thought it would be good for me. I thought it would be good, too, but it's hard when you're nine years old to be taking figure skating lessons.

"It wasn't perceived as a macho thing to do. I took a lot of heat from my friends about that. All the other boys were out playing baseball and basketball, and even street hockey. So they made fun of me about that."

Barrasso went to hockey games with his dad regularly. "When I was growing up, I watched college games. When I was first in high school, we'd go to see Harvard, Boston U., Boston College and Providence College. As I got a little older, I went with some of my teammates."

I mentioned to Barrasso that his parents seemed to play a big role in his early development as a hockey player.

"At first, they knew nothing about hockey," he said. "They were huge baseball fans, especially my mother. She knew who all the good players were, especially the pitchers. She knew pitching stats. I can see her with her transistor, with that plug in her ear, sitting in a chair, listening to the baseball games. My dad still can't ice skate, and my mother never tried. They were very supportive of my efforts to play hockey, though. I don't think my dad ever missed a game of mine until I was playing in the NHL."

I've been told that Barrasso's father became obsessed with the idea of his son being an NHL goalie once Tom demonstrated the dedication and talent needed to become a big-time hockey player. He built a rink in the backyard of their home so his son could practice more.

They attended hockey games together nearly every night of the week at one point. It smacks of *Fear Strikes Out,* the book and movie about Jim Piersall, a high-strung Boston Red Sox ballplayer (played by

Tony Perkins in the movie) who was pushed by his father (played by Karl Malden) to become a big league ballplayer. Piersall had a nervous breakdown during his major league career. He was pushed too far.

Barrasso would never buy that analogy, understandably enough.

"I am a product of Boston at that time," he said. "Everybody wanted to be No. 4 — Bobby Orr — or Phil Esposito, or someone like that." Except Tom Barrasso, of course. He wanted to be like Gerry Cheevers.

"The only three people I watched at all were Jacques Plante, who was in the twilight of his career, and Cheevers, who was playing goal along with Eddie Johnston for the Bruins. Plante was a pioneer guy in many respects. He was the first to wear a mask, and he was known for going out of the nets, instead of just stopping the puck. Cheevers liked to roam out of the net and handle the puck. He took a more active role in the whole game than goaltenders had traditionally done. That appealed to me. I also liked Eddie Giacomin of the Rangers, who was an active goalie.

"We had seats behind the home team's goal (for two of three periods). I can always remember Orr coming in behind the goal, getting the puck and setting up the play. Or he'd just take it up the ice himself, all the way. They couldn't catch him.

"When I was about eight or nine, we had season tickets for three hockey teams in Boston: the Boston Braves of the American Hockey League, the New England Whalers of the World Hockey Association, and the Boston Bruins of the National Hockey League. They all played in Boston Garden. I saw a lot of hockey games as a kid.

"Our seats were in the first balcony, second row, the first two seats on the aisle. I don't know if you've ever been in Boston Garden, but that's really a terrific seat. You can see everything."

I told him I had covered games involving the Islanders and Rangers, as well as the Knicks and Nets, at Boston Garden. I always thought it had great atmosphere. It was a hot house, crowded and steamy and smoky. The rink was the smallest in the NHL, the parquet floor the most distinctive in the NBA. The rafters were full of pennants, some belonging to the Bruins, but most of them celebrated championships by the Celtics.

Barrasso was a student of the game, at an early age. "When the puck was behind the Boston goal, someone would swoop in and cut across behind the net, someone like Phil Esposito," said Barrasso. "Orr would be back there, readying for a control break. If Orr had his stick down on the ice behind the puck that was a decoy, and the guy swooping in would take the puck. If Orr's stick was up, that was a decoy, too, and that indicated that he'd take it out himself. His teammates knew by where his stick was just what he wanted them to do. I have vivid memories of that. I don't know anyplace else I'd have rather been. I thought it was the greatest place in the world. You'd go in and get a hot dog and a Coke, and then watch the game.

"When I was real young, we'd go sometimes by train right to North Station, then go upstairs to the Garden. We lived in Burlington, about 20 miles from Boston. We lived there till I was 12 or 13. Then we moved farther out, to Stow. And we'd drive in. But I liked being in Boston the best. There was always excitement there.

"With the players the Bruins had, you never knew who'd make a great play. When one of the stars would get the puck the noise level went up like it does here when Mario gets on the ice. It would happen when Orr got the puck.

"The fans — same as they are now — really booed the crap out of the opposition. They were really hard on the opposition. When I went to hockey games as a kid, I was almost transfixed. I shut out everything, and focused in on nothing but the game."

It is Barrasso's ability to do just that which had made him such an effective goalie, one of the best in the game.

"If I don't want to hear anybody," he said, "I have a good ability to ignore them."

"I knew I could play in the National Hockey League."
—Tom Barrasso

Barrasso was such an outstanding hockey player in high school that he set his sights on playing in the NHL as early as his sophomore season. He graduated from Acton-Boxboro High School in May of 1983 and played in his first NHL game in the NHL on October 5, 1983 for the Buffalo Sabres.

He was the fifth choice in the first round of the NHL in the 1983 entry draft, the highest a goalie has ever been drafted. He met with instant success. He won the Calder Trophy as the NHL's rookie of the year and the Vezina Trophy as the NHL's best goaltender. He was first-team all-NHL as a rookie.

"I don't remember much about the first game," he said, when I asked him about his pro debut. "We were playing the Hartford Whalers at the Aud in Buffalo. My dad and my brother, Jim, were both there. I remember the second or third save was a decent one. After stopping that, I remember something clicking in my head. 'You're ready; you can play.' I knew I could play in the NHL."

His brother, Jim, three years younger, gave up hockey while playing at the University of Connecticut.

Tom continued as one of the NHL's top goaltenders for the next few seasons, but the Sabres soured on him early in the 1988-89 season, and sent him packing to Pittsburgh in a trade. Scotty Bowman was his boss in Buffalo and he was obtained in Pittsburgh by former NHL goaltender Tony Esposito, then the Penguins' general manager. Esposito gave up Doug Bodger in the deal.

"We had players there who were looking to blame somebody else for the team's problems. The first person you have to look at is yourself.

Tom Barrasso is at his best when protecting goal and visiting youngsters with life-threatening illnesses in Make-A-Wish Foundation of Western Pennsylvania program.

Few can do that. That's why it's always the other guy's fault. My personality is what made me successful at a young age. If I wasn't like that, I don't think I'd have made it," said Barrasso.

"I'm not second-guessing myself. I've done everything I had hoped to do, and I'm only 29. The only award I haven't won that I could would be the Conn Smythe Trophy (as MVP in the Stanley Cup playoffs). That would have been a nice by-product of our team's success."

It was a positive move for Barrasso and the Penguins, one of the best deals in Penguins' history.

Barrasso has been the greatest goaltender the team ever had. In his first full season (1989-90) with the Penguins, Barrasso helped the team reach the playoffs for the first time in seven years. His outstanding play helped the Penguins win back-to-back Stanley Cup titles, including a shutout in Game 6 for the Pens to win their first-ever NHL championship.

Many of Barrasso's biggest achievements were accomplished while he was coping with the life-threatening illness of his daughter, Ashley. She was six years old in the summer of 1994, and her cancer had been in remission since she had undergone a bone marrow transplant when she was two years old.

In February, 1990, in the middle of the NHL season, Barrasso asked for and was granted a leave of absence to join his wife, Megan, and their daughter in Los Angeles, where Ashley was to have her bone marrow transplant.

Ashley miraculously survived the illness that took the lives of most of her hospital friends. Her struggles and comeback have been an inspiration to her father, both personally and professionally. He was inspired to do his part to find a cure for cancer. That's when he established a foundation in his daughter's name.

Barrasso has also helped a number of worthwhile causes including St. James Church in Sewickley, the Cystic Fibrosis Foundation, Make-A-Wish Foundation of Western Pennsylvania; Wheeling (West Va.) Boys Club, Diabetes Society, Pittsburgh Public Theater, and the New York Athletes Against Drunk Driving. Barrasso was honored in 1994 by being named one of the Ten Outstanding Young Americans by the U.S. Junior Chamber of Commerce.

Barrasso said he will never forget how he felt right after the Penguins had won their first Stanley Cup in 1991.

"The moment that sticks out in my mind is when I first saw my wife after we had won. She had flown into Minnesota for the game. We had gone through a period where, the year before, I had played 23 games and left the team for over a month to go to Los Angeles to be with my daughter. I genuinely didn't know if I would come back after that. I didn't know what that was going to do to my career. We'd gone from such a low to such a high that it was a pretty emotional time for us."

The Barrassos have three daughters, Ashley, 6; Kelsey, 4, and Mallory, 2. "I enjoy going to the movies with the kids, and playing with them," said Barrasso. "I've played less golf as they've gotten older, and are easier to play with."

"What I do on the ice gives me everything else in my life."

Concentration is critical to a goalie. It is important to think only about the game, the puck, before you. You cannot allow your mind to wander, to worry about what you have to do tomorrow, or what you forgot to do yesterday.

"That's easy," said Barrasso with a big smile. "The thing I always keep focused in my mind is that what I do on the ice gives me everything else in my life. For myself and for my family.

"I don't think I appreciated this early on. It's a great opportunity to play at the level at which I'm playing. I didn't always take advantage of that. Compared to that, the other things don't really matter. I do what I enjoy doing, and I have to be properly prepared and focused to achieve something. If you're digging a ditch and you don't want to be out there, it'll be tougher to dig that ditch.

"Most other athletes don't have to concentrate as long as goaltenders do. Most of the other hockey players are on the ice about a third of the time, the best half the time, and the superstars a little more than that. But they all get a break. As a goaltender, you don't get a break.

"If there's five minutes left in the game and we're winning three-nothing, the biggest worry a forward has is 'Can I get another goal?' My focus is different. I don't want to give up that first goal. Or two. I don't want to let them get a spark, to get back in the game. It can happen.

"Being a goaltender is like no other position in sports."

I asked Barrasso if he had watched the World Cup action on TV earlier in the month. "Not at all," he replied with a touch of Barrasso tartness. "To me, that's like watching paint dry."

It's the uniqueness of the demands that appeals to Barrasso. "There's no challenge quite like it," he said. "You are solely responsible for the direct success or failure of your team. You can't make any mistakes. If a forward makes a mistake, the defenseman can make up for it. If a defenseman makes a mistake, I can cover up for it. If I make a mistake, a red light goes on. If I make a mistake, most of the time the officials are taking the puck back to center ice to drop it.

"As the game goes on, the pressure gets magnified. If you can do it, there's no feeling like it. The mental aspect is more important than the physical aspect. You can win and feel you played poorly. You can lose and feel you played well. It's a very controlling position. You have the most impact on the game. You can't get that thrill from any other position.

"Nothing should matter except playing the game. Practice is part of the preparation for playing the game. You have to make sure you prepare thoroughly enough. When you ride the bike, lift weights, skip rope, it's all to ready yourself to play in the game. When the time comes, you have to be prepared.

"You shouldn't have to worry about your body. Your body should be doing things almost automatically. I have to stretch 20 to 30 minutes every day in order to do the sort of splits I do to stop shots in a game.

"On game day, I can't worry about anything but the game. We have three kids and my wife has to take care of them. My job is to get focused to play. I don't have time for anything else; I don't answer the telephone. It's time to get ready; I can't sit down in my office and write checks.

"When you get up at 8, the only thing you should be concerned about all day is being ready to play that night. You might have fleeting thoughts about other things, but that's all they can be. Fleeting thoughts.

"When we're at home, I go to bed about 10, and on the road I make sure I get to sleep by 11 or 11:30. I'm at the Arena the day of the game and on the ice by 9:30. We'll skate till 10:30 or 11, have a team meeting, shower and eat lunch. I get home by 1. I try to read for an hour. I go to bed for about two hours, from 2 to 3:50. The first hour is easy; I have trouble sometimes sleeping that second hour. Then I'm up and back down to the Arena at 4:35. I don't get home until about 11:30."

I asked Barrasso if it is any advantage having an ex-goalie like Johnston as his coach.

"He should appreciate the problems more," he said. "But any coach should know when a goalie is playing well or playing poorly. The easiest thing for you to do is point the finger at the goaltender. That's what people's attention is focused on. It's easy to get caught up in that mentality. E.J. knows you can be great in goal, but if you lose it's not that important. There's always satisfaction in doing your job well. You're part of the team. It's not an individual performance."

I asked Barrasso what sort of books he enjoyed reading. Mario Lemieux has always said he doesn't read books, and that has always nagged me. Barrasso said he has read everything written by Tom Clancy and is also a big fan of Robert Ludlum.

"I also have read some of the things I was supposed to read when I was in school, but never did," he added. "Like I read *Moby Dick* for the second time, and I read *Tale of Two Cities*. I try to improve myself. As a kid, I didn't read much. I remember reading a book called *Goaltending* by Jacques Plante that my parents gave me. I've still got it. As a kid, all I cared about was making it to the National Hockey League."

I asked Barrasso if he would ever go to college once he finished playing in the NHL. He had talked about doing so earlier in his pro career. "I don't see how I need it now," he said. "Tom Barrasso is a multi-million dollar industry. I've dealt with people who went to college. By dealing with them, I've learned about investing, and insurance, and what I need to know to look after my own money.

"I personally am a multi-million dollar business. I'm making a million or whatever a year as a hockey player, plus some money on the side. I don't know what I would need to go to college for.

"What I'd like to do someday is some form of philanthropy. I'm interested in that. There are a lot of people in a community like Pittsburgh that need assistance. Athletes have an ability to help raise funds for those people, and I think that's an important responsibility.

"If I lend my name to a golf tournament you can charge people a $1,000 apiece to play, whereas a doctor doing the same thing might not be able to command more than $200 a player. We held a golf tournament for three years, and we raised nearly $500,000 over that span for the Ashley Barrasso Cancer Research Fund.

"People talk about what people like me owe the fans, and I don't buy what they're saying. What I owe the fans is my best performance on the ice. They should feel like they're getting their money's worth as an entertainment dollar. It shouldn't be about shaking hands after the game. What I'm talking about, participation in serious fund-raising events, is more important than the perceived obligations of athletes."

Barrasso has been challenged off the ice as well as on it. He gained much recognition for the way he and his family dealt with his daughter Ashley's life-threatening illness.

"They need money to do cancer research," Barrasso said. "They may never be able to find a cure for cancer. They may work for 60 to 70 years and they may never come up with any answers. But it needs to be done. Look at what they've done in research for cystic fibrosis. They're on the brink of discovering a cure. That's one of the Penguins' big interests. They have discovered the gene that causes it.

"We dealt with a lot of people when my daughter was sick. We met nurses who dealt with a lot more negative stuff than positive things. They're not there for the money or any medals. They want to help. It's a far more noble cause than playing hockey."

"I don't think we should dwell on the disappointment of the past two seasons. I'm grateful for having won those two Stanley Cups. I look back with pride, almost awe, at those two years. But those two years have no bearing on the past two years or the future," said Barrasso.

"I have everything I have ever wanted in my life. I have three great kids and a great wife. I have a house that's too big. I find it amazing how people want to break that down and take that away from me. If I could go back and change it, I wouldn't want my child to have cancer. But my family has grown and become more solid.

"People should worry about their own lives. My wife and I have both been through so much. We had been so low — when our oldest daughter nearly died — and I didn't know if I'd have the desire to do it again. We went from not making the playoffs and having a daughter who was gravely ill to winning it all and having Ashley doing all right again. When you're climbing a mountain you have no idea what it's going to feel like when you reach the top.

"If you go through a war with someone you'll always have a bond. There will always be a bond with my daughter, and there will always be a bond with my wife. They are far more important than anything I do in hockey.

"Winning the first Cup was more emotional. The second time was more gratifying professionally. We've all been through too much to toss it away now. My family is the most important thing in my life."

I asked how Ashley was doing. "She still has a bunch of medical problems. She's been doing OK, but if it comes back — and it could — she'll die. There's no middle ground.

"She had a very serious condition. It's fatal for 90 percent of the cases. The treatment she received was a last-ditch effort. She's made it through that and she's four years out of a bone marrow transplant. There are no new signs of any cancer growth. But there have been side effects from the chemotherapy and radiation treatments she received. She'll be in the second grade this coming year. She's a tough kid, very emotional, and very, very determined.

"People shouldn't feel sorry for Ashley. My daughter has been dealing with disease before she could form a sentence. She looked forward to days when she was good, and dealt with days that were difficult. It fazes us more. To her, it's her way of life."

I asked Tom if he felt at one point that he was surrounded by cancer. His coach, Bob Johnson, died from brain cancer. His teammate, Mario Lemieux, was found to have Hodgkin's disease, a cancer of the lymph nodes.

"Bob's situation was tough. You could see his motor skills deteriorate. He was such an active, energetic, enthusiastic guy and it was all being taken away from him. You'd go to the hospital, and it was pitiful to see him in that situation.

"With Mario — after the initial shock — I said 'Mario will breeze through this. He'll be fine.' People wondered what I was talking about. Once you heard the doctor's report, you knew he'd be fine. What he had was perfect as far as getting him proper treatment. They found it early enough, it hadn't spread, and they knew how to treat it. It was frightening to Mario, at first, but once he started dealing with the doctors he knew what had to be done. The treatments were tough on him, for sure, but he knew he would be better off in the long run. It was not going to dominate his life. My reaction 30 minutes after I heard it was that he'd be great. People thought it was a peculiar way to look at it. But if there was something I knew outside of hockey it was cancer."

"Hockey is an hour or so of hell."
—Glenn Hall
Hall of Fame goalie

Bruce Bennett Studios

Tom Barrasso and Mario Lemieux led Penguins to capturing second straight Stanley Cup, which Barrasso proudly hoists at special celebration at Three Rivers Stadium in the summer of 1992.

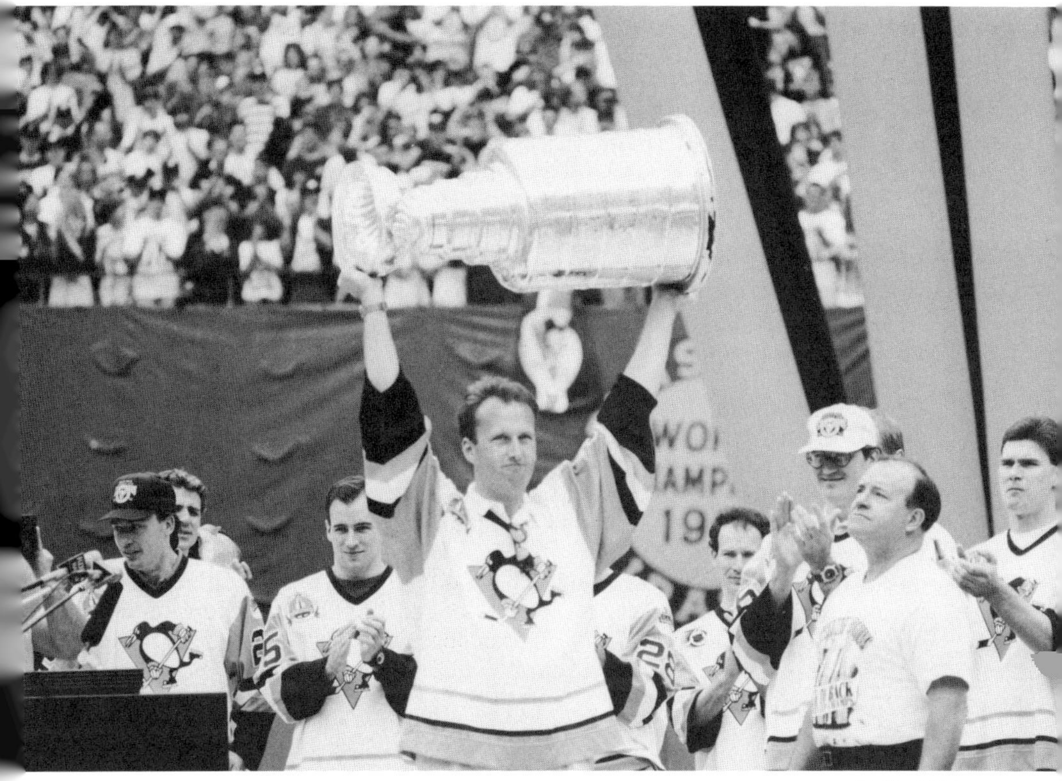

Jim Cunningham

Craig Patrick
From a Hall of Fame family

*"I'd like to go back and just play games,
when they were just fun,
and there was no pressure."*

Craig Patrick has a pedigree unparalleled in professional hockey. His heritage is a Hall of Fame one. His family helped to fashion and popularize hockey in this country, from coast to coast. No one was a rink rat earlier than Patrick, who oversees the operation of the Pittsburgh Penguins as executive vice president and general manager.

His grandfather, Lester, was such a National Hockey League pioneer that the Patrick Division, in which the Penguins once played, was named after him. His father, Lynn, and his uncle, Muzz, were both storied NHL players and administrators. Lester and Lynn are both enshrined in the Hockey Hall of Fame in Toronto. Muzz was also a one-time Canadian heavyweight amateur boxing champion.

"You could say I grew up around the game," offers Patrick with a patrician smile.

It pleases him to no end that he has been credited in a big way for putting the finishing pieces together for a team that won consecutive Stanley Cup championships for Pittsburgh in 1991 and 1992, and it frustrates him deeply that the Penguins bowed out early in the playoffs in the two seasons that followed. Talk of a dynasty dwindled quickly, like an ice carving at a splendid banquet.

Not with Patrick, however. "To win the Stanley Cup, yes, that's our goal for next season," he said. "With the team we have, we should win the Stanley Cup. To me, the challenge of the NHL — to be successful on a continuing basis is something I admire tremendously."

Patrick is proud of his heritage. He realizes now that he had a unique upbringing, that he had entree early on to a magic world which he still enjoys immensely. "Winning was always important in our family," he said. "You didn't have to be good, but being good was important."

Patrick appeared more relaxed than usual, sitting in a plush gray chair in a corner of his spacious office in the Penguins' administrative complex, just to the left as you enter Gate 2 on the floor level of the Civic Arena from the Centre Avenue side of the building. He smiled several times, and was relatively animated. Not much, but moreso than usual. I had flipped through hundreds of photos of Patrick at various press conferences through the years, and his expression seldom changed. It was usually deadpan. Impassive and phlegmatic fit Patrick like tight hockey skates.

He had a healthy tan. He wore a Kelly green knit golf shirt, brown slacks, brown loafers sans socks. He looked like a dentist on his day off. It brought Bob Prince, the Pirates' legendary broadcaster, to mind.

He used to wear loafers without socks. "I didn't have to attend any business meetings today," explained Patrick, "so I dressed casually."

Patrick was born in Detroit, grew up in New Haven, Boston and Montreal. He now lives in Fox Chapel, one of Pittsburgh's poshest suburbs to the north of the city. Patrick looks the part. He looked like he had walked out of a window at Eddie Bauer.

His office had a definite hockey look about it, beginning with a huge tapestry of the Penguins logo over a long gray couch where visitors are invited to sit. There's a large photo showing a boat spraying water on a turn just off Point State Park, a framed montage memorializing the late Bob Johnson, the beloved coach he hired who inspired the Penguins to win their first Stanley Cup, pictures celebrating both championships, hockey memorabilia, some plaques, a few books, some autographed hockey sticks, many family photos both on his desk and the handsome wall unit behind it. The white-walled room was like a mini-Hall of Fame.

There are framed photos in a reception area outside Patrick's office: reprints of the front pages of the *Post-Gazette* when the Penguins won the Stanley Cup, pictures of championship banners being hoisted at the Civic Arena, a large color photo showing, from left to right, three of Pittsburgh's championship leaders: Bob Johnson, Chuck Noll and Chuck Tanner. There are large signatures done with Magic Markers under the likenesses of Noll and Tanner. Johnson must have been dead by the time it was put up. There are signs of success everywhere. Reminders of what has been.

We are interrupted soon after we start to talk by a telephone call from Patrick's daughter Erin, 20, who had just finished her second year at the University of California at Santa Barbara, where she is an outstanding swimmer. She is calling from California. Patrick congratulates his daughter on a recent honor her mother told him about. Patrick tells me to stay, but I leave the office so he can talk freely with his daughter. I eavesdrop out of habit. "I don't get to talk to her very often," he apologizes. "I've been anxious to hear from her." He calls her "Sweetheart."

He and his wife Sue also have two sons, Cory, 17, who's called C.J., who was looking forward to his senior year at Fox Chapel High School, and Ryan, 14, who would be a freshman. Both would be playing on the same forward line in a first-rate hockey program at Fox Chapel. Ryan was also a lacrosse player.

"They hope to play college hockey someday," said Patrick. "But I hope they don't want to be hockey players. If that makes them happy, though, that's fine with me. I'm like most fathers; I just want my kids to be happy. C.J.'s goal right now is to play on a championship high school hockey team."

> *"Nothing was ever serious.*
> *It was just playing."*
> —Craig Patrick

Patrick's plea that he hoped his children would choose a life other than hockey had a familiar ring to it. Earlier, he had said that his father always advised him not to take hockey too seriously. "When I was growing up, everything was hockey," he recalled. "My parents, though, tried to push me away from hockey. My dad must have told me a million times he wanted me to be a doctor or a dentist."

I asked Patrick if his mother attempted to squelch the constant hockey talk in their home. "She might have," he said. "If she did, nobody listened to her."

His dad married twice and had a son from his first marriage, then a daughter and three more sons to Craig's mother. His half-brother, Les, was six years older. Craig came next, then Karen, two years younger, Glenn, four years younger, and Dean, 11 years younger.

"We had a close-knit family," said Patrick. "I had a great relationship with my father. And we saw our relatives on every holiday, it seemed, and during the summer, or off-season."

That's when there was an off-season in professional sports. "There's no off-season anymore," said Patrick, shaking his head. His thinning brown hair had already been bleached at the ends by a stretch of sunny and super sultry days in Pittsburgh.

"Oh, I've gotten in a little golf. But the next season began the day after our final loss. You have to stay at this."

Eddie Johnston, the coach of the Penguins, stopped in to say hello — he mentioned that he had been out at the U.S. Open at Oakmont the week before a few times — and he had a few private words with Patrick. Eddie had gotten a telephone call from his wife, Diane, and they were going out to lunch together.

Tracey Botsford, an administrative assistant, kept bringing messages to her boss. "He wants you to call him when you can," she'd say.

Harry Sanders, the Penguins' media relations director, and Steve Bovino, his assistant, moved in and out of the offices. There was no break for them, either. "We're busy with the summer teams," said Sanders.

The Pittsburgh Phantoms, in fact, had just finished practice. They were a new entry in Roller Hockey International, a deck-hockey version of the sport. Rick Kehoe, a one-time star forward for the Penguins and more recently an assistant coach, was directing that team. Bryan Trottier, a great player with the New York Islanders and a big contributor to the Penguins' Stanley Cup winners, was playing for the Phantoms, for the helluva of it, perhaps to make up for an injury-plagued comeback season as a player-coach with the Penguins, perhaps to supplement his income, maybe because he wanted to keep his employers happy. Trottier came away from practice and went to his desk in an area where Johnston and Kehoe are also quartered. They were doing their best to look busy.

Jim Cunningham

Dennis Cavanaugh

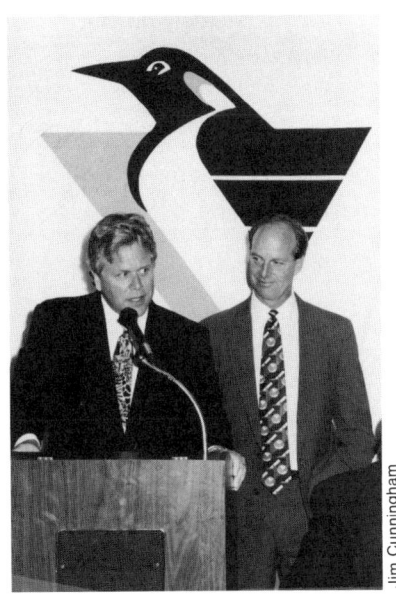

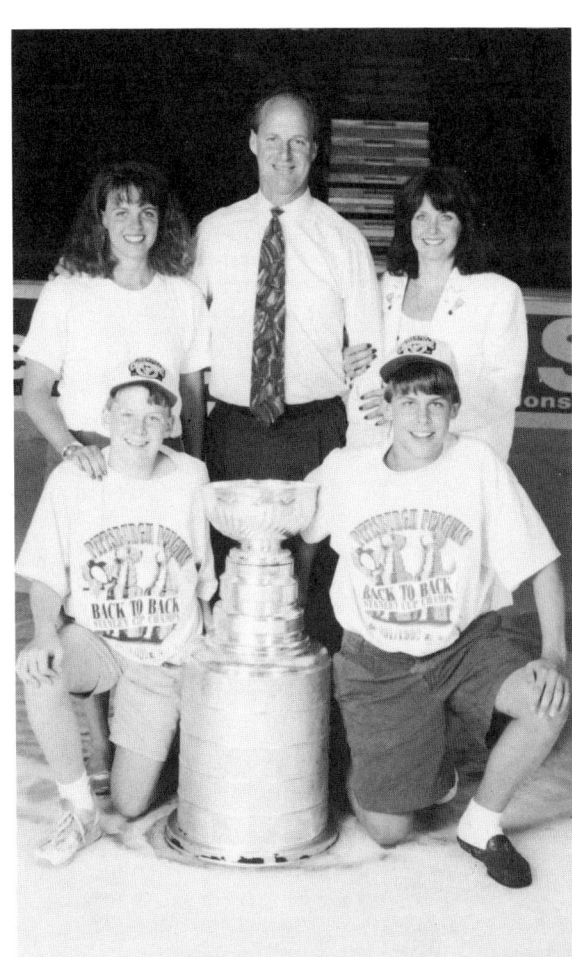

Craig Patrick is introduced by Penguins' owner Howard Baldwin at press conference to announce extension of Patrick's contract as vice president/general manager. Patrick poses with second Stanley Cup in 1992 with daughter Erin and wife Sue and their sons, Ryan and Cory.

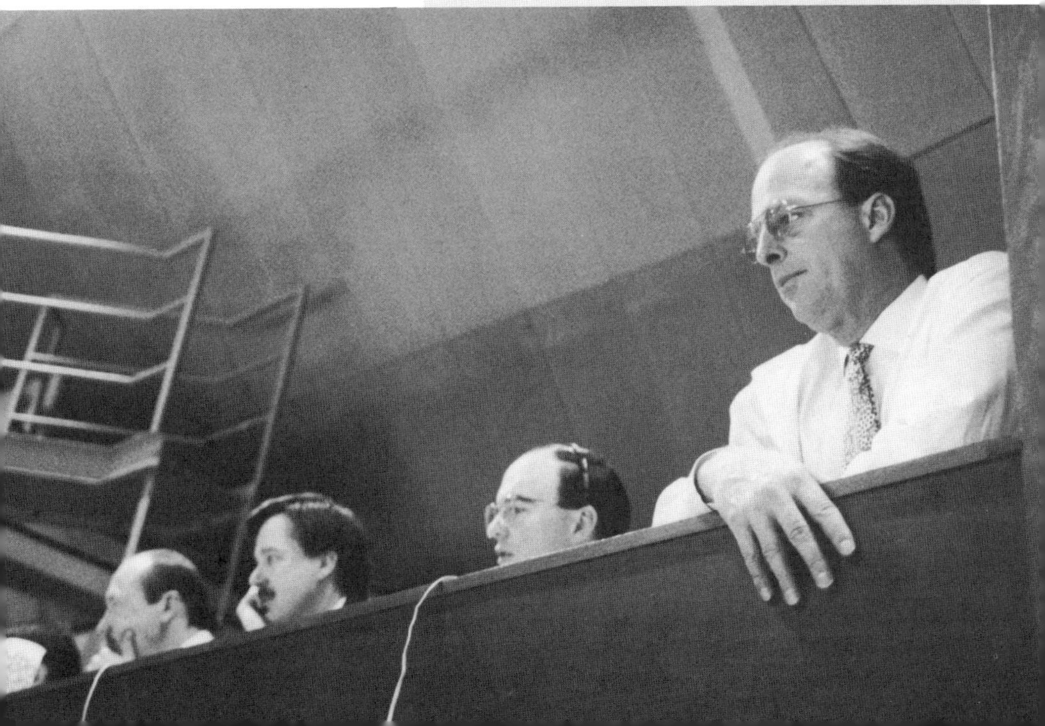

Penguins' president Howard Baldwin and his financial backers had also invested in a team in the Major Indoor Soccer League, a team called the Pittsburgh Stingers, coached by popular ex-Spirit Paul Child. The idea was to have constant sports activity at the Civic Arena.

When I entered the Arena that morning to visit Patrick, I stopped and watched the Phantoms at practice for awhile. From the stands, it looks like the players are on ice skates rather than roller blades. They were playing on a glacier-blue surface in the same area as the ice rink where the Penguins play. The pucks are red plastic. In my lifetime, I had covered indoor soccer and box lacrosse in such settings, but this was new stuff.

"It never stops," said Patrick.

In Patrick's mind, you can't have enough games. He looks back fondly upon his childhood when he enjoyed the best of playgrounds, when he was a kid for all seasons, playing baseball and hockey, his two favorite sports, and basketball and soccer. "We didn't just talk about hockey as kids," said Patrick. "We played everything, including street games. Boston is a great town for sports. I followed baseball and hockey closely in the papers.

"The Red Sox had Ted Williams early on, and Ted Lepcio, Frank Malzone, Jimmy Piersall, Jackie Jensen. When my dad worked in Boston with the Bruins, he was friendly with his counterparts with the other sports teams. We shared the Garden with the Celtics. That's when they had Bob Cousy and Bill Sharman, so I got to go in their clubhouse a lot. We have a picture at home that shows my youngest brother, Dean, that's priceless. It's a picture of the Celtics practicing. They had put down the parquet floor over the ice, but they left an area uncovered in the one end zone, just so my brother could skate. So the picture shows Dean skating while the Celtics were practicing.

"We went to see the other teams play, too. I was in the Red Sox clubhouse, and I got a bat signed by Ted Lepcio, I remember that. But the Detroit Tigers were my favorite team. That's where I was born. I was only four months old when we moved from there, but I always rooted for Detroit teams.

"I was in Detroit last week, and I had never been to Tigers Stadium. So I took my boys to the ballgame. It was great. When I was a kid, I used to play a baseball game myself off the back wall of our garage. My parents' bedroom was above that garage.

"I bounced a rubber ball or a tennis ball off that wall. I would play nine-inning games all by myself. I'd bounce the ball and it would come back at me. I had on my baseball glove, and I'd catch the ball as it came off the wall. If it got away from me and hit certain places it would be a single or a double or a triple, depending on where it hit. If it bounced over the wall behind me it was a home run.

"I tried to catch the ball every time; I never made an error just to create something. I always made the Tigers win, but I wouldn't commit an error to do it. I could bounce the ball as hard as I wanted to when I wanted to. The Tigers always managed to come up with a home run in the bottom of the ninth inning to win the game. They always won."

When I asked him if he wishes he could do the same thing today with the Penguins, he smiled and said, "Of course. The Penguins would always win."

"I was always on the ice."
—Craig Patrick

Patrick seemed pleased to relate these stories. In previous exposures to Patrick, usually in the press box at games, or with other media people around at press conferences, he had always struck me as looking uncomfortable, almost wooden, or stiff. He was accused of being paranoid with the press. They called him "Vague Craig" when he worked with the Rangers in New York. On this visit, however, he seemed relaxed. Patrick was downright expansive in his story-telling. In fairness, I'm sure the topic — his family and his early days in hockey — appealed to Patrick more than the usual fare. He wasn't being grilled about the Penguins' problems or shortcomings, their failure to play up to the great expectations that were held for them. No one was asking him about Mario Lemieux's back. He was so soft-spoken, however, that I had a hard time hearing him from time to time. I found myself leaning forward on the couch to catch his conversation. There are times Patrick appears to be whispering when he's talking to people, like when he stops somebody for a word in the hallway outside his office.

He smiled as he speared the stories out of somewhere, and passed them along. He had been a decent playmaker in his hockey-playing days, and still enjoys competing in celebrity contests. He was doing all right relating childhood memories, too.

"It's hard for me to realize now if I appreciated what I was able to do as a kid," he said. "Now I know how fortunate I was. There were always nice people looking after me.

"I used to like Don McKenney as a player (McKenney would later play for the Pittsburgh Hornets when they won the AHL championship in 1967). And Cliff Pennington was a favorite, too, though he wasn't with Boston long. He taught me how to shoot a puck. I was skating at Boston Garden one day, and he took me aside. I was 10 or 11 at the time. This is the way you shoot,' he said.

"Whenever I wasn't in school, on weekends or holidays, I was always at Boston Garden. I was always on the ice. I looked forward to the Christmas holidays. I'd go in every day and skate all day long. I'd spend the whole day there. I bugged my father for a dollar to go out and get a hot dog or a hamburger across the street from the Garden. That was the only time I was away from the ice. I was always on the ice.

"Usually, I was there by myself. My brothers weren't into it as much as I was. It was usually me and an empty Garden. I'd skate the length of the ice and shoot at the net. I picked spots where I wanted to put the puck, like a certain corner of the net. It was a game I played.

"I'd try to hit the crossbar and see if I could get it to ricochet off the bar into the upper balcony. You had to have accuracy and power to do that. To be able to hit the top of the crossbar and to get the puck into the second balcony was quite a feat. You had to have power behind your shot. I was 11 or 12 at the time, I think. It was great. I couldn't have been happier."

He said his high school had an outdoor skating rink. "I'd go there, too, or I'd go play basketball," he recalled. "Nothing was ever serious. It was just playing."

We compared notes about playing games as kids, and our roles in that activity. I had always organized the games on the street where I grew up in Pittsburgh. At age 13, I had a track and field team with kids a few years younger in the neighborhood as team members. I had a three-man basketball league that played its games in front of my house, and had rigged up spotlights in my parents' bedroom window that shone out on the street. I cleared a ballfield from a vacant lot each spring so we could play baseball and softball. I kept score and statistics, typed them up, and pasted them on my front door. I made up mock newspapers about our activity. Later on, I would call upon business people on the main street, seeking donations for a booster card, collecting money for our uniforms and equipment.

"It's nice when you can make a living out of doing what you did for fun as a kid," opined Patrick.

"I loved the games I played as a kid," he continued. "There was no sense of responsibility. We were just playing games all day. I've talked to women, in my own little survey, and it seems like they don't want to go back to those days. But men do. I'd like to go back to that time. All those silly games.

"There was a feeling of freedom. There was absolutely no responsibility, just being able to play games. And you weren't in school, you were just playing games: ball hockey, baseball. We were always into games.

"I didn't have any interest in school. I didn't want to go to college. But it was the best thing I ever did. I thought it would be so difficult. The first quarter I had straight A's. But I tailed off after that. I didn't give it my best shot. I wasn't a poor student, I simply was not interested in school. I did as much as I had to."

"Do you believe in miracles?"
—Al Michaels

Patrick's personal history, or odyssey to the NHL, is an interesting one. He grew up in Boston, but moved to Montreal as a teenager in the mid-'60s to play junior hockey. His coach with the Montreal Junior Canadiens, coincidentally enough, was Scotty Bowman.

From there, Patrick went off to the University of Denver where he played for the Pioneers and helped them win NCAA hockey titles in 1968 and 1969. After that, he played eight seasons of professional hockey, as a forward with California, St. Louis, Kansas City and Washington of the National Hockey League and Minnesota of the World Hockey Association.

After he retired as an active player, he wanted to be a coach and front-office executive, like his dad and his uncle. One of the crowning achievements of his career in that respect was when he served as an assistant coach and assistant general manager to Herb Brooks for the U.S. Olympic team that won the 1980 Olympic gold medal in a storybook finish. ("Do you believe in miracles? Yes!" cried out Al Michaels on TV after the championship game.)

Following in his family's footsteps, he worked five years as general manager of the Rangers from 1981-86. He hired Brooks to coach the Rangers. The magic wasn't there like it had been in Lake Placid, New York. Patrick was fired and replaced by Phil Esposito. He went back to the University of Denver, this time as athletic director, and worked there for two years. He came to the Penguins on December 5, 1989.

"He's the man to lead us now," said Edward J. DeBartolo, who owned the team at that time. DeBartolo bounced Tony Esposito and Gene Ubriaco in the process.

"It is easy to forget," wrote *Post-Gazette* sports columnist Gene Collier, "that when Patrick walked into the building in December, 1989, the Penguins were worse than a joke. They were an old, bad joke."

Patrick served in a dual role the rest of that season, as coach and general manager. The Penguins, playing without injured Mario Lemieux for six weeks, missed the playoffs by a mere point.

That's when Patrick went to work to put the Penguins' operation in order, and put them in a position to win a Stanley Cup. He hired Bob Johnson as head coach and talked Scotty Bowman into coming to Pittsburgh as director of player development and recruitment.

Patrick took a gamble and used the Penguins' first draft pick to get a young Czech named Jaromir Jagr. At the time, there was no assurance the Penguins could even get Jagr out of Czechoslovakia so he could come to America and play in the NHL. But Patrick pulled it off somehow when a political coup changed things.

He started picking up the players he needed as a proper supporting cast for Lemieux. He got Joe Mullen, Bryan Trottier, Larry Murphy, Peter Taglianetti. Then Patrick pulled off a trade they still talk about with envy at NHL meetings. He sent John Cullen, Zarley Zalapski and Jeff Parker to Hartford (and their GM Eddie Johnston) in exchange for Ron Francis, Ulf Samuelsson and Grant Jennings. The Penguins put it all together and won the Patrick Division and then went on to claim the Stanley Cup, the first such success in the history of the embattled Pittsburgh franchise.

Patrick didn't sit on that Stanley Cup, or keep that championship team intact too long. When the team stuggled at mid-season the next time out, he put together a three-team deal with the Philadelphia Flyers and Los Angeles Kings, in which the Penguins parted with Mark Recchi and Paul Coffey and came up with Rick Tocchet, Kjell Samuelsson, Ken Wregget and Jeff Chychrun. The Penguins were rejuvenated and went on to win a second successive Stanley Cup.

In January of 1992, Baldwin signed Patrick to a new five-year contract. He is believed to make about $500,000 a year. "Quite simply," said Baldwin, who made several big investments in the future of the Penguins in Pittsburgh, "Craig Patrick is the finest general manager in the National Hockey League, and we wanted to make sure he stays in Pittsburgh.

"Craig's hiring of hockey legends like Bob Johnson and Scott Bowman, his astute trades and strong performance in the draft and his quiet, effective and creative leadership have given this city an outstanding professional sports franchise, and one of the best in the National Hockey League."

Patrick wasn't patient when Bowman begged for time to make a decision about whether he would return as coach of the Penguins for the 1993-94 season. So Patrick went out and got himself a new coach — an old coach on the Pittsburgh scene — returning Eddie Johnston to the post. Johnston hadn't coached in ten years, but Patrick had high regard for his ability.

The Penguins were put into the Northeast Division when the NHL realigned for the 1993-94 season and easily won the regular season race. But they just didn't have it in the playoffs, and lost out to the Washington Capitals.

No one took the loss, or the fallout heat, from that disappointment any more than Patrick. He questioned the team's desire.

Considering his heritage and personal background, I asked him if he had mixed emotions when the New York Rangers defeated the Vancouver Canucks in the seventh game of the finals to win the Stanley Cup. It was the Rangers' first Stanley Cup since 1940.

"There were some things that made me want them to win," he said, "and there were some things that made me not want them to win. Part of me wanted them to win because of my family ties with the Rangers. Another part didn't because they're our arch-rivals. But I'm glad they won. Seeing the effect it's had on hockey is great. The coverage it's brought is great for the NHL."

Another reason Patrick was pleased was because he was responsible for drafting the team's two biggest stars in the playoffs, Brian Leetch and Mike Richter. It had been eight years since Patrick had been fired by the Rangers. He hasn't forgotten what it was like to work there.

"I knew how badly they wanted to win in New York. I'd been through all that during my six years there. It all started when the Islanders had that four-year run at winning the Cup. The Islanders' fans started that chant about 1940.

"The Rangers have unbelievable fans. I've never seen such obsessed guys. They have a real passion for the game of hockey."

His grandfather, Lester, served as head coach and general manager of the Rangers and led his team to three Stanley Cup titles. His father, Lynn, was an All-Star winger with the Rangers and served as their head

Jim Cunningham

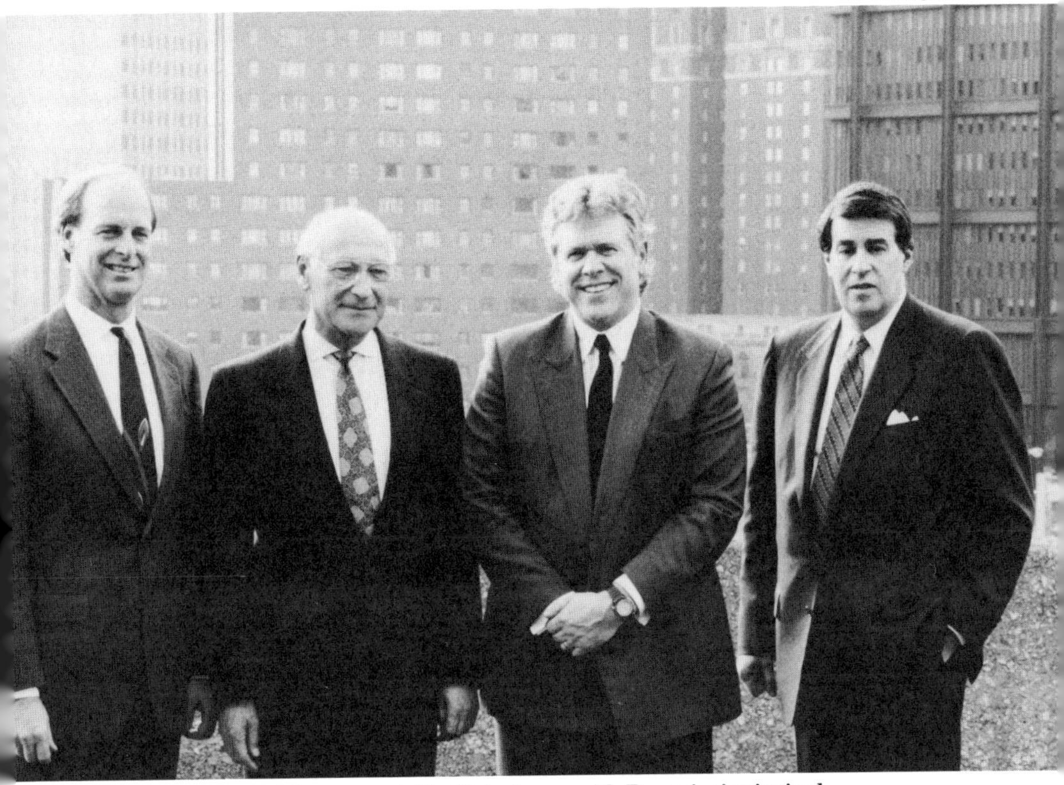

Craig Patrick poses outside Civic Arena with Penguins' principal owners Morris Belzberg, Howard Baldwin and Thomas Ruta.

Dennis Cavanaugh

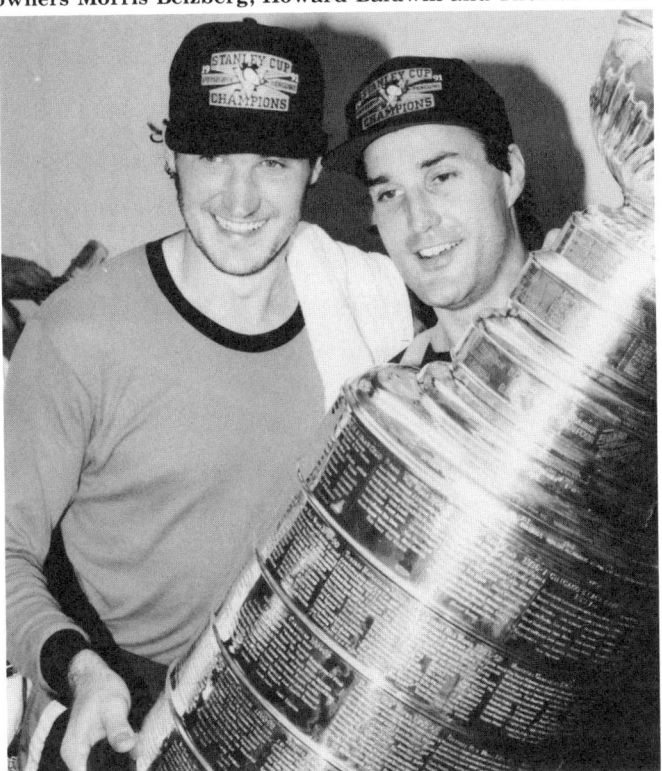

NHL All-Stars Mario Lemieux and Paul Coffey carry Penguins' first Stanley Cup won during Patrick's tenure.

coach from 1948 to 1950. He also was general manager of the Boston Bruins for many years. His uncle, Muzz, was a defenseman for the Rangers and served as their general manager/head coach from 1954 to 1964.

When the Rangers last won in 1940, the names of several members of the Patrick clan were etched on the Cup. Lester was the general manager, Lynn and Muzz were Rangers players. "I thought about them when the Rangers won," Patrick said. "I'm happy for my uncle that he is alive and was able to see it."

And, of course, Craig became the youngest general manager in the New York team's history in 1981. He began his hockey career when his dad was with the Rangers.

"The first time I skated was when I was two years old," said Craig. "I don't remember, but my father told me. It was at the old Madison Square Garden. We moved to Massachusetts when I was four. There was a swamp behind the house where I lived, and we used to go across the street and skate there in the winter months when it would freeze over.

"I used to skate at Boston Garden. I'd go there with my dad. My father had decided after the 1949-50 season that he didn't want to continue as coach of the Rangers. He decided he didn't want to bring us up in New York City. He decided he was going to Victoria, British Columbia, to coach his father's team there.

"The Rangers lost out in the Stanley Cup final to Detroit, losing in overtime in the seventh game. Right after, my father announced that he was going to Victoria. We made the trip all the way to Victoria, and when we got there my father received a telegram from the Boston team. They wanted him to come there, and he decided to accept their offer. My grandfather had originally owned the team in Victoria. My grandfather and his brother had started the Pacific Coast League in the early 1900s. They ended up selling the league to the National Hockey League. They sold the Victoria players to Detroit. He and his brother went to work in the NHL. His brother Frank went to Boston and he went to New York. In 1948, my grandfather went back to Victoria. He was one of 17 children in a family in Drummondville, Quebec. Their family moved to Montreal, and that's when they got involved with hockey. That's where it all began."

Patrick's family has a history of being successful in business, going back to James Patrick, a prosperous merchant in Ireland around 1790. One of his descendants, Tom Patrick, emigrated to America from Ireland. The family owned a general store in Drummondville.

As young men, the Patrick brothers, Lester and Frank, excelled at the primitive hockey of the turn of the century and were coveted by the best teams in their native Quebec. In 1907, however, the family moved to British Columbia where their father amassed a fortune in the lumber business, enough to enable the sons to realize a dream: a professional hockey league on the West Coast.

During its 15-year life, the Pacific Coast Hockey League effectively competed with its eastern rival, the National Hockey Association, winning a pair of Stanley Cups. The league folded in 1926.

That same year, Lester became the first coach of the Rangers and was the leader of the "Broadway Blues" for the next twenty years. Among his players were his sons, Lynn and Muzz, who both became New York stars and went on to follow their father in coaching, Lynn with the Boston Bruins and later the St. Louis Blues, Muzz with his old team, the Rangers.

After the Coast League folded, Frank Patrick served as managing director of the NHL, briefly as coach of the Boston Bruins, and finally as manager of the Montreal Canadiens. Frank was a loner and a dreamer who never really found his niche in the NHL, but he was actually the more brilliant innovator of the two brothers. Together, they restructured the rules and style of hockey into the game as it is played today.

They devised the blue line and wrote new rules and helped shape the post-season playoff system.

The Patrick family legend still lives through the exploits of Lynn's son, Craig. The Patricks have been, indeed, the royal family of professional hockey.

"This is great for me."

After my interview with Craig Patrick, I remained in the Penguins' administration complex for another hour or so, doing some research, making a couple of telephone calls. I spotted Patrick going past the desk where I was sitting. He was moving by on roller blades, and lost his balance when he stopped as I called out to him. "I'm going out for some exercise," he said. "This is great for me."

He was wearing skin-tight teal-colored Spandex pants, like a ballet performer might wear. He was wearing a home jersey of the Pittsburgh Penguins. He had on hockey gloves and carried a hockey stick.

I went up into the stands at the Civic Arena and watched Patrick at play. Workmen were busy mopping up the aisles in the building. Somebody was hammering away at something in the distance. It was quiet otherwise. Patrick had a plastic puck at the end of his stick as he skated up and down the glacier-blue surface, back and forth. Steve Latin, the team's equipment manager, was out there with him, wearing street shoes and standing in front of one of the nets, wielding a hockey stick and feeding Patrick pucks as he flew by.

His sun-bleached hair was flying behind him as he sailed from one end of the rink to the other. He was flicking the pucks into the nets at both ends of the ice. With a plastic puck, it would be impossible to strike one off the crossbar and up into the second balcony. But I wondered whether the thought entered Patrick's mind.

There was a smile on his face. He skated smoothly, easily. Patrick looked at peace with the world. He looked like he was 11 or 12 again, back at Boston Garden. All alone. Skating all day. Just for fun. No pressure. Free, free at last. But he would stay out there just for a half hour, before returning to his office. But for that wonderful half hour, a solo figure skating the length of the ice, doing laps like his daughter does in a swimming pool, he was a kid again.

Dennis Cavanaugh

Craig Patrick enjoys playing for Penguins Alumni Hockey Team.

Hometowns
Faraway places with intriguing names

"You have to remember where you came from."
—Jean Pronovost

The colorfully-named hometowns of many National Hockey League players are like those old radio serials — "The Shadow" and "Sam Spade" and "Inner Sanctum" — in that they leave a lot to the imagination. Think about Flin Flon, Manitoba, for instance, the hometown of Bobby Clarke, the star of the Philadelphia Flyers back in 1975-1976 when I was working the NHL beat for *The New York Post*. Clarke later became the general manager of the Flyers. Flin Flon is named after a legendary figure by the name of Flintabatty Flonaton.

"In Flin Flon," commented Clarke, "you either play hockey or work in the mines. There's no way I wanted to work in the mines."

There were other names, too, just as intriguing, to be found in NHL lineups during that 1975-76 campaign. Don Marcotte of the Boston Bruins was born in Asbestos, Quebec; the Penguins' Ed Van Impe in Saskatoon, Saskatchewan; the New York Islanders' J. P. Parise in Smooth Rock Falls, Ontario; and the Buffalo Sabres' Brian Spencer (who also played for the Penguins once upon a time) in Fort St. James, British Columbia. They also stir the imagination.

But there are more than just intriguing names attached to these towns. There are lifestyles — vastly different and seemingly far removed from what their NHL status would afford them. As a writer, I have long been fascinated by where people come from, their origins, their early influences, how they were shaped by the people and places in their youth.

Spencer's story about his hometown was a good one, for Fort St. James is a rather primitive outpost. In addition to talking to Spencer about his hometown, we did the same with several other NHL performers.

They included Tom Lysiak of the Atlanta Flames, who was born and grew up in High Prairie, Alberta; and Gerry Hart of the Islanders, who like Clarke came from Flin Flon. So did Reggie Leach of the Flyers and Duane Rupp of the Penguins. Bobby Orr of the Boston Bruins came from a place called Parry Sound, north of Toronto. I also talked to Bert Marshall and Bob Nystrom of the Islanders, who grew up in Kamloops, British Columbia; Cesare Maniago of the Minnesota North Stars, a native of Trail, British Columbia; and Derek Sanderson of the St. Louis Blues, who is from Niagara Falls, Ontario.

"We were kind of behind the times in our neck of the woods in British Columbia," Spencer said of Fort St. James. "There was no TV, and not much else in the way of entertainment.

"It would go down to 65 degrees below zero, and we'd get as much as 20 feet of snow. You'd have to live up there and see it to believe it. You don't wake up in the morning and turn on a switch. There was no electricity, and no running water where I lived.

"Frustration built up there. The roads were bad, it was tough to get away, and there was a lot of bitter feelings. I had no chance as a youngster to play hockey there. And my father desperately wanted me to be a hockey player.

"There was a lake there and we learned to skate on it. Eventually, they built an indoor rink, but it was only half the regulation size. It's still there today. We used to travel 80 miles to play hockey in Vanderhoof. That was where I played my first regulation hockey, with referees and all.

"Fort St. James just wasn't very sophisticated. It had been an Indian village, and once it boomed for awhile as a fur trading post. It still is. But it's not booming anymore. It's a lumber town now.

"My dad would drive me down to Vanderhoof in a diesel-engine truck. It was an hour-and-a-half drive in each direction. We might shoot a moose on the way down or back and put it in the back of the truck.

"I didn't have a good background when I got into junior hockey. I might've played five games a whole season. If I had a better background, I might be a better hockey player. Maybe not, though. Maybe it made me more hungry to succeed in major league hockey."

Bobby Orr was thought to have gotten a late start when he obtained his first pair of ice skates at age four from a fellow named Gene Fernie, who was a friend of his father who worked for the Canadian Pacific Railroad. Most of Bobby Orr's friends were skating at age three. "Those skates were so big on Bobby's little feet that we had to stuff the ends of the boots with old paper," his dad, Doug Orr, recalled. "You know, I don't think he ever had a new pair of skates that really fit him until he was maybe fourteen years old."

Orr grew up in a community of about 6,500 people in Parry Sound, situated on the Georgian Bay about one hundred and fifty miles north of Toronto. There's a large sign on the main highway leading to town that proclaims Parry Sound as the "Home of Bobby Orr."

Orr started out skating on the Sequin River, or at Bob's Point, on the sound itself. The winters are quite cold and harsh in Parry Sound. The temperature dips as low as forty degrees below zero during the winter months, causing the ice on the Seguin to freeze three and four feet thick. The average annual snowfall totals more than six feet. And the wind can be fierce, flattening the strongest trees. Some of the locals like to joke that summer means two months of poor skating on the Seguin.

"In the mornings," Doug Orr once told Mark Mulvoy, who authored the biography, *Bobby Orr: My Game*, "some parents would shovel the snow from one section of the frozen river and make an open-air rink so the kids could skate after school."

The Orrs always lived on the other side of the tracks that run through the town. For a short time the Orrs shared an old duplex on River Street that was only a fifty yard walk to the Seguin, but they moved to better quarters for most of Bobby's boyhood, a nine-room white stucco house on a hill, but they could still see the river.

Bobby's father was quite a skater and hockey player himself, and had pro ambitions, but never really pursued it because he had no interest in life in the minor leagues. He was good enough that in 1942, when he was 18, he was offered a pro contract by the Boston Bruins.

"Sure, I think I could have made it," he would later say.

Instead, Doug took a job crating dynamite for Canadian Industries, Ltd., a firm that manufactured high explosives. He worked the night shift, and spent many days watching Bobby chasing a hockey puck on the Sequin. Bobby Orr was often the smallest kid on the ice, but no one could get the puck away from him.

"I never knew how talented Bobby was," his mother, Arva, admitted, "but Doug knew it right away and wasn't afraid to say so. Me? I guess I don't know a hockey stick from a broomstick."

Doug Orr observed Bobby enough to know he had a gift. "Bobby was pretty smart for such a little guy," he recalled. "He used to skate for an hour or so until his face was all numbed from the cold. Then he'd skate off the ice, walk across the street on the toes of his blades, and stand next to our stove for five or ten minutes — or until he was halfway warm. We would say to him, 'Bobby, haven't you had enough for today?' but before we could get the words out he'd be out of the house and on his way back to the ice."

As a young boy back home in High Prairie, Alberta, Tom Lysiak liked to skate over ice-covered streets from his family's farmhouse, which was about five miles from the main part of town, to the nearby river which froze over in mid-winter.

"It was a little tough on the skates, but it seemed like a good idea then," recalled Lysiak, 23 at the time of our interview.

"Maybe people in the States can't imagine a river freezing over, but it frequently was 35 degrees below zero where I lived. A light wind usually kept the river free from snow. We'd skate five miles up the river to a log jam, then skate five miles back home."

High Prairie is located about 250 miles north of Edmonton, the major city in that area, and according to the Flames' high-flying center, there were about 3,000 people in the farming community when he lived there.

Tom thought fondly of those days when he "sat on the old tractor, and slopped the hogs," and tended to chores. "I didn't mind any of it," he said.

"We didn't get TV until 1962 or 1963, and being an English-speaking community, we followed the Maple Leafs from Toronto, which is about 2,500 miles away. There'd be an NHL game on TV every Saturday night at six o'clock.

"Just about everybody watched it. You'd pick up your dinner off the table and take it into the living room. Red Kelly, Bob Pulford and Johnny Bower were big with us, and that's who we pretended to be in our street hockey games. We only knew the Toronto players, except for Stan Mikita and Bobby Hull of the Chicago Blackhawks."

An indoor hockey rink was built in High Prairie in 1957, when Tom was four years old. He learned to skate when he was in first grade and soon after was playing organized hockey.

When he was 17, he left High Prairie, a woodsy area with lots of wildlife, to go play junior hockey with the Medicine Hat Tigers. Medicine Hat was a complete change. "It was an industrial city," Lysiak recalled, "with no trees, no nothing. It was far different from anything I'd known."

Gerry Hart located Flin Flon, his hometown, by saying it's about 1,200 miles due north of Minneapolis-St. Paul. Hart and Bobby Clarke and Reggie Leach of the Flyers were all teammates with the Flin Flon Bombers in junior hockey. Hart, the oldest, was the team captain. His mother, a nurse, often asked Gerry why he didn't develop into a big scorer like Clarke (no opposing player has ever scored more points against the Penguins) instead of being a roughneck defenseman.

Clarke was married to a young woman he met because Bomber teammate, Hart, had been dating her earlier. That's the price one apparently paid for double-dating with Clarke. "We're all still very good friends," said Hart. "We play golf together, go fishing and canoeing together."

Hart recalled of his junior hockey days with Clarke: "It was kind of a sticky thing with Bobby. They knew he had super skills. But he was a diabetic. He didn't have the proper medical attention it required in those days.

"We went on a long road trip and we'd be away for two or three weeks. I remember once, we were on a bus between two small towns, and Bobby went into a slight coma, and we had to take him to a hospital.

"Bobby's father worked underground in the mines for 25 years, and my father for 30 years. It's hard rock mining — for copper, gold and zinc. When you played junior hockey, they gave you a job at the mine.

"We'd practice hockey for a half day and the rest of the day Bobby and I did our jobs at the mine, shoveling rock and mowing grass, stuff like that above ground so there'd be no danger.

"Today, of course, Bobby is the sweetheart of Flin Flon. He could run for mayor and win it. The first year he won the MVP award in the NHL, we had a benefit hockey game there in August for underprivileged kids and Bobby brought some of his teammates from Philadelphia, and everyone who'd played with him in Flin Flon back to participate. They love him there."

George Von Benko Collection

Bert Marshall

Cesare Maniago

Bob Nystrom

Bobby Orr

There are other names, too, just as intriguing as Flin Flon. There's South Porcupine, Ontario, the hometown of Vancouver's Don Lever; Smithers, British Columbia, where brothers Jim and Joe Watson of the Flyers came from; Moose Jaw, Saskatchewan, birthplace of Islanders Glenn (Chico) Resch and Clark Gillies. Ron Greschner of the New York Rangers was born and reared in Goodsoil, Saskatchewan; Rick Blight of the Canucks in Portage La Prairie, Manitoba. They also stir the imagination.

Bobby Nystrom of the Islanders was born in Stockholm, Sweden, but his family moved to Hinton, Alberta, when he was four and remained there for 11 years. It was a community of 4,500 with a pulp and paper mill in the center of it. "It had a good ol' stink about it," Nystrom said of the place.

When the family moved again, it chose Kamloops, British Columbia, a community of 40,000. "It's a nice town and a good climate and pretty rivers," Nystrom said. That is, if you don't mind some good ol' stink. The biggest building in town, it turned out, was also a pulp and paper mill.

"They had a big project," recalled Nystrom, who is still employed by the Islanders, in a community relations capacity, "to carry the smell away. They had it piped up over this big hill there to take it into the next valley. But they didn't allow for the wind or something, and the smell came right back through the middle of town."

Randy Rota of the Colorado Rockies and Nystrom's teammate, Bert Marshall, also hailed from Kamloops. Marshall is a few years older than Nystrom and was born and grew up in Kamloops. He recalls when it was a more comfortable community of 12,000 and how it boomed to where he figured there were about 50,000 residents.

"It's a nice town to be from," Marshall said. It's located 280 miles northeast of Vancouver. Major highways and railroads crossed the city, cattle came and went there, but Marshall said the thing a visitor would remember most was the smell.

"It's awful," said Marshall, now an Islanders' scout. "It's worse now than when they started that project to clean up the air."

When Marshall was in the minor leagues, he played for the Pittsburgh Hornets of the American Hockey League, a farm team for the Detroit Red Wings. When he first came to Pittsburgh in the mid-'60s, he lived in a room above the Pleasure Bar, an Italian restaurant in Bloomfield that was a hockey hangout. He never complained about the smells from the kitchen that wafted their way up to his room.

It's also easy to understand why Nystrom says now, "I love Long Island. I love the good, fresh air."

Vancouver's Cesare Maniago remembered sitting around a big radio listening to "Hockey Night In Canada." He remembers how his dad always had two bits riding on the game, taking part in a poll at the smelting refinery where he worked, and how he won $25 once when Toronto tied Boston, 5-5.

"I'll never forget that Turk Broda and Frank Brimsek were the goalies," recalled the 11-year veteran NHL goaltender.

"We weren't starving, mind you," Maniago pointed out, "but when my dad won that $25, he sent me down to a local store to buy a brick of ice cream. And we celebrated that night."

That was in Trail, British Columbia, which Maniago located as being about 13 miles north of the Washington state border, or a hundred miles directly north of Spokane.

It was a company town, with all activity revolving around the Cominco Company, a smelting firm. "They even provided the recreational facilities, like several hockey rinks," said Maniago.

His dad had a dirty job in the smelter, stripping zinc cathodes. His dad had to wear a mask on the job, just as Cesare did in his NHL career. Only his dad and his co-workers had to worry about their teeth for a different reason: the acid used in the stripping process tended to eat away at their teeth.

"I have two older brothers," said Maniago, "and my dad used to come home and say he didn't want any of us having to do the kind of work he did."

Maniago remembered that there was no TV in Trail when he was growing up and very little radio. Trail was on the Columbia River, and steamboats once brought the ore to be smelted.

"Most of the kids on my block were older than me," Maniago recalled. "I had some ability as an athlete, but I was forced to excel in order to play with the older kids. We played some shinny games in the streets with a tennis ball.

"We used to skate where the wastes were discharged from the smelting company. Some of us used to suck the ice when we were thirsty. God knows what was in that ice, but we didn't know any better.

"Every summer we go back to see my family. I have a summer resort in Summerland, which is about 150 miles from Trail."

Derek Sanderson smiled at the mention of Niagara Falls, for he had fond memories of his youth there. In his early days, he was a Huck Finn type, who fished in the river below the world-famous falls.

"We used to skinny dip in a cove, and wave to the tourists who'd be riding the aerial car overhead. The guide would be telling them how dangerous the river was with its rapids, and we'd confuse them all. It was dangerous about 30 to 40 feet out from the cove where we swam, and I did nearly drown there a few times.

"I first saw the Falls when I was three or four," said Sanderson. "I used to hike down there from my house, which was about a half mile away. As a kid, I couldn't figure out the attraction of the Falls, and why there'd be traffic tied up all over town in the summer. It was confusing. I started to appreciate the Falls, as I got older.

"It's a terrific town. It's serene and gorgeous. It's a very historical area, too. Our gang would get our B-B guns and go to the nearby forts

— there were six of them left over from the War of 1812 — and play soldiers. We'd get chased away by the police.

"The Niagara Falls Park Commission Security Police were always after me, until I made it in the NHL. As a teenager, I was sort of like Fonzie on 'Happy Days' — the black jacket and motorcycle — but those guys all die young, so I went straight.

"It's the honeymoon capital of the world, you know. They still have a June bride ceremony where some lucky bride wins $25,000. I spent the best times of my life in that town, I tell you."

Derek Sanderson during his days with Penguins

"It is scary every time you hear the word 'cancer.' I went back home after I saw them (the doctors) and they gave me the news. And on the way down to my house I could hardly drive because of the tears — and (I was) crying the whole day. It was a tough day in my life. But once I learned about the disease, once I talked to my family and friends ... the more I found out about the disease, the better I felt. I'm very positive, a positive person by nature, and that's not going to change in the future."

—Mario Lemieux
on learning he had
Hodgkin's disease

Dossier
Mario Lemieux

Birthday: October 5, 1965

Birthplace: Montreal

Occupation: Hockey player

Current home: Pittsburgh

Marital status: Married to Nathalie Asselin in summer of 1993. "She's the only girl I've ever gone out with. We've been together since I was 16." They have a daughter Lauren.

Worst job: Sharpening skates

The book I've been recommending lately: I don't read books.

Favorite childhood memory: When I was 13, I got to meet Guy Lafleur. He's the best hockey player who ever lived — at least I think so.

I'd give anything to meet: Johnny Carson

The worst part of my job is: Traveling. We're on the road from October through May, and it takes so much out of you.

My fantasy is: I'd love to be the world's greatest golfer.

The worst advice my mother ever gave me was: She let me leave home when I was 16, and that was much too young.

People who knew me in high school thought I was: Selfish and a loner.

Superstition: Before a game, I always do the same things in the same order: I drink five coffees and then put on my equipment — first the pads, then the socks, then the skates, left side first.

Biggest fear: Getting speared — when you get hit with the end of a hockey stick. It's very dangerous, and it could end your career.

The best time of my life: Playing in the Canada Cup in 1987 against the Russians. I had the winning goal.

The worst time of my life: When I was 16, I went to Russia at Christmastime to play hockey. I was away for three weeks, and I was pretty homesick.

My friends like me because: I'm punctual.

I'm better than anyone else when it comes to: Scoring

Mario Lemieux
The gifted one

*"Since the beginning,
I always loved the game."*

A calm came over Mario Lemieux as he looked back upon a more carefree time in his life, when hockey was pure fun, when his back didn't bother him, when nobody had ever mentioned cancer and his name in the same breath. It was a time when he skated freely, without pain, when he streaked down the sidewalks of St. Henri, heading for the nearest rink to play hockey, the game he loved so much. He was always skating, or so it seemed, and he was happiest when he was on ice, maneuvering the puck on the end of his stick. He was the swiftest, most assured, kid on the block. He sucked in the cold air, saw his breath before him, and could not have felt better about himself. On a clear day, he could see the National Hockey League in his future. It was a boyhood dream. He skated the sidewalks of St. Henri like he owned them.

That's right, the sidewalks of St. Henri. "You have to remember, it gets pretty cold in Montreal in the winter," allowed Lemieux with a smile that hints that he knows something that you don't. Lemieux was a young man, just 29 in the summer of 1994, who was born and bred to play hockey. He not only skated on the sidewalks as a youngster, but there were also times that his parents packed the front hallway of their home with snow from wall to wall so their three sons, Richard, Alain and Mario, could continue to skate at night, or when it was too cold outside, or so the story goes, anyhow.

"I guess when you're young, you just go out and have some fun," said Lemieux. "There were outdoor rinks everywhere. I didn't feel a whole lot of pressure when I played midget and peewee hockey. The pressure and expectations grow. The older you get the more pressure comes with it."

Hockey is a way of life for many children in Canada, and few pursued it with more passion than the Lemieux family. Mario was born on October 5, 1965, in Montreal. His parents, Jean-Guy and Pierrette Lemieux, lived in a working class section of the city. Jean-Guy was a construction worker, and Pierrette stayed at home to raise their three children. They were French-Canadian. Like a lot of people in Montreal, they spoke French, not English. Some speak both languages. It helps. Mario Lemieux did not learn how to speak English well until he started playing for the Pittsburgh Penguins.

Lemieux lives in a storybook mansion in a stately section of Sewickley, near the Sewickley Academy, a private school that attracts students from all over the Pittsburgh area. Some of the most exclusive country clubs and golf preserves are situated in Sewickley.

Sewickley is just west of Pittsburgh, along the Ohio River. Lemieux moved there in 1993 from Mount Lebanon where he lived in a more modern home, the largest on a cul-de-sac, and one that attracted Penguins' fans at all hours of the day. Lemieux couldn't leave his home to water his flowers, or to get his mail, without being asked for an autograph. He sought more privacy — something he constantly seeks — in Sewickley. "I'm such a private person," he said. "I'd rather stay in the background."

He and his wife Nathalie, and their daughter Lauren, just over a year old in the summer of 1994, are at home there. It is the sort of home one is accustomed to seeing only on Robin Leach's TV feature series, "Lifestyles of the Rich and Famous."

Sewickley is an older, established community, one of the tonier towns that surrounds Pittsburgh. There was a controversy that drew attention to Sewickley at the time that I interviewed Lemieux, in early July of 1994. Some Hollywood types were in Sewickley shooting a movie, and they had constructed a McDonald's Restaurant just for the movie scene. Some local citizens objected because they didn't think that a McDonald's fit into the look of the local main street. They didn't care that it wasn't there to stay; it simply didn't look good. It was a subject for local radio talk show fodder that week, and people called and spoofed the snooty stereotypical Sewickley resident. As if no one from Sewickley would be caught dead with a Big Mac.

Lemieux is one of the grandest athletes ever to perform in Pittsburgh, a place often referred to as "The City of Champions" because of the Super Bowl success of its Steelers and the World Series and division championships of its Pirates. Because Pitt won the college football championship in 1976.

He led the Penguins to Stanley Cup championships in 1991 and 1992, and won every significant individual award of the National Hockey League. Yet he likes to be left alone.

"He's just a very quiet guy," said Eddie Johnston, his coach and the man most responsible for drafting Lemieux when he was the general manager of the Penguins back in 1984. "He's very reserved; he's always been quiet. Like a loner, you know. Some people object to that. They think he should be more outgoing, but he's not. That's not him."

It struck me that Lemieux suffered in that respect the same way as Chuck Noll, the former coach of the Pittsburgh Steelers. Noll was not what others, particularly the press, wanted him to be. He wasn't as gregarious or glib or as colorful as they would have preferred. He was just himself, a solid, hard-working coach who believed his team's record spoke for itself.

Johnston had yet to coach a championship team, but he was far more popular with the press than his predecessor, the dour Scotty Bowman, or Noll, for that matter.

No one is more comfortable in a crowd, or a better mixer socially than Johnston. He enjoys people. But he accepts Lemieux for what he is — the greatest hockey player he ever laid his blue eyes on. And that's saying something, because Johnston also grew up in Montreal, and

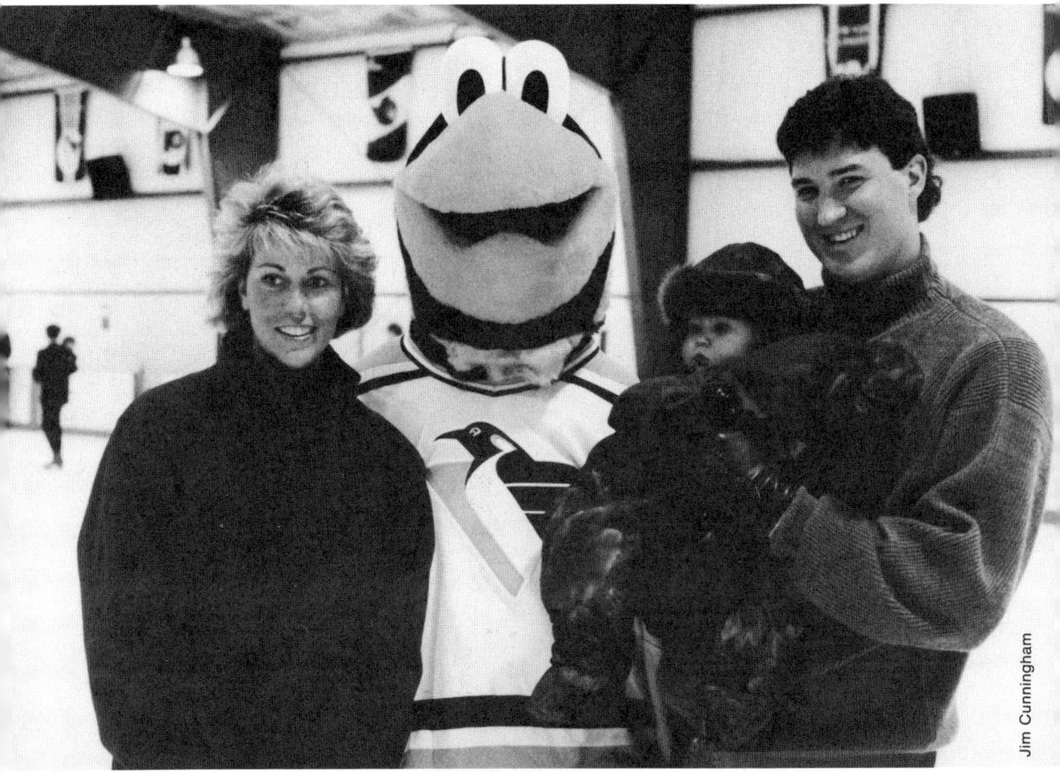

Jim Cunningham

Nathalie and Mario celebrate 1993 holiday season with Penguins' mascot Iceburgh and daughter Lauren. They joined Mario's parents, Jean-Guy and Pierrette, and brother Alain after Penguins won second Stanley Cup championship.

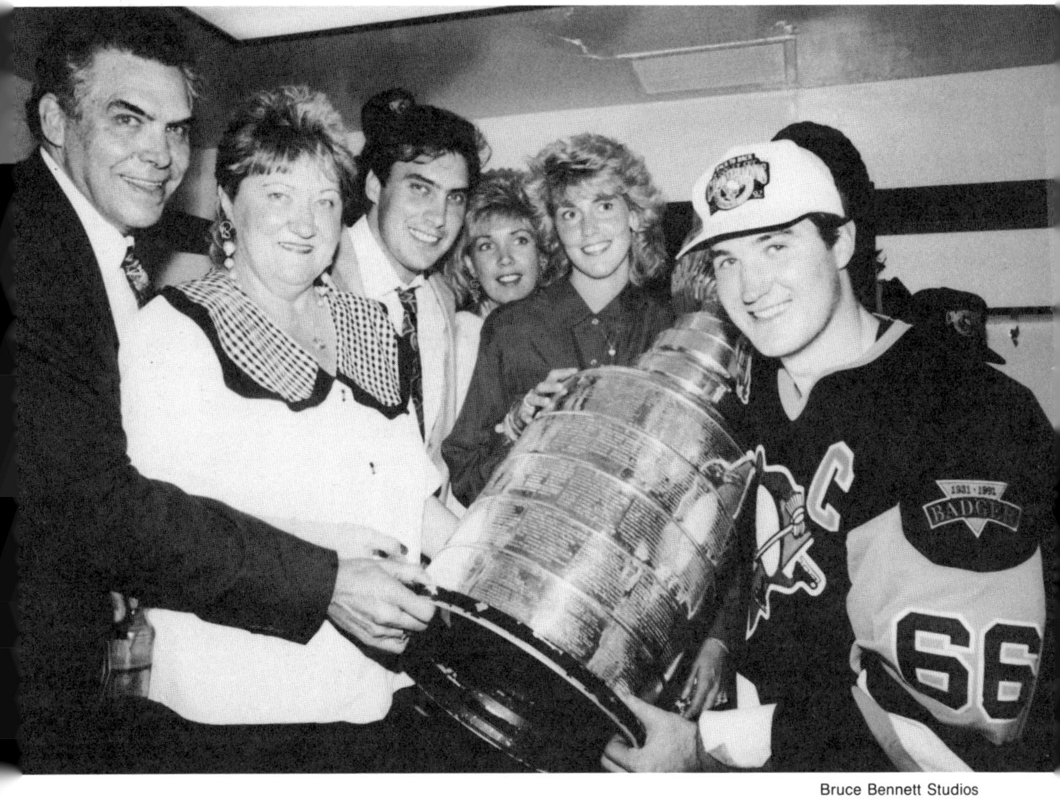

Bruce Bennett Studios

idolized Maurice "The Rocket" Richard and Jean Beliveau, and remains a good buddy of Bobby Orr, his one-time teammate on two Stanley Cup championship teams in Boston.

Johnston always knew that Lemieux was different, a unique individual, something special.

When I mentioned to Johnston that I learned in my research that Lemieux scored a goal the first time he touched the puck in a regular season NHL game, at Boston in the season-opener in 1984, and that he scored on his first shift in the Penguins' home opener at the Civic Arena a few days later, Johnston just smiled.

"I'll go better than that," added Johnston. "He scored the first time he took the ice in his first practice with the Penguins, and he scored on his first shift in our first exhibition game. He's always come up big in the big games: the Stanley Cup finals, the All-Star Games, in international play. He's just got the gift, that's all. He's one of the great ones."

Lemieux's parents knew he had the gift. Their oldest son Richard had been a good local player, but he gave up on the game as a teenager. Alain was good enough to make it in the NHL himself. He was skating, in fact, for the Pittsburgh Phantoms of Roller Hockey International in the summer of '94. The parents recognized early, as did everyone else, that Mario was the most gifted of the Lemieux children when it came to playing hockey. They pampered him and nursed him along the way. They always made sure things were just right for their Mario.

"They were at every game I attended when he was in junior hockey, and I attended a lot of his games," Johnston said.

"I haven't played without pain for the past five years."
—Mario Lemieux

I interviewed Lemieux a few days before the All-Star Baseball Week in Pittsburgh in July of 1994. It was a week when baseball seized hold of the city like it never did before, and when the late Roberto Clemente was the center of attention as a statue was being unveiled in his memory at Gate A of Three Rivers Stadium. Hundreds of thousands of baseball fans filled the city for week-long activities. I had written a book about the Pirates' Hall of Fame outfielder, and 12-time All-Star Game performer, called *Remember Roberto*. I was struck by the similarity of the situations that Lemieux and Clemente encountered when they came to Pittsburgh. They could be the two greatest athletes ever to play for Pittsburgh teams, yet they were often misunderstood, misrepresented and not as popular as they might have been in Pittsburgh.

Both came from cities outside the U.S.A. mainland. Both spoke a different language. Clemente came from Spanish-speaking Puerto Rico, and Lemieux from the French-Canadian community of Montreal. Both had back problems early on, and both were sidelined with back problems from time to time. Both were criticized for their style of play. Former

NHL coach and TV analyst Don Cherry described Lemieux as "a floater," for instance, and Clemente was criticized for not always going all out, when, in truth, he hustled harder than any of his teammates on a consistent basis. "You call Pete Rose 'Charlie Hustle,'" complained Clemente after he starred in the 1971 World Series triumph over the Baltimore Orioles. "I hustle just as much, and you call me nothing." Both had problems communicating when they first came to Pittsburgh, and both had difficulty adjusting to a new culture. Both had great pride in their ability, and wanted acclaim and recognition. At the same time, they wanted to be left alone, to go their own way. They could be aloof, distant. They were called loners. They were called worse. When they said they were unable to play, some observers questioned their resolve and team spirit.

"It's unfair," said Paul Martha, when he was managing the front office of the Penguins for the DeBartolo family. A former classmate of mine at Pitt where he was an All-American football player and a three-sport performer, later a defensive back with the Pittsburgh Steelers and Denver Broncos, Martha had always been comfortable with the media.

"People don't seem to appreciate that this guy is the greatest hockey player perhaps in the history of the game. But he has a back that acts up and won't permit him to play, plus he learned that he has Hodgkin's disease — that's cancer, no matter how you might mask it. How would anyone react to that? I think he's handled it pretty well. But that's a lot to deal with, for anyone. And Mario has always been a private person. That's just the way he is."

Martha liked Lemieux, the man and the player. He'd been on enough teams to recognize the genuine article.

Lemieux often played with pain, as did Clemente, yet they were criticized as malingerers. Clemente was more openly critical of the media than Lemieux. But Lemieux has gone long periods when he refused to discuss his situation with the press. He was tired of going over old ground. He didn't get into the nose-to-nose disputes with the press as Clemente did. There were times he simply said he had nothing to say, and dismissed the press. He could be petty. He refused to grant interviews to Sam Nover of WPXI-TV for a long period, which mystified Nover because he felt he had always treated Lemieux in a big league way. But someone at Sam's station had offered a critical report about a Lemieux indiscretion and Lemieux, according to Nover, told him, "Sam, someone has to pay and it's going to be you." In time, Lemieux consented to interviews with Nover and the rest of the Pittsburgh press pack. In fairness, the Pittsburgh media had been most kind to Lemieux through the years, and were seldom critical, and weren't out to dig up any dirt about him. He was treated kinder than he would have been in bigger NHL markets.

There was something else about Lemieux that made the comparison to Clemente a valid one. In addition to their greatness at their respective games, both were extremely handsome men who cut classy figures in and out of uniform. They looked at home in tuxedos as well as their game jerseys. Both had winning smiles, and great appeal for all fans.

Baseball Commissioner Bowie Kuhn eulogized Clemente after his death in an airplane crash on New Year's Eve of 1972 by saying he "had a touch of royalty about him." The same could be said of Lemieux. There is just something about his look. The great ones have it: like Joe Louis, Joe DiMaggio, Joe Greene, Franco Harris, Jack Dempsey, Muhammad Ali, Wilt Chamberlain. It's something about the way they carry themselves. And perhaps it says something about the way we see them, the way we admire them, the way we address them.

For one thing, most people have to look up to Lemieux. He is 6-4 in his bare feet in the locker room at the Civic Arena, where he has the honor of having the last locker on one side of the locker room area. Tom Barrasso has the last locker directly across the room. In his skates, Lemieux stands 6-7, and looms over most NHL players on the ice. He stands out in any crowd.

Mario Lemieux, living in a grand mansion in Sewickley, looks the part of a prince or a duke in some European duchy. Mario Lemieux has a movie star's aura about him.

Lemieux was looking forward to a trip to Europe, and playing golf at some of the world's greatest courses. He loved golf now the way he loved hockey as a child. It was his newfound passion, and he drew understandable criticism from fans and media alike for continuing to play golf. His critics felt that if he had back problems they could only be aggravated by playing golf. They wanted him to put his golf clubs away until he retired from playing for the Penguins.

His status was uncertain in the summer of '94. Penguins owner Howard Baldwin had stated publicly that he believed Lemieux would be back to play for the Penguins in the 1994-95 season. But Lemieux was playing a wait-and-see game.

He wasn't sure.

"I'm going to do everything I can to be ready for the next season," said Lemieux. "I haven't played without some pain for the past five years. That gets old. I can't continue to play that way."

Barrasso offers the following observation about Lemieux:

"When he feels healthy, he feels like he could accomplish just about anything," said the Penguins' goalie. "He's very conservative with what he has to say with people he doesn't know. He doesn't want to make a statement that people will misunderstand. When you are at the top of your profession, people always look for ways to bring you down off the pedestal. Mario enjoys a private life and he's done a good job of maintaining that."

Civic Arena crowd shows its support for Mario Lemieux, after he appeared at press conference with club owner Howard Baldwin when it was revealed that Mario had Hodgkin's disease, sobering everybody in aftermath of Stanley Cup championship seasons.

> *"I have no sympathy for goalies. None whatsoever. My job is to score goals on them."*
> —Mario Lemieux

*"I got a lot of publicity,
even when I was ten years old."*
—Mario Lemieux

Lemieux seemed relieved to talk about his beginnings in hockey, rather than the usual questioning about his back, his future, the disappointment of the playoffs the previous two seasons, when the Penguins were bounced unceremoniously from the Stanley Cup playoffs in the first round rather than continuing as champions of the NHL, as observers believed they would after they won it all in 1991 and 1992.

I asked him when he first realized how gifted he was as a hockey player.

"We were winning championships in tournaments," he began. "We were in a lot of tournaments. I was under ten years old. There was a lot of attention when I was younger because of all the goals I was scoring. I got a lot of publicity, even when I was ten years old. A lot of people came to the rink to watch me play.

"We played all over Montreal and Quebec City. We'd travel, sometimes as long as two or three days, to play in tournaments. We'd sleep in hotels, we'd have some parties. All the parents would come, and it would be a big weekend for us. It was special.

"Since the beginning, I always loved the game. When you grow up in Montreal, one day you want to be a professional hockey player. When I was six or seven, I knew that was what I wanted. Guy Lafleur was my idol when I was younger. He was the best in the world at the time. I had a chance to meet him when I was 12 or 13. We had a chance to see him on a Saturday night at The Forum. We spoke in French, of course.

"I didn't get a chance to go see the Canadiens play much. We didn't have the tickets. I saw them play in person about three or four times when I was a teenager. I was there when Lafleur scored his 1,000th point.

"I sat behind the bench of the Canadiens, and I showed up in a picture of Lafleur, showing him with his teammates after he'd gotten his 1,000th point, in the next day's newspaper. We cut out that picture and kept it in our house for a long time. I was shown applauding Lafleur. That was pretty cool."

Lemieux sounded so young when he said that phrase: "That was pretty cool."

I asked him to again go back to his beginnings. "I used to skate on a lake near Montreal. I'd go there at sunup and stay till it got dark. I'd just skate forever, for four and five hours at a stretch. I'd have a puck, make some passes, but most of all I was simply skating. It was a place called Chateau Gay, near Montreal.

"I played on the same team as my oldest brother, Richard, for awhile. He quit when he was 14 or 15. He didn't like the game as much as I did. He was a good defenseman. He just never loved the game like Alain and I did.

Mario Lemieux as a hotshot 11-year-old player in 1976.

"I had a strong interest in hockey. I had a lot of posters of the Canadien players on the wall of my bedroom. I had hockey cards. I had a lot of trophies from tournaments on display."

Even as a youngster, Mario had a strong desire to win. Whatever the game, basement hockey, cards, Monopoly, computer games, you name it, Mario wanted to come out on top.

"If Mario lost, it would be as if a hurricane went through the basemen," said Jean-Guy Lemieux.

At 16, he joined a junior hockey club in Quebec called Laval. He was two years younger than Alain had been when he joined the same club. In his first season, Mario scored 30 goals and had 66 assists for 96 points. A year later, he pumped his total up to 84 goals and 184 points. In his third season, 1983-84, he scored 133 goals and had 149 assists for 282 points in just 70 games. That's when the Penguins picked him as the first player taken in the 1984 draft.

Even then, he knew he had the potential to be one of the greats of the game. He was already being hailed as the next Wayne Gretzky. Gretzky, known as "The Great One," as Roberto Clemente was called late in his career with the Pirates, was thought to be the best player in professional hockey. Lemieux was already skating in good company.

He wasn't old enough to have seen Maurice Richard or Jean Beliveau play, two of the Montreal greats who helped establish the game in his hometown. "I only saw them on tape when I got older," recalled Lemieux. "I've met them both. I still call them Mr. Richard and Mr. Beliveau. They still have a real aura about them. They are true sports heroes in Montreal, and throughout Canada. Beliveau was a vice president of the Canadiens for a long time, so he's still on the scene."

Someday Lemieux will command that same sort of attention and respect from younger players and fans.

His face is already painted at the top of an office building in Downtown Pittsburgh. He is depicted in a mural with Roberto Clemente, Bill Mazeroski and Franco Harris. In Quebec, he is known as Le Magnifique, a hero in the leading province of the world's leading hockey nation.

"It's not as enjoyable when you have to cope with pain in every game."

I asked Lemieux about his parents, and the role they played in shaping his successful career.

"They were very supportive. They used to get up at 5 in the morning to get me to practice at 6. My dad and mom were always up, my mom always made breakfast for us. I never had to take a bus, like some of the other kids. They'd take me wherever I needed to go. Most of the kids had to take the bus."

I told Lemieux that Greg Malone told me he used to wear his hockey gear to bed some nights, when he knew he had to get up particularly early, so he'd be ready to go as soon as the alarm went off.

Lemieux laughed at the picture it inspired. "No, I never did that," he said. "I'd get up in the morning and put my pads on."

Did Lemieux ever pretend to be an NHL player when he went out to practice?

"Sure I did. Even in games, I used to think I was Guy Lafleur. Every kid had a dream to play professionally."

I mentioned that Craig Patrick, the general manager of the Penguins, told me he often yearned for those days of his youth, when he could skate the length of the rink alone, pretend to be a popular pro, and just play the game, just have fun.

"It's much easier when you're young," said Lemieux. "You have no responsibilities. You just have to go out and have some fun. Now you have the bills, all sorts of responsibilities."

Time-out. I had to laugh to myself when I heard Lemieux mention about having to pay the bills. That would hardly cause him much stress, considering that his contract called for something over seven million dollars a year. Even with the mortgage on a million dollar plus mansion in Sewickley, there must be plenty left over to take care of the bills.

"Now you have responsibilities, a family and kids. It's become different. I've had a lot of problems."

There I could emphathize with Lemieux. I love to play basketball. I can't play it well. I never could, but I could shoot a lot better when I was younger than I can now. But I enjoy running the court for two hours with an over-the-hill gang in my neighborhood every Saturday and Sunday and holiday morning in the spring and summer. In the summer of 1994, I was experiencing off-the-court pain with my knees. I would get a piercing pain, like my knee was locking up on me, just standing in line in a supermarket. It scared me. I was 51, and not very good at playing basketball. But I didn't want to quit playing. I went to see Dr. Jon Tucker, an orthopedic physician and the grandson of Joe Tucker, a popular Pittsburgh broadcaster of both Steelers and Hornets games once upon a time. Dr. Tucker took good care of me, checked out my X-rays, told me about a deteriorating condition, some rheumatism and mush in those knees, gave me a prescription, and cleared up my problem pronto. Peter Pan was able to return to playing basketball after a two-week layoff.

It made me wonder what it would be like to be 29, to be the greatest hockey player in the world, and to be worried about your back and about Hodgkin's disease, and have to wonder whether you would ever be able to play again. That would throw most people for a loop.

He had soreness in his lower back even as a teenager. "He was growing so fast, we figured it was because he was so tall and had to bend over so much when he skated with the puck," recalled Eddie Johnston.

Lemieux has had good reason to wonder whether he would be forced to retire from hockey. It's a question that has confronted him for sometime now.

"It's always difficult to give the game up," allowed Lemieux. "I always thought I would play as long as I was healthy. Nothing else matters. Your health is most important. My back has been an issue for five years. Then there's the cancer. A lot has happened, a lot of obstacles.

"It's not the same anymore for me. It's not as enjoyable. When you have to cope with pain every game for five years, well, it gets old after awhile. I can't remember the last time I played without pain."

I questioned Lemieux about continuing to play golf when his back condition is so fragile. Many professional golfers are plagued by back problems because of the physical demands of the game.

"I think golf is a big part of my life," said Lemieux. "Winning a tournament some day would be a very satisfying thing. I think I could get the same sort of rush out of golf that I get out of hockey. My back has given me a lot of problems, and I don't think it will ever be right again. I'm trying to do the best I can with what I've still got."

Lemieux alluded to the time and effort he put forth as a youngster to hone his skills, to become the hockey player he became. He admitted, however, that there were others who worked just as hard, some even harder, who never made it to the NHL, or who had less than satisfactory experiences as pro hockey players. Did he realize that he had a God-given talent and knack for the sport?

"Yeah, I think I knew that early on," he responded. "God gave me a talent. I used it to the fullest, and I am proud of that. I practiced a lot, but so did a lot of other guys I knew. They loved the game, too. But they didn't have the talent I do. They didn't end up in the same place."

I was told that Craig Patrick was hoping his two sons would pursue careers other than in professional hockey. At the same time, Patrick said he ignored similar advice from his own father.

"I'm open-ended about that," said Lemieux. "We have a little daughter. Since she can't play hockey, I don't have to worry about that."

I reminded Mario that the Phantoms had a woman playing goalie. Her name is Erin Whitten. There was a woman playing goalie for another team in Roller Hockey International, too. He smiled, as if to say he didn't see that in Lauren Lemieux's future. But it might be in the blood...

"If I have a son, I'll let him decide what he'll do. I'd expect him to want to play sports, but it might be golf or tennis, rather than hockey."

There were two bizarre stories commanding much attention in the sports world at the time of our interview. Former pro football, TV and movie star O.J. Simpson was accused of brutally slaying his wife and a male friend of hers, and the case had dominated the news for weeks. If that wasn't unreal enough, a soccer star in Colombia was killed because he accidentally scored a goal against his own team in a World Cup loss to the United States. Gunmen who faulted Colombia's Andres Escobar for losing the game shot him to death after an argument at a nightclub in Bogota, Colombia.

"This is the saddest day I have ever witnessed in football, in a World Cup or any other competition," said Sepp Blatter, general secretary of world soccer's governing body. "If something happens by accident, you can say it was the will of God. But when people deliberately shoot and kill somebody because he made a mistake in the game, something is wrong.

"The popularity of our game has two faces. The first face produces joy and enthusiasm and brings people together as we have witnessed at the World Cup. And on the other face, the game mirrors our life. It has violence, tears, corruption. Like life, it has all its problems."

Lemieux learned the lesson much earlier that sports is not a refuge from the wrongs or illnesses of the world. Even so, he refutes the idea that youngsters should not hold athletes up to special attention and adulation.

"I think it's fun to do, to pretend that you're somebody in sports," said Lemieux. "I think it's fun to go to the park and pretend you are somebody great. For me, Lafleur was a tremendous person. If you try to be like somebody, you should be careful you pick somebody who is truly special, not just as a player, but as a person."

Jim Cunningham

Bespectacled Mario Lemieux lifts Stanley Cup high overhead at Three Rivers Stadium celebration to mark team's second title.

Ron Stackhouse
Unsung hero

*"Maybe it was because of my style . . .
or rather my lack of style."*

Ron Stackhouse was often booed by fans at the Civic Arena. He was a solid defenseman, a terrific playmaker, a strong point man on the power play. But there was just something about Stackhouse that incensed people. Maybe it was his size — 6-3, 210 pounds — or the fact that he seldom tossed his weight around. He wasn't physical enough to suit some. "Maybe it was because of my style, or rather my lack of style," said Stackhouse.

Maybe if the fans knew where Stackhouse came from, and what a difficult road he had to travel to get to the NHL, they might have been more sympathetic. Maybe not.

He was a widow's only son for a time. He lived in Ontario's West Guilford, a village of, perhaps, a hundred people. That's where he first learned to skate and handle a stick.

"In the winters, there was nothing else to do but play hockey," said Stackhouse of his hometown. "When the tourists went home, there we were, three hours north of Toronto, with not much else to do."

It had its advantages and its disadvantages, but Stackhouse said he wouldn't have it any other way. "I think that's the best way to grow up," he said. "I really enjoyed it, yes I did."

He would often return to that area during the off-season. "After five or six months of travel, life in the big cities, and so forth, I'm ready to go home," he said during his Penguins' playing days.

Stackhouse set club records for a defenseman during the 1975-76 season with 71 points and 60 assists when he won the team's Unsung Hero Award. He also set a club mark on April 3, 1976, when he fired 14 shots on goal against the Washington Capitals. He was the team's co-MVP in 1974-75.

Asked about an unforgettable moment in hockey, Stackhouse said when he was playing junior hockey he was asked by his coach to play goalie on a penalty shot. He had to do it twice because he came out of the crease prematurely on the first shot, and had to try it again. He thwarted both shots.

In his first game with Pittsburgh, after being acquired in a trade with the Detroit Red Wings, he scored the game-winning goal.

Ron Stackhouse is in the crease and on the ice against New York Islanders in fateful 1975 playoffs. Islanders' Ed Westfall (18) scored game-winning goal in seventh game of Stanley Cup series in one of the most memorable games in Penguins' history.

"Penalty killing is as much a part of the game as scoring. It's not as glamorous. But if you kill all of your penalties on the course of a season, you'll win a lot of games."
—Ron Schock

Photos by George Gojkovich

Jean Pronovost
Still a class act

*"They realized I was giving
it my best shot,
and they respected that."*

Serenity. Sincerity. Thoughtfulness, Genuineness. Class. Those were a few of the words that came to mind when I considered my conversation with Jean Pronovost about the days when he played for the Penguins. Talking to Pronovost was such a distinct pleasure; I felt better for it. "I really enjoyed this," I said as I was set to hang up the telephone from my home in Pittsburgh. "So did I," replied Pronovost from his home in Terrasse Vaudreuil, Quebec, just outside of Montreal. And I knew he meant it.

Pronovost displayed such a different temperament, and self-effacing perspective than one finds in most people, certainly most professional athletes, and he reminded me of talking with Willie Stargell of the Pirates. His voice was soothing. He sounded like a man at peace with himself and an ever-changing and ever-challenging world. Ol' No. 19 was still a class act.

There was a real wisdom, a vision, a tone, a way of stating things, a philosophy by which we could all benefit if we listened carefully, and followed his lead. Pronovost felt that, at age 48, and away from playing for the Penguins for 16 years, he was better able to appreciate the specialness of what he had experienced. He looked back with bright eyes, and warm feeling in his heart.

I had the feeling that we had known each other for a long time. I knew all about Pronovost's distinguished career with the Penguins. I knew his numbers. But I followed him, for the most part, the same way I had just been talking to him — by long distance. It was easy to appreciate Pronovost just the same.

I met him and watched him play during his rookie season of 1968-69. It was a season in which he showed great promise with a poor team. That was the last season I edited and co-published a tabloid newspaper called *Pittsburgh Weekly Sports*, an energetic, often irreverent sheet we managed to hold together for nearly five years on a shoestring operation. We carried a headline story about Pronovost and John Arbour, two husky newcomers who had been obtained from the Boston Bruins before the Penguins' second season by General Manager Jack Riley. It was a deal that rated right up there with the purchase of Manhattan from the Indians for $24 worth of goods and trinkets.

Riley got them from Boston in exchange for the Penguins' No. 1 draft choice. "I'd make a deal like that every day," said Riley. Riley said it then, he repeats it now.

I left home in the summer of 1969 — and moved on to Miami for a year and New York for nine years, and by the time I got back to Pittsburgh — in the summer of 1979 — Pronovost had completed his ten-year stay with the Penguins, and had been dealt, by his own desire, to the Atlanta Flames. Remember the Atlanta Flames?

No one had a more productive decade in a Penguins' uniform than Jean Pronovost. Unless Mario Lemieux comes to mind.

Going into the 1994-95 season, Pronovost had played more games in a Penguins' uniform than any other player in the team's history. His 753 games is a record that could last through the ages. Rick Kehoe came closest with 722, Ron Stackhouse with 621 and Ron Schock with 619. Then Lemieux (599). In that regard, Pronovost is the Roberto Clemente of the Penguins. Clemente played one more game (2,433) than the legendary Honus Wagner, who held the record for games played as a Pirate for a long time.

Only Lemieux scored more goals (494) than Pronovost's 316. Only Lemieux (1,211) and Kehoe (636) scored more points than Pronovost (603). Few were more productive in a Penguins' uniform than Jean Pronovost. Then again, seeing Lemieux's totals for a similar ten-year span, and realizing he had missed a lot of games in recent seasons, makes one realize why Pronovost is prudent to avoid comparisons. Outside of Wayne Gretzky and Bobby Orr, there's no one like Lemieux.

But Pronovost was the best the Penguins had to offer before Lemieux showed up in 1984. Pronovost was the first Penguin to score 50 goals in a season. He led the team in goal-scoring five times and in points twice, and recorded 20 or more goals in nine of his ten seasons with the Penguins, while playing in over 70 games in eight of those ten seasons.

Jean joined former Penguins coach Bob Johnson and teammate Rick Kehoe as charter members of the Penguins' Hall of Fame. Kehoe and Pronovost participated in enshrinement ceremonies prior to a Penguins' game at the Civic Arena on October 22, 1992.

Pronovost rates the 1975-76 campaign as the personal highlight of his professional career. That was the season in which he had 52 goals and 52 assists.

His "most cherished moment" was when he assisted as a right wing on the winning goal against Sweden as Canada won the bronze medal in the World Cup in Prague, Czechoslovakia. His linemates, reported Pronovost, were Marcel Dionne of the Los Angeles Kings and Pat Hickey of the New York Rangers.

He also looks back with pride on the 1969-70 season in which the Penguins made it to the Western Division playoff finals before bowing to the St. Louis Blues. That was as close as the Penguins ever got to the Stanley Cup finals before the Lemieux-led team won it all in 1991 and 1992.

Connie Hawkins had played basketball for the Pittsburgh Pipers the year before Pronovost came to Pittsburgh. I told Pronovost that Hawkins had once told me, "I was Dr. J before Dr. J was Dr. J."

I suggested to Pronovost that, as far as Pittsburgh hockey fans were concerned, he was Mario Lemieux for the Penguins before Mario Lemieux was Mario Lemieux, or *Le Magnifique*.

Pronovost was polite in his wording, but he didn't buy into that at all. "In a sense, maybe," replied Pronovost. "But I can't be compared to Lemieux. I didn't have the same talent. I wouldn't want to compare myself to him. He's more of a natural goal-scorer. I was more of a hard worker.

"I remember when I first played at Pittsburgh, they used to flash a sign that said, JESUS SAVES — PRONOVOST ON THE REBOUND. It was appropriate. I got a lot of my goals on second shots, in scrambles, in traffic, the hard way. I never considered myself a 50-goal scorer. I could play hockey — I could play hockey with the best of them — but I was no Mario Lemieux. He's a superstar. If a guy like him had come along when I was playing that would have helped me."

Pronovost prides himself on putting things in their proper perspective. He has a deep faith in God that gives him added strength and an ability to see things differently than he did when he first came to Pittsburgh, an awkward, large-boned lad, a friendly French-Canadian kid coping with a new culture and trying to learn the English language, or at least the way Pittsburghers expressed themselves.

He played in Pittsburgh during a period in which the Pirates and Steelers were so successful, when the city became known nationally as "The City of Champions." When its citizens were thumping their chests to the world. Even Pitt won a national collegiate football championship (1976) during that span, and the kids from Lawrenceville cleaned up every year in the national marbles championship in Wildwood, New Jersey, and were winning international matches as well. Pittsburgher Bruno Sanmartino was the world's professional heavyweight wrestling champion. Pittsburghers like Joe Schmidt and John Unitas were inducted into the Pro Football Hall of Fame during that decade. But the Penguins were not part of the city's success. They were still outsiders, outcasts of sorts.

It gnawed at the competitive soul of players like Pronovost. The Penguins had some terrific players in those days, and they remain among the most popular athletes ever to perform in the area. They came close, but they were never consistent winners, and Pronovost decided it was time for a change of scenery because he couldn't see things changing for the better at the Civic Arena.

"It took me some time to adapt to the city of Pittsburgh," said Pronovost. "I reported to the team's training camp at Brantford, Ontario. Then I remember coming to Pittsburgh, being surprised by the cobblestone streets I saw everywhere. I remember checking in at the old William Penn Hotel. I had such a small room, a dimly-lit affair. I was a little disappointed. My dream was shaken up by this.

"But I tried to stay focused. I had made the National Hockey League; that was what was important. None of us were making much money. We had to rent places in those days, something we could get from September to April. It took a little adjustment. I was a French-

Penguins' scoring star Jean Pronovost is shadowed by masked goalie Chico Resch, above, and J.P. Parise (bottom) in memorable 1975 Stanley Cup playoff series with New York Islanders.

Photos by George Gojkovich

Canadian. I knew English enough to get around. But I was a stranger in a strange city.

"We grew fond of Pittsburgh. I played better and produced, and the fans recognized my contribution. I enjoyed some adulation. They realized I was giving it my best shot, and they respected that.

"That's the reason I wanted to win the Stanley Cup so bad. But the trend wasn't there. In the ten years I was there, we'd have a year in the playoffs and a year out, and a year in and a year out. There was no consistency.

"During my ten years there, there were five different coaches, three general managers and three different ownership groups. It's no wonder there was no consistency.

"Everyone knows you don't build a team from the ice up. You build from the front office down, from management down. I kinda asked to be traded. Baz (Bastien) said, 'No, we want to keep you.' Baz finally granted my wish, and sent me to Atlanta. I look back now and I think I made a mistake. Who knows? Life has many mysteries."

"She should win a medal for courage."
—Jean on his wife Diane

In preparation for doing this book, I sent questionnaires to many Penguins from the past. Some of them responded right away, some later on. Some required a second inquiry. Some simply ignored all communications. Some filled out the questionnaire in more detail than others, some in a sketchy manner. Some sent the photos I requested, the signatures I sought. None went about the task with more pride and interest than Jean Pronovost.

In response to my request for a recent family photo, perhaps a Christmas card, Pronovost took his family to a local photo studio and had a new family portrait taken. I believe it points up Pronovost's immense pride in his family.

He had been married to his wife Diane for 27 years. "She should win a medal for courage," Pronovost wrote in an updated biographical sketch he personally prepared for me.

He provided information about his four children. Eric, the oldest at 24, was a computer analyst and married to Nadia, a social worker and new mother, with Keegan Patrick, who was four months old at the time of our correspondence. So Jean Pronovost — how time passes when you're having fun — is a grandfather.

Martin, 22, is a university student and political science major. Sara, 13, "born in Cheverly, Maryland, U.S.A.," is a good pianist, as is Amy, 10, born in Montreal.

Pronovost was looking forward to his seventh season as the hockey coach at McGill University in Montreal. "I almost got a job coaching a junior team this past year, but I'm still at McGill, and it's great," he said.

Pronovost Family Album

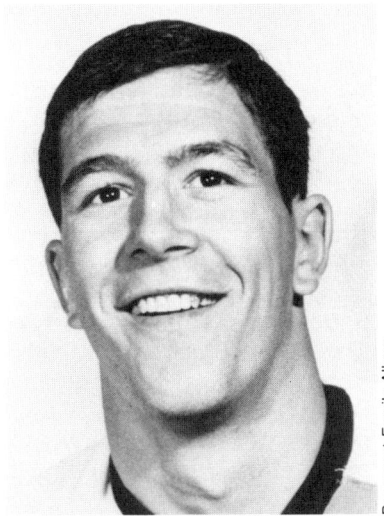

Jean Pronovost in playing days.

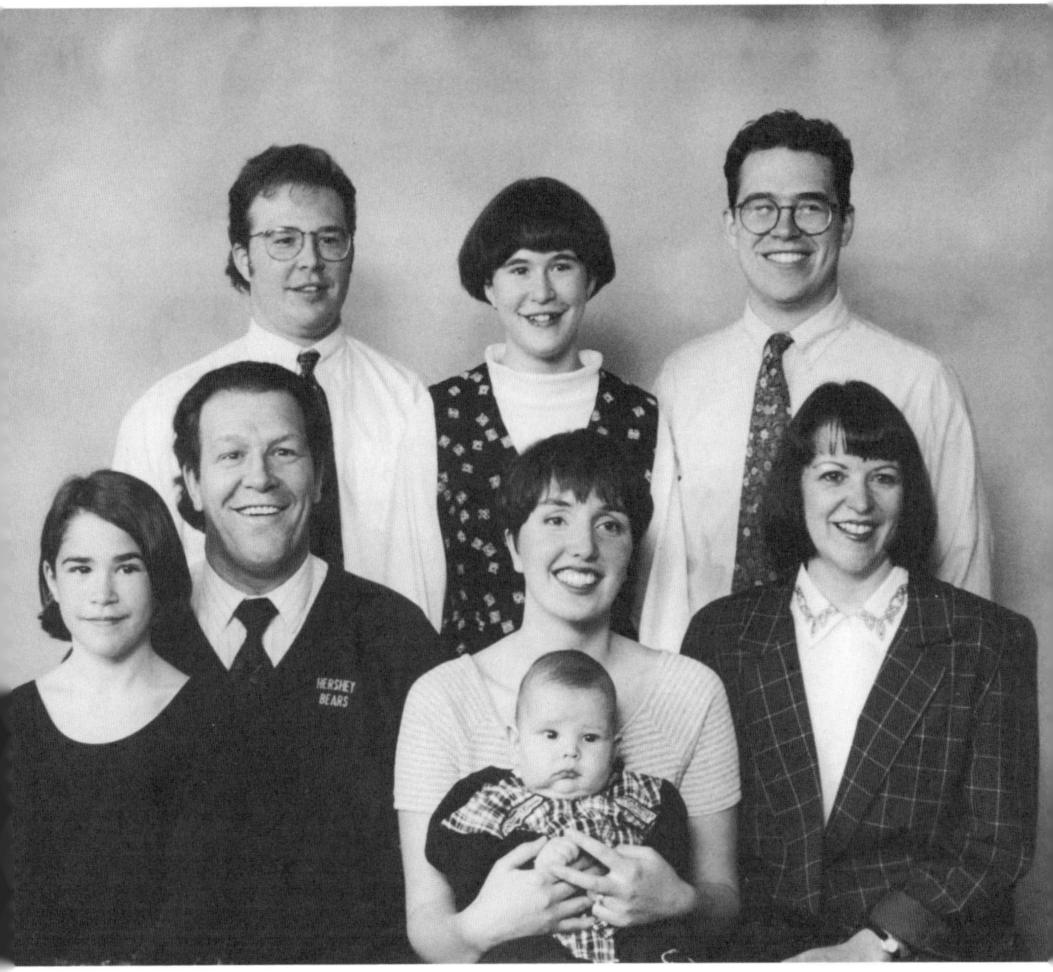

Jean Pronovost proudly shows off his family (left to right front row): daughters Amy and Nadia, holding her child, Keegan Patrick, and Jean's wife Diane, and (rear row) daughter Sara flanked by Martin, left, and Eric.

"It's a great university, very renowned. For the past six years, we've always had a better than .500 record. Last year we missed the playoffs for the first time. We're always competitive.

"You need good marks to get into McGill. It's like getting into Harvard or Princeton or Yale. I have to recruit, and that's difficult. Hockey is played most seriously outside the school system. High school hockey is not very popular. Most good players play in junior hockey. The ones who really want to make it in the NHL often go directly from high school to the junior ranks. This puts a lot of pressure on the kids. Their life is focused completely on hockey. It affects their academics quite a bit. They're just not as interested in school, the way they ought to be. If we catch them early, and get them focused on going to college, we can get some good ones. Many of the kids who want a pro career don't think about education. That's the unfortunate part of it. The kid who comes out of Harvard or Cornell or McGill has a good education to fall back on, too. It's very tough academically at McGill. So I don't know what I'm doing here."

> ### *"He looked like a little boy, and he was out there doing great things."*
> —Pronovost on Michel Briere

When Pronovost was discussing the difficulty the Penguins experienced in competing with the six established teams in the NHL in the year right after the league had expanded and doubled in size, he said, "Parity in the NHL wasn't there like it is now. Now you've got new teams like the Florida Panthers and San Jose Sharks holding their own with anyone. The Florida Panthers came in here to Montreal this year and won twice. The parity wasn't there when I was playing. They kept all the best players on the original six clubs.

"Our goal was to keep it close. We were satisfied if we could make it look good, lose by 2-1 or 4-2. That was an achievement in some places. They come in today and they think they can win."

I asked Pronovost to reflect on some of his teammates during his tour with the Penguins. Under the category of players he most admired from those days, he had listed Bryan Watson ("He came to play every night"), Syl Apps ("great playmaking ability") and Lowell MacDonald ("complete player"). Watson was the surprise for me. I knew him best as "Bugsy" Watson, a real character, and a rough-and-ready combative type who spent as much time in the penalty box as he did on the ice. Pronovost, Apps and MacDonald formed "The Century Line" — so labeled by Penguins' publicist Terry Schiffhauer — because they totaled 100 goals in a season.

On Bryan Watson: "Bryan had some great qualities," Pronovost said when I told him I was surprised to see Watson topping his personal list of players he admired the most. "He was definitely a team man.

He would do anything for the team. He wasn't the biggest guy, but he had a big heart. I liked his attitude. He was a player's player. He put the team first. He sacrificed his body to accomplish that. He was limited talent-wise, but he lasted because he was willing to pay the price."

On Syl Apps: "It was funny how we clicked so quickly, right from the first game. I didn't even know who Syl Apps was — I mean, I knew him as a player for the New York Rangers, and that was it — when we were put together on the same line. We just played well together. We 'read' each other well. When we added Lowell MacDonald, he was the stabilizer. Syl and I knew he'd be back and that we could take chances. It allowed Syl and I to go like gangbusters. Syl was so unselfish. Look at his assists (349, second in team history only to Lemieux's 717).

On Lowell MacDonald: "He is a gem as far as hockey is concerned. He was a very talented individual, a very bright man. Syl was not a dumb player, either, but MacDonald was especially smart. He was a team player, too. He would do what he had to do to make us a better line. He accepted his role. Some guys can't do that. Some won't do that. After all, they talk about the goal-scorers, not about the checkers. They pay the goal-scorers. But MacDonald did what our team needed him to do."

As far as favorite characters on the club are concerned, Pronovost pointed out two, Robin Burns, a leftwinger who played for the Penguins from 1970 through 1973, and Les Binkley, a goalie, the original Penguin, who played from 1967 to 1972.

On Robin Burns: "He's now the president of I-Tech, which makes hockey visors and net protectors, and other hockey-related items, that is based in Montreal. He's done quite well. He kept us loose. He was great for team morale. He always kept us in the right frame of mind."

On Les Binkley: "He was not your typical goaltender. It seemed like a goal didn't bother him. Other goalies, it bothers them. Goalies are a different breed. Goalies are like test pilots. They have a different image. They're thought of as flaky. It's a hard position, very lonesome. But Binkley was definitely one of the boys."

Of all the Penguins he played with, the one he will never forget was a teammate for only one season. That was Michel Briere, No. 21, who was badly injured in an auto accident following his rookie season with the Penguins and remained in a coma for 11 months before dying. Pronovost was a frequent visitor to Briere's bedside at a hospital in Montreal.

He was Briere's best friend on the team. They were the Penguins' only French-Canadians.

"He was a good guy," said Pronovost. "It was hard to know him, though, because he was quiet. He was proud. He had hockey on his mind and he worked hard to make the team. He looked like a kid, he looked like a little boy, and he was out there doing great things."

To show you the difference in times, Pronovost was working as a helper at a brewery in Montreal that same summer that he kept a vigil at Briere's bedside. He was unloading and loading beer trucks. It was a job just like Eddie Johnston had during the off-season when he was a pro hockey player.

"We will know what is going to happen when Michel wakes up," Pronovost said that summer. But Briere never did come out of that coma. He never did wake up. He died at the start of the next season.

"You have to remember where you come from."
—Jean Pronovost

I asked Pronovost what it had meant to him to be inducted into the Penguins Hall of Fame two years earlier. "What I have tried to do, what I always tried to do, was keep a good perspective about my situation," said Pronovost. "It's nice to be recognized, and nice to be famous, sort of. You have to remember where you come from. Sometimes, because of the adulation of the crowd, we forget we're people.

"I can't lose the fact that I'm a person. A problem with a lot of athletes is that they lose sight of their true importance. Or their lack of importance in the true scheme of things. Humanity gets lost in the shuffle. You have everyone telling you how great you are, and you begin to believe it.

"Being a pro hockey player, or a pro athlete, is a great time of your life. I played 16 years as a professional. That's such a short span, as far as a percentage of your total life. It's fun, it's gratifying, but it's not an end-all. You reap what you sow. You have to pay attention to the people around you. Then you won't lose sight of who you are.

"I didn't make a million dollars a year, far from it. Toward the end of my career, $100,000 a year was big money. Money has really changed the game. Worse yet, it has changed the players. I detect a different attitude about a lot of things. Too many of the players are too busy for everybody else. They think they're too important for the little people.

"I try to treat people the way I want to be treated, which is another way of stating the golden rule, I suppose. You'll only get back what you put in."

I pointed out to Pronovost that there was a Hall of Fame basketball coach at Pitt when I was a student there in the early '60s. His name was Doc Carlson, and he had been an All-American football player at Pitt as a student, a nationally-recognized basketball coach later on, and was the director of student health services during my student days. He used to talk to me about "blessed boomerangs," that if you tossed out good things, then good things would come back to you.

Pronovost approved of that message as well.

"Life is too short," said Pronovost. "You can't isolate yourself. The more money they make, the more they isolate themselves. It has become a real big business. I'm 48, and my view of life is not the same as it was when I was playing. But even at that age, I tried to treat people the way you wanted to be treated."

I asked Pronovost if he had benefited from the fact that one of his older brothers was a great hockey player. Marcel Pronovost was inducted into the Hockey Hall of Fame in 1978.

"Not a whole lot, because there was such a difference in my brother and I in age. We saw each other very little. The one thing he told me was 'don't lose sight of your importance.' That's the danger, and moreso now. Like Scott Stevens has signed a contract for $17 million. Nobody should make that kind of money. You're playing a sport you love to play, and you're not worth that much. Most players would play for a lot less, a lot less. It's a great life."

"I was always Jean Pronovost, Marcel's little brother."

Shawinigan Falls, Quebec was where Jean Pronovost came from. "It's a little town, of maybe 35,000 or 40,000 people, about 100 miles east of Montreal," said Pronovost. "We moved from there when I was about eight years old. I'm 11 of 12 children. I have eight brothers, and three sisters. I remember a river, the St. Maurice, where all of us kids used to swim. All that I recall is that it was a lot of fun. I remember vividly, when we were still in Shawinigan Falls, watching my brother Marcel on television. We didn't have a television ourselves at the time. We went to a neighbor's home and were looking through the window, watching their TV. They didn't even know we were there, at first. My brother was in the playoffs in Detroit. The family caught us and made us come inside and watch the game. Otherwise, we'd have been home listening to the game on the radio.

"You really didn't have to have a brother in the NHL to grow up and be a hockey player. Most Canadians think about hockey as a career at one time or another when they're young. It would be like the kids in the United States wanting to play football or baseball or basketball someday. It's natural. It might have helped that we watched Marcel play on television; that was a big thing. Maybe the only thing we had to do sometimes. I was always Jean Pronovost, Marcel's little brother. I took a lot of pride in my brother because there were only six teams then and everybody knew if he was playing in the NHL he had to be really good.

"We weren't really a hockey family, though. Only three of us boys played hockey. My brother, Marcel, of course, and my brother, Claude, who was a goaltender. I was never overly encouraged; by that I mean pushed to play hockey. I wasn't discouraged, either. I was on the ice every day after school.

"I never stopped to think I might not make it in hockey. Oh, I did a little construction work when I was young, and I worked at a bank once. But the thought of anything else besides hockey never entered my mind."

Did he realize most of the goals he set for himself as a hockey player?

"When you start out, I think you always have in the back of your mind that you would like to play with a Stanley Cup winner. You can break all the records you want, but the guys who win the Stanley Cup are the ones who get the real recognition. Winning the Stanley Cup was always in the back of my mind.

"One of my fondest memories of that period with the Penguins was when we went seven games in the series against the Islanders — even though we lost in a heart-breaker after being up three games to none. Scoring my 50th goal was a big thrill, but it didn't last very long. I thought it would mean more to me than it did. I guess I was a little disappointed because it happened and that was it and it didn't stay with me very long."

That was just one of the lessons Pronovost learned from his NHL experience, and one of the things he tries to pass along to his children and the young players at McGill University.

"Discipline and consistency and attitude are three major learning points," Pronovost said. "In those early expansion days, we lacked in all three departments. I have learned to focus more on those aspects.

"Also, the measure of success is not measured on how many awards you receive, but on the way you play the game."

Pronovost pointed out something that another Hall of Fame basketball coach, UCLA's John Wooden, once said, "If you truly do your best — and only you will know — you can consider yourself successful."

Summarizing his stay with the Penguins, Pronovost said, "In retrospect to my days in Pittsburgh, I can add that I have met and made many good friends, and the time invested in Pittsburgh has been a very positive experience and, even though I am away, I am there in spirit."

Lineup at Penguins' training camp at Rostraver Township in September, 1976, were (left to right) Bob "Battleship" Kelly, coach Ken Schinkel, Jean Pronovost, Pierre Larouche and Syl Apps.

Line changes began in Pittsburgh
New and surprising development
History was made in Oakland

Professional hockey prides itself on being the fastest sport in the major leagues.

Its fast pace is maintained because fresh combatants are constantly being sent into action, while their teammates skate off the ice to sit down on the bench for a while to catch their breath and give their weary ankles a rest.

Lineup changes on the run are unique in ice hockey, but it is intriguing to consider the possibilities in other sports. Imagine a running back coming off the sidelines and getting a handoff or pitch from a teammate who was tiring. It would be like a relay race in track.

Hockey did not always have personnel changes with such frequency, and in the so-called "old days," the game was for ironmen only, and the players paced themselves to conserve their energy. As the game wore on, the action dragged, just as it did in those old 25-round boxing bouts.

It was, interestingly enough, the original Pittsburgh professional hockey team that revolutionized the sport, way back in 1925, and gave the game much of the zip it sells itself on today.

Called the Pittsburgh Pirates, it was that club which originated the multiplicity of forward lines. In that era it was considered a passing freakish departure from custom.

In the first season of their brief National Hockey League existence, the Pittsburgh club began tossing on forward line replacements at a speed that is now normal, but then was bewildering.

For then the hockey fashion was a single forward line, with a couple of replacements, really utility men. Even the double forward line wasn't in complete existence. Group changes of players in the course of action were most infrequent.

The move was done in expediency, rather than as an experiment. The team was really an amateur team, in a broad sense of speaking. It had been playing its games in the shabby old Duquesne Gardens as a unit in the U.S. Amateur League, and was now stepping up into the fastest hockey league in the world.

The late J. Odi Cleghorn, a former scoring great with the Montreal Wanderers and Canadiens, was the playing-manager of that green Pittsburgh team. He had a good defense and some pretty fair forwards like Hib Milks, Harold Darragh, Duke McCurry, Tex White, Herbie Drury (a high-speed skater who raced around with his cap on backwards), Louis Belinsky, Alf Skinner, Jerry Lowery, Johnny McKinnon, Ty Arbour and Hal Cotton, according to yellowed newspapers of that era.

Odie felt that if he didn't have quality, he had quantity, and so hit upon the idea of three forward lines. Suddenly, the Pittsburgh bench was flooding the ice with forward lines at intervals of a couple of minutes.

It was a new and surprising development, but it wasn't long before the other teams adopted the idea, in some degree, and so developed the climb to hockey at its present sustained speed level.

Pittsburgh came into the National Hockey League in 1924-25, which made it a seven-team circuit. They had Roy Wolters in the nets, Lionel Conacher, Roger Smith and Jesse Spring on defense their first season. Very little was expected from this amateur group, but they surprised everyone by finishing third in a 36-game schedule. Five years later, however, their record dipped to five wins, three ties and 36 losses in a 44-game schedule. Conacher was inducted into the Hockey Hall of Fame in 1994.

One NHL record which was established at the Duquesne Gardens lasted until 1977 before it was broken. In a game between Toronto and the Pirates on November 19, 1929, Johnny McKinnon, a Pittsburgh defenseman, and Hap Day, a Maple Leaf defenseman, both scored four goals apiece in a game won by the Pirates, 10-5. Their mark is still in the record books today as one of the second-best efforts of goals scored in one game by an NHL defenseman. It is the record for most goals scored in a game by opposing defensemen.

It's something of a curiosity to learn in researching this story that Pittsburgh's professional hockey history dates back beyond that of Montreal. Around the turn of the century, Pittsburgh was in the professional International League. Teams were stocked with the cream of Canadien talent, and produced some of the roughest, toughest hockey in the history of the game. Some books even boast that Pittsburgh was the birthplace of professional hockey, just as it has a legitimate claim as the birthplace of professional football.

The Casino, located at the Forbes Avenue side of Schenley Park, near where the Frick Art Museum is located today, was the first indoor hockey rink in Pittsburgh. It opened in 1894. A four-team league, stocked with many of Canada's top players, was formed in 1902. The teams were called the Victorias, the Pittsburgh Athletic Association, the Bankers and the Keystones, and some of the players were paid for their services. So they are regarded as the first pro hockey teams.

"I don't know why I'm such a good fighter. Maybe it's because I punch harder than most guys."
—Bob "Battleship" Kelly

Hank Bassen

Joe Daley

"They're like a jury sitting on its hands waiting for something to happen."
—Jack Riley commenting on early Penguin fans

Bob Dillabough

George Konik

Red Sullivan
Retirement reflections

"All this losing eats you up."

Pittsburgh had a pretty bad sports year in 1968. All the teams in town were mediocre. Looking back on it now, I realize why I jumped at the chance in the spring of 1969 when I was offered a job to cover the Miami Dolphins for *The Miami News*. I had been editing and publishing a tabloid called *Pittsburgh Weekly Sports* for five years and doing daily sports commentaries on WEEP radio, and I was dealing with pretty dismal stuff. It was a good time to get out of town.

The Pirates were 80-82 and finished sixth in Larry Shepard's last full season as manager. The Steelers lost their last five games of the season to finish at 2-11-1 in Bill Austin's last season as coach. They would be 1-13 the next year under a new coach named Chuck Noll. The Pitt football team went 1-9 for the third straight year under Dave Hart, and Pitt bought out the final year of his contract.

Not a pretty picture, and the Penguins fit right into it. The Penguins were in the midst of their second season, and it was proving to be much worse than their debut effort. They won only two of their first 15 games, and even the squinty-eyed Red Sullivan could see the writing on the wall, or at least on the banners which were posted all over the Civic Arena. Back in those days there was room to put up banners and signs of all sorts — there wasn't a seat stuffed into every nook and cranny of the building — and fans were encouraged to express themselves with sign language.

One of the signs that was posted in late November of 1968 said simply SULLY MUST GO.

Sullivan said it didn't bother him. "Are you kidding?" he said. "No way. The only thing that bothers me is losing."

He said he was still confident in his club, and felt that things would get better. But he admitted, "All this losing eats you up."

They would finish with a record of 20-45-11.

Here's the best example of how pitiful the Penguins' situation was that winter.

Dave Hart brought his Pitt football team to a Penguins game near the tail end of his third consecutive 1-9 season. He had been a highly-successful high school coach in Johnstown when Jack Riley was running the minor league hockey franchise in that Cambria Country community. They became friends.

"I feel sorry for Jack," Hart told me one day when I was talking to him in his office at the Pitt Field House.

"Dave, how can you feel sorry for anyone?" I asked him in return.

My remark made Hart laugh. "Hell, we have to stick together," he said.

I told this story to Sullivan, and he had to smile. He was happy to have a reason to smile. "I know how they all feel," said Sullivan. "Hart, Austin and Larry Shepard last summer. You can't even be civil with anybody, and nobody can be civil with you."

Sullivan was a tough cookie. He was also a survivor. He had been speared in the gut and nearly killed seven years earlier by Doug Harvey, a Hall of Fame defenseman for the Montreal Canadiens, and came back from that.

George "Red" Sullivan was never a superstar during his nine-year NHL career. He played for Boston, Chicago and New York. He was a second line or third line center. But nobody messed with Red Sullivan. He was a battler. He was once described as "fiery and tough, just the kind of man we need," by Rangers' general manager Emile Francis when he hired him to coach the Rangers. Two years later, when the Rangers were mired as deep as ever in the muck of the NHL's lower echelon, Sullivan was fired.

Francis took over as coach and sent Sullivan out scouting talent all over Canada for a year. Sullivan was always given another job. Everybody in hockey liked him.

Expansion in 1967 gave him another opportunity to be a coach in the NHL. But the same thing happened to him after two seasons in Pittsburgh. He was fired once again. He and Riley remained good friends through the years, however, and have kept in touch on a regular basis. "If you see Jack Riley," said Sullivan, "please give him my best."

Sullivan retired for good following the 1992-93 season after serving as a scout for the Philadelphia Flyers, and resides with his wife, Marion, in Indian River, Ontario.

Sullivan said the highlights of his career in Pittsburgh were being hired by Riley as the first coach of the Penguins and the opening game at home against the Montreal Canadiens in 1967. That tells you all you need to know about the performance by the Penguins in his two-season stay.

His most cherished memories of his playing days were "When I was named captain of the New York Rangers and playing in my first All-Star Game, plus the relationships I still have with my teammates."

He counts his blessings. He is still married to Marion, and they have four children, Dan, 43 years old at the time, Jane, 40, Suzanne, 36, and Kate, 32.

The two players on the Penguins he admired the most were Les Binkley and Andy Bathgate. "Bink played great in goal and Andy led our team in scoring."

His favorite character on the club was young defenseman Billy Speer: "He was a barber by trade and gave us all free haircuts," said Sullivan.

What he learned from his experience with the expansion Penguins: "You must have patience and work closely with your general manager."

Looking back on his brief Pittsburgh experience, Sullivan says, "My wife Marion and our family really enjoyed our stay in Pittsburgh. The city is great and the owners at the time were very supportive.

"I grew up in Peterborough, Ontario, Canada and being a Canadian kid I played hockey at an early age and loved it and I said to myself, 'I want to play hockey for a living.'"

Red was the youngest of eight children. His dad died when he was 12. His mother, Regina, a dedicated card and bingo player (much like Eddie Johnston's mother), never saw Red play in a pro hockey game. "She was afraid I'd get hurt," said Sullivan.

"I turned pro with Boston in 1949 and was connected with the NHL until 1993, as a player, coach and scout and enjoyed every minute of it.

"We have 12 grandkids and I feel at this time we have five or six potential hockey players."

Sullivan Family Album

Sullivan clan includes (left to right) son Dan and daughters Suzanne, Jane and Kate. Among them they have 12 children.

Sullivan as Rangers captain ...

... and as Penguins coach

Tom "Scoop" Saulsbury
He always knew the score

"I was just happy being around hockey people."

Tom "Scoop" Saulsbury was a big part of the professional hockey scene in Pittsburgh for a long period, going back to the Hornets at Duquesne Gardens and at the Civic Arena, and continuing through with the Penguins.

Scoop always seemed to be there, hanging around the front office, running errands or doing favors for Baz Bastien or Joe Gordon, going out to pick up the paper, to the airport to pick up a player, or somewhere to pick up a Christmas tree for the team's holiday party. He was even Santa Claus because he was well-suited for the role, and he was the sort of fellow who would do anything for the cause.

He was heavy-set, heavy-jowled, a jolly sort. He wore eyeglasses and there was always a glint in his eyes. He loved to talk. Chatter would be more like it. He could get along with just about anybody, well almost anybody. He mentions a few Penguin front-office types he was at odds with through the years, which helped prompt his resignation as a minor official in 1982 after he'd had a bad night. That and failing vision. He had started wearing bifocals, and it caused him to blow a call as a goal judge at the Arena one night. Scoop said he lost sight of the puck when he looked down into the reading part of his eyeglasses. One club official in particular gave him such a rough time about his mistake that Scoop thought it was best he just say goodbye.

Jack Riley, for the record, was not one of those front-office types. Scoop still reveres Riley, the original GM of the Penguins, who has remained on the Arena scene in some capacity or another ever since. "He was the best," Scoop said.

Scoop no longer frequents the Arena, he's not fond of the current cast of players — "they're too busy for everybody," he snarled — but he watches every televised game the Penguins play, and listens to radio broadcasts every chance he gets. He is still a fan, only in a different way.

He loved hockey. He loved the Hornets. He loved the Penguins. When he was in seventh grade, he showed up at Duquesne Gardens and made himself useful, helping out in the clubhouse, doing anything to assist anyone who asked.

He began to help out in earnest in 1952 at Duquesne Gardens. He served as a stickboy and assistant trainer. Back then he lived in Swisshelm Park, at the eastern end of town, and was graduated in 1946 from Taylor Allderdice High School, where he had been the manager for the football team.

Personal service was something he just did naturally. He liked looking after the needs of other people.

"I was just happy being around hockey people," he recalled. "I became friends with all the players. I got to know Baz. Baz took a liking to me. I was always there."

He was in the insurance business, at least that's what it said on his business card. He was an insurance adjustor. Exactly when he worked was hard to determine.

I remembered him as a restless sort, always in motion, constantly pacing, wearing out the carpet while talking on the telephone, speaking in a machine-gun manner, smiling and laughing easily, and enjoying the hell out of himself. He could never stand still; he was an animated individual.

He served as an assistant clubhouse boy, an assistant trainer, a practice goalie, radio announcer, a game statistician, goal judge, timekeeper, and, at his peak, supervisor of minor officials for NHL games at the Civic Arena. He and the late Frank Tyson and Bob Ferons worked together as off-the-ice game officials for many years

He was paid for his work only during one period, during a short span when Tad Potter operated the Penguins, getting $10 a game, and he's not certain whether or not it was his paycheck that caused the club to declare bankruptcy, the first post-war failure of a franchise in the NHL.

Scoop even showed me a copy of the bankruptcy filing, and another document that showed that one of the team's stars, Syl Apps, was making $125,000 a year from the Penguins during the 1975-76 season. That was $125,000 more than Scoop's salary. The team was sold for $3.8 million that year.

"DeBartolo never paid us a dime," he said, speaking about former club bankroller Edward J. DeBartolo. "We got a pair of tickets and a parking space, and that was it. The ushers back then were making $25 a game, and we were getting nothing. And we were making decisions that helped determine the outcome of the contest."

Then again, Scoop was never in it for the money.

He showed me a copy of *Sports Illustrated*, in which he appeared in the background, working as a goal judge, of a photograph of an NHL Stanley Cup playoff contest between the Philadelphia Flyers and the New York Islanders. Scoop always had the best seat in the house.

At the time of my visit to his home, in late July of 1994, Scoop was 66, retired for four years from Kemper Insurance Co., where he had worked for 14 1/2 of the 34 years he was in the insurance business. He wasn't feeling too well. He was more antsy than ever, and his hands were shaking as he showed me photographs and press clippings, and game programs he had stored in a box. He had Hornets and Penguins programs, and paraphernalia, and each evoked a story from Scoop.

He spoke in a stream-of-conscious manner, jumping here and there. It only added to his confusion and mine. He was scheduled to see a doctor to get checked over later that afternoon. Two days earlier, he had had a lapse of memory, suffered dizzy spells, cold sweats, high blood pressure and perhaps a mini-stroke. Doctors wanted him to check in at a local hospital, but he chose not to. He had a dinner date with two priests, which he felt compelled to honor — "I promised them a good meal, and I didn't want to disappoint them," he said — and he called me to make sure I was coming. He asked me to come earlier in the morning, so he could go to the doctor later in the day.

He was eager to see me as well, though I was willing to postpone our meeting if he wasn't feeling so good. His wife, Arlene, whom he had married when he was 44, made a nice lunch for us, grilled ham and cheese sandwiches, with plenty of pickles, iced tea, ice cream. Scoop, whom I knew to always enjoy a good meal, only ate half his portion. That was a sure-fire tip-off that he wasn't up to snuff. Arlene was concerned about her husband and her mother, who lived just up the street in West Mifflin, in a hilltop area that overlooks Kennywood Park. Both were in poor health.

Scoop profusely apologized for not being himself.

Arlene and Scoop went to mass that morning at a nearby church. Officially, Scoop is still a member of St. Anselm's in Swissvale, near his former home on 120 Whipple Street where he lived for nearly 50 years. Scoop goes to mass every morning. He has his pick of St. Rita's in Whitaker, which has a 7:30 a.m. mass, or Resurrection in Homeville, which has an 8:30 a.m. mass, or St. Theresa's in Homestead Park, which has an 11 a.m. mass. It all depends on when Scoop gets up and gets going each day. Arlene accompanies him whenever possible.

Scoop would have gotten along beautifully with Art Rooney, the Steelers' owner, who was also a daily communicant, and liked to keep company with priests. Plus, Rooney was a hockey fan.

"It was heaven for a hockey fan."
—Scoop Saulsbury

Scoop seemed to brighten up when he recalled his hockey history, when he harkened back to better days, the best days of his life. "I used to plan my vacation every year so that it fell at the same time as the hockey team's summer training camp, and that's where I'd spend my vacation," he said. "It was the greatest vacation in the world."

He reflected on those so-called vacations, when he'd accompany the Hornets to their summer training camp at Niagara Falls. "We used to stay at the Foxhead Hotel, and there'd be three or four other teams staying in the same place, like the Hershey Bears and the New York Rangers. I'd eat with the team, and make myself useful.

"That's when there were only six teams in the National Hockey League, and they'd all practice, as did their top minor league clubs, in a 50-mile radius of Niagara Falls. I remember players like George Armstrong, Gordie Howe, Sid Smith, Tim Horton, Andy Bathgate, Rocket Richard, Jean Beliveau, guys like that. We were a farm team of the Toronto Maple Leafs back then.

"The teams would have scrimmages against each other. There was a game somewhere in the vicinity every night of the week. It was heaven for a hockey fan.

"I never missed training camp until 12 years ago. I went to training camp with the Hornets every year from 1952 to 1956. Then we didn't have a team for five years, until they opened the Civic Arena. I still went up. I stayed with Hershey. Baz Bastien and Frank Mathers headed up that team. Mathers was a real favorite of mine. Up until Mario Lemieux came here, I felt that Frank Mathers was the finest player ever to perform for a Pittsburgh hockey team."

This prompted Scoop to tell me his all-time Hornets team. It included Willie Marshall, Bob Hassard, Bobby Solinger, Les Duff, Sid Smith and Willie Marshall as forwards, Gil Mayer and Baz Bastien as goalies. He had Frank Mathers and Bill Juzda on the backline. I had never heard of Juzda. "He was built like a fireplug," said Scoop. "He met you at the blue line and defied you to go by him."

After the Hornets were folded when Duquesne Gardens was leveled to make room for an apartment complex in Oakland, many of the players ended up in Hershey. And do did Scoop, from time to time. "Hershey was a great town; the players loved to play there," said Scoop. "It was a storybook community. It took about four hours to get there in those days, when the turnpike wasn't what it is today. They won some AHL titles there, too."

I asked Scoop if he was aware that Hershey Gardens was modeled after Maple Leaf Gardens in Toronto, with the seats set up in a steep incline. He didn't. I mentioned that was where Wilt Chamberlain set an NBA one-game scoring record by pouring in 100 points there one night (March 2, 1962) against the New York Knicks. "I don't know anything about basketball; that's not my game," said Scoop.

"Everybody knew everybody there."
—Reflection on Duquesne Gardens

He remembers Duquesne Gardens fondly. He remembers it was next-door to St. Paul's Cathedral. "I'd stop in the church before every game and say a prayer," said Scoop. To him, the Duquesne Gardens was a holy place as well. He said a few prayers there, too.

"Everybody knew everybody there," he said.

He went and watched as they lowered the boom on the building. "I cried like a baby when they knocked it down," he recalled. "It was a sad day in this town, that's for sure."

My buddies back in Hazelwood always called me "Scoops," because I was the sports editor of the local bi-weekly newspaper. Even today, I can be in some distant city, and hear someone screaming out "Scoops," and I know I'm being tailed by one of the boys of long-ago summers.

I asked Scoop about his nickname. Scoop came by his name when he was a student at the Pittsburgh Institute of Mortuary Science near Magee Womens Hospital on Forbes Avenue in Oakland. He remembered doing an apprenticeship at the O'Toole & O'Connor Funeral Home in Hazelwood, and we started talking about Steve O'Toole and his son-in-law John O'Connor, who operated that mortuary. Their front doors were lined up directly across Second Avenue from St. Stephen's Church, and many a Hazelwooder made the direct trip.

"I was the editor of a monthly newspaper we had at the Mortuary Institute," explained Scoop. "It was called 'The Merry Mort.' I had a gossip column that put Dorothy Kilgallen to shame. It was called 'Peekin' in the Coffin.' Because I was writing a newspaper column, the guys started calling me Scoop."

Before that, he had been called "Digger" for obvious reasons. So Scoop wasn't so bad, by comparison.

"With guys who lived in my house, I could put together a better team than what they have now.'

The home he shared with his mother for so many years was always a refuge for Hornets and Penguins looking for a place to stay. Scoop recalled babysitting for Mark Messier — star performer for the New York Rangers when they won the Stanley Cup in 1994 — when he was an infant and his father, Doug Messier, was playing for the Hornets in the second year the team played at the Civic Arena.

"I often would hunt up a house or an apartment for a new hockey player in town," said Scoop. "That's another role I performed in those days. Back then, I could get a two-bedroom apartment for someone for $125 a month. People would go to Florida for the winter, and would let me rent out their homes. I lined up a lot of guys at the Baldwin Apartments. They rented furniture as well as the apartment.

"Val Fonteyne lived with me for awhile. Some stayed a night, some stayed a weekend, some stayed a few weeks or months. Some stayed a whole season. My home was always open to them. I could put a team together of guys who stayed in my home that would be better than what they have now."

With little prompting, Scoop came up with his all-time team, restricted to guys who called his home their home during their stay with the Penguins.

His goalies would be Al Smith and Les Binkley. His defensemen would include Sheldon Kannegiesser and Jimmy Morrison. His centers would be Earl Ingarfield, Syl Apps, Wally Boyer and Rick Kessell. "My wings would be Fonteyne, Dean Prentice, Nick Harbaruk and Ken Schinkel."

Scoop still stays in touch with Fonteyne, Morrison and another former Penguin favorite, Ron Schock. "Schock and I talk to each other every year at Christmas time," said Scoop.

His all-time owner would not be John Harris. Harris owned the Hornets when they were at Duquesne Gardens and again when they were at the Arena. I recalled visiting his office once and thinking the place was strange looking, with a weird color scheme. He appeared dressed like a homeless person, rather than a rich man.

"Everyone was scared to death of him," recalled Scoop. "He was a strange man. He was such a damn slave driver. Bill Torrey, who ended up as the president and general manager of the New York Islanders when they won the four Stanley Cups, got his start under Harris. Harris would call Torrey at three in the morning and say, 'I want some apples. Go out and get me some apples.' He married skating star Donna Atwood and built the Ice Capades around her. That started out with girls skating between periods of the hockey games at the Gardens, and then he created a full-fledged ice show."

"Hockey and big bands were my two hobbies, my two passions."

How did he get hooked on hockey?

"I started going to games when I was in grade school. I could get a ticket for 65 cents at the Garden, and you'd be sitting right behind the goal — the best seat in the house.

"Hockey and big bands were my two hobbies, my two passions. And I still enjoy both. Every Saturday morning, I'd go Downtown to the Stanley Theatre. They had big bands come in for a week, somebody like Brad Hunt and his band. We're talking about 1940-41, when we were in World War II.

"You might not believe this, but talk to your mother about it. I'd haul ashes on Saturday morning for the neighbors, cleaning out their home furnaces for a nickel a bucket. I'd do that until I could get a dollar.

"Then I'd take the streetcar Downtown. I'd get three carchecks for a quarter. I'd go to the White Tower and buy eight hamburgers for a nickel apiece. If you got to the theatre before 12, it cost only 25 cents. I'd have ten cents left over, which I'd use to buy two Cokes.

"It sounds unbelievable, but I could ride the streetcar to and from town, get eight hamburgers and two Cokes, and get into the theatre, all for a dollar. All I needed to make my day was a dollar. I'd see and hear the band, see a stage show, stay and watch the movies, then check out the band again. Afterward, I would get autographs from everybody in the band."

Then Scoop showed me some materials from a cruiseship tour that featured a "big band" theme that he and Arlene enjoyed earlier in the year. There were four bands aboard the ship, with two of them entertaining each evening. They included the bands of Jimmy Dorsey, Les Elgart, Warren Covington and Ray Anthony. Scoop showed me a quiz about big bands which he had filled in, and told he was so proud that he had the third highest score of all the people on the ship. His program had the autographs of all the band leaders scrawled on it. There were personal inscriptions to him.

Taking her cue perhaps from her husband, Arlene advanced to the table and produced an autograph book, and some scraps of paper, which contained the autographs of some pretty famous Pirates of the past.

She showed me the autographs she acquired as a young fan, shadowing her dad to Forbes Field in the '50s. She had the signatures of Honus Wagner — "I'm told that's worth about $250," she said — Kirby Higbe, Cliff Chambers, Rip Sewell, Clyde McCullough, Ed Fitz Gerald, Ralph Kiner and Monty Basgall. She showed me ones she obtained just the year before — from Bill Mazeroski and Ralph Terry — the hero and goat, respectively, of the 1960 World Series between the Pirates and Yankees.

"My dad taught me how to keep score properly at a baseball game," she said. It might have been destiny that she ended up with Scoop, a scorekeeper for the ages. "We're both sports fans," she said. "We enjoy our sports."

Photos from Saulsbury Collection

Tom "Scoop" Saulsbury joins Don McKenney at Penguins party in 1967, and children of Penguins players, like Lowell and Lane MacDonald, at far left, when he dressed as Santa Claus for team's holiday party.

"It's more fun winning than losing."

Doug Harvey was one of the greatest defensemen ever to play in the National Hockey League, starring for a string of Stanley Cup championship teams in Montreal. He is in the Hockey Hall of Fame. He joined the Pittsburgh Hornets for a brief spell in their final Calder Cup championship season of 1966-67, and I remember having the pleasure of taking him out to lunch and interviewing him.

"There's no use playing this game if you're not trying to win," said Harvey. "For one thing, it's more fun winning than losing. You should never say tomorrow we'll be all right if you lose a game or two, because the first thing you know the season's over and it's too late. With Canadiens, we always concentrate on tonight's game. The boys are pretty well known in Montreal. Anytime they lose a game, even on the road, people on the street want to know what the hell happened — in two languages. It's the same all summer: you can have a pretty good summer when you win in the spring."

Doug Harvey

Hall of Famers
They played for Pittsburgh

"It's tough to give it up."
—Don McKenney

It was a transition year. Pittsburgh was giving up a championship team in the Pittsburgh Hornets of the American Hockey League, and taking on a new team in the National Hockey League called the Pittsburgh Penguins. On the one hand, it was tough to let go of the familiar, and die-hard fans struggled with that one. But the AHL was a minor league. The Penguins would be playing in the NHL — the big leagues, at last. It was the major leagues and, hey, Pittsburgh was a big-time, major league city.

It was 1967. Some great players represented Pittsburgh that year, helped popularize the sport, and lent class to the professional hockey scene in Pittsburgh.

They were Doug Harvey, who played for the Hornets in their last season, Leo Boivin, who played for the Hornets during their days at Duquesne Gardens, and Andy Bathgate, who had been one of the NHL's biggest scorers and played for the Hornets in their final season. Both Boivin and Bathgate were members of the Penguins' first team in 1967.

Harvey, Boivin and Bathgate are all in the Hockey Hall of Fame. They didn't get there for what they did while wearing a Pittsburgh uniform, but it was nice to know that players of that caliber suited up for the home team at the Civic Arena once upon a time. For the record, Tim Horton, a classy defenseman who played for the Hornets at Duquesne Gardens and for the Penguins during the 1971-72 season, is the only other former Penguin who has been inducted into the Hockey Hall of Fame.

"He's been good for our hockey team."
—Baz Bastien

Doug Harvey was a great hockey player for more than a decade with the Montreal Canadiens, and would play for the New York Rangers, the Detroit Red Wings and the St. Louis Blues toward the end of his 20-year NHL career.

It was while he was with the Wings that Harvey was farmed out to Pittsburgh for part of the 1967-68 schedule. In Montreal, he was an icon. There he was loved and admired, and recognized by everyone in the streets. In Pittsburgh, he was a forgotten old man.

Harvey was the fifth defenseman in the Hornets' line-up. He was paired with Doug Barrie, who was born the same year (1947) that Harvey first established himself with the Canadiens. There are two defensemen in a game at one time, and usually two lines alternate, and the third gets spot duty. That meant Harvey was playing about ten minutes out of 60. He turned 43 in December of that 1966-67 season with the Hornets, making him the second oldest professional hockey player, behind goalie Johnny Bower of the Toronto Maple Leafs, who was two months older.

I caught up with Harvey one day as he was kicking around the lobby of the old Roosevelt Hotel, wondering what the hell to do with himself. That's when the Roosevelt housed the business offices of the Pittsburgh Steelers.

Baz Bastien, the general manager of the Hornets, had referred to Harvey as "a nice chap," and said this of him, "Nothing seems to bother him. My feeling was that we went pretty well with the other four guys to win the championship. But when we call on him, he's ready. He's been good for our hockey club."

Bastien said Harvey had put on some weight, and that he had slowed down considerably. "It's the legs that go," said Bastien. "Every time he takes the puck and goes four or five steps he passes beautifully. But if he's standing still and they take it off him, he can't recover."

Harvey said you have to play to remain sharp, while admitting that he had put on a few pounds because he wasn't playing regularly. "I lose six pounds out there a night, if I'm playing," explained Harvey.

"I have to be fair," he went on. "Baz took me and I try to do my best and be ready. It's difficult, but I do all I can to win. I've had my years."

That he did. Harvey was first-team All-NHL defenseman for nine of ten years, and he was the only unanimous choice of the voters in 1957-58. He was named the greatest defenseman — winner of the James Norris Trophy — four straight years and seven of eight years through 1962.

He succeeded the great Maurice Richard as captain of the Canadiens and played in 14 Stanley Cup playoffs. Only three men had played in more at that time, namely Richard, Gordie Howe and Ted Lindsay. He was 12th in scoring in Stanley Cup history with 68 points in 129 games with eight goals and 60 assists. Only three men had more assists at the time and they were all on attacking front lines. He once had three assists in one period against Boston in 1957.

"He's the best I've ever seen," said Toe Blake, his coach with the Canadiens.

Ab McDonald, a Pittsburgh favorite who was with Montreal when they won the Stanley Cup in 1960, and was a member of the Hornets' AHL champions in 1967, said of Harvey, "He was something to watch. The best by far. He ran the game everytime he was out there. Montreal had one of the greatest power plays in the game. When the other team got a penalty and was short-handed, Montreal scored. And it was Harvey who started the play."

Don McKenney, another Hornet in that final season, had been to the big dance, too. He was with the Toronto Maple Leafs when they won the Stanley Cup in 1964.

"He was the greatest that ever lived," McKenney commented when he heard Harvey's name mentioned in a question. "He could do everything. It seems a little silly to be playing hockey when you're almost 43-years-old, but if that's what you've done for 30 years it's tough to give it up. He just enjoys the game."

Harvey didn't enjoy sitting on the bench, though. He had always been a fun guy, and liked a good laugh. Team joker. But his heart wasn't in it. And he didn't enjoy living in a hotel by himself. He didn't like being a loner, either. The problem, as McKenney explained it: "All the single guys on the teams are kids. The older guys have their families here."

Doug's wife and their six children were in Montreal.

He had been doing a heckuva job as a player-coach with the New York Rangers a few years earlier, but couldn't stand the player-coach relationship. One of his players was Andy Bathgate.

"He wanted to be one of the boys," one teammate said. "That's what killed him."

Harvey gave me his best hang-dog look, and allowed, "I've always been one of the gang. Sort of difficult for me hanging around a hotel."

"It's like being hit by a freight train."
—Doug Mohns

Leo Boivin was often described as a fireplug defenseman in the NHL. The brawny Boivin said that timing was the key to a crunching check. And Red Sullivan, his coach on the Penguins, loved guys who could check the opposition.

He was 5-7, 190 pounds — if you can picture that — and you knew it when he hit you. He looked as tough as they come. So it was difficult to picture Boivin as a homesick young man back in September, 1951, when he walked out of a Maple Leafs' training camp, calling it quits in favor of a job back home as a carpenter's apprentice.

Boivin left St. Catherine's and went home to Prescott in order to be near his boyhood sweetheart, who became Mrs. Boivin.

Conn Smythe, the boss of the Toronto club, got Harold Cotton, Boston's chief scout and the man who found Boivin playing hockey on one of Prescott's ponds, to go to Boivin's home and talk him into coming back.

Smythe didn't want to lose Boivin, a natural body-checker, who made forwards keep their heads up at all times. He became quite popular with the fans at Maple Leaf Gardens as he battered opposing attackers. Boivin had them crossing the Toronto blue line as if they were skating on eggshells. He was for real and a throwback to the days when defensemen disregarded the puck in favor of battering the forward.

He was with the Leafs for two seasons and part of a third under manager Hap Day and coach King Clancy. Sidelined by a shoulder injury, Boivin was due to return to the Leafs lineup when Smythe decided to lend him to Boston for a season, back when such things were done in the NHL.

The Bruins franchise was in trouble then, and Smythe was trying to return a favor. Boivin became such a favorite in Boston that the late Walter Brown, who was the Bruins' club president as well as the founder of the Celtics, wrote Smythe telling him it would do hockey irreparable damage if the Leafs recalled Boivin.

He put in most of the next 12 seasons with the Bruins before being dealt to Detroit for Gary Doak and Bill Lesuk with 16 games left in the 1965-66 campaign. Leo played 12 playoff games with the Wings that spring.

Detroit kept him one more season and then let him go in the NHL's expansion draft. He was still an intimidating brute. He seldom got the stick, elbow or knee in his checks, taking the opposing player cleanly with the hip and shoulder.

"You better keep your head up at all times when that Boivin is cruising the blue line," said Doug Mohns of the Chicago Black Hawks. "When he sticks a shoulder in your middle it's like being hit by a freight train."

> ### *"When Bathgate is on, there isn't a better player in the league."*
> —Gordie Howe

Up in Canada, where hockey was born, they called him Mr. Stickman. The magician of the hockey stick. He and Gordie Howe were the best right wingers in hockey. Andy Bathgate was his name. He was known as a superb technician. No one more put more oomph on a shot. "Bathgate had the hardest shot in the league," said Montreal's Jacques Plante, hockey's best goalie at the time. "I once lost an 80-foot blast by him. Wow, what a blast!"

Bathgate was the best show on Broadway at one time, when he was the leading scorer of the New York Rangers and the MVP of the NHL. He commanded a high salary. He won the Hart Trophy in 1959 as his team's MVP and had been the runner-up for the award the year before. He was twice the runner-up for the Art Ross Trophy that goes to the top point-getter in the league, finishing behind Chicago's Bobby Hull in 1962 and Detroit's Gordie Howe in 1963.

"When Bathgate is on, there isn't a better player in the league," said Howe.

The other big men in the league, superstars like Maurice Richard and Bernie "Boom Boom" Geoffrion, envied his ease of movement. "He doesn't even have to pay attention to what his feet are doing," raved Richard. To which Geoffrion added, "I have to work harder — push myself — to get where I want to go."

That was Andrew James Bathgate. In 1959, at the age of 26, Bathgate hit the jackpot. He scored 40 goals, the highest total in Ranger history, and he added 48 assists for 88 points. The 6-foot, 175-pound speedster beat out Howe for the right wing position on the all-star team and won the league's MVP award.

How did Bathgate end up playing for the Penguins late in his pro career? He was 35 at the time, and had played 13 seasons in the NHL. He had scored 314 goals. When the Penguins came to their 17th draft pick, Red Sullivan couldn't stand to see his former teammate's name still on the board. He had to take the chance.

"I can't help but think there's still some good hockey left in Andy," said Sullivan. "I think he can still score the goals."

How did Bathgate end up playing for the Hornets in the American Hockey League?

Bathgate was playing for the Detroit Red Wings by then, and things weren't going well for him or the Wings. Gordie Howe wasn't scoring like Gordie Howe. Neither was Alex DelVecchio playing like Alex DelVecchio. And the shots weren't going into the net for Andy Bathgate.

"We're paying him to be a goal-getter," said Sid Abel, Detroit's general manager, "and he's not getting any goals." The Red Wings were in last place when they dispatched Bathgate to their top farm team in Pittsburgh.

Bathgate, Ab McDonald and Bob McCord all came together from Detroit to Pittsburgh. Bathgate set up two goals his first night at the Civic Arena and the Hornets beat Springfield, 5-1. That was November 30. The Hornets promptly went on an eight-game winning streak.

"They want me to be shooting," Bathgate said. "But I've always had a lot of assists. When I had 40 goals that year, I had 48 assists. If I'm not playing good enough for them, well, that's all right. The team comes first. If I came down here and thought I was better than the other guys it wouldn't be good for the team. The only fun is in winning. I'm satisfied if I'm playing and doing well."

You looked at Bathgate sitting there, in street clothes in the front office of the Penguins, and you remembered reading about him in *SPORT* magazine when you were 16 and he was the Big Man on Broadway. It was a funny feeling like the first time you saw Mickey Mantle up close in the Yankees' clubhouse.

Andy Bathgate had dark hair, blue eyes, a bold, straight nose and a firm mouth housing a set of even white teeth, the upper half of which were the finest money can buy and were left in a paper cup in the locker room when he went out to play. "In Canada," he would tell you, "you're not a hockey player until you've lost some teeth."

And you recalled the night Bathgate was playing against Providence in the Civic Arena. And how you wanted to punch the loudmouth sitting a few seats away, who heckled Bathgate the first two periods. "Get the Geritol line in there, Baz!" he'd holler, smiling at his date because he thought he was so damn clever. "C'mon, Pro. Show us something."

And everything down on the ice was going bad for Bathgate. "When you get off to a bad start," said Gordie Howe, "everyone starts fighting it, fighting the puck like crazy." Bathgate had bad memories of those nights. "Everything I did was wrong," he said a week later. "I had the puck under my skates half the time. People expect you to do so much. Some of the fans come to be heard and noticed. It's tough getting used to the tempo and rhythm down here. Even Bobby Hull would have trouble adjusting to this league.

"These people just don't know the difference there is in the National Hockey League. I'm used to the other league where you could break fast. The movement and passing isn't the same here."

In the third period, Bathgate was in time with the tempo, and he rammed home two goals: The go-ahead goal and the clincher. The loudmouth was hollering, "Atta way to go, Andy!" Another fan was up honking his horn.

A few horns and a few loudmouths do not make a major league atmosphere. "It's really quiet here," said Bathgate. "Game seems dull. Most places we play in, they're really shouting and hollering. Even the boards seem dead here. Puck doesn't come off with a zing. Enthusiasm is generated by the fans. Too many people just sit there."

Some of the younger players on the Providence team who wanted a shot at the big-time were taking shots, cheap shots, at Bathgate that night, too. One slapped Bathgate in the forehead with his stick and Andy, in turn, laid about five well-placed punches on his head and stomach. It was the best fight seen in the Civic Arena since Sugar Ray Robinson and Joey Archer went at it.

Bathgate did not care for extreme rough play in hockey, but he was the wrong guy to tangle with at the same time. Under extreme provocation, he once beat up Vic Stasiuk of the Boston Bruins, a tough guy who would later become coach of the Hornets in Pittsburgh. And Bathgate beat him up twice in the same night!

By the time he came to play for Pittsburgh, however, they were saying Bathgate was beginning to slip, like his kneecaps did if he turned too sharply. He considered quitting way back in 1959 when they wanted to operate on both of his legs, and he was ready to give it up rather than become a cripple. He had a steel plate put in his left knee in 1952. He had a trick right knee, too. When he had to play too many games on consecutive nights, fluid would build up in his knees.

On the day I spoke to him in the office, he was trying to find out whether he would be staying in Pittsburgh, or whether he would be going back to Detroit. His wife was still in Detroit, and he was getting tired of living in a hotel at home as well as on the road.

"I don't want to keep jumping around at my age," he said. "I want to get organized and be with my family by Christmas. I just phoned home last night to wish my little girl a happy birthday."

Bathgate glanced at his watch and said, "She's five-years-old today," he said. Her name is Sandy, and there's a little boy, Billy, 3. "I don't like being away from my wife and kids," said Bathgate.

"I'd like to be with them some time around the holidays. It's tough on the family. I've never been home for Christmas. Just awhile during the day. Can't be with them for New Year's, either."

Bathgate had built up a sideline for the day when he had to quit playing hockey. He was a golf pro in Canada during the off-season and owned a driving range on the outskirts of Toronto. He once shot as low as 63 — and with the same sweep that powered his slap shot — he once drove a 325-yard green.

Bathgate played in all 74 games for the Penguins in the first season and led the team with 59 points on 20 goals and a team-high 39 assists. He was the leading scorer in the Western Division (composed of six expansion teams) in the National Hockey League. He scored the first goal by the Penguins in team history in the home opener with the Canadiens.

Bathgate's knees were too bad for him to play the next two seasons with the Penguins, but he returned, unbelievably enough, for the 1970-71 season. He was the team's third-leading scorer with 44 points (15 goals, 29 assists) to Bryan Hextall's 48 points and Jean Pronovost's 45 points. That was his swan song in Pittsburgh.

Bathgate got into the Hockey Hall of Fame in 1978. Harvey got into the Hall in 1973 and Boivin in 1986.

Leo Boivin   Andy Bathgate
These Hall of Famers both wore Pittsburgh uniforms

Where Are They Now?
Gregg Sheppard (1978-82)

"I gained the ability to adjust to difficult situations."

Present home: North Battleford, Saskatchewan

Present job: Realtor, general partner, Westland Agencies, Inc.

Family information: Wife, Karen McMillan. Children: Tami Sheppard, 25 and Brent Sheppard, 22. Karen's children by previous marriage are Ty Claypool, 22, and Tatum Claypool, 16

Personal highlight of Penguins' career: When I was traded to the Penguins in 1978.

Most cherished memory of playing days: Being a member of the Boston Bruins when they won Stanley Cup in 1972. My first league game against the New York Islanders when I scored three goals!

Players you most admired on your team (and why): Bobby Orr (leadership), Randy Carlyle (game player), Rick Kehoe (scoring ability)

Your favorite character on that club: Mario Faubert

What you learned from your experience with the Penguins that served you in good stead during your lifetime: I gained the ability to adjust to difficult situations.

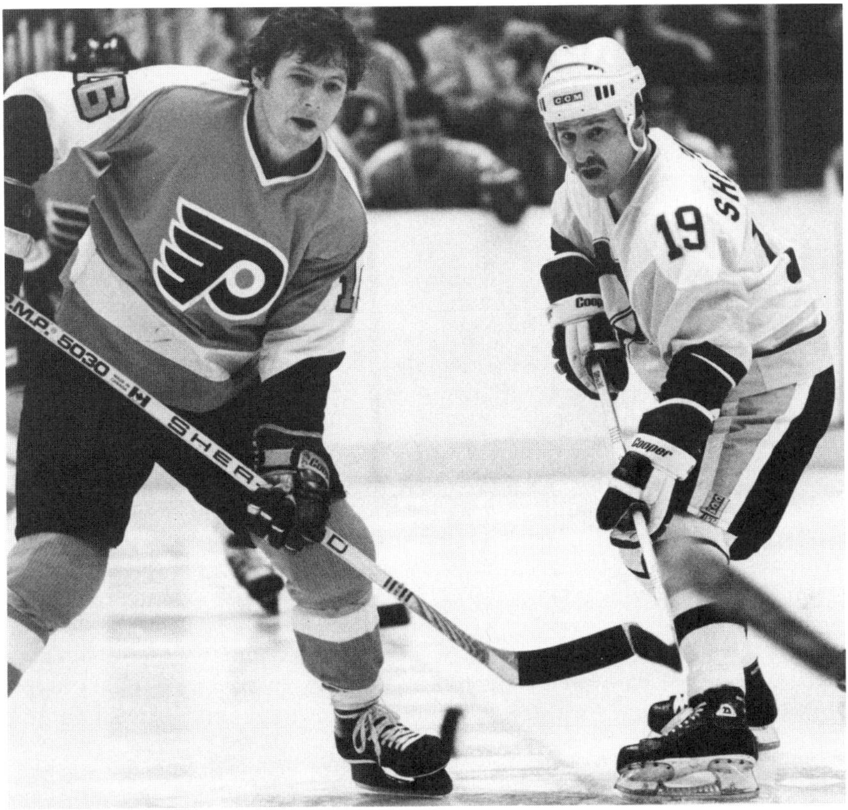

Tom Saulsbury collection

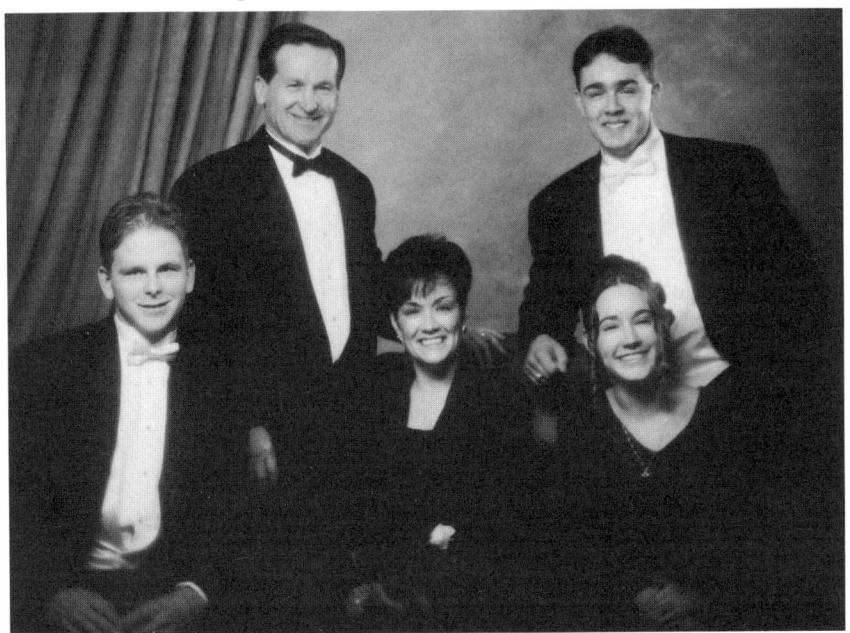

Gregg Sheppard (19) contends with Philadelphia's great Bobby Clarke for possession of the elusive puck.

Sheppard Family Album

Gregg Sheppard stands with stepson Ty Claypool, while his son Brent Sheppard, front row left, wife Karen McMillan, and his stepdaughter Tatum Claypool.

Duane Rupp
A throwback to another era

"I wish I could have played forever."

Duane Rupp represents a different period in Penguins history, in National Hockey League history for that matter. He came up when things were different, when there were only six NHL teams, when it was extremely difficult to get to the top, when the money did not matter, because there was not much of it being tossed around, when the dressing rooms were crowded, when conditions were sometimes downright shabby.

Spend a few hours and a few beers with Rupp and you realize it was not so bad. Rupp loved nearly every moment of it — except maybe those two months he labored under the whip of Eddie Shore at Springfield, Massachusetts in 1961 — and he missed it dearly.

Rupp played pro hockey for 18 seasons, and was a defenseman for the Penguins from 1968 to 1973. He remained in Pittsburgh after his playing days were over.

At age 56 in the summer of 1994, Rupp confessed, "I wish I were still playing. I wouldn't want to be coaching, but I'd like to be playing. I wish I could have played forever. There was a time when I thought I would."

Rumors were making the rounds that Mario Lemieux might retire because of persistent back problems, and Rupp hated to hear that, though he knew better than most Penguins fans how an injury could bring it all to an abrupt end. It happened to him, but he was much older than Lemieux when he had to give up the ghost.

Rupp was relaxing, sitting at a corner table in the back room at Atria's, a neighborhood sports bar on Rt. 19 as Dormont turns into Mt. Lebanon, where Rupp resides with his wife of 18 years, Genie, and their three children. Genie, a former teacher, works as a waitress during the day at Atria's. When they first met, she was working as a waitress during the summer school break at a restaurant just down Banksville Road, near the Dormont Pool and nearer to Downtown Pittsburgh, called the Jamestown Inn. It was popular with pro athletes, the Steelers, Pirates and Penguins, and it was frequented by some sportswriters as well. Several Steelers assistant coaches could be found there following practice at Three Rivers Stadium, just six miles away. It was the first watering hole heading to the south suburbs through the Fort Pitt Tunnel, and some automobiles automatically turned into its parking lot on the way home.

"It was a good place to let off steam," said Rupp. "And their 'Michael's Fantastic Clam Chowder' was the best ever."

He mentioned that Dunc McCallum, Les Binkley, Brian Hextall, Rick Kehoe and Bob Woytowich were among the regulars. I remember bumping into Paul Gardner there a few times. Former Pirates pitchers

Duane Rupp

Dave Giusti and Steve Blass, Steelers coaches George Perles, Woody Widenhofer and Dick Walker were frequent patrons. *Pittsburgh Press* sports editor Pat Livingston used to hold court in "The 'Rhoid Room." Pitt assistant coach Joe Moore liked to argue sports, or anything else.

That was when athletes and coaches hung out and relaxed together, when they were not afraid to eat and drink in the same spot as sportswriters. I know, because I used to frequent the Jamestown Inn when I returned to Pittsburgh from New York in 1979.

Its owner, Jim Breen, sold out to Burger King in the mid-80s, took the money and ran to southern climes, and the Jamestown was leveled in favor of another fast-food joint, just what the neighborhood needed. Some of the crowd moved uptown to Atria's, owned by Nick Atria. Sports pennants from nearly every college in America form a crown molding of sorts. There are pictures of Forbes Field and Three Rivers Stadium, pictures and posters of legendary Notre Dame figures — Notre Dame is very big at Atria's — the 1963 Pitt football team that went 9-1 and never got to a bowl game, some Penguins pictures, and several of athletes and teams from Mt. Lebanon.

This was a Wednesday night, and Rupp was sitting under a framed photograph of the 1991 Penguins team, shown celebrating after winning their first Stanley Cup.

Duane Rupp really looks like a guy from a different era. He has the kind of sweeping wave in his hair some women had to use a hot iron to fashion, thick arched eyebrows and a thick mustache. His mustache was more flamboyant when he was playing for the Penguins. It's all auburn, with dark eyes to match. He looks like he should be wearing a safari jacket and leading natives through a jungle, or a blouse and wielding a sword, battling at the side of Errol Flynn on a pirates' ship. Rupp and Kchoc could be a dueling duo.

Rupp smiled at the suggestion.

Rupp regards today's professional hockey players, particularly the Penguins, with a jaundiced eye. They may be making more money, travel better (the Penguins charter their own airplane), live in better homes, drive better cars, have a more spacious and comfortable clubhouse, and have better conditions in every respect, but they are missing something, as Rupp sees it.

"We used to be like one big family," recalled Rupp. "We ran together, we partied together, our families were close, our wives went shopping together. I could see the changes toward the end of my career. Guys started going their own way.

"We used to live in the same apartment buildings, or have houses in the same neck of the woods. There'd be 20 of us, all Canadians, in a strange city, all foreigners in a sense, and they were like a family. We stuck together. Sure, we'd make some new friends and have some acquaintances, but mostly we hung together.

"I loved playing. I can't say I had a teammate I ever disliked. I may have gotten into a confrontation with a few individuals, but I worked it out.

"I went to the rink . . . I loved playing. You'd go to war for the guys. There was a family kind of closeness, on and off the ice. We were a team."

I reminded Rupp that players in the NHL have more varied backgrounds and origins these days, with so many players in the NHL from Europe and Russia, and so many more American-born players. And they can now afford to live wherever they want to live.

"When I first started, the big guys were defensemen."

Penguins coach Eddie Johnston said Rupp was a good guy and "a stay-at-home" defenseman.

"Back in my time," related Rupp, "that was basically how you had to play to stay on a team. A defenseman played from blue line to blue line, and you seldom rushed in on goal. You stopped at their blue line and kept things in the offensive zone, and you didn't back in on your own goalie. You gave him room to see the puck. Bobby Orr changed that style.

"I was playing for Joe Crozier, Red Sullivan and Red Kelly, and they all coached the same style of defense."

I asked Rupp how he became a defenseman in the first place. "I think my size (6-1, 195 pounds) had a lot to do with it," Rupp responded. "When I first started, the big guys were defensemen. The little guys were a little quicker, and usually a little better at handling the puck, so they were put on the forward line. The guys who couldn't skate were stuck in goal.

"I played a little bit of forward in my career. Eddie Shore was determined he was going to make a left winger out of me. I spent two months under his hellish regime at Springfield. I used to kill penalties as a forward for a few teams I played for."

"I've never been a whiner about hurting."
—Duane Rupp

Rupp recognized a growing interest in hockey among the youth of Pittsburgh, and in 1972 — while still playing for the Penguins — he opened Rupp's Sporting Goods on Washington Road in Mt. Lebanon, just above The Korner Bar and catty-corner from St. Bernard's Catholic Church. He did so well, within a year he opened similar stores on Perry Highway in the North Hills and in Kittanning. He specialized in hockey equipment. "There were only a few sporting goods stores in the area that carried any hockey equipment in those days," he said. "All we carried was hockey equipment. On our signs, we had hockey sticks in place of the 'p's in my name. It started off very well.

"Then, unfortunately, my first marriage ended in divorce, After I left, my hockey store went to my wife and my daughter and son. My son runs it now. They closed the store in Kittanning and the one in the North Hills, but they opened a new one on McKnight Road a couple of years ago. They also moved the store in Mt. Lebanon to a shopping/restaurant complex on Cochran Road. It's a much better set-up. It had been a nightmare for our customers to find parking at our place on Washington Road. I work for my son now, out of our warehouse on Campbell's Run Road in Robinson Township. That's where we store our hockey equipment and where we handle our mail order business.

"I was in the restaurant business for 15 years after I got out of hockey and coaching. I was the manager for the Ground Round Restaurant, the one near The Galleria in Mt. Lebanon, for nine years."

Rupp remains a catalyst for hockey activity in the area. "I still play," he said with more than a hint of pride. "I played on as many as four teams this past year. I play in an adult league in Mt. Lebanon, and an adult league in Beaver, both with my oldest son, Rich, who's 32.

"We have a Penguins Alumni team, and Integra Bank sponsors a celebrity team. I play on that team with Jack Lambert, the old Steelers' linebacker. He's our big star. We play NHL alumni teams and celebrity teams. We played against Buffalo in Erie last year, and against Washington out at Rostraver. I'm an officer of our alumni organization. We don't have a lot of ex-Penguins living in Pittsburgh, so we have to recruit some other players. Like Larry Richert of KDKA-TV plays for us."

Bill Eiler, the public relations manager for Integra Financial Corporation, got his company involved with the celebrity hockey team. He previously worked in a similar capacity at the Pittsburgh Brewing Company, which was heavily involved with local sports-related promotions.

"We raise funds through our hockey games for the 'Courage To Come Back' program at St. Francis Health Foundation, and for the Lupus Foundation, which Lambert has looked after. We play about four or five games against teams in the area, and we play in places like Johnstown and Greensburg. Our Integra managers are acting coaches. It works out well for us. You should see Lambert. He's a good hockey player, you know. When he comes down the ice, he's a little intimidating."

Rupp gets a kick out of Lambert. "He's the only guy who takes it more seriously than I do," said Rupp. "Jack's a real trip. He fits in well with our guys.

"Some of the Penguins from the past who still live around here who play for us are George Ferguson, Kim Claxson, Alan Lemieux, Randy Hillier, Warren Young and Mark Kachowski. The most enthusiastic guy we had on our team was Craig Patrick, the Penguins' general manager. He missed only one game; I didn't miss any."

There was a period, soon after he retired, when Rupp stayed away from the rink.

"When you are first finished with professional hockey," he explained, "you have to completely get away from it for awhile.

"I quit as a player when I was with Winnipeg in the World Hockey League when I got my shoulder smashed up. They put three pins in my shoulder that were 4 1/2 inches long. My shoulder shriveled to the point where the pins were protruding through the skin. Guys on our club were hanging their clothes on my shoulder, like I was a coathanger."

Rupp is from the old school that ignored injuries and just kept playing. "You never wanted to sit," he said. "I've got a hip that hurts like hell after I play. Some nights I can't sleep, sometimes I can't sleep for a week. I used to have a hand that hurt and kept me awake, but that problem has gone away. I'm hoping it will go away with my hip, too."

I mentioned an orthopedic doctor who helped me when I had a knee problem. Rupp wagged his head. "I don't know," he said. "I've never been one to run to doctors. I've never been a whiner about hurting.

"Back when I played, you played whether you were hurt or not. You were afraid someone was going to take your job.

"Nobody goes out to lose. Every athlete is a competitive person. It's the nature of the beast. You can't turn it on and off. If you try to take it easy that's when you get hurt."

"Maybe I'm in my second childhood."
—Duane Rupp

"I coached at Rochester with the Americans from 1975 to 1979. We went from having six owners to having 26 owners. Each year they knew more about hockey; they became experts in a hurry. We had about twenty 20-year-olds with the Boston organization — they wanted to develop the young talent in a hurry — and we were supposed to win. When we didn't, they let me go.

"I was out of hockey for nearly a year. I told my wife, 'I'm done.' And she said, 'Yeah, till the phone rings.' Just then the phone rang and the next day I was coaching the Syracuse Firebirds in the American Hockey League.

"That was in 1980. The next year they moved to Quebec. I didn't speak French; they didn't invite me back. I went for about six or seven years, and I didn't even want to see a game, or be around it, anything. I got back into it about five or six years ago — maybe I'm in my second childhood or something. Someone calls and tells me about a game and I grab my bag and I'm gone. I really enjoy it.

"If I didn't play, I'd probably weigh about 240. I played a couple of pounds under 200. I'm probably about 210 now. But I could get heavy in a hurry. I could easily be 230 or 240."

"Someday I'll be there."

Rupp grew up in one of the storied hockey communities, a place called Flin Flon, Manitoba, 1,200 miles north of Minneapolis-St. Paul. Bobby Clarke and Reggie Leach of the Philadelphia Flyers and Gerry Hart of the Islanders were all from there.

"My first year (1956-57) as a junior, we won the Memorial Cup, which takes in all of Canada in junior hockey competition. It was the first time a team out west had won it in 20 years. It set us off on a glamorous start. We owned the town for the rest of our junior days there. I played one more year in Flin Flon, and we got the royal treatment.

"Our team was sponsored by the New York Rangers, so we automatically belonged to them. There was no draft back then.

"It was a mining town of about 25,000 people and they loved their hockey. There wasn't a whole lot to do there for entertainment. It was an isolated place. I walked three miles to school and then home for lunch, back to school again and then home again. And sometimes it was 60 degrees below zero. My kids say, 'Sure, sure,' when I say that. But it's true. There was a great desire to get as far from Flin Flon as possible, and the NHL provided that possibility."

There were only six NHL teams when Rupp first came up. There were great players like Bobby Hull, Gordie Howe and Jean Beliveau. "You were in awe when you stepped on the ice with them," recalled Rupp. "They were legends, and playing with guys like that was, well, like a dream come true.

"When you were a kid, you'd sit and listen to Foster Hewitt doing the games on the radio from Toronto's Maple Leaf Gardens. Every kid in Canada said, 'Someday, I'll be there.' I was one of those kids and I made it. I ended up playing in Toronto. I started out with the New York Rangers and then played for the Maple Leafs.

"I didn't go to New York directly from the juniors. I started off in Fort Wayne, Indiana in the International Hockey League. Then I played in Kitchener, Ontario in the Eastern Hockey League. I went to Springfield of the American Hockey League, but lasted only two months. I played for Vancouver in the Western Hockey League, Baltimore in the American Hockey League, then two years in the NHL before I was traded to Toronto. It was called the Andy Bathgate trade, and I was just another player thrown into it. I spent the rest of the year there, and three with the Rochester Americans in the AHL. It was difficult to get into or stay in the NHL in those days.

"Al Arbour was my partner as a defenseman at Rochester. We played together for three years. We both made the AHL All-Star team, but we couldn't make the NHL. Not then. I did short stints with Toronto then, but nothing long-term.

"Frank Mathers was one of my favorite coaches. When I became a coach, I said that — good or bad, live or die — I was going to be that kind of coach.

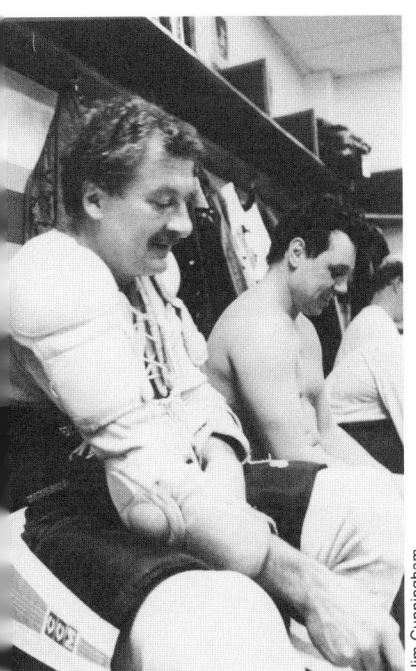

Jim Cunningham

ıane Rupp dresses alongside Pierre ırouche at Penguins Alumni hockey ntest.

Rupp Family Album

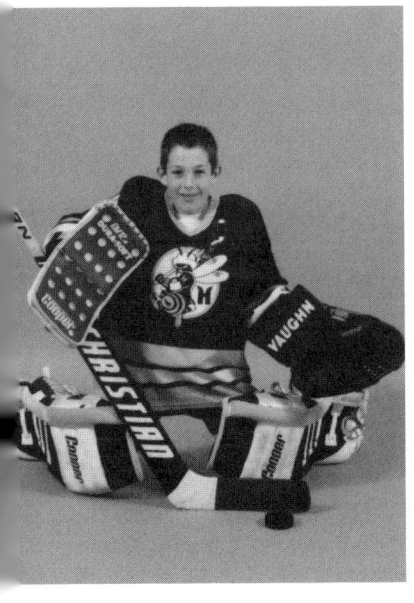

Two of Duane's sons are enthusiastic hockey players. Brad, shown above as a junior at Mt. Lebanon High School, and Brennan, left, an 11-year-old who was playing with the Hornets in Mt. Lebanon Peewee Division.

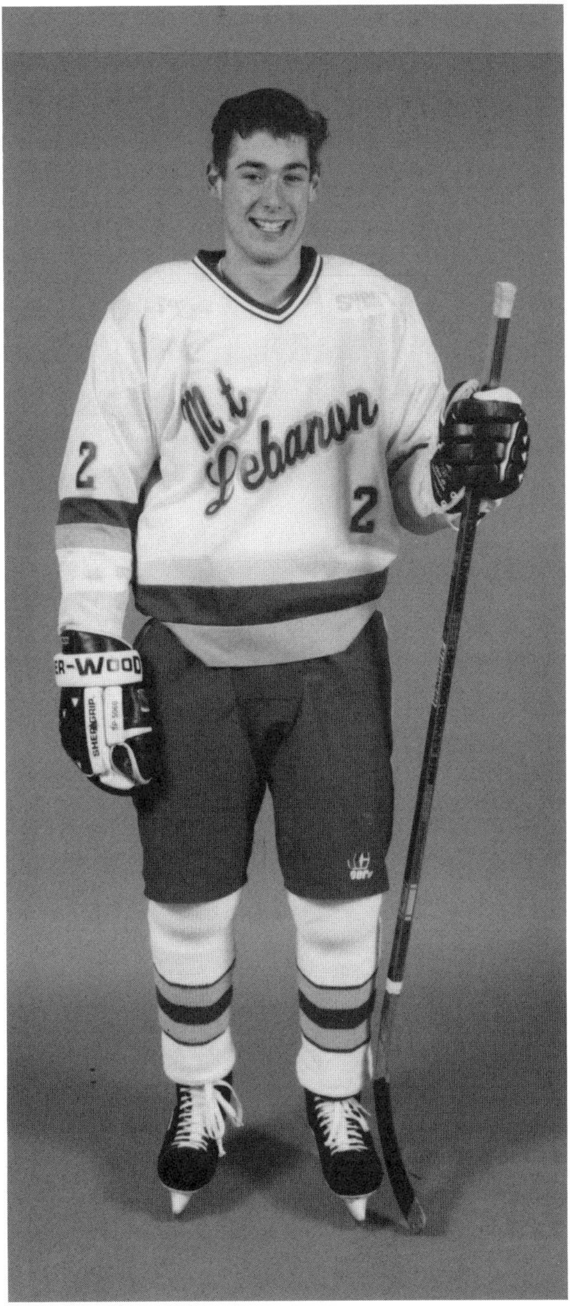

"I remember the first time I ever took the ice at Maple Leaf Gardens. The crowd wore suits and ties, and they probably sat on their hands. There was no jumping up and down, or banners and all that stuff. You'd get a little clap if you did something good. There'd be a little murmur going through the stands.

"Today, you see situations like Chicago where they don't even let them finish the National Anthem before they start going crazy, and it's quite a contrast to the fans who were in the Maple Leaf Gardens in those days.

"I was 39 and playing for the Calgary Cowboys in the World Hockey Association when I had to quit. My shoulder was killing me.

"I always thought goalies were a little different."
—Duane Rupp

Brad Rupp, 17, one of Duane's children, was about to start his senior year at Mt. Lebanon High School. He played for the club hockey team at school, and also for the Pittsburgh Junior Penguins. One of his teammates with the Junior Penguins was Craig Patrick's oldest son, Cory. Brad was 6-1, 195 pounds "and growing," as his dad put it.

"He plays defense; that's where he wants to play. I told him, 'If you just do what I tell you — not that I could do all that I'm telling you — you'll make it.' "

Several weeks after our interview with his father, Brad decided to skip his senior year at Mt. Lebanon High School in favor of a junior hockey program in Helena, Montana. He had considered doing the same in Canada.

His second son by his second marriage is Jordon, and he was 13 at the time. "He's my scholar," said Rupp. "He could care less about hockey. He's going into ninth grade and he's very good in school. My youngest is Brennan. He's 11, and he plays goalie for the Mt. Lebanon Hornets in the Mt. Lebanon Peewee Division. I always thought goalies were a little different, and he fits the mold. At first, he didn't care about the puck. He just wanted to run into people. He's been a goalie now for three years, and I can't talk him out of it."

Speaking of goalies, I mentioned Eddie Johnston, and Rupp reacted by smiling and telling me a standard story. "I scored my first NHL goal against him," said Rupp. "I don't let him forget it. When I see him, I mention it to him all the time. I played against him, and I've met him, but I don't know him that well. I'd say he knows his hockey. He's been around for so many years, he has to know his stuff. For some reason, goaltenders make good coaches. As a goaltender, he was pretty steady."

Greg Polis
A boy and his dog

"The game just came naturally to me."

Try to picture Greg Polis playing hockey as a child with his dog. One-on-one on the ice near his home in a prairie outpost called Dapp, Alberta, population 75. Kids were hard to come by so Polis played against his Labrador retriever, a sporting dog for sure on a frozen pond near his home.

It also helps explain why Polis didn't take himself too seriously as a prospect. "I never really thought of pursuing hockey," he said. "The game just came naturally to me.

"I wasn't a real fan, but I still watched the Saturday night game on television. In high school, I was always planning ahead and I was pretty well set on studying engineering, or something like that. I hadn't decided what type."

He described Dapp as having "a downtown that filled almost 300 yards" of western prairie with a general store and hotel, and a bar complex. He said only a youngster with exceptional natural ability as a hockey player would get noticed.

Polis was just such a hockey player. When he was 16, he decided to give hockey an earnest shot.

This background helps one appreciate why Polis was such a delightful hero in the National Hockey League's All-Star Game midway through the 1972-73 campaign. It was the third straight appearance by Polis in the league's showcase contest.

When he was chosen to the team by Billy Reay, the coach of the Chicago Blackhawks, Polis publicly said he didn't deserve to be on the team. He had played on two previous All-Star teams under Reay, which helps explain his selection. He and Jean Pronovost had become the Penguins' first 30-goal scorers the season before, but Polis didn't feel he had been scoring enough to deserve such an honor this time around.

In fact, he didn't even feel he was the best leftwinger on the Penguins at that point in the season. Lowell MacDonald, who had been shifted from the right wing to that side for the first time in his career, and had made a spectacular comeback the year before after being out of hockey for two years with a knee injury, had been more productive.

As it turned out, MacDonald did make the team, filling in at the last moment for injured teammate Syl Apps. Polis nearly missed the game at New York's Madison Square Garden. He was at the Greater Pittsburgh Airport, preparing to fly to New York for the game when he received a telephone call informing him that his wife, Llewelyn, who was two weeks past due, was going to have their baby.

Llewelyn had gotten some publicity in the Pittsburgh newspapers prior to that event because she did volunteer work, teaching ceramics at a home for men with incurable diseases.

So Polis drove from the airport to Pittsburgh to be with his wife at the hospital. She gave birth to a seven pound, 14 ounce baby boy, Jason Gregory Polis. That was on a Monday. Polis stayed in Pittsburgh overnight and made a second attempt at getting to New York the next day. He bought some cigars to pass out en route to New York.

He arrived at Madison Square Garden less than four hours before the All-Star Game. He decided to dedicate the game to his newborn son. He was hoping to score a goal, so he would have a puck to present to his son upon returning to Pittsburgh. Someday he would be able to explain its significance.

Polis ended up scoring two goals and being named the Most Valuable Player for the All-Star Game even though his West team lost to the East, 5-4. Teammate MacDonald assisted on his first goal.

He had played in an All-Star Game with the likes of Bobby Orr, Phil Esposito and Bobby Clarke, yet he came away with an automobile as an award for his spectacular outing.

The 23-year-old Polis had been something of a puzzle for the Penguins, and more so for their fans. He was the first player picked by the Penguins in the 1970 amateur draft. He was one of a handful of players in the National Hockey League who never played a game in the minor leagues, jumping right from his junior club, the Estevan Bruins, to the NHL. He had finished second in scoring twice during his junior career while scoring 123 goals in three years.

He had a cannon-like slap shot. He was used on the power play and to kill penalties. But he just never seemed to convince Pittsburgh hockey fans that he was playing his best. He was criticized for not being more physical, especially because he was square-shouldered and built along the lines of a linebacker in football. He didn't go into the corners to come up with the puck. Penguins fans usually saved their booing for defensemen like Duane Rupp and Ron Stackhouse, but they were seldom polite in showing their displeasure with Polis.

Yet he made the All-Star Game his first three seasons. During his fourth year in Pittsburgh, he was traded, along with Bryan Watson and a second round choice in the 1974 draft to the St. Louis Blues in exchange for Bob Kelly, Ab DeMarco and Steve Durbano. He spent one season with the Blues and then went to the New York Rangers, where he averaged nearly 20 goals a season. He had a four-goal game against Minnesota while playing for the Rangers in 1975.

He was with the Penguins less than four years, but he was a star, something of a shooting star perhaps, a comet that flamed briefly across the Pittsburgh sky, then disappeared.

Greg Polis

Pierre Larouche

"I'm from a family of ten. I have six sisters and three brothers. One brother died young. My mother is the one who spoiled me because I was the youngest. She really spoiled me. But that is love. The only time I can't play good hockey is when she is in the crowd. I get very nervous. Sometimes she sneaks in the game. I don't know. I play good."
—Pierre Larouche

Peter Mahovlich

Bob Paradise

Ulf Samuelsson
A Swede who goes to war

"I'm glad he's on our side."
—Mario Lemieux

Sweden is a neutral country. Swedes are supposed to be blond, blue-eyed, smiling, peace-loving postcard people. Ulf Bo Samuelsson hardly fits the stereotype. He has dark blond hair and blue eyes, and that's about it. He goes to war every time out as a feisty, hard-hitting defenseman for the Pittsburgh Penguins. He is an offensive defenseman even though he does not often lug the puck into the offensive zone or score many goals. He's just offensive, that's all, unless he's doing his rough stuff for your team.

Then he's the greatest.

He came to the Penguins from the Hartford Whalers late in the 1990-91 campaign, and contributed in a big way to winning two consecutive Stanley Cup championships. He quickly became one of the fans' favorites at the Civic Arena.

They love to chant "Ulf! Ulf! Ulf!" whenever he touches the puck, or pushes an opponent into the boards, or pummels somebody. They have put up signs in the balcony which have read "Cry Ulf!"

Built like a boxer, at 6-1, and a well-muscled 195 pounds that runs from coathanger shoulders down to a slim waist, he has a reputation for being more than a rough player. *Sports Illustrated* did a story on him a few years ago called "Mr. Dirty."

"I'm not going to say I'm a clean player, because I'm not," said Samuelsson in a candid interview with *SI*. "I do whatever it takes to stop the other guy. Whatever it takes to win."

Later, reflecting on the piece and the response to it, Samuelsson conceded, "Even my mother says I'm a dirty player."

Penguins' defenseman Kjell Samuelsson, his friend and countryman, said, "Ulf isn't your average Swede, that's for sure."

Ronnie Francis, who has been a teammate in both Hartford and Pittsburgh, put Samuelsson's situation into its proper perspective: "He plays very tough, physical, and when you play that way you're bound to have guys run at you and try to hurt you.

"He has a zest for life. I've been playing with Ulf for ten years, and I still shake my head at the things he does. He's as crazy as ever."

Badger Bob Johnson loved Samuelsson's style of play. Johnson once called him the toughest hockey player he had ever seen.

"A competitor!" Johnson was fond of calling him. "That's the thing I like about Ulf. He loves to play the game. He competes."

Samuelsson wears oversized shoulder pads and a partial face shield, and he assumed the image of a linebacker for the Penguins, their answer to Steelers' Hall of Famer Jack Lambert.

Ulf Samuelsson seems a lot tamer on the golf course, at Penguins' annual outing at Fox Chapel Golf Club to raise funds for Pittsburgh amateur hockey leagues, than he does when he's in action on the Civic Arena ice.

Photos by Jim Cunningham

The Penguins pay Samuelsson $800,000 a year to play the way he does. That's his role with the team.

His father, Bo Samuelsson, and his childhood friend and teammate Tomas Sandstrom, helped shape him. How'd Ulf get the way he is today? Bo knows.

His father gave him his determined spirit and Sandstrom gave him his agitating style. Samuelsson irritates the hell out of everybody he plays against. They hate him.

Samuelsson grew up in Fagersta, a steel city in central Sweden, so he is at home in Pittsburgh, still reputed to be a steel city, even though it's more myth than reality these days. Then again, the nearest skyscraper to the Civic Arena is the foreboding USX Tower, once known as the U.S. Steel Building. Samuelsson started out playing soccer, but was convinced to give hockey a fling by his buddy, Sandstrom.

They were both hell on ice wherever they played. The Swedes play on larger ice surfaces, and they normally play a kinder, gentler game. It's more of a finesse game, with the emphasis on skating and stick-handling and passing skills. In short, they play it the way it was supposed to be played, not NHL style. There is little checking and almost no fighting. The knock against European defensemen in the past when they came into the NHL was their questionable work ethic.

Samuelsson and Sandstrom were teammates on the Fagersta FAIK juniors, and they were upsetting their opponents with the way they played the game: checking, shoving, elbowing, swapping punches when anyone resisted or protested. They were playing like alley cats. Like Canadians and Americans.

Sandstrom says it was Samuelsson who started playing that way, but Ulfie feels it was the other way around.

"We had some good coaches," said Samuelsson. "But I think the best coaching I got was from my dad. He took that upon himself as his life's job."

Discipline was strict at the Samuelsson home, and Bo would swat his son if he got out of line. Bo knew how to handle his son, and he did not need a hockey stick to do it.

"We sat up many nights and talked about things," recalled the young Samuelsson. "He got me motivated. He told me I had a chance. Everyone by human nature is lazy. I'm a little lazier than most people. I was. But he got me into good working habits."

If Ulf came home pouting from a loss, he suffered another loss. "I got whacked a few times by my dad afterward," he admitted.

"He really, really helped me out. I really didn't have much talent when I was much younger. I was one of the slower guys. He didn't push me or anything, but, when I was 14 or 15, he started to help with some off-ice programs and then he pushed me a little bit because I was lazy. I got things rolling a bit. He always had some advice for me when I needed it."

Almost to a man, Penguins point to their father as the driving influence in their lives, with their moms providing strong support systems.

Sometimes the fathers seemed almost maniacal in the demands they made upon their sons to skate and excell at the ice sport. Their fathers seemed a lot more involved in their games than one finds in interviewing football players. Steelers Hall of Fame coach Chuck Noll had a theory that strong mothers made strong sons, and that strong fathers tended to breed weaker sons. Then again, Noll's father was ill a great deal during his developmental years, and his mother, a teacher, was the stronger influence in his life. It was what Noll knew, and what worked for him.

Bo Samuelsson was a stout-hearted soccer player whose pro ambitions were cut short by rheumatism at age 25. He was a fierce competitor, downright nasty at times — sound familiar? — and drew more than his share of flags from the referees.

"He was a tough guy," said Sandstrom. "*That* Ulf got from his dad."

Ulf's competitive spirit was what caught the eye of Swedish scouts when they saw him playing junior hockey in his hometown. Ulf was only 17 when he was promoted to play with Leksand, about a 1 1/2 hour drive north of Fagersta, in the Swedish Elite League for the 1981-82 season. After that season, he was chosen in the second round of the NHL entry draft by Hartford.

"I'm almost diseased with winning."
—Ulf Samuelsson

Ulf Samuelsson came to the States in 1984, dividing his first professional season between the Whalers and their American Hockey League farm team in Binghamton, New York. He may have been in a foreign land, but he did not retreat from the style he had displayed back home. He rang up 92 penalty minutes in just 36 games in the minors, and 83 minutes in 41 games with the Whalers. He raised a lot of eyebrows around the NHL.

Samuelsson drew a high-sticking penalty and caused a commotion in Halifax, for instance. The next time the two teams met, the Halifax players jumped Samuelsson. Better yet, they jumped him during the pre-game warmup.

"The whole team came after me," recalled Samuelsson with a smile. "Cops came with dogs, everything on the ice. It was a riot."

At the same time as Ulf was finding his way in the NHL, his buddy Sandstrom was breaking in with the New York Rangers, and was on a similar roughhousing rampage. "They said, 'Where did these guys come from?'" recalls Samuelsson.

He remembers growing up with Sandstrom, and the effect they had on each other. "We almost lived at the hockey rink," said Samuelsson. "Even if we didn't have practice, we would be up there playing games, like hide-and-seek or whatever. We were always up there because we lived fairly close. We would go right after school and watch the big guys play. Then, as we moved up in school, we had a pretty good gang going at school with all different ways to find to get into trouble at school. We had pretty good grades — all of us — but we were a little crazy in school.

"Tomas was a quieter guy, but he was the guy who would always do something; fix with something and have things going for him. He would get caught in trouble as much as I would because he was always there. We were a bunch of four or five guys, who did some extra time in school and had to sit after and clean some toilets and washrooms and things like that.

"We were on all the teams in school and we were good athletes. We were on the football — I mean soccer — team, ice hockey team, basketball team, handball team, track and field and we did a lot of things together. I think people liked us. We really wanted to have a good time and we didn't like to be mean to anyone or anything like that. We just played some practical jokes."

Sandstrom remembers something else about Samuelsson's style and what was said about him back in Sweden. "I saw him rough up a lot of players." recalled Sandstrom. "Everyone kept saying that he was going to get killed if he played like that when he went to the NHL."

"You love him when he's on your team."
—Kevin Stevens

Bill Clement, once a member of the Broad Street Bullies of Philadelphia, and more recently a color analyst on Flyers' hockey and on ESPN telecasts, said of Samuelsson: "He would fit right in with the Flyers of the '70s, with guys like Eddie Van Impe, Dave Schultz and Moose Dupont. He's crude, but Dick Butkus was crude, and he's in the Pro Football Hall of Fame. To me, Samuelsson is like a linebacker on skates."

Rick Tocchet was a tough guy who played for the Flyers when he first squared off against Samuelsson, and then joined him as a teammate on the Penguins. He saw Samuelsson from both sides of the fence.

"No, I didn't like him," said Tocchet, reflecting on his days in Philadelphia. "In fact, like most people who don't know him, I hated him. But now he's probably one of my best friends on the team. I'd do anything for the guy." Now that Tocchet has been traded to the LA Kings, it will be interesting to see how he and Samuelsson get along.

Kevin Stevens added, "I never liked playing against him, either. He hits you head-on, and every time you turn around, he's right in your face. You love him when he's on your team and you hate him when he's not. He can make you cringe even he's playing with you. He just plays with such reckless abandon."

> *"He's Jack Lambert on skates."*
> —Ron Cook, Columnist
> *Pittsburgh Post-Gazette*

Surprisingly enough, Samuelsson became expendable late in the 1990-91 season, which was a lucky break for the Penguins. Craig Patrick was seeking to add stability and to improve his defense, and he dealt high-scoring center John Cullen, along with Zarley Zalapski and Jeff Parker to Hartford in exchange for Samuelsson, Ronnie Francis and Grant Jennings. It was a trade that is pointed to as Patrick's masterful move, and one that directly led to consecutive Stanley Cup triumphs. At first, many Penguins' fans were upset by the deal, but they came to love it.

The Penguins had a good idea of what they were getting in Francis, a two-way forward who was the most popular player on the Whalers, but Samuelsson was even better than advertised. Maybe Pittsburgh and the black and gold uniform and the fans brought out the best (or worst) in him.

Ron Cook, columnist for the Pittsburgh *Post-Gazette*, quickly dubbed him "Jack Lambert on skates." Lambert loved that. So did Samuelsson when he came to appreciate the comparison. So did the Penguins' fans.

In an interview with Cook, Samuelsson said, "You have to have a guy who can play the kind of hockey I do. Some nights, I'm sitting there sore in a few places and I still have to go out and play my game. There are times I wish I could put myself in an offensive-minded player's body, but I don't have those skills and I know it. I'm just trying to maximize myself to help us win.

"That's what this is all about, winning. I have enough money. I'm not saying I don't want more, but I have enough to settle in Sweden tomorrow if I wanted. It's just that I'm almost diseased with winning."

I knew Dave Lewis from his early days as a solid defenseman for the New York Islanders. He's always had a reputation as a good guy. As an assistant coach with the Red Wings, however, he wished he had a defenseman in Detroit like Samuelsson.

"It's hard to think of anybody you would rather have on your team," said Lewis. "You hate to play against him, yet you admire him for what he does for his team. Ulf battles, sticks up for himself. He has a mean streak, he is a little dirty, and he always seems to be paired up against the other's team's best player. When Pittsburgh plays us, he's out there against Steve Yzerman. With Boston it's Cam Neely, with Chicago it's Jeremy Roenick, and so on. He gets under your skin and throws your game off, and that's what you want in a defenseman. He has been very successful, and it's very frustrating to play against him."

Don Sweeney, a defenseman for the Boston Bruins, offered begrudging praise for Samuelsson: "One thing about him, he always comes back for more. No matter what you dish out, he comes back. It's like he's a glutton for it, or something."

Neely, who's gone at it with Samuelsson on several occasions, was less diplomatic: "I don't really respect the way he plays. I don't like the guy."

Mike Milbury, former bench boss of the Bruins who moved upstairs to the front office, offered, "Jerk that he is, he's always wearing that smirky grin that makes you want to punch him in the face. Then you do it, he takes it, and you're the one in the penalty box for two minutes, feeling like a fool. He's not often called for retaliation and that, probably more than anything, is why people can't stomach the sound of his name."

Samuelsson answers questions about his reputation for dirty play:

"I have got a reputation for being a guy who causes trouble and stuff," he said. "Some might call me a stick man or whatever. You have to remember that one of my main jobs as a defenseman is to help the goalie and to clear the area around the net.

"I have to get the opposition's good players and throw them off their games and I think I do a pretty good job at it. Unfortunately, I've always had that problem (of using the stick recklessly). And I'm really trying to work on it. I can give other kinds of shots at the opposition beside high-sticking them. I know they're going to get back at me and that's something I can live with. I can live with a few sticks and bruises if I can get them distracted in front of the net. Then I feel I'm doing a good job."

Asked about his favorite hockey player, he said, "When I was younger, it was Borje Salming because he was the guy who broke the ice barrier between Sweden and the NHL. He did a lot to make it easier for us. Now it's so easy to break in for almost anyone. Particularly, in years past it was tough for Swedes or Finns to break in; NHL players saw them as people who would come here and take their jobs. That's what they were thinking.

"Now my favorite has got to be Wayne Gretzky, even though in one game he told me he was going to hit me hard some place I can't mention. He's the greatest player I've ever seen"

"You want to be able to lead a normal life when you are done with your career."
—Ulf Samuelsson

When Ulf came to America he brought his girlfriend with him. Her name was Jeanette Pellas, and she was from Leksand, and she was 16. It would be less lonely here with her at his side.

"It's a big step, to take everything and move to a new country," he told Chuck Finder of the *Post-Gazette*. "You hardly know what you get when you order from the menu. I remember my wife, my girlfriend at the time . . . about the third time she got her food, she just started crying."

Ulf Samuelsson stretches to block shot in front of goalie Tom Barrasso, and stoops to pull son Philip, who was 15 months old, when his mother Jeanette brought him to the 1993 Penguins' Christmas party.

Photos by Jim Cunningham

Samuelsson came to America with a college business degree from Leksand. Ulf and Jeanette settled in Rosslyn Farms, and they have a son Philip. The Samuelssons go back to Leksand each summer. Jeanette's family lives there. Ulf's mother and his sister, Britt, live in his hometown of Fagersta.

His father died in November, 1991, after being ill for a long time with kidney problems. He misses his dad dearly. It's one of the reasons Ulf has served as a poster boy for Pittsburgh's kidney foundation.

Ulf finds himself sometimes rummaging through a family scrapbook, that contains clippings of his father's soccer heroics. There are articles his father sent him for inspiration.

"I still pick up the phone, especially in the car, I don't know why, like I am calling my father. I forget," he told Finder. "It's a big part of my life missing right here. I had no one to spill my guts to, as far as hockey. That was . . . a tough thing . . . to go through."

He's a throwback to athletes like his dad. He doesn't stay sidelined long when he's injured. He has a history of coming back fast from physical ailments, bruises and hurts. He will take pain-killing shots to help him get back to the lineup. He said it has to be a personal decision, and he doesn't push his philosophy on anyone else.

"I'd never blame anyone for not taking the painkillers," he told Cook. "You only have one body. You want to be able to live a normal life when you're done with your career. Sometimes I wonder why I take the shots. But it's just like a poison with me. When it comes time for the game, I'll do what I have to do to play. If it means taking the needle, I'll do it."

Asked how he would like to be remembered, Samuelsson said, "I'd like to be remembered as a guy who came and played every night. I'm a guy who was really good defensively, a good penalty-killer, and had some offensive talents.

"I'll probably be remembered as a guy who was always joking around and was never taking anything seriously. That's how they're going to remember me. Guys who play with me, though, know how serious I am when it comes to the games."

Samuelsson is well-acquainted with NHL referees.

Syl Apps
Followed his father to NHL

"Millions of people would love to be in your shoes just once."

My memories of Toronto are mostly of Maple Leaf Gardens and banks. That's right, banks. There seemed to be a bank, a large, grand bank, with huge pillars, on every corner in midtown when I visited there. "You must've been walking where I work," said Syl Apps. "There's a pretty close financial community. There's a small downtown corridor of banks and financial institutions in the business district of Toronto." And Apps, one of the best players to ever perform for the Pittsburgh Penguins, is a vice-president for the bond brokerage firm of Shorcan International Brokers Limited on Adelaide Street. "I've been a bond broker for 12 years, and it's pretty demanding," said Apps. "I'm pretty well established now, and I'd like to move off the desk and the trading, and into more of an administrative post before long. It's a grind when you're on the desk all the time. It's a business you can't do forever. I'd like to keep my sanity.

"There is life after hockey. It's a reasonably difficult transition," Apps admitted. "There is a certain void there. There's a certain excitement and glamour in hockey. In the business world, it's not quite the same. Your highs and lows are long term. In sports, it's a series of momentary thrills. You miss that."

He lives in the suburb of Unionville with his wife Anne and their three children. Toronto is his hometown. It is where his father first put the family name in the newspapers, as a Hall of Fame player for the Maple Leafs in a ten-year NHL career that spanned the '30s and '40s. Syl Apps or Sylvanus Apps has always been a grand name in the professional hockey world, and one that rates a knowing nod and a smile throughout hockey-crazy Canada.

Syl's memories of Pittsburgh tend to focus on the mid-'70s when the Penguins had a pretty good team on the ice, but were a dismal mess in the front office, where the owners had a bad case of the shorts. Those beleaguered owners could have used a friend at all those banks in Toronto. They simply prayed a lot between paydays hoping the checks wouldn't bounce as high as an Apps' slap shot off the top bar of the goalie's cage.

Apps had marked his 47th birthday just a fews days before we talked over the telephone, and he was 14 years removed from the NHL. So perhaps he was able to view those days in a positive, more mature frame of mind than he might have appraised or accepted them at the time.

I had last seen and spoken to Syl during the summer of 1993 at the Penguins Carnival at the Civic Arena when he came back to the building where he'd been a popular star to sign autographs for the fans at a day-long pre-season celebration of hockey.

His once dark mane — Penguins fans from that period can remember his long hair and those bushy sideburns he brandished — are silver-streaked now, and so are his reflections. He can even see a silver lining in that crammed Penguins' clubhouse at the Civic Arena where he once dressed and stored his personal belongings.

"We were going through financial problems, but we made the best of it," said Apps with a light-hearted voice, and it was easy to picture his handsome smile. "We went through stuff like not having enough sticks. Some guys were lucky if they had two sticks they could call their own. Some guys had one pair of skates and that was it. They were rationing towels in the clubhouse. Some people would have said it was crummy. Even so, it was a great place for me to be at that time in my life.

"There is a time in your career when security and comfort come into line, and that was the case for me in Pittsburgh, in a strange way. We certainly weren't secure in our jobs, as far as the franchise's future was concerned, and there weren't many creature comforts in our clubhouse, but somehow I felt good there."

For one thing, Apps was among the best paid of the Penguins, making at least $125,000 the season (1974-75) the club declared bankruptcy. For another, he was in good company.

"We had a good group of guys," said Apps. "And we made the best of it. I remember once being interviewed by a Toronto television station before the (1977) playoffs. They were asking me questions about the Maple Leafs. I had to speak in very general terms, because we had no scouting reports, no game film, no insights into what they were doing. We'd see the lineups before the game, and that was what we knew. They knew all about us, but you had to be a little bland or general in your answers about them. We'd say stuff like, 'It doesn't really matter who's in goal tonight . . . as long as we play our game.' Hey, it would have been nice to get scouting reports like the other teams had on us. It would have been nice to know something about their power play. It would have been nice to have better equipment. We knew how well we were treated when we were in other buildings. It must have been difficult for our clubhouse guys because they didn't have the budget to offer much in the way of amenities in our clubhouse or the visitors' clubhouse."

(I mentioned Syl's story to Anthony Cagliano, a clubhouse attendant who has served the Penguins since the team first came into being. Cagliano laughed. "We used to have to wash the towels in two home-size laundry machines during each period so we'd have clean ones when they came in at intermission," said Cagliano. "But we had a lot of good boys on that team. They didn't complain much.")

Apps went one step farther, and said something that would cost him his players' association card these days. "We had good owners, too. They were making an honest effort. That's when Tad Potter was running the organization, and had a local group of investors. They were likable, enthusiastic guys. They did everything in their power to stave off going bankrupt. They were trying; they didn't want it to turn out that way."

Syl Apps was one of Penguins' smoothest skaters.

"It's always something I'll look back on."
—Syl Apps

When Apps assessed his days with the Penguins, he pointed to the 1975 All-Star Game in Montreal as the personal highlight of his ten-year career. Apps was the MVP and won a brand new Dodge for helping the Wales Conference defeat the Campbell Conference, 7-1.

"The year before I was supposed to go to the All-Star Game in Chicago and got hurt, and that was a disappointment, and I had missed out because of an injury of playing in the All-Star Game in New York two years earlier," said Apps. "To go up there and do well, it's always something I'll look back on. I had a couple of goals and hit a couple of posts. I nearly had a third goal. Maybe they liked the way I hit the post."

His mother and father were in attendance, and his father said afterward that it was the thrill of his life, to see his son be the star of the All-Star Game.

"It was kind of fun," said young Syl. "The only time I usually got to play in front of my family was when we played in Toronto. I remember scoring a penalty shot there once (against Bernie Parent on February 9, 1972) in my second year with the Penguins, and my mom and dad were in the stands. That made it even more special.

"To go to the All-Star Game for the first time was a memorable experience. There was a certain amount of excitement, indeed, and I was fortunate to get a few goals. You never forget certain games. I remember my first game with Pittsburgh. I scored a goal and assisted on another, and did well the first few weeks. In short, I got off to a good start there. What if I hadn't? How would that affected what I did the rest of the year? You wonder about stuff like that."

Apps may have felt pressure to get off to a good start in Pittsburgh because Penguins fans were not happy when the team traded one of their favorites, Glen "Slats" Sather for Apps, then a 23-year-old castoff, and defenseman Sheldon Kannegiesser, from the New York Rangers. Sather, more recently the general manager of the Edmonton Oilers, was the sort of aggressive, defense-minded forward the Rangers needed. The Penguins needed an offense-minded center to fill the void left by the death of Michel Briere just before the season started.

Apps may have seen a sign that was hung out in the Civic Arena that night. It was directly across the ice from the Penguins' bench and it asked simply:

WHY SLATS?

Apps answered the question by coming away with two points against Jacques Plante, a Hall of Fame goaltender. He was named the No. 1 Star of the Game in his debut on January 27. "We were playing against Toronto, and took them, 3-1. Jean (Pronovost) fed me on a breakaway for a goal, and I had an assist on a power play, out to (Greg) Polis in front of the net. You remember those things. Those first couple of games set my momentum for the year."

That goal, on a magnificent deke of Plante, was announced to a Canadian television audience by his own father. "I was being interviewed on the telecast of a game at Montreal that night," said the elder Apps. "They handed me a sheet of paper which had Syl's goal on it. Believe me, it was one of the greatest thrills I've ever had when I announced it."

Apps was 23 at the time. Kelly had put him on a line between left wing Greg Polis and right wing Jean Pronovost.

Young Apps had it all. He was a solid six footer, weighed 195 pounds, and had an accurate right-handed shot. He looked good, on and off the ice, and had a sophisticated air about him.

He had been a member of the superb Scarborough Lions peewee team that won every tournament in sight a decade earlier. New York Rangers' All-Star defenseman Brad Park was on the team and his father, Bob Park, coached the team. Apps played Junior B hockey in Kingston and then attended Princeton University.

"I was at Princeton for one year and played freshman hockey," said Syl. "I didn't have an especially good year. The players weren't too strong and sometimes it's more difficult to look good with bad players than it is with good players. The bad ones tend to get in your way."

Apps returned to Kingston where he attended Queens University and played with the Kingston Aces in the Ontario Hockey Association Senior Series. He turned pro with Omaha in 1969-70, recording 16 goals, 38 assists during the schedule. In the Central League playoffs, he exploded with a 10-9-19 ledger as Omaha won the title. He then shifted to Buffalo and helped the Bisons win the American Hockey League title. He cracked the Rangers lineup in 1970-71.

"A job worth doing is worth doing well," his father often told him.

"He always used to throw that line at me," said young Syl. "When I mowed the lawn, it seemed like eight acres, although it only took me about an hour and a half to complete. I used to cut the grass in the shape of flags and stuff. When he came home — zip! — I'd go out the back door. 'Wait until it rains,' I'd tell my father, 'you'll never know the difference.'"

Apps broke into the NHL with the Rangers. "I was in awe of playing in the NHL, and being around players I'd heard about or watched play on TV," Apps said. "The Rangers had a good chance at winning the Vezina Trophy (for the best goaltender in the league). Their top goalie, Eddie Giacomin, was having a good year. We'd be up 7-1, and Francis was still reluctant to use a rookie like me. He was reluctant to put in young players. He felt he owed it to Giacomin to go with his best lineup, not to let the other team get a cheap goal or two."

Apps played 31 games for the Rangers that year, and 11 with their farm team in Omaha, before he was dealt to Pittsburgh. In 31 games with the Rangers, Apps had one goal and two assists. In the same number of games, but with more playing minutes, he came up with nine goals and 16 assists in Pittsburgh.

The following season, Apps led the Penguins in scoring with 59 points, on 15 goals and 44 assists. In 1972-73, Apps again was the

Penguins' top point-maker with 85 (29 goals, 56 assists), in 1973-74 he was tops again with 85 points (24 goals, 61 assists). In 1974-75, Apps was runner-up to Ron Schock's 86 points with 79 points (24 and 55). In 1975-76, Apps was third behind Pierre Larouche (111 points) and Jean Pronovost (104) with 99 points, with a club-record 67 assists and 32 goals. The Penguins had three players in the top ten in scoring in the NHL for the first time in club history.

Checking out those numbers, it is easy to see why Apps rated being named to the Penguins Hall of Fame, and was to participate in induction ceremonies at the Civic Arena in October of 1994. He would be joining Pronovost, Bob Johnson and Rick Kehoe, who were honored in the charter class of 1992. Going into the 1994-95 season, Apps was second in career assists (349) only to Mario Lemieux (717) and among the top ten in several offensive categories of the club's all-time lists.

Apps centered for "The Century Line," with Pronovost at right wing and MacDonald at left wing. The trio accounted for 203 points and 84 goals in 1972-73, 239 points and 107 goals in 1973-74, 214 points and 94 goals in 1974-75, and 276 points and 114 goals in 1975-76.

And then it ended. MacDonald played just three games in 1976-77, 19 games the following season and was finished. Pronovost got frustrated and pushed for a trade and was dealt to Atlanta in 1978, and Apps was sent to Los Angeles in 1977.

"He's a late bloomer."
—Syl on his son

Syl and his wife, Anne, have three children, a son, Syl, 18, and two daughters, Gillian, 16, and Amy, 10. At the time of our interview, young Syl was looking forward to his final year of high school. His father says he is a good hockey player. "He plans to play hockey on a college level in the States," said his father. "He's always been small, and is just starting to grow. He's a late bloomer. I was one of those. I didn't turn pro until I was 21 or 22. I think he'll make out fine. His team came in third, and his team won the Ontario championship. He's serious about his hockey and his studies. He wants to get an education. The girls are both good students, too. I went the university route and he sees the wisdom of doing the same. I started out at Princeton, but just didn't feel right there, so I went to Queens (in Kingston, Ontario) and got my degree there. The odds of making the NHL and staying in the big leagues are slim to start with. I won't push it. If it works out, that's great. If it doesn't, you've still had fun playing college hockey, and you have something to show for it."

Syl Apps competed with the best of them, such as Hall of Famers Denis Potvin (5) of New York Islanders, at right above, and Frank Mahovlich (27) of Montreal Canadiens. Apps is now in Penguins' Hall of Fame.

Photos by George Gojkovich

"We had a lot of fun."
—Syl Apps

Apps has fond memories of the Penguins he played with, particularly Jean Pronovost, Lowell MacDonald, who teamed with him to form "The Century Line," and Dave Burrows, Ron Schock, Bryan Watson and Bob Paradise, just to name a few.

He pointed to Paradise as the player he most admired on the team. "He was just a good guy," explained Apps. "I broke into the pros with him at Omaha. He and Davey Burrows. I hung out with both of them. Bobby was a good leader. He didn't put up with anybody's b.s. He wouldn't stand back and ignore something that was bothering him. He'd speak his piece. But he was a good guy and a good team man."

Apps picked Watson as the character on the club he would not soon forget. "He brought a different element to the team," said Apps. "He was very supportive of everybody. He egged people on; he could get the best out of some guys, one way or another.

"We had a lot of fun. We had such a mix of personalities, just on our line alone. Prony had a boat-load of talent, and would voice his opinion. Lowell was quiet and went about his work. I was a little bit of a tyrant; I guess I could be pretty demanding at times. Lowell was something, considering he couldn't see twenty feet in front of him, yet he could find the corner of the nets with his shot."

"The Century Line" was known for passing the puck around a lot before anybody would unleash a shot, and sometimes drew criticism for over-passing. "Forget all those 'drop passes,' they'd say," recalled Apps. "They'd say it wasn't in the game plan. I didn't have a great shot. I wasn't going to take three steps over the blue line and beat anybody. I didn't think so, anyhow. Lowell wasn't a big shooter, either. Prony had the best shot of the three. Psychologically, maybe we just thought 'we'll get a little closer and have a better chance of getting the puck in the nets.' Prony knew if he could get to a certain spot, I'd look for him. And he'd look for me the same way. Lowell laid back a little, and covered for us both defensively."

When I asked Apps what he learned from his experience with the Penguins that has served him well since then, he said, "Team play. It serves one well in all of life."

"He wasn't quite in the same mold as everybody else."
—Apps on Pierre Larouche

When Pierre Larouche came to the team for the 1974-75 season it sent shock waves through the team. He was young, at 18, and brash, with tremendous talent, and upset some with his high salary, off-the-ice shenanigans and cocksure attitude.

Pierre Larouche   Vic Hadfield

"He wasn't real popular, but he had some talent," said Apps. "He wasn't quite in the same mold as everybody else. No one else had the same sort of elite junior career he had in Canada. He came in saying, 'I'm here.' Some people liked him for it, some people didn't."

Vic Hadfield came that same season, and he helped keep Larouche in line. "He was a great leader, a great guy all the way around," said Apps. "He was having trouble with his knees. It was unfortunate. If he had been healthy, he could have taught everyone a lot."

Hadfield came to the Penguins from the Rangers. Apps recalled another ex-Ranger in the same mold as Hadfield who was with the Penguins when Apps first joined the team. "Andy Bathgate was there," said Apps. "What a class individual he was."

"I led a charmed life."
—Syl Apps

I asked Apps what it meant to him to be named to the Penguins Hall of Fame, something Howard Baldwin instituted soon after he bought the team from Edward J. DeBartolo. "I feel honored, very much so," said Apps. "It's nice to be appreciated for what you've done. If you've been in a place long enough, you'd like to think you made a contribution to that sport in that city. I had so much fun there. I enjoyed that situation so much, despite the difficulties. I started out in New York, and finished up my career in Los Angeles, and Pittsburgh is where I had fun.

"When I look back on it, I led a charmed life. I was lucky to get a college education, and I was lucky to be traded to Pittsburgh where I had an opportunity to play in the NHL, and to play with some pretty terrific guys. I have friends who wonder what it was like, who wish they could have experienced what I experienced. My friends say, 'I'd like to just warm up in Chicago Stadium.' Millions of people would love to be in your shoes just once."

"Bloodlines are a wonderful thing."
—Red Kelly

His father was 80 at the time, and living in retirement in Kingston. "His health isn't that great," Apps reported. "He's always been proud of the fact that I did so well."

No more than that night in Montreal when the 27-year-old Syl won MVP honors for getting a goal and an assist in a 7-1 victory for the Prince of Wales team over the Clarence Campbell Conference team. There were 16,997 at the Montreal Forum for the NHL's 28th mid-season classic, but none was more excited than Syl's father.

Young Syl was two-and-a-half months old when his father had a goal and an assist in the first NHL All-Star Game. Apps took the opening faceoff in that showcase contest in 1947.

"I've had a lot of thrills in hockey," said the elder Syl, "but this is one of the greatest thrills I've ever had, watching my boy tonight."

His boy had been a late scratch in the two previous All-Star Games because of injuries. Apps had been added to the January 21, 1975 game by Bed Guidolin, the coach of the Kansas City Scouts.

"It was my first All-Star Game, and I was afraid to make a mistake in front of all the best hockey players," said young Syl. "I didn't want to be embarrassed in front of my family and all those people watching us on television."

Red Kelly, young Syl's first coach in Pittsburgh, had played against his father. "He was a great name, a great guy, a great player," recalled Kelly. "He went around me that first time as if he had jets. He went around me so fast I looked like a post on the ice. That was the year young Syl was born. He's got the breeding, you see. Bloodlines are a wonderful thing."

Syl's father was a center for the Maple Leafs from 1936 to 1948, and was the captain of three Stanley Cup winners. He was reported to have been an elegantly stylish player who was one of the best skaters in NHL history.

Frank Orr of the *Toronto Daily Star* wrote: "The name of Syl Apps recalls an era when life was simpler. He was the epitome of the clean-living, splendid-example-to-youth athlete, a non-cussing, let's-win-one-for-the-old-team leader who always contended for the Lady Byng Trophy as the big league's most effective gentleman."

He had been a graduate of McMaster University and a pole vaulter on Canada's 1936 Olympic track and field team.

Sylvanus Charles Joseph Apps was a member of the Ontario provincial parliament, and the owner of a brick company after his hockey career was completed. His son's name was Sylvanus Marshall Apps, but people just started calling him "Junior," even though he was not really a junior.

"The only advice I ever gave him," said the elder Apps after that 1975 All-Star Game, "was to skate hard, hit hard and don't get hurt."

Young Syl had to laugh lightly at the mention of his father's remarks. "He never pushed me in hockey," he said. "I was two or three years old when I started to play. But he pushed me in school.

"Dad always said keep your nose to the grindstone, your shoulder to the wheel and your ear to the ground and all will be well. But you can't do everything at once. My Dad also used to tell me there are a lot of opportunities in this world.

"It was inevitable that people were going to compare me to him. Although it didn't bother me that much, I'm sure I worked harder to succeed in hockey because my father was such a famous player."

Glen Sather

Bryan Watson

"The thing about being an agitator is to get the last word in and, above all, don't make sense. That really confuses them."
—Bryan Watson

Russ Anderson

Denis Herron

Welcome to Pittsburgh
Robitaille also has Reich connection

"I'd love to play with Mario."
—Luc Robitaille

Luc Robitaille and his family found Pittsburgh to be better than they anticipated, and thought they might very well prefer it to living in Los Angeles. Their first impressions were positive ones: the skyline was impressive, Luc liked all the rivers, and his wife said she was relieved to be away from forest fires, house burglars, race riots and earthquakes. They shared this in personal interviews. But in some respects, Robitaille had to recognize right away that, in some ways, Pittsburgh would be a lot like LA.

As impressive as his high-scoring credentials were after eight seasons with the Kings in the National Hockey League, Robitaille would still be playing second fiddle in Pittsburgh to Mario Lemieux. In LA, everybody bows to Wayne Gretzky.

There was even the possibility that Lemieux might not be playing for the Penguins, and he would still command the most attention among the hockey literati. Runner-up was the best Robitaille could hope for, just like in LA.

ESPN had released a stunning report a few days earlier that indicated Lemieux might pass up the entire 1994-95 NHL campaign, or a large part of it, to properly rehabilitate his back and to deal with problems from his Hodgkin's disease. Or, he just might retire altogether. Lemieux was in Europe, and Penguins officials were reluctant to comment on the report until they could meet with Lemieux, and find out what was on his mind.

That was the background when the Penguins called a press conference on August 3, 1994 to introduce Robitaille to Pittsburgh.

Robitaille brought his beautiful wife, Stacia (pronounced Stosh-ah), and his six-year-old stepson, Steven, to Pittsburgh within a few days after learning that the Kings had traded him to the Penguins for Rick Tocchet and a second-round draft pick in 1995. They were in Pittsburgh to meet the press, and to possibly pick out a home.

Stacia is a country blues singer, tall and stately, with long blond hair and huge blue eyes. Steven was cute and all smiles, and hammed it up whenever a photographer drew near. "He can smile that same smile every time on cue," remarked his dad. Otherwise, Steven wrapped himself around his dad's leg as his father stood and spoke to newsmen. This was a family direct from Hollywood casting. Yet Lemieux managed to steal the show, and he was *in Scotland* playing golf that day.

More time was devoted to debating about Lemieux's golf game, or his insistence on continuing to play the game when his back problems

Jim Cunningham

Luc Robitaille and son Steven and wife Stacia appear at press conference at Civic Arena soon after Penguins obtained Luc from LA Kings.

persisted and sidelined him during the hockey season, than to what Robitaille's presence might mean to the Penguins' chances of reclaiming the Stanley Cup.

The Robitailles shared a dais at the Igloo Club of the Civic Arena with another forward, John Cullen, who had been a scoring star for the Penguins a few years earlier but had been traded to the Hartford Whalers in a March, 1991 deal thought to have solidified two Stanley Cup championships for the Pens. Ron Francis, Grant Jennings and Ulf Samuelsson came to Pittsburgh in that deal in which the Pens also gave up Zarley Zalapski and Jeff Parker.

Cullen had not fared as well in Hartford or, in turn, Toronto and was thought to be damaged goods. He had been hurt most of the two previous campaigns, and had a career-low 30 points to show for his last season. But the Penguins thought they could use another center, whether or not Lemieux might be able to play, and that it made sense to sponsor Cullen's comeback. He was available and the price was right. Cullen was devastated when he was dispatched to Hartford, in the first place, and welcomed an opportunity to return to a team with which he had enjoyed his greatest success. The Boston U. grad had 92 points with the Penguins in 1989-90, and 94 points in 1990-91.

"There's a lot of ice time for everybody," cautioned Craig Patrick, the Penguins general manager. "We overuse people because of their talent. Now we just have to spread it out a little, so we're using rested people. That was our biggest problem at center. We were thin, we didn't have a lot of experienced guys there. Bryan Trottier was hurt most of the year. Mario was hurt most of the year. Ron Francis got overused."

Media who had followed the Penguins for a long time called out to Cullen, smiled or winked, shook his hand heartily and made him feel like he'd come back home. He even got some hugs from front-office workers. Cullen was all smiles. By comparison, the Robitailles looked a little nervous under the camera lights. They were all smiling, at no one in particular, straining, it seemed, eager to make a good first impression, eager to be accepted. They were, naturally, a little ill at ease in a roomful of strangers.

With Robitaille, a proven big-time goal-getter and seven-time NHL All-Star, and Cullen, the Penguins had pumped up their firepower. Tocchet was one of the most popular Penguins, and the fans would miss him, but a back injury had limited Tocchet to 51 games the previous season, and he remained a question mark. The 30-year-old Tocchet, who put in seven-and-a-half seasons with the Philadelphia Flyers before coming to Pittsburgh, had been great two years earlier when he came up with a career-high 48 goals, 61 assists and 109 points. The year before, he joined the Penguins in mid-season, in time to help them win their second straight Stanley Cup.

Tocchet had been a tough cookie, and someone who looked after Lemieux. He had undergone back surgery in Philadelphia in June and had resumed skating, and was thought to be ready for training camp.

He was also thought to be an *old* 30.

There was speculation Kings' star Wayne Gretzky had lobbied to get Tocchet. The word is that Gretzky gets what he wants in LA. He didn't care for Robitaille for whatever reasons.

Robitaille knew better than to talk about that subject. "Personally, I wouldn't want to get into that," he said, begging off. And he was equally careful about what he said about Lemieux. No one had to tell Robitaille his role alongside Lemieux in the Penguins' scheme of things.

"I'd love to play with Mario," said Robitaille. "He's one of the greatest players ever to play the game. But it's really up to him. Nothing I can say or do is going to make any difference. I guess he feels a lot of pressure to come back, but if I was him, I'd just be worried about living to be 60 or 70 . . . and enjoying all that money."

Some suspected that the Penguins got Robitaille and Cullen, a small center, as insurance in case Lemieux might not play. They credited Patrick for perhaps pulling off another steal in swapping Tocchet, suspect back and all, for Robitaille, one of the NHL's most consistent scorers throughout his career with the Kings.

The 28-year-old Robitaille had set an NHL goal-scoring record for left wingers during the 1992-93 season with 63 and finished the season with a career-high 125 points. He had 44 goals and 42 assists in 1993-94, and had scored 50 or more goals three times and 44 or more goals eight times. Luc could score, but how would he fit in?

"With Luc and Kevin Stevens, we now have the two best left wingers in the National Hockey League," pointed out Patrick. Robitaille and Stevens both scored more than 40 goals the year before.

Robitaille, 6-1 and 190 pounds, was more resilient than his reputation as strictly an offensive player might suggest, having missed a total of only eight games during his eight seasons in the NHL. He was an immediate hit, winning the Calder Memorial Trophy, as the NHL's best rookie in 1986-87, recording 84 points (45 goals and 39 assists).

I remarked to Robitaille that Penguins' fans, at first, said, "This is a steal!" Then, on second thought, they asked, "What's wrong with Robitaille? Something must be wrong."

Robitaille smiled at the remarks. "There is nothing wrong with me. I'm healthy, I can assure you of that," he said. "But in six months, they might say, 'Hey, we got screwed.' I have to give extra, and even more than that. If we win, that's all that matters. People will say it's a good trade."

Asked if he might prove helpful to Lemieux, he said, "I don't know how I can help Mario, except maybe that I'm also from Montreal, and I speak French, too. Maybe that will make him more comfortable with me."

The Penguins had improved themselves one way or another, no one doubted that. The Penguins might lack a bodyguard for Lemieux with Tocchet gone, but gifted scorers are harder to come by than henchmen in the NHL ranks. Tocchet, though, was a tough guy with talent. They had brought back Marty McSorley from LA the previous year, but that didn't work out. The Penguins still needed to get some "grinders" and "muckers," in hockey parlance, to complete their lineup.

If reputations mean anything, Robitaille was regarded as a scorer who did little checking and left the combat for others. As first impressions go, he looked like a Russian ballet star when he entered the Igloo Club. He is handsome, almost elegant, lithe, pale, hollow-cheeked, on the soft side, as appearances go. At the same time, he was friendly, cooperative, doing his best to fit in. He could be a tiger in disguise.

"I'm here to prove that I'm more than a goal-scorer," said Robitaille.

> *"That was out of a movie script. That was from a dream sequence."*
> —Tom Reich on Mario's return from radiation treatment

Luc Robitaille shared the same agent as Lemieux. Tom Reich (pronounced Rich), a Pittsburgh-born and bred attorney who now lives in Los Angeles, entered the room after the initial introductions. He stayed away until his client had completed his interviews. Reich needed no introduction. Now 56, he had represented Penguins and Pirates through the years, and was well known to all the media. His nephew, Steve, a 33-year-old attorney, looks after Lemieux's needs in Pittsburgh out of the Reich, Werner & Alexander law firm at One PPG Place.

The Penguins had tried to avoid turning this coming-out party for Robitaille and Cullen into a Lemieux press conference. Even before Patrick introduced the principals at the dais, Penguins' publicist Harry Sanders had instructed the media that questions would not be fielded from the floor, as was the usual procedure. Rather, everyone could do their own one-on-one interviews.

Patrick was obviously wary that the media would start asking questions about Lemieux's status, and it might make Robitaille and Cullen uncomfortable. After all, they weren't exactly chopped liver.

In making the announcement, Patrick said, "We are extremely pleased to add Luc to our team. We feel he will give us additional scoring punch. In acquiring Robitaille, we had to part with a player who has been a great asset to the Penguins, during the past three seasons."

The Penguins put on a first-class luncheon. They always do. After they finished their meals, the media surrounded Robitaille and Cullen to do their interviews. They abandoned both, however, when Reich entered the room.

Reich looked like he was representing the Los Angeles Raiders. He was wearing a smart-looking light gray double-breasted suit, a black pocket handkerchief, and an oatmeal-colored tie that wasn't up to snuff with the rest of his classy attire. His hair and beard were a well-coordinated black and gray, with streaks of silver. His eyes shone behind dark-rimmed glasses. He would have drawn approval from Raiders' owner Al Davis for his natty wardrobe.

Reich is confident and comfortable in the company of reporters, especially familiar ones from the newspapers, TV and radio stations of his native Pittsburgh. It is a sign of the times in sports today that agents command more attention than players in such a setting. They always have more to say.

"I can tell you this," remarked Reich in the way of openers, alluding to Lemieux's playing status. "A decision has not been made.

"His ability to come back the same way he did (in 1993) after he completed the radiation treatments, scoring a goal in Philadelphia just hours after his final treatment, was not reality. That was out of a movie script. It creates expectations that are unrealistic. That was something out of a dream sequence. That's not reality. He didn't have a back problem until the second game of the playoffs; that probably cost us the Islanders' series. The reality of Hodgkin's disease is that we have to review his situation every year.

"If he can play in safety and in comfort, he's going to play. He's a hockey player. He understands the risks. The steps we're going to take him through are so that Mario can make the most informed decision he can make regarding his well-being. That's what we're doing. He'll be evaluated by all the doctors in regard to his back and his Hodgkin's disease. He doesn't make this kind of decision in a vacuum. After we get fresh medical information, we'll make a decision."

On that last line, with the "we" reference, Reich reminded us of one of those cornermen in boxing who say things like "We'll take his best punch."

It had only recently been disclosed that Lemieux became anemic during the playoffs in April, 1994. He was no longer anemic, but it was a source of concern.

"There will be a battery of tests, both on his back, and in relation to his Hodgkin's," said Reich. "When he developed anemia, that was obviously very serious. If you or I develop anemia, it's no big deal. But when somebody with Hodgkin's disease develops anemia, it's a whole different ballgame. Even when it returns to normal, which it did, it's cause for concern. The downside of his back is one thing, but the downside of Hodgkin's is something quite different, something we don't even want to belabor at this point; it's the end game none of us want to deal with. This is not a blip on the screen; it requires a decision.

"Obviously, it's a decision that affects a lot of people. If he doesn't play, there's no one here who will be sadder than me. If he doesn't play we'll have a situation of deepest depression. This is not fun. Coming here for Luc Robitaille, that's fun. You have a new player in town.

"Mario told me that he felt worse on the ice this past season than at any other time in his life. I don't want to belabor this, but this guy has had two people in his family who have died of Hodgkin's disease. There's a tremendous amount of uncertainty. I don't want to overplay it — there's limited data on it — but it's cancer. There's a 95 percent remission rate — that's not a cure rate — and ten percent die from it. This is no game. This is way more serious. It ain't the flu.

"He was out with the back injury when they learned he had Hodgkin's disease. Mario has been here for ten years, becoming one of the greatest hockey players of all time. When healthy, he's probably the greatest hockey player who ever lived. He couldn't have approached that without a lot of hard work. He has worked hard. And he can do it again if necessary to resume playing. If he hadn't had problems relating to his Hodgkin's disease, he'd be in a normal off-season regimen.

"Do you realize the level of fitness it takes to play hockey? You know it's higher than baseball, right?"

He spoke of the Catch-22 situation with what Lemieux is dealing with. "When you have that, you're supposed to rest," he said. "He gets criticized for playing golf, but that's his r. and r. (rest and recreation). If you can deny him that, there's something wrong with your thinking. Golf is therapy for him. It's something he needs for himself, to get away and do what he enjoys. It's good for his body and good for his mind. If the time comes when he has to apologize for some r. and r. — playing golf or taking his family to the Cayman Islands — everybody can go to hell. We also have to worry about how all this will affect how he gets around in his second life, after sports.

"He's gone through things that are unbelievable to me. I can't believe, considering what this man has done, what he's accomplished, how he's enriched this city, what he's done for charity, some of the shit that I've been reading. I've read that he simply ought to retire, or that the Penguins should trade him while he still has value. Where does he deserve that? I probably wouldn't be in this business anymore if I had not met Mario Lemieux."

Reich negotiated a $42 million contract in 1992 that was fully guaranteed. "If he's able to play, the contract speaks for itself," said Reich. "If he's not able to play, it will be worked out with the Penguins the way we always work things out with the Penguins, amicably and cordially."

When someone pressed him for details of the contract, saying the public wanted to know whether or not Lemieux would be paid regardless of whether he could or could not play, Reich shook his head. "I'm not going to tell you that anymore than I'm going to tell you what I learned about O.J. Simpson out in LA."

"What do you know about O.J.?" a reporter shot back.

"Don't be looking for him in any old-timers' games for awhile," replied Reich, unable to restrain himself.

Once upon a time, the Penguins were the poor boys on the Pittsburgh sports scene. Times change. Reich arrived back home just days after Pirates officials had put the team up for sale. They put the mayor on notice that he had six months to find a local owner, according to the terms of the ballclub's agreement with the city and its stadium lease, or they would put it up to the highest bidder, who might take the team elsewhere. Then, too, the baseball players had set a strike deadline of August 12. "There's no way the ballplayers will ever accept a salary cap," said Reich. "I've represented enough baseball players, and I know how they're thinking. Forget that."

Reich may live in LA these days, but he's always been a Pittsburgher at heart. He remembers watching the rookie Ralph Kiner break in at Forbes Field back in 1946. Reich said, "It would be a massive, abominable blow to the city if Pittsburgh loses the Pirates."

"Life is so much bigger than hockey."
—Luc Robitaille

Robitaille was excited about playing for the Penguins. "They're a good team and they have a chance to win the Stanley Cup," remarked Robitaille, when assessing the situation. "They have a lot of scoring power up front, a good defense and a great goalie. That's what you need.

"They have great talent here, a great team. They had a great year for 80 games last season. They just couldn't get untracked in the playoffs.

"There's nothing good enough if you don't win the Cup. I'd be happy with 30 goals if we won the Cup. There comes a time when you really want to win it. For me, that time is now."

He mentioned how much he had enjoyed playing for the Canadian team that won the World Championship. This tournament is held every year in April, the same month the NHL playoffs begin. Canada can only send players from teams that don't make the playoffs or are eliminated in the first round.

"We all had terrible years," recalled Robitaille, "which accounted for us being available to play. We talked to ourselves in preparation for the games, and we said, 'We're not losers. Let's do something we can be proud of.' And we did. Hopefully, I won't get to go to the World Championships again for a long time."

Asked to account for his availability in a trade, considering his super stats, Robitaille shrugged. "It had a lot to do with new management," he said. "I don't think the reason was on ice. It doesn't matter anymore. This team wants me. Mr. Baldwin and Mr. Patrick want me. And I want to prove I'm more than a goal-scorer. I want to win.

"Last season was hard in Los Angeles. A lot of things happened, mostly off the ice. It's hard when somebody doesn't want you.

"Sometimes you gain the respect of your teammates by paying the price. You take a check in the corner or a beating in front of the net. I know I gave everything I had. I'm happy to be here. I think it will be a big break for my career. I talked with my wife about that, and I told her this will be best for my career."

Asked about the possibility of teaming up with Lemieux, he said, "Mario is the best player in the game. He's been through a lot. No one can understand what Mario has gone through unless they're Mario. He had to deal with cancer and a bad back. I've had injuries and I've had things happen to me, but this is different. It has a lot to do with life. Life is so much bigger than hockey.

"I think he has to make his own decision. Only Mario can make this decision.

"I'd love to play with Mario. He's one of the greatest players ever to play, the greatest now. His situation is a hard situation. I don't think anyone would want to be in his shoes. I can understand how he has to take his time. He has to make sure he takes care of himself."

He had been given a quick introduction to what he might expect in Pittsburgh from his agents.

"Having Tom Reich and Steve Reich representing me, I knew a lot about the city," related Robitaille. "Knowing Tom and Steve, it was easy for me to ask questions about the city."

The Robitailles had arrived in Pittsburgh the night before. They were picked up at the airport by Steve Reich. They had the usual visitors' reaction when they came through the Fort Pitt Tunnel and had Pittsburgh burst upon them. The lights were on at Three Rivers Stadium as they crossed the Fort Pitt Bridge. Elton John and Billy Joel had joined up on a concert tour, and they had drawn nearly 40,000 to hear them sing. I was at that concert, and it's a shame the Robitailles weren't there to get the proper introduction to Pittsburgh and its people.

"I had been here for four days for the All-Star Game (in 1990), and I always liked it," said Robitaille. "But we were looking at it with a lot more attention this time. It's beautiful at night. I love water, and we're surrounded here by three rivers, right?"

Regarding his reputation as "a soft player," Robitaille remarked:

"I love to play the game, and I consider myself a winner. A lot of people have classified me as strictly a goal-scorer. I'll do whatever is necessary to win. I'm looking forward to the change. The whole situation in Los Angeles was hard last year."

Wouldn't he miss the glamour and glitz of LA?

"It becomes a time when you get enough of that," he said with a smile. "I consider it safer here."

When their car came through the Fort Pitt Tunnel, Stacia was startled. "The first thing I thought about was earthquake," she said. "In Los Angeles, you don't go into tunnels. We were in such awe when we saw the city all lit up at night. Steven said, 'Oh, my god, it's so beautiful!' I was shocked. I came here once before for Tom Barrasso's golf outing to raise money for his daughter's cancer foundation, but I never really saw the Downtown before. I'm excited.

"We are staying at the William Penn Hotel. I said, 'Luc, I'm so happy. I don't have to worry about earthquakes anymore.' We went through the riots in LA, we were robbed in our home as we were sleeping — which was so scary to think about — and we had the forest fires this year. I don't have to worry about anybody at my back anymore."

Stacia spooks easily, it seems. She confessed that during their first night at the William Penn, a refurbished old hotel, she said to Luc, "Oh my, God, I'll bet there are ghosts in this hotel."

During our conversation in the Igloo Club the following day, she disclosed, "We're going to look at houses today in Sewickley, and I'm looking forward to that. I'm told it's a nice area. I'm a country blues singer, and Nashville is a lot closer to Pittsburgh — I'm told it's an hour and a half flight — than it is to Los Angeles. That should be good for me and my career, too."

She wasn't sure how the cold weather would affect their pot-bellied Vietnamese pig, Wilbur. She said they had two horses, two goats, one pig and two dogs. Sewickley as well as Washington County, out where the Penguins were building a new training complex at Southpointe, could accommodate a menagerie like the Robitailles were bringing with them.

With the kind of money he makes, Robitaille could afford the kind of layout necessary to unload Noah's ark.

Agent Tom Reich explains Mario Lemieux's physical problems.

303

Where Are They Now?
Paul Gardner (1980-84)

"Pittsburgh is still a favorite city of mine."

Present home: Scarborough, Maine

Present job: Assistant coach of Washington Capitals development team, the Portland Pirates of the American Hockey League, and co-coach of New England Stingers of Roller Hockey International.

Family information: Son Scott, 12, and daughters Ashley, 10, and Lindsey, 8, all born in Pittsburgh. Paul married Sherri Largent in June, 1994.

Personal highlight of Penguins' career: Being first Penguin to score four goals in a game (against Philadelphia on Dec. 14).

Most cherished memory of playing days: First NHL goal in first NHL game in Montreal vs. Kenny Dryden. Scoring goal in Penguins' game the day after my son was born (Dec. 19, 1981)

Players you most admired on the team: Greg Malone and Rick Kehoe — good friends, good teammates and they worked hard.

Favorite character on the club: Gary Rissling, always upbeat, great team player.

Role model: Ken Schinkel was an excellent influence off the ice, both as an advisor and friend.

What you best remember about Pittsburgh: Pittsburgh is still a favorite city of mine, and I visit it every summer at least once.

Paul Gardner
Growing up in a hockey family
"It's a great lifestyle."

The ruddy face was a familiar one. He had last played for the Penguins a decade earlier, yet he looked and felt right at home in the Civic Arena. Paul Gardner grinned through a thick mustache, auburn going gray. Gardner greeted two old friends, Jim Rooker and Jackie Powell, who had been talking to each other.

This was Monday evening, August 15, 1994, a few minutes before the final regular season game in the second season of Roller Hockey International. The home team was the Pittsburgh Phantoms, a first-year franchise owned by Howard Baldwin and the same investment group that bankrolled the Penguins.

Gardner was the co-coach of the visiting New England Stingers. Rooker was a former Pirates pitcher and broadcaster who was there to sign autographs, take a bow at mid-rink before the face-off, and toss a few rubber baseballs to the fans. Powell had been the goalie judge for the Hornets and the Penguins from 1937 to 1991, and had come out of retirement, at age 82, to perform the same job for the Phantoms.

They were gathered alongside the north end of the rink, in an area just outside the hallway that leads to the locker rooms. I was seated nearby and came over to say hello to all three of them.

As he approached me and shook my hand, Powell pointed back at Gardner, and shook his bald head. He remembered how Eddie Johnston, in his first year as general manager, had sent Gardner to the minors during the 1983-84 campaign.

"Gardner was one of the guys E.J. got rid of, and it was a mistake," said Powell, who always speaks in a whisper directly into your ear like he is sharing a secret or scoop. "He came back after breaking both his heels while working on his house to score 17 power play goals. You'd think you'd find a spot for a guy like that."

Powell returned to where Gardner was talking to Rooker. Gardner and Rooker knew each other from frequenting some of the same watering holes in Pittsburgh in the early '80s.

"This is what I've come to," said Rooker, who had been released about six months earlier from a high profile position as a member of the Pirates' broadcast team, after 13 years as a color analyst on radio and TV. The well-tanned Rooker remained a handsome devil, but he looked a little ill at ease at being part of a three-ring circus.

Rooker was wearing a too-snug Phantoms' jersey with No. 7 on the sleeves. He was going to be the "celebrity captain" for the evening's entertainment. Rooker received a lengthy introduction over the p.a. system, including the fact that he had been one of the heroes of the Pirates' 1979 World Series triumph over the Baltimore Orioles.

Remember Rooker in Game 5 after the Pirates had lost three of the first four games? He gave the Pirates a chance to come back and win it all.

Rooker had ripped the Pirates' management bitterly when he was dismissed. He had burned all bridges behind him. He still ran Rook's East Side Saloon in Ambridge. He was still blond, and he still had that winning smile.

Under normal circumstances, the Pirates would have been on the road that night, traveling on an open date from Miami to Los Angeles — no one would have enjoyed a Florida to West Coast tour more than Rooker — but the Major League Baseball Players Association had called a strike four days earlier. Suddenly, roller hockey was the only game in town. At least on this particular evening. And Rooker was a lounge act.

Gardner also greeted former linemate Rick Kehoe, who was coaching the Phantoms, in addition to serving as one of Eddie Johnston's assistants on the Penguins. Kehoe was wearing a silver-gray double-breasted blazer, color-coordinated with his carefully-combed hair, and a burgundy shirt and black tie and black slacks. He was wearing the Phantoms' colors. Gardner was more casual in a white cotton knit jersey with a subtle team logo over the left breast, with dark slacks.

"This is our last game of the season," said Gardner, with more than a hint of relief. "I get two weeks vacation and then hockey camp opens again."

Gardner's main job is as an assistant coach for the Pirates of Portland, Maine and the American Hockey League, the top farm team of the Washington Capitals. The Pirates were owned by the same people who owned the Stingers, so Gardner was asked to stay on and coach them as well, along with Barry Trotz.

The Pirates had won the Calder Cup as AHL champions, while the Stingers were simply playing out the string. The season had not gone well, the team hadn't drawn many fans, and Gardner had to wonder whether the team would be back for another season in Roller Hockey International.

Gardner had spent the afternoon telephoning old friends and watching TV, shows like Donahue — just "killing time," he said with a shrug — at the Hyatt Hotel across Centre Avenue from the Civic Arena. Since the Stingers were staying in the same hotel where many NHL visiting teams are accommodated, I asked Gardner if it was anything like traveling with an NHL team.

"No, it's not the same," said Gardner. "It's a laidback attitude in this league. The players make $180 a game, so it's not taken that seriously. Five or six of our guys didn't have much of a chance to get used to roller blade skating because our ice hockey season lasted so long, and we dug ourselves a hole. They don't play it with the same intensity, they don't take losing as badly. For most of the team, it's a matter of staying in shape, and picking up a little extra money.

"It's different from ice hockey. You can't stop and go like you normally do. You can't stop on a dime like you do on ice skates. Here, you have to make a quick circle. It's a lot slower pace than most people thought it would be. It's wide open, with four on four instead of five on five. There's no blueline, so there are fewer offside calls. There are four 12-minute quarters instead of three 20-minute periods."

Ticket prices are different, too. They range from $11 to $9 for adults, and $8 to $6 for youngsters 12-and-under. Many in the crowd wore NHL game jerseys, just like they do at Penguins' games. There were a lot of young people in the stands.

"I played about five games myself this season," said Gardner, "and it's not the same game. It takes some getting used to."

"I really enjoyed the dressing room and the guys."

Paul Gardner played for the Penguins from 1980 to 1984. He was acquired along with Dave Burrows from the Toronto Maple Leafs for Kim Davis and Paul Marshall — a real steal of a deal — in November of 1980.

He was with them when they went from being a fairly competitive club to an embarrassment for the NHL.

Gardner was the team's third-leading scorer that first season, with 34 goals, 40 assists and 74 points in only 62 games, trailing Kehoe (88 points) and Randy Carlyle (83 points), as the Penguins finished third behind Monteal and Los Angeles in the five-team Norris Division.

During the 1981-82 season, Gardner shared the team lead with Mike Bullard for most goals with 36. He was fourth in scoring for the Penguins with 69 points.

He led the team in 1981-82 in power play goals with 21 and again in 1982-83 with 20.

In that 1982-83 season, he was sixth in scoring in his last full campaign with the Penguins with 55 points. The Penguins finished sixth and last that year in the Patrick Division.

Gardner played only 16 games with the Penguins the next season, and scored no goals, when he was demoted to the minors. The Penguins, coached by Lou Angotti, finished with a 16-58-6 record for 38 points, their worst record ever and the worst overall record in the NHL. It gave them the No. 1 selection in the 1984 entry draft and the chance to draft Mario Lemieux.

There was a big difference for Gardner between that first and last season in Pittsburgh.

Soon after he joined the Penguins, he became the first player in club history to record four goals in a game, scoring them against the Philadelphia Flyers on December 13, 1980. "It was like my tenth game with the team, and it was a big thing in helping me fit in and feel comfortable," recalled Gardner. "They had gotten me to help on the power play, and to score goals, and I proved in a hurry that I could do just that."

Gardner, like most of the former Penguins interviewed for this book, expressed positive thoughts about his experience in Pittsburgh. He liked the city, the fans and, most of all, his teammates. Looking back, the record didn't seem to matter. "I really enjoyed the dressing room and the guys," he said. "There were never any fights in the dressing room. We had a great group of guys and we got along well.

"In all my years here, the games that stand out the most were two deciding playoff games we lost. The one we lost in my first year here came in the second overtime in St. Louis in the preliminary round, and the next year we lost to the Islanders in overtime in the deciding game of the preliminary round. We were leading with six minutes to go, and lost at Nassau Coliseum. They were both losses, but both memorable games.

"Rick Kehoe was my linemate the whole time I was here. At first, we played with Ross Lonsberry, and he retired, and then we played with Pat Boutette. Kehoe was great to play with. I played for Eddie Johnston for three years, and then with Lou Angotti for one year. Eddie was great to play for. He was an upbeat guy, lots of fun. And he wanted to win in the worst way. He's a hockey man all the way."

I asked Gardner what it was like playing for the Penguins in the pre-Lemieux period.

"It was frustrating in my last full season," he said. "I got hurt during training camp, I was home on a day off, putting in storm windows. I fell off a ladder and broke both of my heels. I missed four weeks of the season. At the end of the season, they sent four or five veteran guys to the minors — I was one of them. They wanted to revamp the team and build for the future, so they got rid of many veterans. I had scored 200 goals (201, in fact) and it hurt to get sent down like that. I went with Jimmy Rutherford, Roberto Romano and Ted Bulley. We had a good team in Baltimore.

"Then I signed with Washington; they were struggling with their power play, and thought I could help."

Gardner signed with the Washington Capitals as a free agent for the 1984-85 season. "When Bob Berry became the coach of the Penguins, he called me to see if I wanted to come back to Pittsburgh, but I had already signed with Washington, and he wasn't aware of that. I've often wondered what it would have been like to have played with Mario. And what might have been. He's brilliant to watch. He makes the game look so easy. He's in control. But I ended up as a scout and then coaching for the Washington Capitals, so I can't complain. The Capitals have treated me well. Maybe it was meant to be.

"I was with Washington for two years, but played mostly with Binghamton in the American Hockey League. Then I went to Buffalo for a short span."

Altogether, he was in the National Hockey League for seven seasons. Then he became a player-coach with the Rochester Americans.

"It's been wonderful," said Gardner. "I wouldn't trade it for anything. I've been fortunate to make a good living. It's a great lifestyle."

I asked him what he thought would happen to Lemieux. "The word around hockey is that he'll sit out this season," said Gardner. "People think he'll take a long time to evaluate his situation, to see how bad his back is, and the other stuff. They think he'll sit out the whole year."

He mentioned two of the bright lights in addition to Kehoe in his stay with the Penguins, namely Ken Schinkel and Greg Malone.

"Schinkel was a great influence on me," said Gardner. "He was a real special friend. We were close, even though he was in upper management. We played a lot of golf together. He was like a father away from home for me. I go out of my way to see him whenever it's possible.

"Greg Malone and I played junior hockey together at Oshawa. When I came here, he was the guy who took me around. Greg and I stayed here in summers, and played golf together — we loved to play in all those charity golf outings — and became good friends. We traveled everywhere together."

"It was wonderful having a hockey dad and a hockey brother."
—Paul Gardner

Gardner has been able to do just what his dad did, just what his big brother did, what he grew up hoping he might be able to do someday. His dad was Cal Gardner, who played in the National Hockey League with the New York Rangers, Toronto, Chicago and Boston for a total of 12 seasons (1945-46 to 1956-57). He was with two Stanley Cup championship teams in Toronto (1949 and 1951).

Paul's older brother, Dave, played seven seasons in the NHL, with Montreal, St. Louis, California, Cleveland and Philadelphia (1972-73 to 1979-80).

"Dave was four years older than me, so we never played together on any real teams when we were growing up," said Paul. "But he was there to go watch. He was a big help. When we played in the street, I was always the littlest kid, and I got to play because of Dave. He looked after me.

"There were just us two boys. We grew up in Toronto, and my dad and mom (Mary) are still there. They are both 70, and they are both in good health.

"My mom and dad were a big influence on me. It was wonderful having a hockey dad and a hockey brother. We were a hockey family. Dad and Mom both stressed education. That was the No. 1 rule: school was first. Dave and I both did well in school. If you didn't do well in school, you didn't get to play hockey. It was that simple.

"Dave got to see Dad play late in his career, in the American Hockey League. Dad finished up as a player-coach with Springfield. Then he coached a year in Cleveland in the late '50s.

"So I really followed in my dad's footsteps in so many ways."

"It was called the Civic Auditorium, and the principal tenant was the Civic Light Opera."

The scene at the Civic Arena brought back many memories. They opened the roof of the Civic Arena, something that's rarely done, even though temperatures had dipped into the mid-50s, and it brought a bit of a chill for some fans seated in the upper reaches. I visited the press box at the top of the building, directly under the opening in the roof. The view from there was stunning. It's the city skyline from the opposite side from where it is normally viewed and pictured. The sky was dark blue and provided quite a backdrop for all the familiar skyscrapers.

The Civic Arena opened in 1961. Only then it was called the Civic Auditorium, and its principal tenant was the Civic Light Opera. The $22 million facility was designed for the Civic Light Opera's productions. Having a steel roof that opened to the stars was going to be an added attraction.

It was there that I saw Civic Light Opera stage productions — mostly musicals — and remember seeing the same with my sister Carole at Pitt Stadium as a youngster. I don't think I had been in the Arena when the roof was opened for over 30 years.

Built from 2,950 tons of Pittsburgh steel, the mammoth dome opens and closes in two-and-a-half minutes.

I had seen lots of events over the years at the Civic Arena, but this was the first time I had ever witnessed a professional roller hockey game.

There was a boisterous crowd of 5,141 on hand, which I thought was quite good. That was about the size of some of the weekday crowds that came to see the Penguins play when Gardner was on the team.

It wasn't hockey, but it was an interesting summer diversion, an excuse for an evening out at the Civic Arena. The Phantoms ripped the Stingers, 18-6. I think there were two goals scored in the first 30 seconds of the game, one by each team. Deck hockey is much more difficult for goalies.

The crowd gave its loudest cheer each time Bryan Trottier was mentioned over the p.a. system. Trottier played for the Phantoms, but only at home games, which tells you all you need to know about the intensity or casual approach of Roller Hockey International. Trottier had played for six Stanley Cup winners, four with the Islanders and two with the Penguins, and had been a player/coach with the Pittsburgh team the previous season. He was playing as a favor to his boss.

Warren Young, who served as Kehoe's assistant, had started playing for the Phantoms the week before. No one ever benefited more from playing on the same line as Mario Lemieux. A journeyman player in the minors most of his pro career, Young was signed as a free agent by the Penguins and had 40 goals and 32 assists to finish second in scoring only to Lemieux for the 1984-85 season. It was the only time two rookies ever scored 40 or more goals for the Penguins. Both made the NHL's All-Rookie team.

Pittsburgh's Civic Arena

Pittsburgh Penguins

Trottier had two goals and four assists, and Young picked up a goal against the New England team.

Alain Lemieux, brother of Mario, was missing from the Phantoms' lineup. He hadn't dressed for six games, and had not been at practice in recent weeks. Kehoe said he didn't know of Lemieux's whereabouts. Alain's absence didn't rate the same sort of media attention as the possibility of his kid brother doing the same with the Penguins.

The Phantoms had a strange season. It included an eight-game winning streak at the outset of the season, and a seven-game losing streak in the stretch run. They finished the regular schedule with a 13-9 record and would open the playoffs against the Chicago Cheetahs.

The Chicago Cheetahs . . .

The Phantoms had a woman goalie, Erin Whitten, and a black forward, Bruce Coles, a swift skater who scored two goals, and their own cheerleader/dance team. There was something for everyone in the Phantoms' production. Every time there was a break in the action, somebody was dancing, competing in some kind of skills contest, or music was turned on to the max and shook the building. There was everything, but a quiet moment for reflection.

The Chicago Cheetahs . . .

I had seen the Pittsburgh Pipers and Pittsburgh Condors of the American Basketball Association play at the Civic Arena — most of the sideshows seen in sports today started with the ABA — the Pittsburgh Hornets of the American Hockey League, Pitt and Duquesne and high school basketball games, Bruno Sammartino and his wrestling colleagues, the Pittsburgh Triangles of World Team Tennis, the Pittsburgh Spirit of the Major Indoor Soccer League.

Now there was another new team bankrolled by Baldwin & Co. called the Stingers of the two-year-old Continental Indoor Soccer League. It was coached by Paul Child, who had been a popular and productive performer for the Spirit.

I had two seats on the aisle, third row from the rink, and I was watching my first Phantoms' game with my oldest daughter, Sarah, who would soon be 21 and starting her third year at the University of Virginia. Sarah started watching sports when she was about three or four years old, and tagging along with me, when I was covering the New York Islanders and New York Nets at Nassau Coliseum.

What next? I had covered jai-alai, horse and greyhound racing and alligator wrestling when I worked in Miami. I remember covering a professional box lacrosse match at Nassau Coliseum. I had written about ping-pong players, all kinds of Olympic sports. I had played pool with Willie Mosconi and Jackie Gleason only a block away, when Gleason was staying at the William Penn while promoting his "Great One" TV series. Remember Gleason and Paul Newman in "The Hustler"?

I was back in a building where Billie Jean King and Evonne Goolagong and Kenny Rosewall and Gordie Howe and Jean Beliveau and Bobby Orr and Bobby Hull and Connie Hawkins, Dr. J and Rick Barry and Wilt Chamberlain and Norman Nixon and Billy Knight and Calvin Murphy and so many sports superstars had played or performed.

I had seen Sugar Ray Robinson, Sonny Liston, Muhammad Ali and Floyd Patterson box there. And when the roof opened at the Civic Arena, I saw all those stars all over again.

Gardner was right. Playing in Pittsburgh was a great thing to do.

Paul Gardner and his new wife Sherri Largent (they were married June 25, 1994) with his son Scott, 12, Ashley, 10, and Lindsey, 8. All three children were born in Pittsburgh.

Red Kelly on working

Even as a youngster, laboring on his dad's southern Ontario farm during the tobacco harvest, Red Kelly learned something about coaching, which served him in good stead during his three and a half seasons with the Penguins (1969-1973). A field boss before he was 16, he realized the importance of creating harmony with the men who worked with him.

He harvested crops for 20 years with the benefit of machinery. "It was tough work," he said. "We would put up 1,200 sticks of tobacco a day, which amounted to two tons of cured tobacco. The work would give you a strong back and legs, and helped your wrists, too."

He reported to training camp eight to ten days late to complete the annual harvest, but he would catch up in a hurry to what his teammates were doing. "I was always in playing shape, or working shape," claimed Kelly.

Pittsburgh Penguins

Why Red Kelly Preferred Pittsburgh to Los Angeles

"I wouldn't want to have continued in Los Angeles. We lived about a mile from where Sharon Tate was murdered. My family didn't like it and we had our house broken into. They stole my family stereo and my wife's jewelry. And there were mud slides and fires not far away. Hang, I'll take snow and mud any day."

On Home-Ice Advantage:
*"It's an advantage
in knowing the curvature
of the rink and the
resiliency of the boards.
You have to know how
the puck comes off them.
You use the boards
like a pool table.
It's almost as if
they were another man."*
—Red Kelly

Paul Martha
Insider's view

"It would be a shame if the sports tradition of this city were allowed to die. Things can be done to prevent Pittsburgh from becoming a ghost town as far as sports are concerned."

—Paul Martha, 1992

Paul Martha's ominous warning about Pittsburgh's bleak sports future was fresh in my mind as I motored through the once-bustling milltowns of Rankin, Braddock, Duquesne, Munhall, Homestead, Hays and my hometown of Hazelwood.

It was an overcast gray day in January of 1992 and the landscape did nothing to brighten my spirits. I had been spending time the previous few days near my old neighborhood attending a funeral in our family, and I was in a funk.

Passing through ghost towns will only darken your mood.

So many empty buildings, so many rust-coated roofs and equipment, rusty skeletons, an eerie stillness in the railroad yards below, whole units of once-familiar and foreboding mills missing on the horizon. Where were the proud buildings and busy, soot-stained, lunch bucket-toting, hard-hatted workers of my youth?

There was some white smoke in the sky over the USX Edgar Thomson Works in Braddock, but that was about it. No one in decades had referred to Pittsburgh as "the steel capital of the world," "Steel City" or "the smoky city," unless they were ill-informed travel writers or politicians just passing through and failing to check out the skyline.

Mesta Machine Company in West Homestead, where my father and two of my uncles and my brother Dan all worked, was gone, having given ground to Sandcastle, a water-ride amusement park along the Monongahela River.

In my youth, I used to pass through all these milltowns traveling on a streetcar from Hazelwood to Kennywood for summer picnics, and it was always an impressive view. The mills loomed so large on the western Pennsylvania horizon back in those days.

I recalled how a few years earlier, I had taken John Underwood, one of the nation's top sports authors and a former feature writer at *Sports Illustrated*, on a similar tour.

Underwood had telephoned me from Florida to ask if I would be so kind as to take him around the mill areas to do interviews and research for a book he was doing about religion and the dying milltowns. He said he remembered that I had been "a good guide" in driving him around Pittsburgh back in 1963 when he came to town to write about Pitt's highly-successful 9-1 football team, led by Martha, an All-

American running back, and the school's chancellor and most renowned cheerleader, Dr. Edward Litchfield.

I first met Martha in 1960 when he was the star of an undefeated (6-0) freshman football team at Pitt that was coached by Lou "Bimbo" Cecconi and Bill Kaliden. That was the same fall when Billy Mazeroski hit a ninth inning homerun to beat the New York Yankees in the seventh game of the World Series right across the street from the Pitt Student Union at Forbes Field. Martha and I were in the same freshman class, and occasionally were in the same classrooms in the Cathedral of Learning over the next four years. We sweated through several Spanish classes, I recall. For me, Spanish class was equivalent to working in the mines or Mesta Machine Company.

Martha was always one of my favorites. He was a fine infielder on the school's baseball team, started for a freshman basketball team where the other four starters went on to play in the NCAA and NIT tournaments as upperclassmen, while he concentrated on football and baseball. He came through in the clutch with touchdown runs to win games for the Panthers. He was successfully boosted by Beano Cook, Pitt's sports publicist, for national honors. He was a writer's dream.

He was easy to promote. He was always smart, handsome, well-connected, fun to be around, and a tremendous competitor. He could mix with the poorest and richest people in Pittsburgh and never miss a beat. It's a trait he still possesses.

He had been wearing a white warm-up outfit when I visited him earlier that day in his well-appointed formally-furnished office at the Civic Arena, and he was scheduled to play tennis afterward at the Racquet Club in Monroeville.

He looked good, as always, even if he, too, was in a bit of a funk, still distressed by all that had gone down in his life during the just-ended 1991. He looked in great shape, though he said one of his knees was aching from an old football injury. His heart was aching a little, too. His role at the Civic Arena had recently been diminished, and he wasn't sure where he stood in a lot of respects.

"1991 was the worst year of my life," said Martha. "My mother died in August. We won the Stanley Cup, but the real joy of such an achievement was stolen away because I knew beforehand that the team and the Arena operation were going to change hands. I knew in December of 1990 that, because of negative economic developments affecting the real estate business, the DeBartolos wanted to sell the team. I had a falling-out with the DeBartolo family, and they blocked my bid to be one of the owners of the Penguins. I lost my position as head of the Arena, and I'm no longer associated with the 49ers. And our coach, Bob Johnson — one of the greatest guys I've ever known — died in October as we were starting a new season. 1991 was just awful, as far as I was concerned. After all that we had gone through to build what we built here, and then to have to give it all up. Spectacor, a Philadelphia group, took over control of the Civic Arena in Pittsburgh. That just shouldn't happen. Some people got fired. It was very disruptive. People I was close to got fired."

He was retained by the new owners as executive vice-president of the Penguins. But that changed quickly, and he left his office at the Arena to join the law firm of Eckert, Seamans, Cherin & Mellott, which handled legal affairs for the Penguins. Martha was still linked to the Penguins, but in a minor way. Martha's attempt to buy the Penguins put him on the outs with the successful bidder, Howard Baldwin.

Martha believed a letter of agreement with Baldwin, dated August 23, 1991, gave him and his group of Pittsburgh-based investors a legal right to buy 50 percent of the hockey team.

A group led by Baldwin and Morris Belzberg had negotiated a deal to buy the Penguins from Edward J. DeBartolo Sr. for $31 million. Baldwin backed off his original agreement with Martha.

Martha detailed the financial problems of Pittsburgh's pro sports franchises — the Pirates, Penguins and the Steelers — when we spoke and predicted that teams here would have a difficult time competing with teams from bigger markets like New York, Chicago, Los Angeles, Boston, Philadelphia and Atlanta.

Then, too, Martha thinks that Pittsburgh lacks the kind of inspired political leadership to lift the city and its sports franchises out of their doldrums. "David Lawrence and Richard Caliguiri could get things done in this city," said Martha. "They knew how to get big business behind their projects.

"The Pirates couldn't sign Bobby Bonilla and it's unlikely they can sign Barry Bonds. They're losing their best players." He said it was hard for the Penguins and Steelers to generate the kind of revenues needed to keep up with the ever-escalating salary structure in pro sports.

"We don't have a collective bargaining agreement now in hockey," he continued. "Some hard decisions have to be made, if we're going to maintain some sort of economic sanity. Right now, we don't have a collective bargaining agreement in hockey or football. That means there can be no free agency compensation and there can't be a draft. The salary escalation in baseball could kill all of us. It has a trickling-down effect in every professional sport.

"I'd like to see the business of professional sports put in a structure so a city like Pittsburgh can maintain its sports tradition. It would be a shame if the sports tradition of this city could be allowed to die."

There could come a day, he emphasized, when the stadiums and arenas are abandoned by some of our pro teams. They would be unused and empty. "You're really close to that with Three Rivers Stadium," said Martha. "Can you imagine Three Rivers without the Pirates' 91 home games? That could really happen in the '90s. I know the business."

If that doomsday prediction sounded outrageous in 1992, it seemed less so in the summer of 1994 when the Pirates put a "For Sale" sign up for the ballclub. And anyone who didn't consider that the Pirates might be purchased and relocated elsewhere must have their head buried in the sand at Sandcastle. Just think about all the abandoned mills along the three rivers. Looking back twenty years ago, did that ever seem possible?

Paul Martha, at right in both photos, admires first Stanley Cup along with Craig Patrick and Penguins owner Edward J. DeBartolo, and was among those in the Penguins party who were recognized by President Bush at special ceremonies at The White House. Others visible in photo, from left to right, include Mario Lemieux, Peter Taglianetti, Joe Mullen, DeBartolo, Bryan Trottier, Bob Johnson and Rick Kehoe. In the summer of 1994, Martha was named to a special 8-person advisory board, which also included movie actor Michael Keaton, by Penguins' owner Howard Baldwin.

Photos by Dennis Cavanaugh

I remember a conversation I once had with Art Rooney Sr. He said the Pirates were more important to Pittsburgh than the Steelers. "They have so many more dates at the Stadium than we do," said Rooney, whose first sports love was baseball. He loved to walk to the Stadium from his home on the North Side to see the Pirates play. He liked the fact that they played so often because he enjoyed getting out and being around people as frequently as possible.

"Without the Pirates, there wouldn't be big league baseball in Pittsburgh," said Mr. Rooney. "But even if the Steelers weren't here you'd still have big-time football out at Pitt."

Martha said there was a time in 1983 when DeBartolo wanted out of hockey. "I went to the mayor and other civic and county leaders and we got things done that enabled Mr. DeBartolo to remain here," said Martha. "So I know how to do what needs to be done.

"You need people who realize what sports means to a city's major league image and its quality of life. Once upon a time here, you had Davey Lawrence and Richard K. Mellon, and they got great things accomplished. You had the Renaissance, and Dick Caliguiri got the corporate support to pull off Renaissance II. Things can be done to prevent Pittsburgh from becoming a ghost town as far as sports are concerned.

"People have to recognize it is a serious problem. Pittsburgh has huge potential. With the new airport and the opening of the European common market, I think Pittsburgh will become an international hub. It's already an international city. You see more and more foreign-owned companies setting up shop here. The Germans love Pittsburgh; they're bringing companies here, like Miles. We need to put some shine back on the skyline."

> *"I hope he realizes what*
> *he's gotten into."*
> —Paul Martha
> on Mark Sauer

"I think the economic mechanisms have to change for a city the size of Pittsburgh to compete," said Martha. "The Pirates have become a minor league team for no other reason than they can't compete with bigger economic markets."

After Carl Barger resigned as president of the Pirates in 1991 to lead an expansion franchise in Miami, the Pirates interviewed Martha to fill the void. "It was a no-win situation," said Martha. "They interviewed me and Mark Sauer, and that was it. I hope he realizes what he's gotten into."

Martha had similar foreboding feelings when media speculation mentioned him as a candidate for the vacant athletic director's position at Pitt during the same period. Martha loves his alma mater, but has been distressed at the decline in standards for the sort of student now representing Pitt in athletics, and the lack of leadership and commitment to return the school's programs to what he regards as achievable lofty levels.

"Plus, I'd have had to take a major slash in salary," said Martha. "Pitt doesn't have the financial resources right now to do what's necessary to become competitive again. But the school has such a strong medical program — more organ transplants are done there than anywhere else in the world — and other fine professional schools, and they should be using them as bait to attract the finest student athletes in the world. There's a great opportunity there to do something special. You can't guarantee grad school acceptance to athletes when you recruit them — it's against the NCAA rules — but there should be slots open that are earmarked for athletes if they are qualified.

"I think football players should go to school and do well. When I was on the selection committee to pick a coach (Paul Hackett), I was disappointed when they laid down the guidelines for the kind of players they wanted on the football team. I felt Pitt was being compromised. Maybe I was naive."

"I ran the whole thing."
—Paul Martha

Paul Martha has long epitomized the best in Pittsburgh sports. He first made his mark at Shady Side Academy, where he starred in several sports. He was a true student athlete at Pitt, and was good enough to be the Steelers' No. 1 draft choice in 1964. He played defensive back for the Steelers in the NFL from 1964 to 1969 while attending law school. He obtained his Doctor of Law degree at Duquesne University in 1969 and played one more year of pro ball, with the Denver Broncos in 1970, before retiring to practice law on a full-time basis back home in Pittsburgh.

Martha, 49 as we spoke in January of 1992, joined the Penguins' organization during the summer of 1978 after the DeBartolo Corporation assumed control of the franchise. He was named vice-president prior to the 1978-79 season and handled the club's legal matters as general counsel until 1992, and also served on the NHL's Board of Governors. He is now on a Penguins' advisory board.

Martha wore many hats in his service to the DeBartolo family. With his background in law and professional football, he was selected to serve as neutral arbitrator for the NFL in 1982. He and Steelers' president Dan Rooney were credited with having a big influence in resolving player-owner differences that year and settling a 57-day strike that had halted play.

He also served as president of the defunct Pittsburgh Maulers in the USFL during their one season of operation — the Rooneys were really upset about their existence — and he has handled legal work for the San Francisco 49ers of the NFL. He became involved with the Major

Indoor Soccer League as well, serving as vice president for the Pittsburgh Spirit. Spirit owner Frank Fuhrer is his cousin ("He's certainly made his contribution to the Pittsburgh sports scene," said Martha.).

Before the DeBartolos sold their rights to the operation of the Civic Arena in 1991, Martha served as vice president of the Civic Arena Corporation and headed day-to-day operations of the entertainment facility. "I ran the whole thing," he said.

He and his wife Bobbie reside in Fox Chapel and are the parents of three sons, J.P., Christopher and Richie.

"It doesn't look good for him."
—Bobbi Martha on Bob Johnson

I recall a Saturday afternoon in September of 1991 when I took my wife Kathie and our daughters, Sarah and Rebecca, on a lunch/shopping trip to Shadyside. While walking on Walnut Street, we bumped into Bobbi Martha.

It was only a few days after the news first broke that Bob Johnson had brain cancer. He had undergone emergency surgery to remove part of a brain tumor on August 29 at Mercy Hospital. Within a few days, it was disclosed that there was a second tumor. "It doesn't look good for him," she told us. "Paul talked to the doctors and they are not very optimistic."

In Pittsburgh, a prayer vigil was begun by fans for "Badger Bob," a lovable figure.

No coach was ever more closely tied to a team's success than Bob Johnson, who lifted the Penguins to a Stanley Cup championship in his first and only season in Pittsburgh. The Penguins grabbed hockey's Holy Grail with an 8-0 victory over the Minnesota North Stars in Johnson's hometown of Minneapolis on May 25.

"Bob's the reason we were able to win the Cup, but he meant more to us as a person," said defenseman Paul Coffey. "I've never met a better man."

Johnson, indeed, was a bubbly sort who pumped up everyone's spirits. He made former Pirates manager Chuck Tanner come off as a gloom and doom guy by comparison, and you recall that Tanner was knocked for being such a positive person.

"It's a great day for hockey," Johnson liked to say, with the same spirit and smile of Ernie Banks, the one-time great of the Chicago Cubs who always said, "It's a great day for a doubleheader."

Both put sunshine in other people's lives.

Johnson was 60 when he died at his home in Colorado Springs, Colorado.

"What he's done for this city and this hockey club in one year is pretty incredible," team leader Mario Lemieux said. "Nobody would have thought we'd win the Cup last year, but with Bob Johnson, everything was possible."

"He's inexhaustible."
—Paul Martha on
Edward J. DeBartolo

Edward J. DeBartolo Sr., of Youngstown, Ohio, is one of the nation's richest men. His DeBartolo Corporation is the nation's largest developer and manager of shopping malls, and he owns and operates many sports enterprises, especially thoroughbred racing tracks.

The San Francisco 49ers, led by his son, Edward Jr., won four Super Bowls in the '80s, succeeding the Steelers as the sport's most-successful dynasty.

Martha worked with the father and son for 14 years. "I now have a strained relationship with the family; it's unfortunate," said Martha. "I had a signed deal with Howard Baldwin to be a partner in the new ownership picture, but Mr. DeBartolo Sr. blocked that. He didn't want an employee being part of management."

Asked how Mr. DeBartolo Sr. had been so successful in his business endeavors, Martha said, "He's a hard-working, tenacious businessman. He's inexhaustible.

"I'm thankful to him for giving me the opportunity to develop a career as a sports and entertainment executive, which is very enjoyable. I have been exposed to so many different situations. I know this business. There have been a lot of good times, and there have been some bad times."

How about his relationship with Eddie Jr.? "He and I were good friends," said Martha. "We, in some way, will always be good friends. We went through a lot together. We went through some things we won't soon forget."

Martha will miss being associated with the 49ers and the NFL. "I felt I was a part of it, particularly in the beginning," said Martha. "I remember the hard times that Eddie Jr. and I went through.

"I was involved with selecting Bill Walsh as the coach. He was the perfect coach for the 49ers, a local guy who had coached at Stanford and been in the pros. He fit in perfectly in the community. He enabled Eddie to win the Super Bowl four times."

One of the most upsetting aspects of the 1991 campaign was the illness and death of Penguins' coach Bob Johnson. In his only year as coach of the team, Johnson directed the Penguins to a Stanley Cup triumph, the first in the history of the franchise.

"There are certain people you meet in life," said Martha, "and after a period of time you know they're very special. I didn't know him that well, at first, but I got to know him. He and Craig Patrick and I played golf together a few times, and we spent some time together.

"He was a special human being. He always found good in everything. He totally astounded people, particularly the players, because somehow he could find something good in a 9-to-nothing blowout. It made him a special person.

"My father-in-law was a special person."

Martha's deceased father-in-law was Edwin H. Gott, who had served as president, chief executive officer and then chairman of U.S. Steel.

"He was a very honest, forthright person at a very difficult time in U.S. Steel's history," noted Martha. "He went to Peabody High School, and worked his way up through the ranks at U.S. Steel to become its top executive. I learned a lot from him. He had integrity; I remember him being very critical of some of the perks that went to top executives. He didn't think it was right.

"Art Rooney Sr. was a special person. All of his faults aside, you realize that he was special. Bob Johnson was that way, too."

Then Martha paused a moment, and said, "I would be remiss if I didn't mention my parents. My dad, Al, and my mother, Dorothy, had a lot to do with my success, as well as the success of my sister and our brothers."

His sister, Lynda, was a national baton-twirling champion during her high school years. His brother Richie was a running back at West Virginia University. He has two other brothers, Albert and David.

"Our parents came to all our games and activities, and carted us all around in their cars so we could do all those things," said Martha.

Switching subjects, I asked Martha what it was like to win the Stanley Cup after so many frustrating seasons.

"It was an interesting experience," said Martha. "It's something I'd like to experience under different circumstances. The ownership problems and sale of the franchise and the management position at the Arena took the glow off what could have been an exhilarating experience."

In short, with everything that was going on, he couldn't enjoy it. "No, I couldn't," said Martha.

What was he thinking as he saw the Penguins skating around the ice in Minnesota on May 25, 1991 after winning the clinching game?

"I was thinking it's really too bad because next year somebody else will own this team."

There was a book about the topsy-turvy financial world on a table near his desk called *Going For Broke*. It could have been the title for the Penguins' Stanley Cup campaign.

"This is all a little unbelievable," said Paul Coffey in the midst of the ownership squabble in November of 1991. "I've never seen a championship team be involved in the turmoil that's faced our team."

It wasn't too long before Coffey and Mark Recchi, two of the team's top stars and popular players who had big roles in the Penguins' Stanley Cup championship, were traded away. The Penguins struggled all season long just to qualify for the playoffs. Just when the playoffs were to begin, the NHL players went on strike.

"We can't be isolationists."
—Paul Martha

Sometimes Pittsburghers take their own for granted. Paul Martha is one of those. He is a Pittsburgh treasure, yet he is often more valued and commands greater respect on a national basis than he does in his hometown.

Martha is often mentioned when top jobs come open in the sports world, and it doesn't matter whether you are talking about football or hockey or even baseball. He is regarded as somebody who can run a sports ship in a storm.

Martha has lunch just about every day of the week with his longtime friend and fellow attorney, Steve Stepanian II, who has his law degree from Harvard. They once worked together at Reed Shaw Smith & McClay, Pittsburgh's top law firm.

On this particular day, Martha drove me in a blue Cadillac to the Gateway Towers where Stepanian lives in one condominium apartment and has an office in another apartment on another level. For lunch, Martha picked the Grand Concourse Restaurant.

This is a unique restaurant, another Pittsburgh treasure. It is set in the Edwardian splendor of the Pittsburgh & Lake Erie Railroad terminal built in 1901. It's part of the Pittsburgh History and Landmarks' Station Square restoration. It's on the Monongahela River just across the Smithfield Street Bridge, with a grand view of the Golden Triangle.

Japanese businessmen took up three nearby tables. It pleased us to see that they all ordered Iron City Lite draft beer, and toasted with it. "This is becoming an international city," said Martha, repeating a favorite theme of his. "The sooner we realize that, the better off we'll be.

"If Japanese interests wanted to buy the Pirates and keep them here, we should never turn our backs on such an offer."

At the time, Japanese interests were running into a snag in their bid to buy the Seattle Mariners of the American Baseball League because baseball commissioner Fay Vincent felt that it was not in the best interest of our so-called national pastime to have foreign ownership.

"We can't be isolationists," said Martha.

"The Pirates just signed two ballplayers for a total of $9 million, and for one year in both cases," he said, alluding to new contracts for Barry Bonds and Doug Drabek. "That's bad business. Next year they'll be back for more, and the Pirates can't afford to pay more. We might need somebody to come in and buy the Pirates because the local corporations who own it now will not want to stay involved."

The Edwardian splendor of the Grand Concourse must have reminded Martha of what he had been reading lately. He talked about a book he was reading by Winston Churchill, and was in awe of Churchill's precise use of words, and the vast extent of his vocabulary.

Martha pulled out a slip of paper of words he had written down just that morning from Churchill's book. He tested us on a few of the words to see if we knew the meanings. Martha likes to read in the morning before starting his workday.

Stepanian is also a voracious reader, and said he had just re-read a book by Jimmy Breslin, one of my favorite writers, on Damon Runyon, a legendary Broadway columnist whose characters inspired shows like *Guys and Dolls*.

It was easy to see from the conversation why Martha and Stepanian get along so well. "Our wives accuse us of spending more time with each other than we do with them," said Stepanian, who serves as an advisor to Martha and helped him put together the group that wanted to buy the Penguins.

"We had a signed agreement to purchase the Penguins," said Stepanian, "but DeBartolo couldn't stand the idea of an employee buying the team from him. So he blocked the deal. It's too bad, because the team would be better off with local investors."

What drives Martha to keep climbing new mountains?

"I don't know if there's one thing that drives people," he responded. "Other people telling them they can't accomplish things, I suppose. I was told I couldn't play major college football, then I was told I couldn't play pro football. I was told I was too small."

When Noll dispatched him to Denver, I asked, did he regard it as a rejection?

"I wasn't able to completely celebrate the championships the Steelers won because I was disappointed I still wasn't a part of it," he said.

"I had been there with Joe Greene and L.C. Greenwood, Andy Russell, Rocky Bleier and Ray Mansfield. They were still there when the great things started to happen, and I wasn't."

It's strange, but a similar thing happened to him with the Penguins. I felt badly for Martha as I watched the parade at Three Rivers Stadium that celebrated the Penguins winning their second Stanley Cup championship. Martha was nowhere to be seen, suddenly a forgotten man in the organization. It hardly seemed fair.

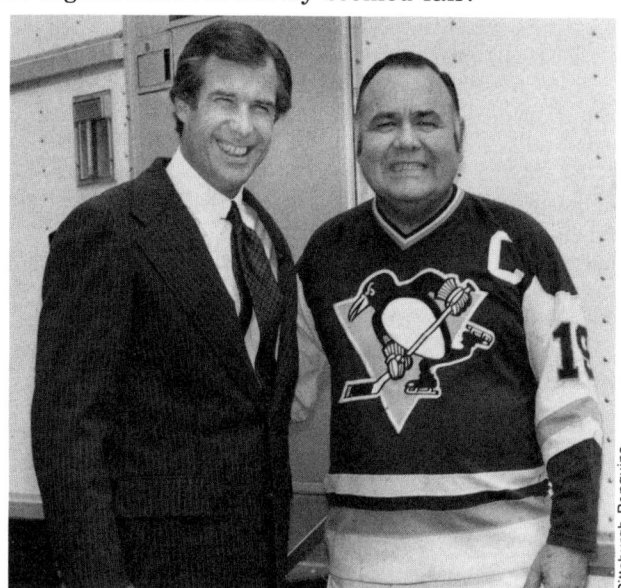

Paul Martha meets his match in smiling department as comic Jonathan Winters puts on Penguins uniform in 1978.

Keith McCreary

Tim Horton

"When you're a player, you never want to quit playing. You grow up all your life dreaming about being a hockey player, and now you've got to let the dream go. It's not an easy thing to do."

—Craig Patrick

Bryan Hextall

Eddie Shack

George Von Benko Collection

Jackie Powell
His "peepers" still shining

*"I played the game.
I loved the game."*

Jackie Powell probably saw more hockey games than anybody in Pittsburgh. His life and the history of hockey in his hometown were intertwined.

Powell never tired of telling stories about the Pittsburgh Yellow Jackets, the Pittsburgh Shamrocks, the Pittsburgh Pirates, the Pittsburgh Hornets of Duquesne Gardens, the Pittsburgh Hornets of the Civic Arena, the Pittsburgh Penguins. Soon he would even be telling stories about the Pittsburgh Phantoms. He knew them all.

Yes, there was a hockey team called the Pittsburgh Pirates that played once upon a time in the National Hockey League. The Pittsburgh Pirates was also the original name of the Pittsburgh Steelers when they first had a franchise in the National Football League, back in 1933.

It gets confusing, so it is helpful to have a friendly fellow like Powell around to sort it all out. Powell is about 5-6, a burly, pink-cheeked chap who usually covers a bald head with a brown fedora, and is an animated chatterbox.

"I played the game," said Powell. "I loved the game." He also loved to tell stories about his experiences.

From 1937 till 1991, Powell served as a goal judge for whatever professional hockey team was playing in Pittsburgh. Before that, as a youngster growing up in Shadyside, all the way back to 1923, Powell was a stickboy for visiting teams at Duquesne Gardens in nearby Oakland. It was like being a batboy for the Pirates or a waterboy for the Steelers. It made a kid feel special to sit alongside pro athletes.

He was always an insider, with the best seat in the house, whether he was a stickboy sitting at the end of the visiting team's bench, or in a catbird seat directly behind one of the goalnets. The seat was a free one at that. He knew and mixed with the hockey players from Pittsburgh and the visiting teams through the years. He was quick to smile, to share a story or a cigar, and he seemed to be having the time of his life.

He can close his eyes and see the Gardens, the smoky air, the railings around the box seats, the rickety steps, the rats that ran around unchecked in the clubhouses, the fans. He remembers unruly fans tossing chairs onto the ice from the box-seat sections to protest an unpopular referees' call. He can still see the great ones skating toward him, and scoring goals.

He remembers every player from the first Hornets' Calder Cup championship team in 1951-52: Leo Boivin, Tim Horton, Frank Mathers, Coach King Clancy, Gil Mayer, Bob Solinger, Johnny McLellan, Bob Hassard, John Ashley, Andy Barbe, Bill Ezinicki, Chuck Blair, Gordie

1948-49 Pittsburgh Hornets Hockey Team — First row (left to right) Ed Rafferty, Sid Smith, Stan Kemp, Coach Bob Davidson, Pete Langelle, John "Peanuts" O'Flaherty, Baz Bastien. Second row — trainer Socko McCarey, Bill Benson, Stan Psutka, Bob Dawes, Pete Backor, Frank Mathers, Eldie Korbussen, GM John Mitchell. Third row — Phil Samis, Les Costello, Fleming MacKell, Rudy Migay, Eric Pogue, Ray Ceresino.

Glenn Barton Collection

1951-52 Hornets Calder Cup Championship Team — First row (left to right) Tim Horton, Leo Boivin, Frank Mathers, Coach King Clancy, Pete Backor, Bob Solinger, Gil Mayer. Second row — Baz Bastien, John McClellan, Bob Hassard, John Ashley, Andy Barbe, Bill Ezinicki, trainer Socko McCarey. Third row — Chuck Blair, Frank Sullivan, Ray Hannigan, Gordie Hannigan, Rudy Migay, Phil Maloney. Hornets posted 46-19-3 record as Western champs enroute to Calder Cup triumph.

Hannigan, Frank Sullivan and Phil Maloney. Baz Bastien was the business manager and Caleb (Socko) McCarey the trainer. McCarey was also an area scout for the Boston Red Sox, and a colorful character who frequented Frankie Gustine's restaurant during my student days at Pitt.

"I've seen all the great ones here," said Powell. "The only one we really missed was Rocket Richard. We never saw him here." Aside from the great star of the Montreal Canadiens, Powell could point to a lot of Hall of Famers he first saw playing in Pittsburgh.

He saw Howie Morenz, Auriel Joliet, Gordie Howe, Jean Beliveau, Jacques Plante, Gump Worsley, Bobby Hull, Bobby Orr, Phil Esposito, Guy Lafleur, Mike Bossy, Wayne Gretzky and, of course, Mario Lemieux.

Orr and Hull were his early favorites — "I used to say a few extra Hail Marys when the old Blackhawks came to town" — and Mario and Gretzky were his contemporary favorites.

The highlights of his career as a goal judge were serving in that capacity for the 1967 Stanley Cup finals won by Montreal over St. Louis, and the 1990 All-Star Game at the Civic Arena "when Mario went wild (four goals and MVP award)."

Powell came out of retirement in the summer of '94 after a two-year layoff, at age 82, to serve as a goal judge for the Phantoms in Roller Hockey International. It's deck hockey in a big-league setting, a wide-open, high-scoring summer diversion and Powell found himself turning on the red light to signal a goal nearly three times as often as he did in National Hockey League and American Hockey League games.

Powell has never been paid for his services, unbelievably enough, except for a short stint in the mid-'70s when Tad Potter was the principal partner in the Penguins' ownership group, and Powell and other minor officials picked up $15 or $25 a game. "Heck, I don't count that," said Powell, raising his bushy eyebrows to emphasize that he didn't consider that significant compensation. Potter's largesse, on the other hand, may have been a contributing factor to the team going bankrupt in 1975.

"Other teams paid their minor officials, but not in Pittsburgh," Powell pointed out. He was not complaining. For him, it was strictly a labor of love, and he thought he was lucky to be sitting where he was sitting. "We got two tickets and a parking space. That's so your wife would have someone to sit with."

His wife of 38 years, Fran, was a big sports fan, so she liked the setup. "She loved it when we'd travel to some other city during the playoffs," said Powell. "During the playoffs, the minor officials worked in other cities, so the crews would be neutral. That was always exciting."

The only one who came close to Powell for personally witnessing hockey games in Pittsburgh was Frankie Tyson, who also served as a timekeeper and minor official dating back to the early Garden days, until his death a few years earlier. "He was from Homewood and went to Westinghouse High when we first met," said Powell. "He loved and knew his hockey as much as anybody."

> *"I knew a bad egg when I saw one."*
> —Jackie Powell on
> egg-buying skills

I first got to know Powell when he served as a sidekick for Jack Sell, a sports writer for the *Pittsburgh Post-Gazette*, in the early '60s when I was a student sports writer at the University of Pittsburgh. Powell was a go-fer, keeping stats, running copy to the Western Union operator, anything he could do to assist Sell. As a morning newspaperman, Sell was always sweating deadlines, and Powell helped ease the pressure. Every *P-G* beat man back then had such a sidekick, someone to go to the locker room and get some quotes from the coach or manager or the athletes for them. The custom has gone the way of the conventional clack-clack typewriter. Nobody runs copy anymore.

Sell covered college football and basketball, and was even doing high school sports when he first picked Powell to tag along with him on his assignments. Powell was playing football at Schenley High School at the time. Sell talked to him after a game, took a liking to him, and asked him if he wanted to help him out at another game he had to cover that evening."

Powell smiled before he continued his story about that eventful day back in 1929.

"I'll have to wait until I go home and ask my mother," Powell remembers telling Sell.

"How about that?" asked Powell now with more than a hint of pride. "Am I dating myself with that story? I got permission at home, and I met him that night at the press gate. The Duquesne University football team was playing its first night football game. It was at Forbes Field."

Powell has been sitting in on history ever since. Sell covered the Steelers from their inception in 1933 right up till 1973, and retired the year before the Steelers won their first Super Bowl. He had covered the Steelers through so many mediocre seasons, and then he missed out on their first championship season. "Art Rooney flew Sell to the Super Bowl as his personal guest," Powell recalled. "They had been boyhood friends on the North Side, and Art always treated him special."

Jackie's wife, Fran, used to sit in the stands with Sell's wife, Grace, at Steelers' games at Forbes Field, Pitt Stadium and Three Rivers Stadium. "Fran was a baseball fan from the start, and I converted her into a hockey fan," said Powell. "She liked football, too. We never had any children, so we could come and go as we pleased."

Sell has lived on 36th Street in Lawrenceville most of his adult life. It's just a block from where my mother had been living the previous 16 years at St. Augustine Plaza, a senior citizen apartment residence. My mother was 87 at the time, and remained an enthusiastic sports fan. She would enjoy Jackie Powell.

He was a man for all seasons, an aficionado of fun and games. He rooted for the kids from Lawrenceville when they were winning national marbles titles in the '70s. He was a big fan of another local favorite, world boxing champion Fritzie Zivic, and saw him fight at the Gardens.

Even after Sell's retirement, Powell continued to show up in the press box at Three Rivers Stadium for Steelers and Pirates games, and managed to make himself useful to club officials or members of the media. In his 80s, he was still helping to make up the payroll for the ushers at each game at Three Rivers.

His real job for 44 1/2 years was as an egg buyer for what he referred to as the A&P Tea Company. Once again, his eyes — or "peepers," as he frequently referred to them — served him in good stead.

"I could tell freshness, a Grade A or Grade B, by holding an egg up to a candling light," said Powell. "I knew a bad egg when I saw one. I used to watch the weather reports. If the weather was bad in the Midwest, and there was a big snowfall, you knew eggs would be scarcer, or late coming in. It meant you had to pick up extra stuff on the local market to make up the difference.

"We had the largest egg candling room around at our 43rd Street warehouse here in Lawrenceville. We had 40 egg candlers there. We didn't use candles; we used lamps."

I asked Jack if, after checking out eggs so closely so much of his life, he still ate them. "I eat 'em every day for breakfast, even though they talk about cholesterol being bad for you and all that junk," said Powell. "They haven't killed me yet."

"We'd go to the Gardens and skate for free."
—Jackie Powell

Powell was a student at Osceola Elementary School in Shadyside, where he met Roy Schooley Jr., whose dad owned the Pittsburgh Yellow Jackets and operated Duquesne Gardens. The Canadian-born Schooley also served as the city treasurer.

"There was always politics involved with the operation of the hockey team back then," said Powell.

His friendship with Roy Schooley Jr. opened the door for Powell to a world he would enjoy the rest of his life.

"His dad's chauffeur, who was also the trainer for the Yellow Jackets, would pick us up after school, and take us to the Gardens," recalled Powell. "Roy's brother, Bobby, played hockey at Pitt. We'd go to the Gardens and skate for free. On Sunday, we'd go to church at St. Paul's Cathedral and then hustle across Craig Street and play hockey from 10:30 till 2:30 in the afternoon. We'd go up to Paganucci's at the corner of Craig and Centre, across the street from the Luna Restaurant, and get a hot dog and something to drink. It was great.

Baz Bastien offers advice to Hornets goalie Gil Mayer.

Hornets 1966-67 Calder Cup Champions — First row (left to right) Don Caley, Bill Harris, Bob Wall, Coach Baz Bastien, Bob McCord, Pete Goegen, Hank Bassen. Second row — publicist Joe Gordon, Terry Gray, Don McKenney, Ab McDonald, Pete Mahovlich, Warren Godfrey, Ted Taylor, Doug Harvey, trainer Danny Wood. Third row — Doug Barrie, Duke Harris, Craig Cameron, Gary Jarrett, Val Fonteyne, Parker MacDonald.

"I was a stickboy when we had a team in the National Hockey League for the first time (1925-30). Roy Schooley Jr. was the stickboy for the home team, and I was the stickboy for the visiting teams."

Powell remembers when Duquesne Gardens was first converted from a streetcar barn to a skating rink, when there were only 2,400 seats. "Then they put in a balcony, adding another 2,000 or so seats. They had netting draped from the ceiling to cover the rafters and scaffolding. It had a low ceiling and it was a real fire hazard. They never gave the real crowd count because they didn't want to get in trouble with the fire marshall. They'd say it was a capacity crowd.

"The visiting dressing room was on the second floor, and you had to go up rickety stairs to get there. There was a firehouse nearby, and some of the firemen used to come over and watch the games. They had a set-up so a bell went off at the Gardens if they were needed to answer an alarm."

Powell has plenty of stories, but he tells them like he's crating eggs — carefully. "Now don't use that one," he'll cry after sharing a spicy story, or when he fears he might upset somebody. Fair enough.

"It was just a different era."
—Jackie Powell

He remembers the Yellow Jackets having a real strong team. They had players like Lionel Conacher, Herb Drury, Roy Worters, Hib Milks, Harold Darragh, Roger Smith, Terry McGovern, Dinny Manners and Dink Madden. They pioneered the pro ice sport here. They paved the way for the Penguins in Pittsburgh.

"Lionel Conacher was called 'Big Train.' He was Canada's answer to our Jim Thorpe," said Powell. "He was a big hero in Canada, and later became a member of the Canadian Parliament. You'll like this ... Conacher also played football for Duquesne University. He'd play football on Saturday afternoons for Duquesne, and then hockey on Saturday night."

I asked Powell how Conacher could do that, and if he were a bona fide student at Duquesne, indeed, if Conacher went to class at Duquesne. "He went to school enough to say he was a student," recalled Powell. "You know what they used to say, 'Duquesne was a school built on The Bluff, and run on the same principle.' Boy, I got into trouble a few times for saying that.

"It was just a different era. Buff Donelli just died, and he coached the Duquesne football team and the Steelers in the same season (1941). Things were done differently in those days, that's all. It wasn't the big deal it is today. Hockey teams would come in and play two games, Friday and Saturday," said Powell. "That's when streetcars ran right up to the Gardens. It was a popular place.

"One time, when the Yellow Jackets were in what was called the United States Amateur Hockey League, our team was so good that they

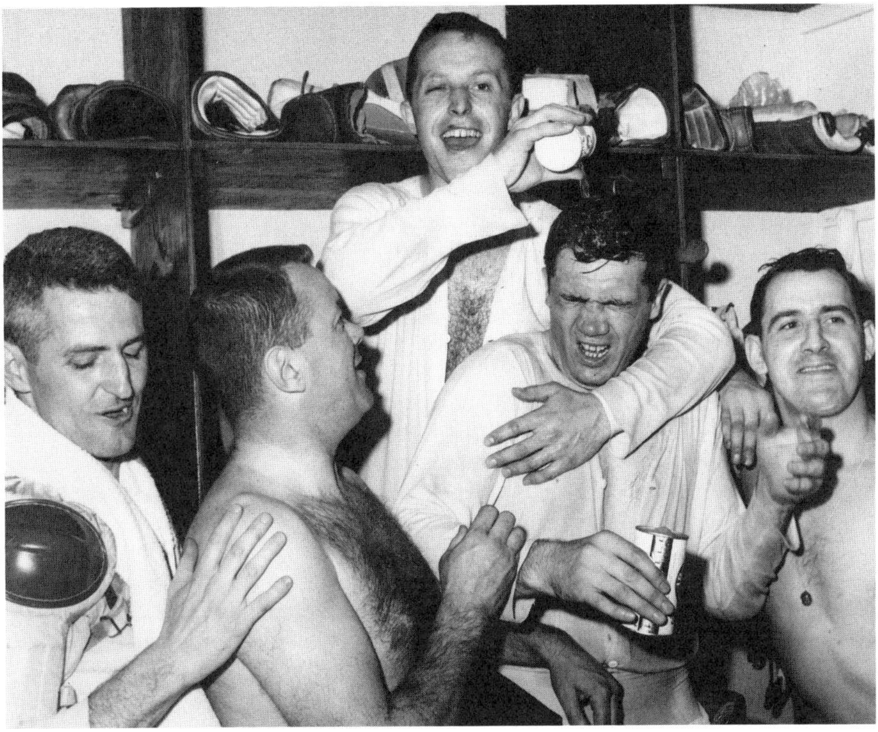

Glenn Barton Collection

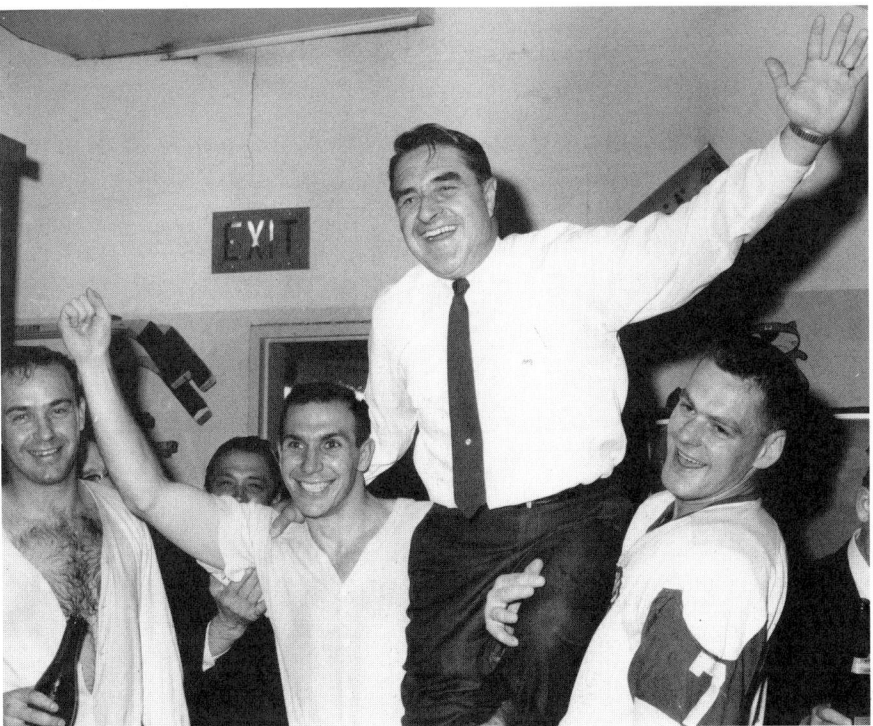

Jubilant Hornets celebrate capturing Calder Cup in team's final season (1966-67) (left to right) Billy Harris, Doug Harvey, Bob Wall, Bob McCord and Pete Goegen.

Bastien Family Album

Calder Cup coach Baz Bastien is boosted in clubhouse by, left to right, Parker MacDonald, Gary Jarrett and Ted Gray.

split it up and had a Pittsburgh team in each of the league's two divisions. That's when the Hornets were born. But we rooted for the Yellow Jackets."

"I was recognized around the league for wearing a hat."
—Jackie Powell

Powell goes back to the pioneer days of pro hockey. He remembers when referees carried bells, like altar boys, holding the clapper between their fingers, and ringing the bell when they called a penalty.

He remembers, if you can picture this, when goal judges stood on the ice, directly behind the goal cages, and stood on the back bar that sat on the ice when the players swept behind the goal cage. The goal judges would wear derbies, and they would wave a flag when a goal was scored.

"I remember seeing that as a kid," said Powell.

"A gentleman named Garnet M. Sixsmith started hockey here, coming from Canada with several other players back in 1902. They later were branded the first hockey professionals. And some people say that pro hockey had its origins right here in Pittsburgh."

Powell was known around the NHL as Jackie "The Hat" Powell because he always wore a fedora when he worked as a goal judge. "That was my trademark around the league," said Powell. "I wore a hat even when I had hair. It was always cold in those hockey rinks, and there was always a draft coming through the tunnel directly behind me at the Civic Arena and at Duquesne Gardens."

"The Gardens had the largest ice skating surface in North America."

Powell remembered when boxing great Benny Leonard took a fling at operating an NHL team in Pittsburgh — the Pittsburgh Pirates — but it didn't work out, and the team was moved to Philadelphia the following season.

"As the stickboy, I'd set at the end of the bench with the two reserves. That's how I met Larry Aurie."

The Pittsburgh Shamrocks played in the International Hockey League in 1935-36. They were put together by Roy Babcock and Associates. They were coached by Sprague Cleghorn, a hockey Hall of Famer, but it was a bad team and the franchise failed after one season.

"Then John Harris put his version of the Hornets on the ice for the 1936-37 season," said Powell. "And Aurie was the coach, and that is when I became the goal judge.

"Harris bought Duquesne Gardens and changed its name to The Gardens. He had a night club, called the Tent Club, on the second floor of the building. The Gardens had the largest ice skating surface in North America. We had Olympic skating trials and speedskating trials there. When we got into the NHL, we had to shorten the ice to meet certain specifications.

"Harris also had the college teams at Pitt, Duquesne and Carnegie Tech, plus some teams from Cleveland, use his facility and he started a local amateur league. He revived the Yellow Jackets in the Eastern Amateur Hockey League. Frankie Brimsek was the goalie for that team. He was a great goalie and became known as 'Zero' Brimsek. I remember him showing up the first time wearing a blue chinchilla overcoat, with a velvet collar, a sweatshirt, blue jeans and carrying a canvas bag. He was an outstanding goalie in the American Hockey League, and went to the National Hockey League. He's in the Hockey Hall of Fame."

Powell prided himself on knowing the best of them. "Willie Marshall was great for us," said Powell. Another one of his favorites was Frank Mathers, a defenseman during the heyday of the Hornets of Duquesne Gardens. "He could play anything," said Powell.

Mathers later became the front-office boss of the Hershey Bears and Powell remembers talking to Mathers one night when Mathers accompanied his club to a Civic Arena AHL match.

"Hershey was affiliated with the Boston Bruins then," said Powell. "Mathers told me, 'We had a kid in our training camp named Bob Orr. You'll never see him in the AHL. He's too good. Just remember that name.'"

I asked Powell if any NHL player had ever given him a bad time about a call he made. "I remember in our first year in the NHL at the Civic Arena, a puck dribbled over the line, and I put on the red light. Cesare Maniago came back and smashed his stick against the glass where I was sitting. I think he was more mad at himself than he was at me."

So most of the memories are positive ones.

"It's been a lot of fun," Powell said. "I still enjoy it."

"Nice talking to you."
—Jackie Powell

On the same day I talked to Jackie Powell, I attended the funeral of Steve Petro, who died a few days earlier at age 79. Petro had been involved with the Pitt football program for nearly 50 years. He had come from Johnstown, Pa., and played for Dr. Jock Sutherland's team's in Pitt's so-called "Golden Era." He was a lineman for "The Dream

Backfield," and a roommate and lifelong friend of All-American running back Marshall Goldberg. He was a Pitt man, a man's man. He loved his University and served it well. I had last spoken to him on the sideline during the alumni game that preceded Pitt's annual spring intrasquad game. He was there with Goldberg and Edgar "Special Delivery" Jones, another of Pitt's finest backs. I loved talking to those guys. I first met the chisel-chinned Petro during my student days at Pitt in the early '60s, and worked with him as a member of the athletic department's executive staff in the mid-'80s. I often talked to him about Pitt football history. People like Petro and Powell are Pittsburgh treasures. They are so much a part of the sports scene we often take them for granted. But we can learn so much from them. I am reminded of something the late Alex Haley once wrote, "When old people die it is like a library being burned down." Jackie Powell sent me a note a few days after I interviewed him. "Nice talking to you this afternoon. I really enjoyed it," he wrote. "Our visit was a genuine pleasure and I hope I helped a little. Call again anytime." I could tell by the handwriting and the sentiment that Powell, like Petro, was from the old school. I filed his letter away for posterity.

Goal judge Jackie Powell of Lawrenceville called the shots for Hornets and Penguins for 54 years.

Fonteyne Family Album

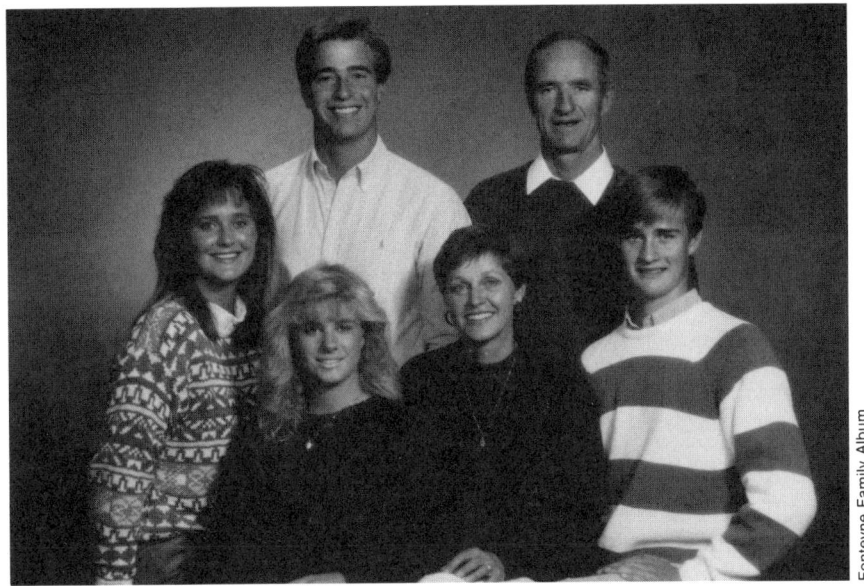

White-collared Val Fonteyne stands next to his son Dean in family portrait. Front row, left to right, daughters Cathy and Patricia, wife Anna, and son Murray. Fonteyne was one of the most popular players with Hornets and early Penguins team.

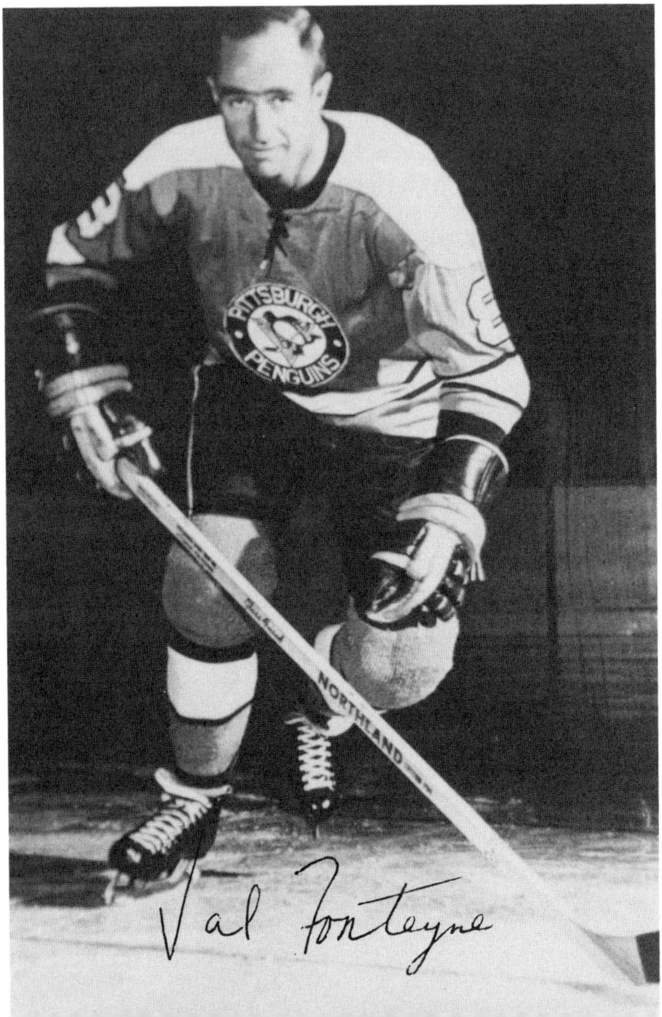

George Von Benko Collection

Dave Burrows
A defenseman's defenseman

"People make the city."

What Dave Burrows remembers best about playing for the Penguins in Pittsburgh is the city and its people.

"All the good people, that's what comes to mind first," said Burrows. "In a few words, the people. I fell in love with Pittsburgh, from the first year I was there. The fans were so good to me. People make the city.

"Pittsburgh, to me — I'm not a city type of person — has everything to offer you'd want from a big city, yet it has a small downtown area. It's just the right size. You could live just outside the city and be in the country."

Burrows boasted about his teammates, special friends, the bond they shared, the highs and lows they experienced together, the chemistry — "that's hard to come by in sports" — and management and front-office types, how everyone was trying to make things work, and talked in a warm manner about the trainers and clubhouse attendants. He appreciated all of them and how they enhanced his life.

He loved playing for the Pittsburgh Penguins in the National Hockey League, and he played during a period when the club was pinching pennies and, ultimately, went bankrupt. It was a period when some NHL players absolutely dreaded the idea of playing for the Penguins. It was considered the pits.

But Burrows loved Pittsburgh and it loved him back. He played seven seasons for the Penguins from 1971-78, was traded to the Toronto Maple Leafs for two seasons, and then reacquired by the Penguins in another trade and came back to Pittsburgh for the 1980-81 season. He put in ten quality seasons in the NHL.

Burrows was obtained in the first place in June of 1971 from the Chicago Blackhawks in the NHL's interleague draft. He was traded to Toronto for Randy Carlyle and George Ferguson in June of 1978. Burrows remembers that the Maple Leafs came to Pittsburgh for the season opener in 1979. His first game in the Leafs' lineup was against the Penguins.

"It was weird, going to the locker room at the other end of the ice; I felt weird. I was in the starting lineup, and when I was introduced over the p.a. system I received a standing ovation from the crowd. I remember that like it was yesterday. It's one of those times you'll never forget. It was very moving. It made me feel so good. It's the people; they don't forget."

He had been born in Toronto — on January 11, 1949 — and playing for the Maple Leafs should have been a boyhood dream come true — yet he felt like he was wearing the wrong uniform. He felt like a Pittsburgher in exile.

Dave Burrows and his wife Carol are now at home at Parry Sound, Ontario, with their sons, left to right, Wade and Bret.

Burrows was one of the best defenseman in the NHL. He always had one of the best plus/minus ratings on the Penguins. He was an old-fashioned defenseman, one who concentrated on stopping the other team from scoring, and seldom strayed into the offensive end of the ice. He knew his strengths. He would do anything to block a shot, and frequently gave up his body, sliding across the ice if he could thwart a goal-scoring effort. His legs were always bruised from top to bottom, and the subject of jokes in the clubhouse.

"I knew I wasn't any offensive threat; I wasn't a goal-scorer," he said. "I always got a thrill out of breaking up a two-on-one break. That was how I got my thrills. I was a stay-at-home defenseman. I was happy with that role. You have to use the ability God gives you."

He was big, at 6-1, 190 pounds, a handsome, quick-to-smile sentry, a lopsided smile at that, dark eyes sunk into hollow cheeks, a left-handed shooter. Seven goals and 22 assists in 1975-76 was a career-best season.

He was one of the most popular Penguins. He was named the team's rookie of the year after the 1971-72 season. He was named the team's MVP in 1972-73, and shared the honor with Syl Apps, Jean Pronovost and Lowell MacDonald in 1973-74. He won the Penguins' Booster Club Star-of-Games Award in 1975-76.

Burrows' ability was acknowledged by hockey purists. He was often among the top vote-getters for the James Norris Award as the league's top defenseman. He played in the NHL's All-Star Game on two occasions, during the 1973-74 and 1975-76 campaigns.

"They were highlights in my career, even though I got hurt in both games. So I'm not sure why I think that way. It was nice to be picked and play with those guys. I dislocated my shoulder in my first game in Chicago, and missed six games, (the first time he was out of the Pittsburgh lineup in three years due to an injury). My shoulder was never right after that. I had to have an operation. In the All-Star Game in Philadelphia, I got cut in the forehead. So the All-Star Game was a good news, bad news thing for me."

That sort of sums up his situation with the Penguins as well. The Penguins had a pretty good team when Burrows was with them, but the club was in dire financial straits.

Burrows refers to himself as a throwback in relation to his style of play, but his remarks about his concern for the club and wanting to keep it in Pittsburgh also points up a perspective one seldom finds in today's athletes.

"We were always aware of the team's financial difficulties," said Burrows. "We were operating on a shoestring. The guys were doing what they could do to help out. The players were willing to go out and make appearances any place where they'd have a Penguin. I was making personal appearances everywhere. For nothing. We weren't drawing many people to the Arena, so we were doing whatever we could do to get people interested in our team. You didn't know if you're going to be there the next year.

"I loved the city so much. I did whatever I could to keep the team there. We went the whole spectrum while I was there, of having few people in the building, the bankruptcy, turning it around, having a good team, getting to the playoffs. It was wonderful to see it turned around. We started getting big crowds for certain games at home. It became a great atmosphere for hockey."

Burrows and his family rented a home in Green Tree that had been owned by Roberto Clemente, the Pirates' great ballplayer. Burrows remembers that Clemente was killed in an airplane crash off the coast of his native San Juan, Puerto Rico on New Year's Eve, 1972, while attempting to transport supplies to earthquake-stricken victims in Nicaragua.

A lot of the Penguins, and Pirates and Steelers, lived in the Green Tree area in those days. It was a close-to-the-city suburb and the rental rates were appealing. "We had a team that got along well together," recalled Burrows. "We were a close-knit group, like one big family. We had a special chemistry."

He remains a Penguins' fan, even though there are few holdovers in the organization from his playing days. "Things have changed," he said. "My heart is still there. I still watch. I don't know any of the people on the team now, but when I see the Civic Arena on TV, and I hear the cheers . . . it brings back good memories."

"Bobby Orr is still very much remembered up here."
—Dave Burrows on Parry Sound

Burrows was talking over the telephone from his home in Parry Sound, Ontario. It seemed ironical that Burrows, a throwback to another era as far as his defensive style was concerned, would be living in Parry Sound. There's a sign out on the highway at the city limits that lets visitors know that Parry Sound is the birthplace of Bobby Orr, the greatest offensive-minded defenseman in the history of the National Hockey League.

"He's still very much on the minds of people in Parry Sound," said Burrows. "Bobby Orr is still very much remembered up here. I don't think he gets up here a lot, but his mom and dad still live here. I work with his dad, Doug, a little, and I hear about Bobby from time to time. He and his dad just got back from fishing for salmon in Quebec."

Burrows, at age 45, was the manager of a youth center in Parry Sound. "Floor hockey is the only hockey we have here," he said. Wedding receptions and dances and various social events are often held there, and Doug Orr handles permits which have to be obtained when liquor is dispensed on the property.

I asked Burrows how he happened to end up in Parry Sound.

"The year I turned pro I bought a property here," said Burrows. "I didn't have any ties here. I didn't know anybody here. It's on a lake, Georgian Bay, roughly three hours straight north of Toronto. There are about 6,500 here year-round. We just felt comfortable here. The year after we bought the property, we built a shell, and the years after that we kept working on the inside, finishing it off. We've had a place here for 24 years. After all the years of summering here, we realized that this was really home. I lived in other places when I was playing, in places like Dallas and Portland in the minors, then Pittsburgh and Toronto, but this is where our kids grew up."

Grew up, indeed. Dave and his wife Carol have two boys. Bret was 23 when we talked, and married and living in Rochester, New York. Wade, 21, was single and in his fourth year as a student at Liberty University in Lynchburg, Virginia. Bret was graduated from Liberty, a Christian-related school founded by evangelist Jerry Falwell.

I had heard that Burrows, as well as his former teammate Jean Pronovost, had become quite deeply involved in religion-related activities, and asked Burrows about that. He had not said anything earlier to promote that involvement. Burrows talked about it only after I asked him.

"I'm a Christian," said Burrows. "I try to lead my life the way the Bible tells us how to live our life. Yes, it's very, very important to me. I wasn't a Christian when I played. I am now. It's made quite a difference to me. It's given me a peace and joy I didn't have — even when I made the big money as a hockey player. I'm not going to preach about that, but you asked..."

Switching subjects again, I asked Burrows about Bobby Orr and the impact he made on the National Hockey League.

"He was absolutely the best," said Burrows. "As a defenseman, I'm prejudiced. I think Bobby changed the game, and controlled the game more than anyone I ever saw. Even with Wayne Gretzky and what Mario Lemieux has done.

"When I look back, and when I see what Bobby did on the ice, he did more than even Gretzky and Mario now. He definitely dominated the game. I'm not taking anything away from Gretzky and Mario. They have tremendous talent. But they didn't change the game as much. Bobby Orr did that. He revolutionized the way the game is played. He was not only a great defenseman, but he was an extra attacker. He controlled the game from one end of the ice to the other end of the ice. He was unreal."

I asked if deep in the heart of Dave Burrows there was any desire to skate and do it like Bobby Orr. "Not really. I was a throwback to a generation before. The way I went at it, my job was to get the puck out of our end, keep them from coming in. I was the goaltender's helper. Bobby played in a different world."

I asked Burrows if Parry Sound had sent any other players to the pros. He mentioned Terry Crisp and Floyd Thomson as two other long-time pro performers from that area.

They had moved to Parry Sound that year from Orangeville, Ontario, where Dave had been the hockey director at a Christian sports camp for eight years. They were in the midst of converting their cottage into a year-round home.

I asked Burrows about life after hockey, and how he was dealing with it.

"I've been thinking about that today, when I was driving home, knowing we'd be talking," said Burrows. "There is a wonderful life after hockey. At the peak of your hockey career, you can't think anything can be better. I loved playing hockey, but I love what I'm doing now, too.

"I've been blessed since I played that I made the adjustment fairly easily. I was ready to retire when I did. I was able to play long enough to satisfy that aspect of my life. It was time to quit. I accepted that. It was time to get on with the rest of my life. Some guys have a difficult time. They can't give it up. Hockey becomes their life."

I mentioned to Burrows that I had spoken to Duane Rupp, another former defenseman for the Penguins, and that he had said he wished he could have played hockey forever. I told Burrows that Rupp was still playing in several recreational adult leagues, and with a celebrity team that included Steelers' Hall of Famer Jack Lambert in its lineup.

"I'd like to see Jack playing hockey," said Burrows. "I think we admired each other's work when I was playing for the Penguins. I met him and we talked about that. Hey, I still play a little bit in NHL old-timers' games. But it's strictly for fun. I don't miss the hits or the competition."

"If the guys don't get along in the clubhouse, it shows up on the ice."
—Dave Burrows

In a form he filled out prior to our interview, Burrows listed Bob Paradise (1973-76, 1977-79) as the player he admired the most from his days with the Penguins.

"He was just one of those super guys," said Burrows, when asked to explain his choice. "Lewie Morrison (1974-78) was another super guy. Lewie didn't play a lot, but he accepted his role. He didn't sit there and complain. He was very supportive of all the guys. Bob Paradise wasn't the most talented guy, but he came to play every night. He was tough. A special guy."

Burrows had listed Dunc Wilson, a maverick goalie (1976-78), as the most unforgettable character on the club.

"He was just one of the funniest guys I ever met," said Burrows. "He was all one-liners. He wasn't a long story-teller. He kept everybody loose with some of the wild remarks he'd make. He was a good spirit."

Talking about Paradise, Morrison and Wilson brought back clubhouse scenes to Burrows.

"Everyone got along very well. We just had a great chemistry. It's tough to get that. You can have a team with talent, but if the guys don't get along in the dressing room, it shows up on the ice. If you don't get along, man to man, or as friends, I don't think it helps you on the ice.

"Prony, Syl and Lowell MacDonald proved that. Those three guys were the most unselfish players I've ever seen. If they had a fault, it was passing too much to let the other guy get the goal. It was a pleasure to play with those guys."

Dave Burrows (4) dives between teammates Ron Schock and Gary Inness to thwart scoring attempt. Burrows has come back, at right below, to perform for Penguins Alumni Team.

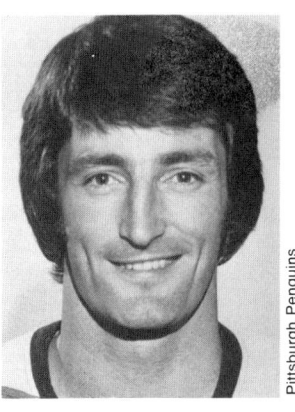

Where Are They Now?
George Ferguson

Present home: Mt. Lebanon, Pa.

Present job: Sales Manager, Scole Engineering Co., Inc. Eastern manager for Los Angeles-based company that manufactures and sells diagnostic medical equipment.

Family information: Married 20 years to Candi. Son Shane Patrick Ferguson, six years old (as of Nov. 16, 1994).

Personal highlight of Penguins' career: Playoff goal against Buffalo to win first round playoff series in 1974.

Most cherished memory of playing days: Of my 12 years in the NHL, my four years and a portion of another season with Penguins were the best. Playing for Johnny Wilson was great.

Player most admired and why: Randy Carlyle, a good competitor, who played every night and was an honest player.

Lesson learned from experience that has served you in good stead ever since: Good management is a key to success.

George Ferguson
Love affair with Pittsburgh

"This was a great place to play hockey."

George Ferguson sounds like a Penguins' fan when he discusses the club and its curent program. "I don't begrudge anybody making money, but the scale is so out of whack now," said Ferguson, who played for the Penguins for just over four seasons (1978-82) in a 12-year career in the National Hockey League. "The salaries have gone through the roof."

Ferguson was seated at the Civic Arena, with two of his teammates on the Penguins' alumni/celebrity hockey team, watching the Pittsburgh Phantoms of Roller Hockey International. He was with Jack Lambert, the Hall of Fame linebacker with the Pittsburgh Steelers, and Duane Rupp, another former Penguins' performer.

The roof had just been partially opened at the Civic Arena, which may have prompted Ferguson's remark about salaries going through the roof.

This was an August evening in the summer of '94.

"We were talking about how there are signs along the boards, with advertisements for one company after another," Ferguson said. "The hockey rink is surrounded by billboards. It's just all money, money, money.

"And they feel like they've got to entertain you every minute. I don't like that music blasting at you every time there's a stoppage of play. They're working too hard at selling you on the game. They ought to give it a rest."

I asked Ferguson if Rupp and Lambert, who are both from the old school, were contemplating future careers in roller hockey. Ferguson laughed. "Lambert is always boasting about how his skating has improved. He practices a lot. He loves to play hockey. So does Duane. Lambert is a big draw wherever we go to play hockey. He's our biggest name."

This sparked a memory. I remember a trip to San Diego with the Steelers in 1980. My brother Dan and I were sharing a room at the hotel where the Steelers were staying. One evening Dan came to the room, all excited, and said I had to come out to the swimming pool. "You won't believe what you'll see!" he said.

When I got to poolside, I saw Jack Lambert skating around the pool. He was on roller skates. When he spotted me, he charged at me and stopped abruptly right at my shoetips. If he had been on ice skates, surely he would have laced my suit with ice shavings.

"I could have been a helluva hockey player," Lambert sneered. Then he skated off, and traveled through the hotel's dining room, stopping to plant a kiss on the forehead of one of his favorites, Jackie Hart.

Anything to get a reaction from the crowd. And this was on the evening of an NFL game with the Chargers.

"I've never met anyone quite like him," said Ferguson. "He's intense, whatever he does. If he had focused on hockey as a kid, who knows how good he might have been?"

Ferguson said he sees many of the early Penguins' fans when he participates with the Penguins' old-timers team in any fund-raising or charity-related exhibitions in western Pennsylvania.

"They say they can't afford the tickets these days to follow the Penguins," said Ferguson. "They have a hard enough time buying tickets for one game, let alone having season tickets like they once did. Even some corporations have a tough time justifying the expense, especially since the tax advantage has been lost. But it's the old die-hard fans I talk to the most at some of the socials that follow our games. Those are the guys I feel sorry for. They have to come see us play in order to see a hockey game. They were the real die-hard fans; they were there long before I got here. When we play in Kittanning or in Mt. Lebanon, we hear a lot of that stuff. If they don't have Lemieux, I think they're going to have to go back to having some 15-game packages, and stuff like that, so people can afford to go see them.

"I can't relate to the kind of money hockey players are making now, and the cost gets passed along to the fans. Ticket prices are out of sight. It's kinda crazy. The difference in salaries for hockey players just in the past ten years is unreal. The money is mind-boggling. And what people have to pay now to see them play is also mind-boggling.

"I also wonder whether players put out as much as they can when they're financially fixed for life. Do they worry as much about the game as they would if they didn't have long-term security? I wonder about that. I wonder about the preparation part. I had a routine I went through before every game. I'd start thinking about the game the night before. I'd get to the locker room early, and get my mind on the game to come. I was always very nervous before a game. I see some of these guys now, right before a game, and they look really relaxed. If they have five or six million in the bank, how hungry can they be?"

"They were just bad."
—George Ferguson

Ferguson was traded to the Minnesota North Stars early in the 1982-83. So he missed out on the 1983-84 season, the worst in Penguins' history, the one that set the franchise up to draft Mario Lemieux.

There has always been talk that the Penguins purposely made sure they didn't win games at the end of that campaign because they didn't want to blow the chance to get Lemieux. He was looked upon as a franchise-builder.

"I never heard talk about throwing a game; I never thought that was a question," Ferguson said. "But they made some personnel changes that weakened their team in the short run, but may have put them in position to improve themselves down the road.

"Plus, the opinion in the hockey world wasn't unanimous about Lemieux. Some thought he was too soft, that he floated, that he wouldn't work hard enough to succeed in the NHL. But Eddie Johnston always believed he was the real thing. But Lemieux was not an automatic first pick.

"There was a controversy about Mario being No. 1: 'He's lazy. He's this and that.' It wasn't a given that he'd be No. 1. I don't know whether they were maneuvering to get him; they were just bad.

"I talked to some of the guys who were on that team. It was pretty dismal — there were a lot of nights when there were 5,000 people in the stands.

"The team went through some dog days when I was there, too. We didn't have any franchise players. We were all in the same boat, about average, some a little better, some not so. The club was always making wholesale changes. They'd change seven or eight guys a year. There was no stability.

"Pittsburgh is a tremendous place to play. I wish I could have played my whole career here."

That sounded odd coming from a guy who was born and grew up in Trenton, Ontario, about 100 miles due east of Toronto. When we spoke, Ferguson still had a summer home there. Ferguson played junior hockey in Oshawa and Toronto, and played his first six NHL seasons in Toronto. That would seem to have been a young boy's dream come true.

"I got tired of Toronto after three years," he said. "I wasn't going anywhere there. They had Darryl Sittler and Tiger Williams, and that's who they wanted to go with. I just wanted an opportunity to play.

"Pittsburgh was an ideal place. The fans weren't tough. As long as you played hard, they accepted you. The media didn't put pressure on you. It was not a critical press.

"But I didn't know it would be so good. I remember being called in Toronto, and being told I'd been traded to Pittsburgh. When they told me Pittsburgh, I said, 'Ah, God, Pittsburgh!' That was the way it was perceived at the time, as a dirty, smoky industrial city. That's when the city was getting a bad rap. But it's a beautiful city, and the people fully adopt you here."

Ferguson didn't come to the Penguins on his own. He was part of a package deal. The Penguins swapped Dave Burrows, a popular and highly-regarded defenseman, to the Maple Leafs for Ferguson and Randy Carlyle, a young defenseman.

I asked Ferguson if he thought the Penguins knew what they were getting in Carlyle, who became an all-league performer.

"I don't think so," he replied. "At least not when they made the deal. A year later they were shocked by how good he was. Obviously, Baz (Bastien, the GM) made a good move. Randy was a good leader; he was made for that."

Ferguson made a fast impression on Penguins' fans, too. In 1979, he won the Three-Star Award from the Booster Club, and the Bill McCracken Memorial Award as Unsung Hero of the Penguins. He was one of the most popular players ever to play in Pittsburgh.

A right-handed shot, he earned himself a spot in Penguins' fans hearts forever when he scored in overtime to eliminate Buffalo in the preliminary round of the 1979 playoffs, two games to none. "That's what people bring up the most when they meet me," acknowledged Ferguson. "That was big in a lot of people's minds."

He also scored a then record-tying three goals in one period in a Stanley Cup game.

Beating Buffalo was a big accomplishment, as far as Ferguson is concerned. "We beat a team that was a legitimate Cup contender. They were absolutely the superior team. Our goalie, Michel Dion, stood on his ear and made saves in that series. He was sensational.

"Pittsburgh was the underdog in every way. We didn't have a big organization like Toronto and Chicago and New York and Montreal. Our coach, Johnny Wilson, did everything. He was a great coach. I loved playing for him. I wish I could have played 12 years for Johnny Wilson. He was fair and he was just. That's all you can ask for. Then E. J. came in. I had played with E. J. in Toronto. He was near the end of his career. He was one of three goalies on the team. He was in a tough situation around 1982 and 1983. There was a power struggle between him and Baz. He wanted to turn things around. He got rid of a lot of the older guys. I was one of them. I can candidly say that things were done here to help assure that Mario came here, but I don't think that included losing games."

Baz Bastien   Johnny Wilson
Two of George Ferguson's favorites were his GM and coach.

Jaromir Jagr
The richest kid in town

"I always play for fun."

A voice on the telephone said she was an AT&T operator and that she was connecting me to a teleconference call. I was in my home office, working on this book, and — like magic — I am listening to a joyful Jaromir Jagr talking about his new contract with the Penguins. He is in his hometown of Kladno, a coal-mining community in the Czech Republic. It is noon, Tuesday, August 9, 1994.

Penguins' owner Howard Baldwin thinks of everything, and money doesn't seem to be an object. Any minute, I expected somebody knocking at my front door, delivering a box lunch. After all, this was a Penguins' press conference. For the record, I am still waiting. But Baldwin never ceases to amaze me. He is a bold sports entrepreneur who wants to win, who wants to prove he's in Pittsburgh to stay.

Baldwin's boldness was pointed up once again by his signing of Jagr, a tremendously gifted young athlete, an impressive broad-shouldered 6-2, 210 pound dynamo who had demonstrated in four seasons at right wing with the Penguins that he could play with the best of them, and twice contributed to championship seasons while still a teenager.

"It's nice to know he's going to be with us for many years," said Penguins General Manager Craig Patrick. "He'll improve; he should only get better."

I recognized voices on the conference call, like Bob Smizik of the *Pittsburgh Post-Gazette*, Stan Savran of KBL, Bob Grove of the *Washington Observer-Reporter*. The most distinctive voice belonged to Jagr, who still struggles, understandably enough, with the English language. Then again, how well would the reporters have done if the interview had been conducted in the Czech language? Enough said.

Jagr (pronounced Yog-ger) repeated every question, oh so slowly, and responded in the simplest of sentences, not always complete sentences, and somebody was typing away on a laptop computer, storing Jagr's comments for posterity, and the annoying rat-tat-tat sound was making it even more difficult to understand Jagr. The radio-types with tape recorders were complaining about the interference, and begging somebody to stop typing. It was comical. They were looking for clean sound bites. The next day those sound bites would be used — how could a sports report on the radio be aired these days without a sound bite? — even though they were mostly muted and unintelligible. Jagr just kept talking. And he laughed lightly every now and then.

Hey, Jaromir Jagr, just 22, was certified as one of Pittsburgh's youngest millionaires, maybe the richest man his age in Pittsburgh, Kladno or Homestead, where he had been living with his mother, Anna, the past few years. He could laugh all the way to the bank.

According to circulated reports, Jagr had signed a new contract calling for nearly $20 million over five years. It's no wonder sports owners want salary caps because, left to their own free-spending instincts, they can't throw enough dollars at the young men who play for them. How can the Penguins pay salaries like this? Why is it necessary? How high can the price of tickets go at the Civic Arena? If they open the retractable roof, the sky is the limit.

Remember the immediate reaction when the Penguins were ousted from the playoffs by the Washington Capitals in the spring of 1994? All media reports stated that Baldwin would be unhappy, and that he and his partners couldn't continue to bankroll the highest-paid team in the National Hockey League if it was going to get bumped out of the playoffs in the first round two years running. Jagr was among those mentioned as high-salaried stars who might be dealt elsewhere in a restructuring of the team.

So what did Baldwin do? For starters, he announced that the Penguins would be building their own practice facility in Southpointe, industrialist/developer Jack Piatt's ambitious business/residential golf community in Canonsburg. Mario Lemieux was going to be a partner in the dual ice rink complex. Those who worried about the possibility of the Los Angeles-based Baldwin pulling up stakes in Pittsburgh should have been comforted by that announcement.

Then the Penguins traded Rick Tocchet to the LA Kings for Luc Robitaille, whose contract called for more money than Tocchet was paid, and free agents like Tomas Sandstrom and John Cullen were signed to new contracts. During a period when the Pirates had lost their best players in the free agent market and the baseball club was put up for sale, Baldwin was signing all the Penguins' top players to long-term contracts, and bringing in reserves to make sure there was depth in the playing ranks. Baldwin was even looking into being a part of the solution to the Pirates' financial problems. Baldwin's initial bid to buy the ballclub was rejected. But he came back a month later with another bid. He also considerably cut the prices for tickets in the upper regions of the Arena.

He deserved credit for making a commitment to pro sports in Pittsburgh. And now Jagr was prepared to do the same. Asked what he was going to do with all that money, Jagr said, "I will be in Pittsburgh the 26th or 27th to look for a house. Now that I know I am staying in Pittsburgh, I want to buy a home."

I pictured Jagr as he appears after most practices or games, bounding playfully about the Penguins' clubhouse, a white towel wrapped around his midriff, always chatting loudly, laughing, carrying on, cutting up. There is no more spirited player in the Penguins' clubhouse. After all, Jagr is just a kid. He loves to play video games and, with the money he's now making, he can afford to make more trips to the gaming tables of Las Vegas, which he said he had done during his summer vacation. Asked by an intrepid reporter if he had lost much money on his visit to Las Vegas, Jagr was smart enough to respond, "I was even." It's unlikely Jagr remembered the flap over Michael Jordan's gambling habits, but it was a smart reply just the same.

Jagr has a reputation for being suspicious of sports writers, or most strangers. He says he's afraid he won't know friends from foes, and wonders what their motives might be. If Jagr was a little paranoid about people trying to take advantage of him before, he should be a real head case now that he is making about $4 million a year.

One of the first questions Jagr was asked was how his role would change if Lemieux were unable to play. And whether he thought he would get more opportunities to be on the ice when the Penguins had a player advantage and were working their power play now that Tocchet, also a right winger, had been traded away.

"If Mario is not back this year...," began Jagr. "I don't know if Mario's going to play or not. If he's not playing, everybody else has to play harder. Mario and Wayne Gretzky are the best players in the world. Everybody has to play better."

Would that put more pressure on him?

"I always play for fun," said Jagr. "If I play for fun, I can do better things. I will still do my best, that's for sure."

He was asked what Luc Robitaille's presence would mean to the Penguins.

"Luc... I heard about it. He's coming to Pittsburgh. He's a goal-scorer, a great goal-getter. He'll be a great player for our team because he can score a lot of goals."

Jagr was coming across loud and clear from Czechoslovakia. He was hardly providing especially penetrating insights, but he was not missing a beat, either.

"I think I can play on the power play," he said. "I would like to play more on the power play."

He was then asked how much it bothered him in the past not to get much playing time when the Penguins had a manpower advantage, when scoring chances are more abundant.

"How much it bothers me? It don't. We have a lot of good players who can score goals," said Jagr. "A lot of players are better than me on the power play. I hope I can play more."

He said he was pleased with his contract. "I got a very good offer," he said. "I want to play in Pittsburgh. We have a good team, a good organization. People are always nice to me. We can win a lot of Stanley Cups. We can win it."

"Without Lemieux?" someone asked over the long-distance teleconference call.

"It will be very hard," said Jagr. "I heard he'll be back for playoffs. It would be nice."

That perked up everyone's interest on the party line. Pittsburgh reporters were prying everywhere trying to get a clue as to what Lemieux might be doing, ever since ESPN released a story a week earlier that he would be passing up the 1994-95 season, or that he might skip the regular season over health concerns, and come back for the playoffs.

"Where'd you hear that?" someone asked.

Jagr said he'd read it in a Czech newspaper. "That's what I read here," said Jagr.

Photos by Jim Cunningham

Jaromir Jagr enjoyed second Stanley Cup celebration with adoring fans at Three Rivers Stadium.

Jagr was asked if he had been worried that the Penguins might not be willing to pay him what he was after, since the team hadn't fared well in the playoffs, and that management was expected to pare the team's payroll.

"I left it up to my agent," said Jagr. "Mike (Barnett) told me not to worry, to just play hockey. That's what I have an agent for."

With the proper cue, Barnett broke into the conversation. He had been asked if the deal had been difficult to negotiate.

"It was easier when my client told me he wanted to stay in Pittsburgh," said Barnett. "As for dealing with Penguins' management, it's a pleasure to deal with Craig Patrick and Howard Baldwin. Jaromir is where he wanted to be from the beginning. He's ready to take more of a leadership role. As annual increases come along, so do expectations for improvement."

Barnett said the Penguins were doing what other NHL teams were doing, tying up their best young talent to long-term contracts. "He can be a foundation for the team for many years," said Barnett, speaking about talented young players in general. "In most cases, players are more comfortable with that kind of security."

Is it any wonder?

"He's a very emotional kid."
—Mike Lange

In recent years, Jagr had been living with a family in a home in Calhoun Manor, a section of West Homestead. They didn't have any children, and they welcomed him with open arms. West Homestead is a milltown, or it was a milltown when Mesta Machine Company loomed large on its riverbank. That's where my father and his two brothers, and my brother, all worked before it was closed down in the early '80s. U.S. Steel had a huge plant in neighboring Homestead. But it closed, too. Before he bought the home he was talking about buying after he signed his $20 million contract, Jagr figured to be the biggest business in the Mon Valley. And he caused a flap a few years ago by getting a refund on local school taxes because he was not an American citizen, and not obligated to pay same. With his salary, his contribution would have been substantial. It might have helped a financially-troubled Steel Valley School District. "He had a legitimate reason for not paying," said Earle Wittpen, editor of the *Valley Mirror* weekly newspaper that serves the area. "It didn't upset the people here." Jagr was first urged to move into West Homestead by Penguins' officials because there was a significant Czech community in the area. It was thought he would be more comfortable there. Other young Penguins had been placed with families in suburbs like Mt. Lebanon, Upper St. Clair and Fox Chapel to help them make the transition to moving to a new city and adjusting to life in professional sports. Lemieux was among those who benefited from such "adoptive" families.

Jagr was 18 when he reported to the Penguins in July of 1990, knew little English, and seemed to need a support system more than most rookies. "He came into the league," said KBL's Stan Savran, "when most kids his age are consumed with getting a date for the prom."

A lot of young women in Pittsburgh were enchanted with the long-haired, baby-faced young man with pink cheeks from Czechoslovakia. They were eager to teach him about the local customs. The police had to be called on a frequent basis to the home where he was living in West Homestead to chase overzealous autograph-seekers and date-seekers.

Jagr enjoyed fast cars and fast girls, and picked up more than his share of moving traffic violations from police throughout western Pennsylvania, and who knows how many times he was dunned by his dates.

"Every young girl in Pittsburgh wants to marry him," said fellow traveler Tocchet. "Of course, every cop in the city knows him, too."

Jagr was the team's No. 1 choice in the 1990 entry draft. Patrick took a risk in drafting Jagr. There was no assurance at the time that he would be able to come to America. Czechoslovakia was in political turmoil at the time, and a revolution against a Soviet-controlled government had broken out.

Expectations were high. "You all know by now," added Savran, "that if you jumble JAROMIR you come up with MARIO JR."

Even after Jagr had been here a few years, he was still feeling his way in the dark. "He's a very emotional kid," said Penguins' broadcaster Mike Lange. "I don't think people realize how emotional he is, day-to-day. We all lose sight of the fact that he's 21. His mom is here with him now, and she's emotional, too. She'll read things in the paper about him and she'll start crying, and we don't know why."

Jagr did his best to explain his dilemma.

"The hardest part for me is, you know, I can watch TV and I can talk to people, but I never find out who is a good person, who is a bad person," he said. "Maybe I will never find out, because I wasn't born here. Maybe I will never speak so good English that I will ever find out. That's the biggest problem, you know. Should you be friends with somebody or should you not? It's hard, you know, it's very hard."

It was evident by those remarks that Jagr, just like most American youngsters, had learned to pepper his comments with the "you know" phrase.

> *"If you scramble JAROMIR*
> *you come up with MARIO JR."*
> —Stan Savran

Mike Barnett of International Management Group, Jagr's agent, was doing his best to introduce Jagr to some of his other clients who might help show him the ropes. In the summer of 1992, Barnett took Jagr on a yachting trip with two of the NHL's top scoring stars, Gretzky and Brett Hull.

"I just appreciate them talking with me," said a wide-eyed Jagr. "They are hockey heroes. I couldn't believe I was there on their boat, in their house, going places with them. They are such great hockey players and such nice people."

No one was more enthusiastic than Jagr at Penguins' practices. Eddie Johnston had to chase him off the ice. He had no bigger fan than Johnston. Jagr led the Penguins in scoring in 1993-94 with 99 points, but Johnston said the best was yet to come.

"He's capable of scoring 50 goals with that kind of talent," Johnston said. "With his speed and strength, he just blows by guys when he has to."

"I'm very happy with the way I'm playing," Jagr told Gene Collier, columnist for the *Pittsburgh Post-Gazette*. "You can never be satisfied with yourself, in hockey or in life. When I first came, and nobody know what I can do, I beat the defenseman. Now, everybody is waiting for me. I'm still only 21. I'll be bigger and stronger still."

Jagr stunned Penguins' fans with some ill-considered remarks he made to a writer from *Sports Illustrated* in the summer of 1992. There was talk at the time that the Penguins might not be able to afford to keep all their high-salaried stars.

"If they have no money, I want to be traded where there's beaches," said Jagr. "I have two Stanley Cup rings. I don't need more rings. I just need money and beaches and girls."

Maybe somebody in West Homestead showed him the local beach, the Sandcastle water-slide park along the Monongahela River, to soothe his frayed nerves. When he drew some skeptical looks and critical comments for driving in the fast lane in Pittsburgh, he said, "I go to the bars; I go to clubs. I don't want to stay home because it's boring. I want to meet people the same age as me. I am just a normal 21-year-old guy."

One of his former teammates, Paul Coffey, came to Jagr's defense. "He's very, very misunderstood," claimed Coffey. "Jags wants to be the best. A lot of times, he's down on himself, and people think he's down on everyone. That's not it at all. He's a great kid.

"It's tough on him. He's not from Canada, he's not from the States. He doesn't trust a lot of guys, and he's trying to figure out who to trust. In the locker room, a lot of things get said, foolin' around, and sometimes he didn't know if they were laughing with him or at him. You know, you don't mature because people say it's time. You do it when you're ready."

Jagr, according to his agent Mike Barnett, has what it takes to be a superstar in sports.

"He has the three characteristics that usually will endear an athlete to fans," observed Barnett a few years back. "He has the skills that allow him to make individual plays that cause people to ask, 'Did I just see what I think I saw?' He has a very youthful approach to the game and to life that people find very appealing. He's like a teenager who thoroughly enjoys playing against men. And he plays on a championship team that brings a lot of media exposure. He loves people and he'll laugh and joke around with anybody. He's so unpretentious."

Jaromir Jagr (68) is high-flying Penguin, who is most comfortable in the company of fellow Czech Martin Straka, and their respective parents.

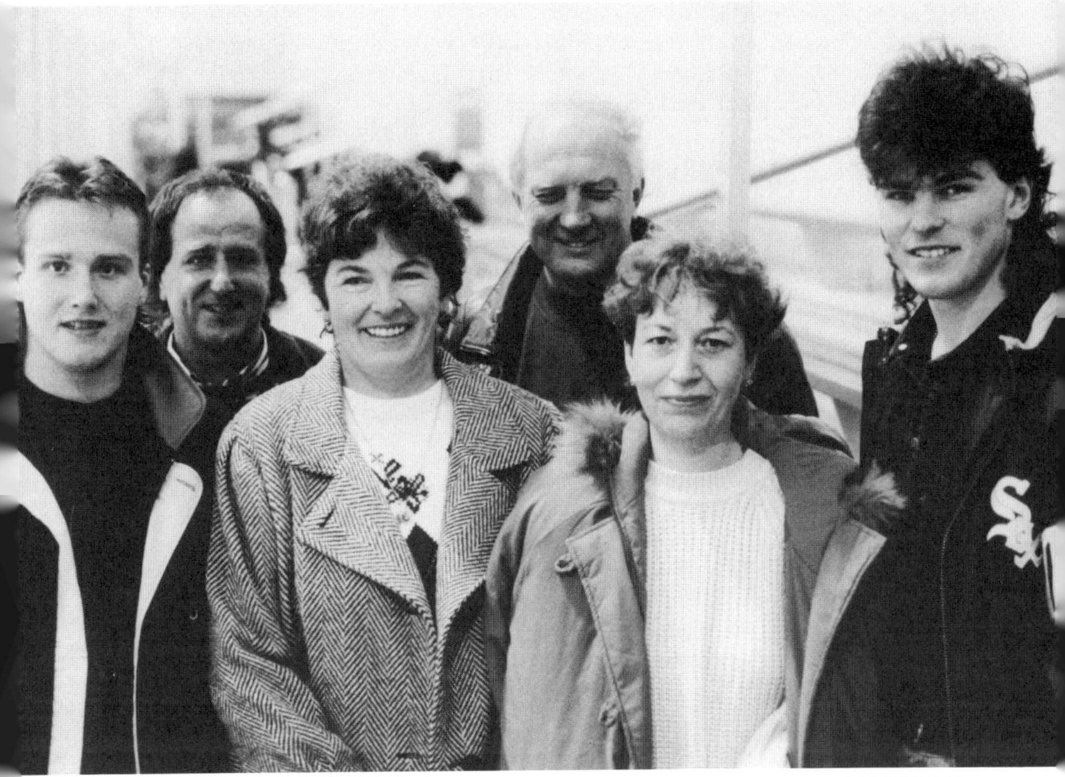

Scotty Bowman, who has seen his share of outstanding hockey players through the years, assessed Jagr in this way: "He's a different type of player than the league has seen in a long time. He has a lot of Frank Mahovlich in him. His skating style and strength make him almost impossible to stop one-on-one.

"When Mario gets the puck, he's always thinking, 'Where can I put it?' He'll pass the puck off and get himself in a better situation to score than he was in. When Jaromir gets the puck, he's always thinking, 'Where can I go with it?' He reminds me of Maurice Richard in that way. They both played the off-wing, and both had so many moves. I don't think either knew which moves they were going to do until they did them. Totally unpredictable."

When Bowman's scouting report was repeated to Jagr, he said, "I just play."

> *"My goal was to play in the NHL, because that is the best hockey in the world."*
> —Jaromir Jagr

As a 12-year-old in Kladno, Czechoslovakia, Jagr had a paramount goal, to come to America and to play in the National Hockey League. He carried a picture of then-U.S. President Ronald Reagan in his school books to remind him of his mission.

This was not a smart thing to do in a Communist country. He was scolded by a teacher for carrying the picture, and told to get rid of it. He did, but later reclaimed the photo. There was no stopping the jingoistic Jagr.

In late 1992, when Reagan's aides heard about the story after the Penguins had won a second straight Stanley Cup, they set up a telephone call between the former chief executive and the emerging NHL star.

"He told me 'thank you' for the nice talk about the U.S.A. and about him," recalled Jagr. "It was my best day. I never talked to a guy like him. Ever."

Jaromir is interested in Czechoslovakian history, spurred perhaps just by what he has learned about his own family's proud heritage.

Jagr's grandmother, Jarmila, told the boy about the first Jaromir Jagr, his grandfather and her husband.

He had his own farm which the Communists took over in 1948. They took all his land, and took most of his livestock. They left him with the house, barn and yard where the family still resides today.

His grandfather was thrown into jail for refusing to cooperate with the Communists. He was imprisoned for two years.

Jaromir Jagr never knew his grandfather. His grandfather died in 1968, four years before Jaromir was born.

"In school, we were always taught the Soviet doctrine," said Jaromir. "We were taught the U.S.A. was bad and wanted war. Russia was a friend and was preventing the U.S. from bombing us. Even my father didn't tell me the truth, because he was afraid I'd say something in school that would get us into trouble. But my grandmother told me the truth."

When Jaromir was six, he practiced hockey with three different age groups, getting three times as much ice time as his peers. "That was my father's idea," said Jaromir. "When I played against other six-year-olds, I was great. When I played against 10-year-olds, I was average. My father wanted me to play where I was average."

His father played street hockey with his son after school. They played in a dirt yard between the family's house and barn, often scattering a dozen chickens that the family kept in the yard.

His dad used an axle off one of his old tractors to craft a homemade set of barbells for Jaromir.

At age 13, Jagr saw Gretzy and Lemieux play in Prague in the World Championships in 1985.

"Those were the only names I knew," recalled Jagr. "But I knew about life in America, and I knew about the NHL. My first goal was to play for the local team in my city. My second goal was to play for the national team of Czechoslovakia, because that is my country. But my third goal was to play in the NHL, because that is the best hockey in the world."

When Jaromir was 15, he was already playing for Kladno in the best hockey league in Czechoslovakia. At 16, Jaromir was making more money than his father, who had a good administrative job at Kladno's coal mine.

When Jagr was 17, he became the youngest member of the Czech national team, which was one of the best hockey teams in the world.

Jaromir had an American flag in his bedroom and two decals of Old Glory on the windshield of his car in Kladno.

He wears No. 68. His grandfather died during a Czech freedom movement known as the Prague Spring of 1968. The Russians marched troops into Prague to put down the uprising.

Czechoslovakia's revolution of 1989 and 1990 overthrew the Soviet-backed government and enabled Jagr to fulfill his lifelong dream of playing in the NHL without having to defect, the way tennis stars like Martina Navratilova and Ivan Lendl did. Jagr was afraid he was going to have to defect to realize his dream, and he knew that Navratilova's name was never in the Czech newspapers for her accomplishments. It was as if she had died. The Penguins made Jagr their first choice in June, 1990, the fifth player taken overall, and Jagr was able to come to America without any red tape.

He entered the NHL's entry draft as a Czechoslovakian citizen and as a free man — the first player from his country to do so.

Jagr liked to go back to his family's farmhouse each summer since he began playing for the Penguins.

He played for the 1990 Czechoslovakian team in the World Junior Tournament, held in Helsinki, Finland, and in the World Championships in Switzerland. He was a member of the Czechoslovakian 1991 Canada Cup team.

Already realizing his boyhood dreams, Jagr is enjoying the best of both worlds.

"He's a very smart guy for his age."
—Jiri Hrdina
Czech Mate

As a rookie, Jagr was placed with a Czechoslovakian family in West Homestead, just south of Pittsburgh. Penguins GM Craig Patrick enrolled him in a Berlitz course, and he brought in Jiri Hrdina, a veteran Czech player from Calgary, to help Jagr adjust.

"I could talk to him about his problems," said Hrdina, who played for the Penguins from 1990 to 1992. "He's a very smart guy for his age. Very unusual to have the goals he does. He wants to be the best player in the game."

Patrick wanted to provide his young protege with all the support he could muster to boost Jagr's sagging spirits.

"He was in the throes of homesickness," explained Patrick. "Realistically, the reason he was in this depression was because he didn't have a grasp of the language. He really didn't know what we were saying to him. He did his best, but it's hard to get along in the streets, and with your peers, if you don't know what they're talking about. You hear people laughing, and it's natural that you start to wonder if they're laughing at you."

Of course, Jagr told people that he learned to speak English by watching the TV sitcom, "Married With Children," which may help explain why he's often made some intemperate remarks that have gotten him into hot water. He also developed an insatiable taste for Kit-Kat candy bars.

"Jags must eat ten pounds of Kit-Kats a day," said former teammate Wendell Young. "He eats them before, during and after games."

Teammates were delighted with his merry manner and youthful ways. "Me and Jags were in a bar one night playing a pinball machine," said Tocchet. "There were, like, a thousand girls and Jaromir. When he needed change, they started throwing quarters at him. When I needed quarters, they told me to get my own."

A playful sort, Jagr even served as a guest weatherman on Radio WDVE-FM, cracking up irreverent hosts Jimmy Kren and Scott Paulsen, the way he'd say things like "A chance of showers. . ."

"There is still a kid inside him," said Tocchet. "I don't know how long it will last, but I hope he keeps it for a long time."

Pittsburgh has many people with roots in eastern Europe, and Jagr has found that a source of comfort. He may be the most popular Penguin with young fans.

Jagr says that can be a problem. "I can't go to the mall in Pittsburgh. I can't buy anything or do anything. Everywhere I go, people want my autograph.

"But I like that way better than if it didn't happen. If it stops happening, it only means you're not a good hockey player anymore."

The best should be ahead for Jagr. He can skate so swiftly, and he handles the puck so smoothly, and he knows where the nets are, without even looking. "Every goal is a highlight film," offers Ronnie Francis.

Jagr has to pinch himself over his success. To him, hockey is such a simple game.

"What I like more than anything in the world is the skating," he said. "Just being there, one-on-one, me and the defender. When that happens it becomes all that matters."

Jaromir Jagr likes to grow a little beard every now and then just for fun. He showed up for training camp in September, 1994, sporting some extra whiskers, but soon shaved them off.

Ron Schock
The captain

"Home and away, I gave the best effort that I had."

Ron Schock had a reputation as a hard-working, non-stop scrambler, a two-way forward who was particularly adept at killing penalties, a likable leader, unselfish and someone who rated the "C" designation on his jersey as the team captain.

Never a great scorer, but someone who could and was willing to set up others, someone who sacrificed for the team. Nevertheless his name remains in the Penguins' record book in several categories for his efforts over eight seasons (1969-1977). Going into the 1994-95 season, for instance, he still held the record for the fastest two assists in Penguins' history. Schock was credited for two assists in a six second span on goals by Wally Boyer on March 5, 1970 at Detroit.

He is still in the Top 15 for career goals and assists. His best season was the 1974-75 season when he led the Penguins in scoring with 86 points on 23 goals and a club-record (to that point) 63 assists.

He played parts of four seasons with the Boston Bruins at the beginning of his NHL career, and was taken by St. Louis in the 1967 expansion draft. He was traded to Pittsburgh for Lou Angotti and a first round choice in the 1971 amateur draft on June 6, 1969.

Schock was born in Chapleau, Ontario on December 19, 1943. He grew up in pre-television days in the wind-whipped isolation of central Ontario, where there wasn't much else to do except go skating and play hockey. The freeze sets in early in Terrace Bay, which is snow-covered most of the year.

Schock says there was a soda fountain shop and a movie house where they changed the pictures every couple of weeks when he was growing up in a village of 1700 on the northern shore of Lake Superior, about 400 miles due north of Chicago.

"There wasn't much else to do, but skate," he said. "I've been skating ever since I was five, the year we moved to Terrace Bay. Everybody skated.

"We did a lot of party-skating, where the boys and girls skated together on the lakes and rivers."

They built an ice rink in Terrace Bay when Schock was ten. "It was a portable rink, exposed to the cold," said Schock. "We spent an awful lot of time sweeping the snow off it.

"I played hockey all the time as a kid. I stayed there until I was about 16 or 17, and went off to play junior hockey. I'll never regret those days."

Schock was the second child in a family of five and the oldest of three boys. His introduction to hockey came on the streets of Terrace

Ron Schock

Vic Hadfield

Photos from George Von Benko Collection

*"Each time I get hit in the face
I get closer to wearing a mask."*
—Les Binkley

Don Awrey

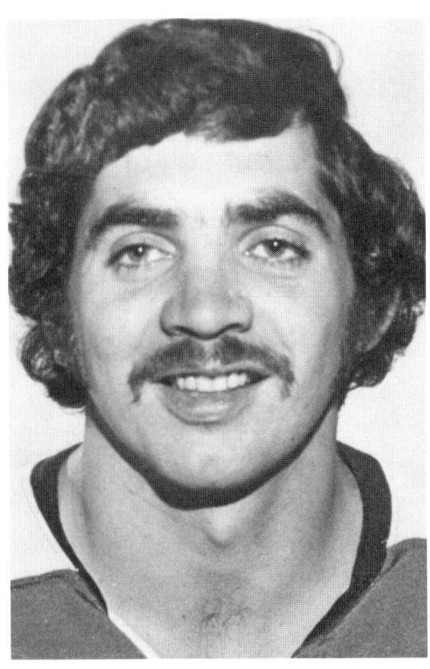

Ron Stackhouse

Bay, playing outside his home with his younger brothers. He continued to play hockey in high school.

"I was on kind of an all-star team," he says. "The best kids in town would play the best kids from other towns in the area. We'd travel to their rinks and then they'd come and play on ours."

Schock said they went to places like Oba, Nipigon, Atikokani, Longlac, Marathon and Armstrong Station. Occasionally, they'd drop in on one of the larger cities in the province, like Thunder Bay, 50 miles across the inlet, and the hometown of Bob "Battleship" Kelly, another celebrated Penguin of that time period.

His father drove him to all his games. "Had there been more to do in Terrace Bay, would my father have had the same interest in hockey?" asks Schock.

He wasn't thrilled about going to Pittsburgh in the first place. He hadn't enjoyed earlier trips there. Plus, he had twice played in the Stanley Cup finals with the Blues, and wasn't eager to leave the league's best expansion team. But he and his wife Jane moved to Pittsburgh, lived in the Green Tree area, and grew to like it, as did their four youngsters.

> *"Hockey wasn't work for me.*
> *Hockey was an enjoyment.'*
> —Ron Schock

Ron and Jane Schock, his wife of 29 years, were living in Fairport, New York, a suburb of Rochester, when I called on them in the summer of 1994. They had four children, two boys, Jeff, 28, and Steve, 26, and two girls, Jody, 24, and Marnie, 21. "That's enough, don't you think?" said Ron Schock.

He and his oldest son own a landscaping business, and do some home repairs. In the winter, they do snowplowing for families in the area. There's always plenty of snow in the Rochester area in the winter. He's been at this for about seven or eight years "The older I get, the longer it seems," said Schock, age 50 when we talked. "We did this once before, too." There was also an attempt at operating a donut shop.

Both of his boys play in recreational hockey leagues, and that's what hockey has been in their lives — a recreation. "It's never been one of their career pursuits," said Schock. "I still play with the old-timers once in a while, with the Buffalo team — Buffalo's about 65 miles from here — and they have an old-timers' team in Rochester. A lot of the guys who played for the Americans have settled here."

Schock said he occasionally catches an Americans' game in the American Hockey League.

"My biggest memory of my hockey days was that I was at a children's banquet in my hometown in Canada, and a little boy asked me, 'If you were to be traded, where would you least like to go?' And I said New York and Pittsburgh.

"That was on a Friday. On Monday it was announced that I had been traded from St. Louis to Pittsburgh. I'd been in Pittsburgh during a hotel strike, and we had stayed in some godawful places there. So I had a bad feeling about the place.

"But my wife and I went down and visited a friend in the Pittsburgh area prior to reporting to the Penguins. I told her, 'If I go there with the attitude that I'm going to hate the city it's going to be a bad experience for us. We've got to give it a chance.' We spent a good number of years there, brought up our kids there, and they were all enjoyable years. I like Pittsburgh. I grew to like it very much."

He became a personal friend, he says, of Tad Potter, who had put together a local group of investors to buy the team in 1971. Potter had been a member of the Penguins' booster club, called the Hockey Hounds, and bought the team along with Peter H. Block, Elmore Keener and A. H. "Peter" Burchfield. The club went bankrupt in 1975, following the team's best season on the ice.

"My wife and his wife Jeannie became good friends. We never talked business. I never had a problem with monies, and I was always treated extremely well. That was Tad's way of doing things. A lot of the problems in the office didn't leak down to the clubhouse. You had to know there were problems, though. We'd get about 11,000 for our games on some Saturday nights, and we'd get about 3,500 on Tuesday or Wednesdays. You could hardly open the building for that kind of crowd. They tried, I know they tried. Hockey didn't take off in Pittsburgh until after I left."

I asked Schock to name some players he particularly admired from his days in Pittsburgh.

"I admired the skills of others, and there were good things and bad things about each person. I was one of those people who sat back, and watched. I admired quite a few of the players. There were some things I didn't like about some of them, but there were probably some things they didn't like about me.

"I think of a player like Pierre Larouche. He comes to mind. I think about how he turned off everyone, at first, but how he changed quite a bit. There was Vic Hadfield; I had a lot of respect for Vic. Les Binkley. Lowell MacDonald. They had a lot of good qualities. I would have liked to have some of their qualities.

"There were very few of the players that you didn't like," said Schock. "Some you liked better than others. We had a lot of good times together. When we'd travel, we might get up a group of ten to 15 guys and go out and have Chinese food. We stuck together pretty well. At home, we'd get together with our wives. I was captain so I had to arrange some things.

"Hockey wasn't work for me. Hockey was an enjoyment. I missed it terribly. I had a good number of years playing, but it was still difficult to walk away from it. I liked practices. I liked everything about the game. It wasn't like going to the office, like 'ah, hell, I have to go to work today.' It was never like that.

"I was a contributor. I gave the best effort that I had, both away and at home. Sometimes it was better than other times. It was the best I had that night.

"I'll never forget the one year (1974-75) there when we had the three-nothing lead on the Islanders in the playoffs, and we lost four straight to get bounced out. I think, as a team during the season, we were never beaten. The Islanders had that same attitude against us. Some games we were behind by two or three goals, but we never thought we were going to lose. It's a feeling you don't have often. We were never out of the game. Not that we didn't get blown out once in a while, but we always thought we could score and make things interesting. There was always somebody who would come up big.

"That team had a real significance to me. The financial problems didn't leak down to me. I was going to work and enjoying it. I wasn't a great newspaper follower, as far as what was happening on the inside. I parked above the Civic Arena, and I'd go through the front lobby, and I'd always see one or two of the owners. Tad would say hello. I just never knew. Maybe I was living in Never-Never Land.

"I guess the only disappointment I ever had was when I was traded from Pittsburgh to Buffalo. Everything else there was pretty much on the plus side.

"I think of myself as a Penguin; that's where I played the longest. I had some very happy times there. I was in Boston when there were only six teams, and in St. Louis when there were 12 teams, and we went to the Stanley Cup finals twice under Scotty Bowman."

I asked Schock if he was close to Eddie Johnston when they were both Bruins. "I lived with Eddie," said Schock. "I roomed with him on the road. I lived with him a year in Boston before I got married.

"If I were in town, he's the type of guy I'd never hesitate to call. We called him Downtown Eddie. He really liked life, and he enjoyed it to the fullest. He was young and full of himself. He's a good golfer, and he knew all the right people."

I mentioned a story to Schock that Johnston had related to me, about the time he was nearly killed by a slap shot by Bobby Orr that struck him in the side of the head during a pre-game warmup.

"I was playing for St. Louis then. I went to the hospital in Boston to visit Eddie. I went with our goalie, Glenn Hall. Goaltenders were always different. They were the ones in the trenches. They liked to talk to one another."

I told Schock that Eddie Johnston and his five brothers had all gone to Ireland for a week of golfing over the summer. "It's a wonder," he said, "they're all not in jail."

> ***"Nine out of ten people would say that the greatest thing about Pittsburgh is its people and that it's a big city with a little city atmosphere."***
> —Mario Lemieux

Ron Francis
Always the big brother

"That's the way I was brought up."

It's OK for kids to have sports heroes, but Ron Francis feels they should be careful. "You have to keep in mind that all athletes are humans and they make mistakes," he said. "They're not perfect."

The Penguins veteran center comes close — he reminds one of athletes from a bygone era with his refreshing approach and appeal — because he is a concerned citizen, a caring person, and a man who learned the right values at an early age, and continued to practice them throughout his professional hockey career. He is handsome in a hard-nosed way, an old-fashioned fellow who fans can relate to, and they like the way he goes about his work. He is dedicated to succeed. His own mother says he has always been a "driven" individual.

He was the most popular player with the fans during his ten years with the Hartford Whalers and caught on quickly with the Pittsburgh populace during his first four seasons with the Penguins. He was named the team's MVP in 1994, and was admired by teammates, management and fans alike.

I spoke to Francis just before training camp opened for the 1994-95 NHL campaign, before he had left his home in Unionville, Connecticut, just outside Hartford where he spent his summers. At the time, there was a continuing controversy concerning sports heroes that was cause for great debate. Former football star O.J. Simpson was accused of murdering his former wife and a friend of hers in one of the most celebrated crimes in history. Simpson had been one of the biggest of sports heroes, and many felt it pointed up the senselessness of young people pointing to sports heroes as models. Others felt there were still sports heroes worth emulating.

"It's a tough call," cautioned Francis. "I don't think there's anything wrong with looking up to an athlete. I don't consider myself any better than anybody else. So I have a hard time dealing with people who tell me that I'm special, or 'you're so great.' As long as it's not taken to the extreme, it's OK. If there's a sick kid out there who'll benefit from a visit or call from me . . . if I can help them . . . that's fine. I'll do that.

"First and foremost, you have to understand that all people are human, and have human frailties. It can be such a blow to a kid who puts all his eggs in one basket, and then sees his sports hero get into trouble, or do something wrong, or fall into disgrace.

"It's OK to set goals, or to model ourselves after someone, to say, 'I want to be able to play sports like him.' Or to be like someone in the entertainment business, a movie star, a rock star. 'I want to be able to be as great as him or her.' But you have to be careful."

Francis, 31 at the time, had never been one to put all his eggs in one basket, or to be a hero-worshipper, or to model himself after someone in sports.

"I was never one to get caught up in that," he said. "I can honestly say I never idolized any athlete when I was a kid. At least I don't remember doing that."

He grew up in Sault Ste. Marie, Ontario, where Phil and Tony Esposito had already gained fame as hockey players when he came along. "Phil Esposito came to my school when I was in kindergarten," recalled Francis. "I posed for a picture with him. It was a classic. He was wearing one of those awful polyester leisure suits and big fat sideburns, and I had a brushcut. We both looked different. I showed that picture to Phil once and we both got a kick out of it."

I had been speaking to a friend in professional sports management that same day, and he voiced the opinion that today's athletes were so much different from when he first got into the business, that they were so caught up with themselves, and spoke mainly of personal goals and self-interest. I mentioned this to Francis.

"I was brought up that if I spoke too much 'me' and 'I' stuff, I got a real tongue-lashing. From both of my parents. I was taught to be team-oriented, to be family-oriented. I was told to do whatever I was doing as well as I could do it, but to share the credit.

"The pro sports issue is no different than anything else. If you have people telling you how great you are, sooner or later you tell yourself, 'maybe I *am* great.' That's where you get into trouble."

Toward the end of the previous season, Francis signed a contract extension that could keep him with the Penguins for another five years. It was for more money than he ever thought he'd make in his entire NHL career.

"The money has made things more challenging in sports," said Francis. "I'm making more money than I ever dreamed of. In 1981, when I signed my first contract with Hartford, I got a $35,000 signing bonus. My dad had worked in a steel mill all his life, and $30,000 was the best he ever did for a full year's work, and that was after 40 years at the job. My family just looked at that check in awe.

"I know I've been lucky. With the kind of money I make, I can do more. I can go more places, have more things, and not worry about where my next buck is coming from. It brings more demands and more pressures, too. From a fans' standpoint, it looks one way. It looks all glorious. From an athlete's viewpoint, it's a real challenge, in every respect.

"Don't get me wrong. I wouldn't trade it for anything in the world, but it's not all that glamorous. There's a great deal of travel involved, for instance, and you're away from your family a lot. I missed my daughter's first steps, her first words. There are the pressures of the game, the expectations, the frustrations when things aren't going as well as you would like. In some respects that's no different from the pressures everyone feels on their job, but ours is public. When we make mistakes everyone knows about it. The bad comes with the good. You read about

 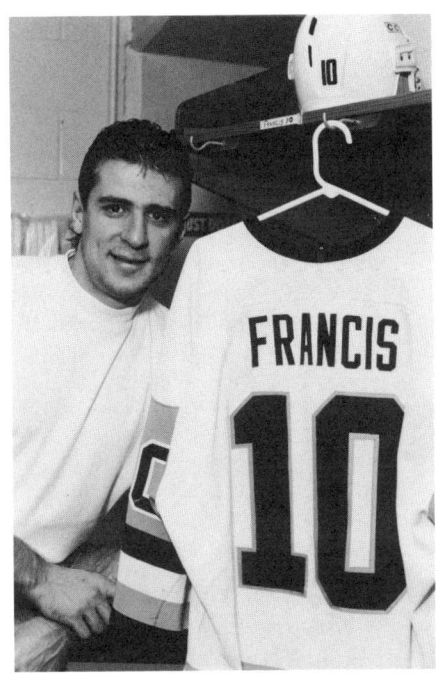

The different faces of Ron Francis, the popular center of the Penguins, who joined wife Mary Lou, daughter Kaitlyn and baby Michael at Penguins' 1993 holiday party.

Photos by Jim Cunningham

your failures as well as your successes in the newspaper each day. Someone in the stands says you're no good. There's lots of parts to the game. We had stretches where our kids were sick, and we were both up all night. Maybe I wasn't in the best shape, or as sharp as I'd like to be that next night in a game. Maybe I didn't play as well as I should've. And someone is shouting that you're a bum. It's not as cut and dried as it appears. You have to live the life to appreciate all the plusses as well as the minuses.

"I try to be nice to people on the way up, because you're going to meet the same people on the way down. I was told that, right? I try not to put myself on a pedestal. Everyone has their own personality and what they want to do. I try to be conscientious about what I do — on and off the ice — because that's the way I was brought up.

"People will remember you as a good hockey player, but that will die out. If you can have them say you were a good person and a good friend, and left them with good memories, that's more important. Hockey will come and go. I can't play hockey for the rest of my life."

Ron Francis says Sault Ste. Marie was a steel mill town. "The majority of jobs there are involved with the steel industry. My dad, who is also Ron Francis, started working in the steel mill when he was 18. He was there for 41 years. He just retired," said Francis.

"He started off with shift work, sometimes 11 to 7, sometimes 7 to 3, sometimes 3 to 11. It depended on the needs of that week at the mill. As I got older, into my middle teens, he had become a salaried worker, and then a foreman, and had an 8 to 5 job. Before that, though, it was always shift work, always a different schedule. If he worked 11 to 7, he'd sleep in the morning when he came home. He'd be up in the afternoon, when we came home from school, and then he'd get some more sleep after dinner before he'd go back to work."

That brought back some memories of the similar schedule at our home. My father worked the 11 to 7 night shift at Mesta Machine Company throughout my youth. My wife's father did the same at Westinghouse Electric Company. It made life different for everyone else in our families. Then again, we didn't know any different.

"He always found the time to participate in our activities," recalled Francis. "He built an ice rink for us in the backyard, and he'd play catch with us. He had a fluctuating work schedule, but he was always there for us when it was time to play."

Francis said there were hockey rinks in the backyards of every third or fourth house in his neighborhood in Sault Ste. Marie. "It wasn't warm enough to have swimming pools," he recalled.

He said there were about 80,000 people in the community, and there were six indoor skating rinks. "Then, too, the city had a public parks program and they put up portable rinks in different playgrounds all over the city," he explained. "They also put up shelters, someplace where you could get dressed, get warm, or take off your skates before you went home. So we had plenty of facilities."

Francis Family Album

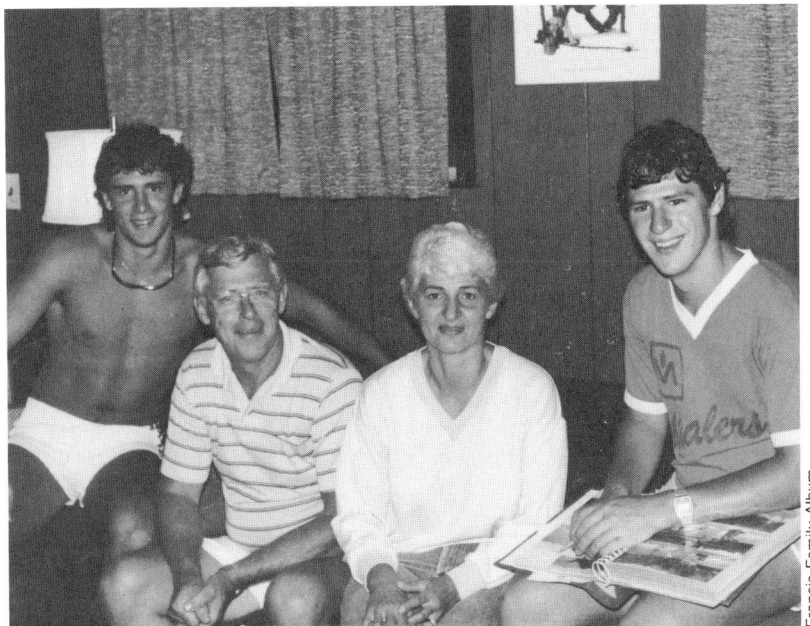

Ron Francis' family includes, left to right, his father Ron, his mother Lorita, and kid brother Ricky, seen at home back in 1983 and more recently at Hockey Hall of Fame in Toronto.

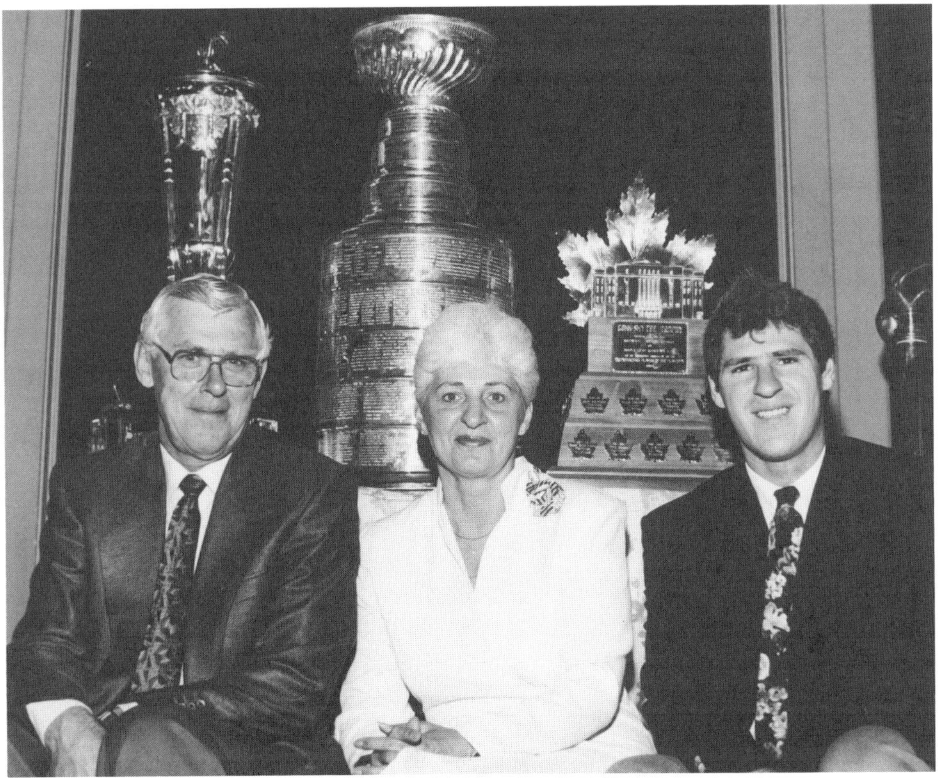

I asked Francis when he first got seriously interested in hockey. "Probably before I realized I was," he said. "I understand I started skating when I was 2 1/2. I started playing organized hockey when I was 3 1/2. My mother had a friend who had a son who was 4 1/2, and she took him to sign him up for the youngest league in our community. You had to be at least four years old to play in it. My mother and I went with her, just to keep her company. She had another son who was my age, also 3 1/2. The lady who was signing up the players asked the other woman about us two little guys. 'What about them?' the lady asked. Our mothers told her we were only 3 1/2. The lady said they were short two players, and they could use us. Our moms thought 'what the heck,' and signed us up. My dad thought they were crazy."

Ron had a brother, Ricky, who was two years younger. "My brother had a learning disability." said Francis. "He couldn't play in our hockey league, but he was very involved in Special Olympics programs."

I asked Ron if that was why he lent his name and efforts to Special Olympics. "I do run a charity golf tournament in my hometown every year to benefit Ricky and all his friends," said Francis. "I did a lot of work in Connecticut when I played there, and I still sit on an honorary board for Special Olympics."

I mentioned that I had a 38-year-old niece with Down's Syndrome who participated each summer in a Special Olympics competition, and what a thrill it was for her to win some medals for running.

"That's what it's all about," said Francis. "You go to those events and you'll never forget it."

He said that the Special Olympics in Sault Ste. Marie included regularly scheduled competition in floor hockey, bowling, soccer, track and field, softball, swimming and cross-country skiing. "They've got more and more kids involved," said Francis.

Francis has often participated in charity-related or fund-raising events, and he came away with a real bonus from such activity. That's how he met his wife, Mary Lou, the mother of their two children, Kaitlyn, who was 3, and their son, Michael, 14 months old.

"We had a fund-raising dinner in Hartford like we do with the Penguins, where the players get all dressed up in tuxedos and serve as waiters," recalled Francis. "It was called 'Tip A Whaler Dinner.' It was to raise money for research to help the blind. Mary Lou had been named Miss Connecticut Eyes, and was representing a local eye foundation. We met there, started talking, and she just wouldn't let me go."

Francis laughed at his own remark, made within earshot of his wife. "Notice I laughed when I said that," remarked Francis.

> *"There was a strong sense of family.*
> *We were all together."*
> —Ron Francis

I asked Ron what influence his brother Ricky had on his young life. "I had to grow up in a hurry, they needed me to help out at home," said Francis.

"When Ricky was young, he used to have 20 to 30 seizures a day. He was a 24-hour-a-day baby-sitting job for my parents. My dad was working different shifts, so sometimes it was just Mom and me to look after Ricky. LSD was considered the wonder drug at the time, but it didn't seem to be working for Ricky. When he was nine, the doctors told my parents that they should put him in an institution, that he would die before he was 12. My parents wouldn't go along with that. Their attitude was that if he's going to die, he'll die at home. My mother learned about some doctors who were doing special research with megavitamin diets out in western Saskatchewan. She couldn't afford to go there, but she had a friend who was going out to see the doctors to have them check her child who had similar problems. My mother sent along Ricky's medical file, and told the doctors she would like them to make some recommendations, and she would pay them for their services.

"They recommended that she take Ricky off all dairy-related products, and they put him on a high dosage of vitamins."

Ron started sounding like a pharmacist as he tolled off the different dosages of vitamins that were given to his brother. "You still remember all the numbers, don't you?" I said.

"No question about it," he responded. "Having been a part of it, I'll never forget it. It made all the difference for Ricky. He's doing fine now. He learned how to read and, to look at him, you'd never know there was anything wrong with him.

"But it was difficult. I remember waking up in my bunk bed as a kid because it was shaking. My brother, in the bed below, was having a seizure. When he'd go bike riding, we'd have to keep an eye on him. I remember he fell off, when he was having a seizure, and got all cut up. We had to keep a constant eye on him.

"Meanwhile I was so active in hockey. And no matter how crazy things were at our house, with Ricky's special needs and my dad's crazy schedule, I was always at all my games and practices on time. My parents went with me on weekend trips, and they brought Ricky along with them. There was a strong sense of family. We were all together."

I asked Ron if he felt that looking after Ricky may have forced him to grow up faster, and may have contributed to his early maturity. "I really don't doubt that," he said. "We all had to deal with it, and how to handle it. I didn't suffer from it, or get ignored in favor of my brother.

"I always had my skates, my equipment. I never missed a game; I never missed a trip. It's crazy when you go through it. My dad's schedule was crazy. My mother was trying to balance everything. It could look chaotic. I remember that my parents never complained about it. That was important. Everything's worked out for the best."

"You fantasized about how much money you'd make."
—Ron Francis

I asked Ron when he realized that he was really a good hockey player, and that he might have what it takes to play professionally. "I knew I had ability; I think at an early age I'd had a lot of success at it," he recalled. "Like every kid in Canada, I dreamed of playing in the NHL. You fantasized about how much money you'd make, and what kind of home you'd live in. I hoped I'd play.

"But I didn't think I had a realistic chance of playing in the NHL until I was about 17. I was turning 18 and I heard I was ranked in the top ten prospects, and that I could go high in the draft.

"Before that I was hoping I could get a college scholarship, and go to school for four years, and enjoy playing the game and getting an education.

"The kids in Canada have to make a decision at 16. You have to find a place to play for a year before you go to college, or you go directly to the juniors. Once you step in the juniors and accept any money you forfeit the ability to get a college scholarship. My mother always hoped I'd go to college.

"When I was in that position, I got several inquiries. I checked out Cornell and I had every intent of going there. I told them I was all set to go there. Then I met with the people from the junior hockey team in my hometown later in the week, and I had second thoughts. I thought, 'If I'm good enough to play in the NHL, I'll find out in a year, rather than four years if I go to college.' I told my local junior team that I'd sign with them if they drafted me, and agreed to pay for my college education if I didn't make it in the NHL. Today, they have a built-in plan for kids in that same position to assure them of a paid education."

He was 18 when the Hartford Whalers made him the fourth player taken in the 1981 draft. They assigned him to the Sault Ste. Marie Greyhounds of the Ontario (Junior) Hockey League.

"I went back to school the first few summers I was in the NHL. I went to Lake State, and did some courses. Then for three summers I worked in financial planning. I got a broker's license and then I got a real estate license. So I have been getting an education, and I have been preparing for life after hockey."

"Mario's decision has to be something he can live with."

Ron Francis had also spent the summer preparing himself for the coming campaign. When Francis first came to the Penguins, he was promptly told by Badger Bob Johnson that he wouldn't have the same role that he had in Hartford, where he had been the "franchise" player. Indeed, in Hartford he had been Ronnie Franchise.

Ron Francis at 3½ with his first team

At 10 with novice traveling team

At 16 in his second year of midget play

Ron in his first year of juniors

"Bob said to me, 'We have a No. 1 center here. Maybe you've heard of him. Maybe you haven't. It's a guy named Mario Lemieux. He's gonna be the No. 1 centerman.' There was no doubt about it."

Francis had to laugh a little at the memory.

Johnson had also told reporters that Francis had suffered in Hartford because the expectations were so great.

"He was supposed to lead them to the Stanley Cup, but he never did," said Johnson. "There was a lot of pressure on Ronnie Francis."

Francis was a fantastic No. 2 center in Pittsburgh, a two-way player who contributed in so many ways, on the ice, in the clubhouse, outside the Civic Arena. But things had changed. Mario had been missing more and more games and, as Francis and I spoke on a summer evening in late August, rumors had resurfaced that Mario might not play in the coming season. Stories had come out of Montreal and Toronto that Mario had made up his mind that he was going to sit out the year to give his balky back and his Hodgkin's disease problems proper treatment. It appeared he simply wasn't ready to return.

There was so much uncertainty in the sports picture in Pittsburgh. The baseball season had been abruptly ended by a players' strike, the Pirates were up for sale, Howard Baldwin was back with a restructured $83 million bid for the Bucs, and was wondering what the reaction would be among the fans and season ticket holders if Mario, indeed, decided not to play.

How did Francis feel about the situation? Was he ready to become the Penguins' No. 1 center on a full-time basis?

"I, as well as the rest of the guys on the team, have learned to deal with that situation. First and foremost, Ron Francis wants what's best for Mario Lemieux.

"If he can get healthy and enjoy the rest of his life, that's my No. 1 concern. From a strictly selfish standpoint, I'd love to see him play. He's so great, and he makes the rest of us better. But you've had to be around him in recent years, to watch him deal with his back problems, his illness, to watch him go through what he's gone through.

"No matter what he does, he should not be criticized. He's done more than his share for hockey, and he has to do what is best for him. So he can watch his kids grow up, and play with them. So he can go out in the yard like my dad did and play catch.

"If he doesn't play, it leaves a big hole. Do I think I can fill it? No. I can help. Everyone has to view it that way. None of us can replace Mario Lemieux. But if we all work harder, and work together, we can help make up for his absence.

"Right now it's still a big 'if' as we don't know what he'll do. I've been told that life is what happens when you're making plans. I remembered that. I don't know what he ought to do. It has to be a personal decision. Mario's decision has to be something he can live with."

"If you play hard in Pittsburgh, they (the fans) appreciate it."
—Ron Francis

I asked Francis how he felt about playing in Pittsburgh after spending his first ten seasons in Hartford. "I was brought up on the loyalty thing, and I wanted to play my whole career in Hartford," he said. "I was disappointed, to say the least, when I was traded to Pittsburgh.

"But I really like Pittsburgh. Coming through the tunnels, and seeing the city burst upon you . . . it always impressed me as a beautiful city. In my first year at Hartford, I lived with Greg Millen, who had played in Pittsburgh. He always thought it was a good place to play.

"I can relate well to the people in Pittsburgh. Pittsburgh's history as a steel city is something I'm familiar with because of where I come from. I know it's no longer the steel city it once was, but there's still a blue-collar mentality, and I mean that in the best sense of the phrase. The people of Pittsburgh have always worked hard, with no excuses. If you play hard in Pittsburgh, if you're trying, they appreciate it.

"If things aren't going well, but they know you're working hard, they can accept that. The city has a history of great sports teams. It's a great tradition. It's a great place to play."

Francis remains one of the NHL's best two-way centers. He is an accomplished penalty-killer and can play defense like a man who truly cares.

"I don't know where we'd be without him," said Eddie Johnston.

Tom Barrasso remarked after a game in which Francis had been the Penguins' outstanding performer: "There is no law, no sign on those dressing room walls, that Mario has to win the game for us. Or that Kevin (Stevens) has to win the game for us. Sometimes people take notice of Ronnie Francis and sometimes people look right past him, but nobody should."

Francis could look in the mirror, check out his usual heavy beard growth and be honest with himself.

"My goal in hockey is to be successful," he said, "and whatever it takes for us to win the Cup, I'm willing to give."

Where are they now?
Orest Kindrachuk (1978-81)

"Give an effort every night."

Present home: Medford Lakes, New Jersey

Present job: Registered representative, insurance agent

Job description: Financial planning

Family information: Wife — Lynn, Sons — Zak, 14, and Jake, 11

Personal highlight of Penguins' career: Being elected captain by teammates. Was captain for three years.

Most cherished memory of playing days: Playing with Ross Lonsberry on my left and Rick Kehoe on my right. It was a line I really enjoyed.

Player you most admired on team: Respected all players on the team as we all know what it takes to play at this level: tremendous drive and dedication, starting at a very young age.

Favorite character on that club: Brian Spencer and his two-ton tank.

What you learned from your experience with the Penguins that served you in good stead during your lifetime:
- Coming from the Philadelphia Flyers and being elected captain, I wanted to pass on what it takes to succeed. To give an effort every night, and never give up. If you do both of these, eventually you will win with regularity. The public will respect you, win or lose.
- Not only to work with your team members, but also with management. I had my differences with management on the treatment of the team. You treat the players without respect, the players will have little respect for management. If you try to cut corners on expenses, it will eventually show on the ice.
- There were quite a few of us traded there (from the Flyers) in 1978 so we had something to prove. We did as we made the playoffs and then beat Buffalo out in the first round.
- Playing in Pittsburgh was a good individual experience. For me, it taught me to be more of a leader and that you had to work every night there was a game.
- Keep the team together on off-days.

Orest Kindrachuk and his family, left to right, sons Zak and Jake with his wife Lynn, as they board cruise ship.

Where Are They Now?
Lowell MacDonald (1970-71/72-78)

*"Perseverance and dedication
do have their rewards"*

Present home: Mequon, Wisconsin

Present job: Athletic director, University School, Milwaukee

Job description: Athletic director at a prep school, similar to Shady Side Academy. I coach the school hockey team, oversee the rink operation, and direct a summer hockey school.

Family information: Wife Joyce is a registered nurse. Sons Lowell and Lane. Lowell graduated from Colgate University, where he played hockey for four years. He played hockey for one year in England. He is now an associate producer for ESPN hockey coverage. Lane graduated from Harvard University, and played for the 1988 USA Olympic team. He was captain of Harvard's NCAA championship hockey team (1988-89), and won the Hobey Baker Award in 1989. He played in Switzerland for a year. He is now getting an MBA from Stanford.

Highlight of Penguins career: Winning the Bill Masterton Trophy in 1973, and being selected to play in two All-Star Games, and runner-up to Johnny Bucyk of Boston for Lady Byng Trophy in 1974.

Most cherished memory of playing days: After two years of not playing a game, being able to come back and reward Red Kelly for his faith in me by having four-and-a-half super seasons before my knee required surgery again. It was the seventh time my left knee had to be cut.

Player most admired on the team: Difficult to choose one. Some you admired for their skill level, others for their dedication, others for their fearlessness, etc.

Favorite character on the club: Again, just too many over an eight-year period, so it's hard to select just one.

Lesson learned from your experience with Penguins: That perseverance and dedication do have their rewards eventually, and that friends stick with you during the good and bad times.

Lowell MacDonald
Still flying high

*"My greatest memory?
I'd have to say the fans."*

Lowell MacDonald overcame a fear of flying and a series of knee operations to make one of the great comebacks in National Hockey League history.

Most hockey people thought MacDonald was finished, and he admits he thought they might be right, when he returned to Pittsburgh in 1970 and — in time — scripted an inspirational story of courage and determination.

MacDonald had first played in Pittsburgh for the Hornets when they were revived in 1962 with the opening of the Civic Arena, and played for them for three seasons in the American Hockey League.

He got a chance to get to the National Hockey League on a full-time basis when the league expanded and doubled its size to 12 teams for the 1967-68 season. He was taken in the expansion draft by the Los Angeles Kings, which turned out to be a good news, bad news situation.

The good news was that his coach would be Red Kelly, who would become the most significant factor in his NHL career and the bad news was that no NHL team traveled more miles in airplanes than the Southern California club. MacDonald dreaded flying, and it led to his leaving the league and withdrawing from the ice sport for awhile.

Kelly and MacDonald hooked up again in Pittsburgh in the early '70s, and MacDonald took advantage of the opportunity to become one of the leading scorers in Penguins' history, and one of the team's all-time most popular players.

MacDonald moved to Milwaukee when he retired from the NHL during the 1977-78 season, and he was beginning his 17th year as the athletic director at the University School, a prep school in Milwaukee, when we spoke in late August of the summer of '94.

He had spent six weeks during the summer in his native Nova Scotia, building a home on a harbor there. He had a cottage by the ocean for a summer retreat for many years, but had sold that in favor of something more permanent, and possibly safer. He had grown up in New Glascow, and his mother and sister, as well as the parents of his wife, Joyce, were still living there.

Joyce is a nurse at the University School. "That works out well for us," said MacDonald. "An athletic director spends a lot of time at school; there's always something going on. There's never an end to athletic events. So we get to see each other during the day."

I asked MacDonald if Pittsburgh still had a special place in his heart since he had enjoyed so much success there.

"No question," he replied. "I remember a few years back when Pittsburgh was named the most livable city in America. I went to a bank here right after that and the people at the bank knew that I had played hockey in Pittsburgh. 'Did you see that story?' they asked me, and they were poking fun at the survey. I don't have to tell you the image Pittsburgh has in other parts of the country. I told them the rating was deserved. I'll never forget the traffic tie-ups and the potholes, but you'll also find the greatest people in the world in Pittsburgh.

"I was there for eight years with the Penguins. My two boys both grew up there. It became home for us. Yes, Pittsburgh still has a special place. We regret that we don't get an opportunity to get back there these days — working out here and scrambling to get home to Nova Scotia for vacations — to maintain our friendships in Pittsburgh."

I asked MacDonald to detail how he came to the Penguins and turned his NHL career around in an unbelievable manner. He went from washout to playing in two NHL All-Star Games.

"I had a major fear of flying; I was in bad shape," recalled MacDonald. "My two years in Los Angeles really took its toll. We flew over 100,000 miles a year, and I remember being on a 16-day road trip. That was before regional scheduling; that would be unheard of today. Then I had a bad flight to our training camp (in 1969) at Barrie, Ontario. I flew from Halifax to Toronto. I missed my original flight, and the plane I was supposed to be on was hijacked to Cuba. Yvon Durelle (a world-rated light heavyweight boxer from Montreal who was big in the 50s) was on that plane. I had a real bumpy flight. It was real bad. I stayed at the training camp for a day or two. But I couldn't get back on a plane after that ordeal. The combination of the bad flight, and the mix-up and the hijacking was just too much for me psychologically. So I got on a train and went home to Nova Scotia. Joyce had even gotten a call saying my flight got hijacked to Cuba. But I called her as soon as I could to straighten that out.

"I needed a year in college to get my b.a. degree. I had gone to summer school for nine years, picking up credits here and there. I went to St. Mary's University in Halifax and they helped me. Half way through the year, the Kings started calling. Larry Regan asked me if I would be interested in going up to Springfield to play — just on weekends. He'd fly me back and forth, said I could play a game or two. He said they wanted me to consider coming back. He offered me nice money as an inducement.

"Here I was back in college with Joyce and two boys, and I decided to give it a try."

Former Hornets and Penguins performer Lowell MacDonald stands behind his family at 1993 Christmas gathering in their suburban Milwaukee home. They are, left to right, Lowell, Joyce with Brooks, the dog, and Lane.

Lane in USA Olympic uniform in 1988

Lowell Jr. in his Colgate days

Lowell as a Penguin

"I check their credentials as human beings."
—Lowell MacDonald

MacDonald played parts of 14 games in Springfield that season. "By this time, Red Kelly had left Los Angeles and was with Pittsburgh," said MacDonald. "He called me. He said they flew only 30,000 to 35,000 miles a year in Pittsburgh. He knew how bad I was about flying. He had tried to get professional people in Los Angeles to help me when we were out there. I said I'd come if he wanted me. So Pittsburgh picked me up from Los Angeles in the 1970 intraleague draft.

"So I came back and I hurt my knee in training camp. I dressed for about ten games that year, and may have taken a shift a game, and that was about it. I had my left knee cut for the sixth time. I went about two years of doing absolutely nothing as far as hockey was concerned. They were lost seasons.

"Getting to the point, I was 31, and that summer when I went home I wondered whether I was through or not. I had to know. I worked real hard, and Joyce encouraged me to give it a try. She said, 'You can't just walk away; you'll have to see if you can continue or not.' I came back and I got four-and-a-half unbelievable years in Pittsburgh. There were some great people up in the seats, who didn't know me to begin with, but really got behind me. They were so supportive.

"When you ask me about my greatest memory there, I'd have to say the fans. I had never played for them before, yet they were behind me. They were nice to Joyce and the two boys. It made Pittsburgh so special. I was able to pay them back for supporting me. I played only 22 games my last year-and-a-half there, when I was operated on for the seventh time, and that was it. I wish it could have ended better, but I have to count my blessings.

"It was hard to walk away the way I did in the end. There were some people in management there who made it difficult, but not Red, let me tell you.

"I had a great coach in the juniors in Eddie Bush (who later coached the Hornets). He was one of the best coaches who ever lived. He had Hadfield, Gilbert and Ratelle in juniors. So I was lucky in that respect.

"I never met a classier individual than Red Kelly. People said he was too easy, but when you look back, only one thing counts — the decency of a human being — and he hung in there with me.

"In all honesty, I was getting to the point where I believed all the people who said I was washed-up. First, you can't fly, then you can't play. Dr. (Charles) Stone, the Penguins' team doctor, operated on my knee. He saved my career physically, and Red saved it for me mentally. Nine coaches out of ten would have said there was no way in the world they could help. I have the greatest respect for Red.

"People look at your record and they want to see how many Stanley Cups you've won. I check their credentials as human beings."

> *"We had a chemistry where we just knew where the other guys were going to be."*
> —Lowell MacDonald

When he rejoined the Penguins full-time, MacDonald scored 34 goals and 41 assists to finish third in team scoring with 75 points, behind his two linemates, Syl Apps (29 goals, 56 assists and 85 points) and Al McDonough (35 goals, 41 assists and 76 points).

The following year he teamed up with Apps (high scorer again with 24 goals, 61 assists and 85 points) and Jean Pronovost (third with 40 goals and 32 assists for 72 points). MacDonald set a club record with 43 goals to go with 39 assists for 82 points.

In 1974-75, MacDonald dipped to seventh in scoring with 60 points (27 and 33), and the next season, his last full one with the Penguins, he was fifth with 73 points (30 and 43). He played only three games the following season and 19 in his final go-round.

"Syl and Pronny and I just clicked, that's all," recalled MacDonald. "We were all right-handed shots. I had been a center in high school, and I moved to right wing at 17 and stayed there. Red said I could make the adjustment and play left wing. That was before the Europeans showed us that you could have right-handed shooters on that left side. Red said I could score with my back-hand shot.

"We roamed all over the place. It was more dangerous running into Pronny and Apps than it was those guys like Schultz on the Flyers. We flattened each other a number of times. But we had a chemistry where we just knew where the other guys were going to be. We had a match-up that couldn't have worked better.

"Pittsburgh was great for us. Pittsburgh was home. I loved playing with the guys I was playing with, and I just wish I could have had a few more years with them. They were pretty good hockey players. We miss the city, no doubt about it. I got a new lease on my hockey life there."

Lowell MacDonald splits New York Islanders' Dave Lewis (25) and Ralph Stewart (16) in 1975 playoffs at Civic Arena.

Larry Murphy
Looking ahead with a clear view

"Before I won, I didn't know what I was missing."

From his office on the 22nd floor of the Koppers Building in Downtown Pittsburgh, Larry Murphy could see the Civic Arena. While he was learning the ropes in the financial investment business during the summer of 1994, he was always reminded of his prime concern these days.

At 33 and approaching his 16th year as a highly-respected defenseman in the National Hockey League, Murphy thought it was high time he prepared himself properly for his future beyond hockey. Preparation has always been important in Murphy's game. At the same time, he was eager for the 1994-95 NHL campaign to commence, and he had high hopes that the Penguins could recapture the Stanley Cup that had eluded them the past two seasons.

"I think we have the talent to have the opportunity to win it all," said Murphy, a member of the Penguins when they won the Cup in 1991 and 1992. "I'm optimistic. It's a long haul, like a marathon run, getting to the finals.

"The situation is different around here the past few years. The heat has been turned up here. With success comes the cost. We're expected to win.

"I've experienced some great ups and downs since I came to Pittsburgh (in December of 1990). The expectations here are very high, deservedly so. When you don't reach the level that's expected it's very disappointing. After we won the Cup those two years, we knew how good it was to win. The last two seasons have been the toughest and most disappointing part of my career. Before I won I didn't know what I was missing."

In his office at D.B. Root & Co., a newly-formed financial counseling firm, there are a few reminders of those great moments. There are framed photographs of Murphy with the Stanley Cup and one of him with former President Bush at The White House, when the Penguins were honored there for winning the Stanley Cup.

Murphy is a partner with an ownership interest in D.B. Root & Co., working with his good friend Dave Root, who had opted to start a new business on his own four months earlier. Root previously was the president and chief executive officer of Bill Few & Associates, a financial counseling firm in the Frick Building. Bill Few is a friend of mine from our days of working with student publications at the University of Pittsburgh, and the host of a Saturday morning investment advice show on WTAE Radio. Few had introduced me to Root several years earlier. Root was one of his original partners.

"Larry sits on our board, and he's learning the business right now," said Root. "But he has some money management experience, and he's fairly sophisticated, with some good money instincts. Right now, though, his focus is hockey."

Making $850,000 a year to play for the Penguins will give a guy more than a nodding acquaintance with money management, I suppose.

Murphy talks eagerly about his new venture. "I believe I've found something I truly enjoy," he said. "Dave's a good friend, and he's the third generation of his family to be in this business. I'm lucky, because I really enjoy this area, and my wife and I have decided this is where we'd like to continue to live when I'm finished as a player."

Larry and his wife Nancy, and their two daughters, Madison, 5 1/2, and Alexa, 2 1/2, spent much of the summer at a get-away home on a lake in Ennismore, Ontario, about an hour-and-a-half drive north of Toronto, Murphy's native territory.

Murphy can move through shopping malls in Pittsburgh without creating a stir. He just blends into the crowd. He has no hang-ups about that.

"I get enough of that," he said. "After you lose, when you pick up your dry cleaning, they want to know what happened. You have to deal with failure as well as success.

"My five-year-old knows I wear No. 55, and my wife points me out on TV," said Murphy. "I think she assumes everybody's dad plays hockey on TV. I don't see myself sitting them down and showing them a videotape. And I'm not much of a collector of hockey memorabilia. By the time they understand, I'll be getting on with whatever else I'm doing."

It appears he is doing that already.

"I have a considerable stake in this new firm, and the hook is into me," Murphy said. "I've made a commitment. I've invested in the company, and I plan to make Pittsburgh our home.

"I'm fortunate to be involved in a business now. I can get some relief from the sports world. When I came to Pittsburgh, my expectations weren't too high. Now we're positioning ourselves to live here for the forseeable future. I find Pittsburgh a relaxing city. I don't feel as much stress here as I did in LA or DC. I lived in northern Virginia when I was with the Washington Capitals, and there was stress in the air. Here, I don't feel it.

"When the day comes when I am no longer playing, I want to be ready. No matter how gracious people are, you no longer belong. That happens the next day. That's the thing that guys find tough. One day you're a hockey player and the next day you're not. That's the thing that a lot of guys have a tough time dealing with. That's why the guys playing today and the guys who played yesterday can't really relate to one another. It's that vicious.

"That's the reality of the situation. If I can get a handle on that, I'll be better off. For some guys it's tough; they can't give it up."

Looking over his shoulder, Murphy could see the USX Tower and beyond that, about four rising blocks from the Koppers Building, the

Civic Arena. "I never lose sight of my bread and butter, and the most important thing in my life right now," he said with a dimpled smile.

"There are things you experience in pro sports that a lot of people don't experience. There's nothing greater than scoring a goal. You can't find that kind of feeling elsewhere. There are obviously great moments in your life, like when your children are born, but you can't replace the special feeling of sports. I'll miss that rush. One day it's all gone."

"I'll never forget I was the last kid picked."
—Larry Murphy

Larry Murphy is dressed in casual summer attire — a white golf jersey, beige shorts and white sneakers — and eating a corned beef sandwich with potato salad and Diet Coke at Augie's American Bistro. This is one of the restaurants in The Galleria, an upscale indoor shopping mall near Murphy's home in Mt. Lebanon. He's leaning on a brass rail with a good view of the lobby below. He can see shoppers and somehow he can also see himself as a young boy back home in Scarborough, a suburban community 30 miles from downtown Toronto.

"It was your typical suburban community, a bedroom community of Toronto, with housing my parents could afford," said Murphy. "My father worked for the phone company, Bell Canada. He was a 40-year man. He's retired now, and they're still living there. There was a definite separation between Scarborough and Toronto in those days, but now Toronto has expanded so much it just swallowed up the whole area. Now Toronto runs everywhere.

"I was like a lot of kids who grew up in that region. I had a great love for the Leafs. I lived and died with them. My favorites were Dave Keon and Eddie Shack, 'The Entertainer.' They were definitely my two favorites. But I knew everybody on the team.

"I still remember when they won the Cup in '67. That was a big day in my life, when they beat Montreal. It was not such a big day for my dad, who grew up in Montreal and is still a Canadiens' fan. We've always had a friendly rivalry in our house about that. I think my dad would love to see me play for the Canadiens before I complete my career."

Larry left the Penguins' training camp in late September to visit his ailing father. Larry's dad got him started in organized hockey the same way Dave Root is getting him started in the financial advisory business, with on-the-job training.

"I remember the first day I went for a tryout for our kids' hockey league," said Murphy. "I was about five or six at the time. I didn't even know what I was getting into. My dad hadn't prepared for it. I had an older brother, and my dad put his hockey equipment on me and we drove off. My brother was trying out, and I was going along for the ride. The way they ran the tryouts was to have all the kids skate in from the blue line, and they watched you.

Photos by Jim Cunningham

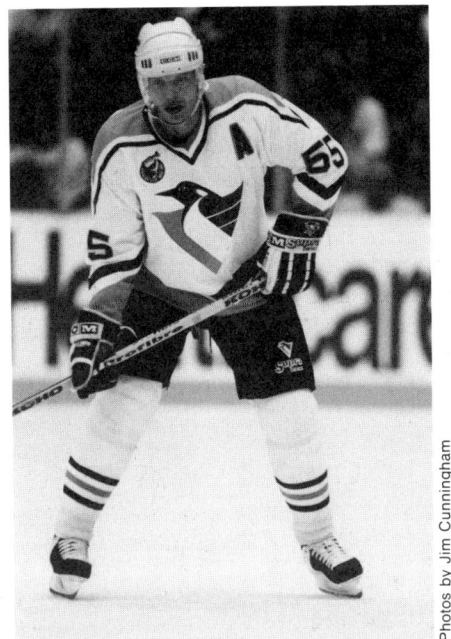

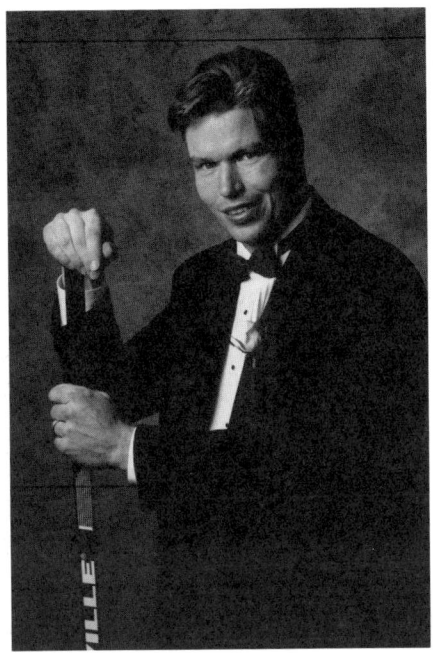

Larry Murphy makes his mark in Penguins' uniform, in tuxedo at team's charity fund-raiser, and children with life-threatening illnesses through the Western Pennsylvania Make-A-Wish Foundation.

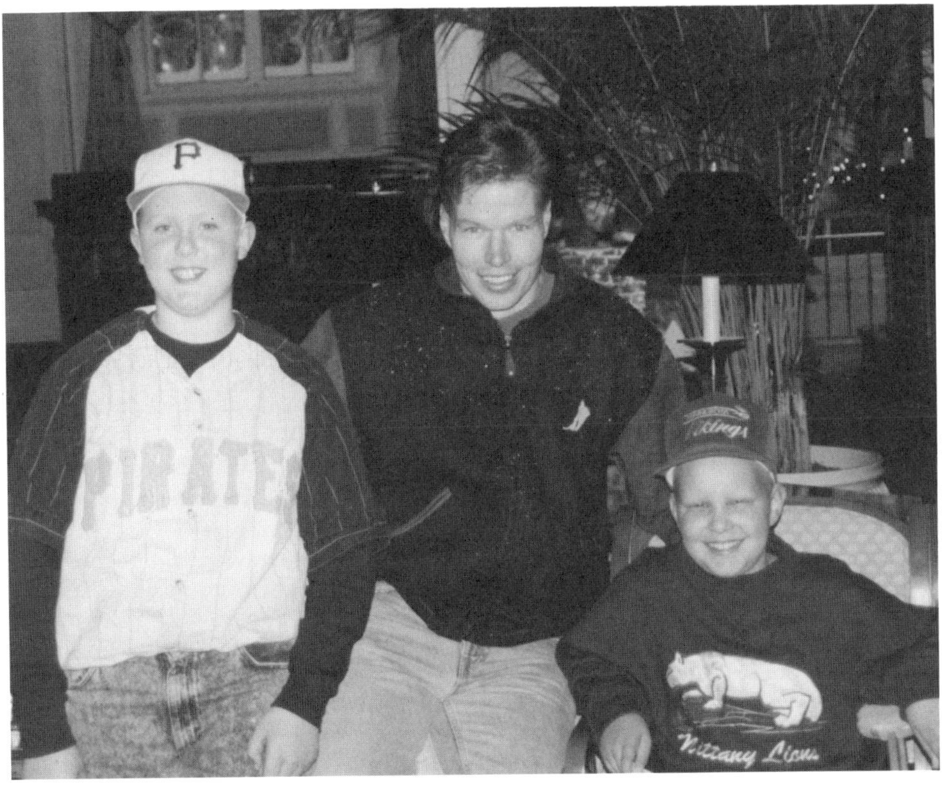

Western Pennsylvania Make-A-Wish Foundation

"There were four coaches and they were choosing up teams. They'd say, 'OK, I'll take him, or him.' Well, I had only been on skates once in my life, and I couldn't even skate. I was just hanging onto the boards for the most part. There were a lot of kids and it was taking a considerable amount of time. I'll never forget I was the last kid picked. I just think they needed some extra players. And I'll tell you, it didn't bother me a bit. I just thought it was so great to be on somebody's team.

"That winter we put an ice rink in our backyard. After that, we always had our own ice rink for three months during the winter. I think that was the biggest reason for my development. I skated every day, and that's the most important part of becoming a real hockey player. There were a couple of backyard rinks in our neighborhood. We had sort of a revolving game; we ended up in a different person's backyard every day. There was never any pressure about the game. My parents loved it and wanted me to enjoy it and they gave me the opportunity to do just that. My dad drove me everywhere I needed to go to play the game."

I asked Murphy if his father had gone to see the Canadiens play at the Montreal Forum when he lived there. "He watched them on TV; he'd never gone to a Canadiens' game," answered Murphy. "He still follows them. He never played himself, but he loved the game."

Murphy's brother, Richard, who was four years older, played hockey until he was 12. "He lost interest in it," recalled Murphy. "He just gave it up. My parents didn't mind. If I wanted to quit, they wouldn't have protested. My brother and I were different in that area. I couldn't get enough of it. A lot of winters I played on two different teams. I played forward and defense, about half and half, in different years. I was playing forward when I was 15, but I switched back to defense full-time when I turned 16, and got into serious competition.

"I was a big fan. I collected hockey cards. I lived and breathed the game. We even had a hockey table game in our basement that we played all the time. I was always plotting how I was going to get five cents to go out and get some new hockey cards."

Nowadays, Larry and his wife collect antique books. "It's tough to find good ones, but it's fun to look for them," said Murphy. "I feel like they're such a huge commodity. You get a sense of history from them. It's like bringing the past right into your living room."

I mentioned to Murphy that so many of the Penguins I spoke to had talked about how devoted their parents were in seeing that they got to practice, to games and did whatever else was necessary to see their sons realize their dreams.

"My mother didn't drive, so my dad had to do all the driving," he said. "In hockey, you have to put some distance on to play games. You had to have someone get you there. No way I could have done it without them.

"Same as putting a rink in the backyard. I couldn't have done that myself. I don't know how you could succeed in this sport without your parents. Other sports are at school, but hockey was not involved with the school. It was separate. My mother and dad went to most of my games. They enjoyed it. A lot of their friends were similarly involved, and they enjoyed getting together."

> *"He does the little things that help you win hockey games."*
> —Eddie Johnston

Never a particularly swift skater or strong shooter, Murphy managed to become one of the NHL's top defensemen. In 1992-93, for instance, he finished third among all NHL defensemen in scoring with 85 points (22 + 63), was a finalist for the Norris Trophy given to the league's best defenseman for the season, and was named second team all-NHL. His 22 goals were one less than his career high set in 1986-87. During the 1993-94 season, he was the Penguins' only offensive-minded defenseman. He carried the load on the blue line since Paul Coffey was traded to Los Angeles in 1992

Coffey is the all-time leading goal-getter among defensemen, surpassing the likes of Orr and Denis Potvin, and Murphy is not the same kind of player as Coffey.

"I don't have blazing speed, so you have to compensate somehow," said Murphy. "I just kind of go out there and play the best I can."

"He's a very, very smart player," said Eddie Johnston. "He does the little things that help you win hockey games."

Murphy got off to a strong start in the NHL. After leading Peterborough of the Ontario Hockey Associaton to the Memorial Cup, Murphy was the fourth player picked in the 1980 draft. He was selected by the Los Angeles Kings, and he finished runner-up to Peter Stasny for NHL Rookie of the Year. He had three solid seasons for the Kings, but early in his fourth season he was dealt to the Washington Capitals. Only two years earlier, he had been named to the NHL's All-Star second team and been a finalist for the Norris Trophy. He competed for the Caps for six seasons, before being traded to the Minnesota North Stars. Midway through his third season there, he was traded along with Peter Taglianetti to the Penguins for Jim Johnson and Chris Dahlquist. He has enjoyed success at every stop.

"Whenever someone mentions my name in connection with the Norris, I'm flattered," said Murphy. "But I know I'll never win it. That's OK. The only thing I care about is winning games. I'm most proud of the two Cups we've won."

Murphy is not the type of player who lifts fans out of their seats. "Using my head, playing the game smart, has always been my strong suit," Murphy has said. He's smart and steady and he contributes to a winning effort, but he's never been a marquee performer.

"I'm just a guy trying to do the best job I can," Murphy told Ron Cook of the *Post-Gazette* in a 1993 interview.

"On this team, because of all the scoring power we have, I just try to get the puck to the forwards. But, depending on the game or the situation, I'll jump into the play. I rely on anticipation and concentration. I rely on being in the right place at the right time."

When he came up with two assists in the Penguins 2-2 tie with the Ottawa Senators at the Civic Arena on November 27, 1993, they were the 645th and 646th assists in his career, and pushed him ahead of the legendary Bobby Orr in the all-time assists listings.

When he moved ahead of Orr in the record book, Murphy's reaction was typical in its temperance.

"Bobby Orr is probably the greatest defenseman to play the game," said Murphy. "By no means do I measure myself equally with him. But still when you're able to have your name in the same sentence as Bobby Orr, that's something I take as a true compliment. It's something I never dreamed I could possibly do when I started this game."

Murphy left it to teammates to gush over his accomplishment of overtaking Orr in the record book.

"That's a tremendous accomplishment for Murph, to be in the same galaxy, if you want to call it that, as Bobby Orr," said Bryan Trottier. "It makes his accomplishment all that much more incredible."

Murphy became a fixture on the right point on the power play in Pittsburgh, distributing the puck to the right player and confounding opponents by keeping clearing attempts in the offensive end of the ice. He has great passing ability. Bob Johnson worked individually with Murphy when he was coaching the Penguins, improving his performance on the power play.

He had scored more points than all but six defensemen in the history of the NHL, and held club records for defensemen with three different franchises.

The *Post-Gazette* carried a dossier about Murphy that offered a few interesting tidbits about him. His first job was as a golf caddy. His secret vice is the stock market. The three words that best describe him: logical, honest, fair. Who would play you in a movie? Ulf Samuelsson. He watches McLaughlin Group on TV. Three things that would be found in his refrigerator: pizza, pizza, pizza.

"Winning the Cup is not a smooth ride."
—Larry Murphy

As he sat at a table at Augie's American Bistro, Murphy was stroking a neat goatee he had grown over the summer, sort of a lark. It was dark and offered a stark contrast to his strawberry blond hair. "It will be gone before I report to training camp," he promised. "I had a full beard for awhile, and I couldn't bring myself to cutting it all off at once, so I cut it down to this. It gave me a different look."

The same could possibly be true of the Penguins by the time they reported to training camp the following month. An announcement had been made that morning by the Penguins that they would be holding a press conference in four days to clear the air on the matter of Mario Lemieux's playing status. Most observers felt he would be sitting out the 1994-95 campaign.

On the same day that I was talking with Murphy, Penguins' owner Howard Baldwin was meeting with Mayor Tom Murphy to further discuss the possibility of Baldwin and his group purchasing the Pirates. They would be pictured together in the next day's newspaper. NHL owners were threatening a lockout of the players unless a new bargaining agreement was signed by the players association.

There was a lot of uncertainty about the sports picture in Pittsburgh. "Our situation is the same as from the first day I got here," said Murphy. "For me, it's been this way since December of 1990. Mario hasn't been able to play every night. We don't have too many on this team who aren't accustomed to that situation by now.

"Obviously, he's a great player and your team is better with him on the ice. My feeling is that he's not going to play. There's one upside to that. We can go into the season knowing it's up to us to succeed. Mario won't come flying in to save us. It's a great opportunity for everybody on the team to step forward and pick up the slack.

"A lot of guys will have their ice time increased, and they have more of an opportunity to show their stuff. John Cullen is with us again. If he comes back and plays the way he did when he was with us the last time (1988-91). If Kevin Stevens comes back strong after being able to work out this summer, and if Jaromir Jagr keeps getting better, and Luc Robitaille continues to score like he did in LA . . . I think we're right there. We have guys who want to win. It's discouraging in one sense if Mario can't play, but it shouldn't prevent us from believing in our ability to win."

I mentioned to Murphy that Jack Riley, the former GM of the Penguins, had ventured the opinion that Murphy was one of several players — including Ron Francis, Kevin Stevens, Joe Mullen and Ulf Samuelsson — who didn't have their legs for the playoffs, that they were simply spent from overwork.

"Things could have been different in our series with Washington," said Murphy, warming up to Riley's remark. "If we could have come up with a period where we had been able to strike fear into their hearts . . . but we never could. It's a game of confidence. They were brimming with it. We were struggling with it. If we had gotten that . . . but it just never happened. "The years we won the Cup, there were times when the team was in trouble. Winning the Cup is not a smooth ride, like every shift is poetry in motion. It's just not that way. Something would turn things our way, and we went on from there.

"As for the business of 'not having our legs,' I don't think that was the issue. As for Mario, from the time he came back nothing ever came easy. It was a struggle for him. You could see it in him; he wasn't pleased with the way things were going."

I asked Murphy if Mario's personal expectations were so high they wouldn't permit him to play at a lesser level, even if he were still better than the majority of NHL players.

"His expectations are high; that's just part of it. There are a lot of other things to go with it. He makes things easier for the rest of us. I've never seen a player who can destroy an opposing goalie's confidence the way he can.

"Usually, the goaltender comes in here flying high because of what he's done in an earlier series. He's carried his team. Within a period, he's crushed. His confidence is gone. So we'll miss that."

Like many who are familiar with the Mario Lemieux soap opera, Murphy, who became the team's player representative before the 1994-95 season, didn't think that Monday's press conference would really certify anything.

"Hopefully, he'll be able to come back at some point," said Murphy. "Maybe he'll change his mind later in the season. It's like Michael Jordan giving up basketball. He had something else to go to. But he could change his mind and come back to basketball.

"From my understanding, Mario will be paid anyhow, that his contract is guaranteed. They've made changes in our roster. The team is looking like we're preparing to play without him. I think Craig Patrick has made the kind of moves to keep us in contention. He's put together the kind of team we need to go without him. They aren't going to play the game watching the door to the dressing room, looking for him to come out and save the day.

"Mario could always win games by himself. Every time he played, you felt that way, that he could do whatever needed to be done to pull us out of the fire. Without him here, it will take everybody to contribute that much more. We still definitely want to win that Cup. I look forward to Monday and to hearing what Mario has to say."

"Whenever you see me, you know the boss is here."
—Chauffeur for Howard Baldwin

Following my interview with Murphy, I paid a visit to the Civic Arena. There was much activity in evidence. Some young people were playing on the light blue roller-hockey surface. Workmen were busy on improvements in the building, just as they had been the previous summer.

Included in the list of renovations and additions were a $3.4 million view replay board/scoreboard; six new superboxes; new upgraded seating areas in the north and south ends; cleaning of the interior of the dome; a new sound system, new lighting, repaving the parking lots; and a Penguins Hall of Fame Wall, according to Phil Langan, the team's vice-president for community and public relations.

I spotted a group of men moving cameras into position in the south end of the rink. On Monday, they were going to start filming a movie starring Jean-Claude Van Damme, the French answer to Sylvester Stallone and Arnold Schwarzenegger. Reports indicated the area would be a scene of some startling activity before long. They'd even be blowing up cars in the parking lots outside. The Van Damme movie is an action-adventure thriller, of course, with a hockey setting that's co-produced by none other than Howard Baldwin. There he is again. I had seen the dark limousine parked outside Gate 9. "Whenever you see me," the chauffeur told me, "you know the boss is here."

I wasn't aware that a press conference had taken place at the Arena just before my arrival at which Van Damme made a personal appearance to announce the shooting. Baldwin was there with his buddy Tom Murphy. Baldwin also helped produce the films "Hoosiers" — one of my all-time favorites — and "Flight of the Navigator."

The Penguins' public relations department didn't want to play its hand, but promised that Lemieux would be making a definite statement about his plans for the coming season. The season opener with the Chicago Blackhawks was set for October 1. The hockey thriller that would be filmed at the Civic Arena would be called "Sudden Death."

In regard to the Lemieux story, Penguins fans wanted to see another "Hoosiers" movie rather than one called "Sudden Death." They wanted a heroic finish. Mario had always spoiled them that way.

Larry Murphy hoists Stanley Cup.

Mario Takes A Rest
Back, fatigue force decision

"I still love the game of hockey."

At a press conference at the Civic Arena on Monday, August 29, 1994, Mario Lemieux made an announcement that he would be sitting out the entire 1994-95 campaign and hoped to make a comeback with the Penguins the following season if his health permitted.

Penguins' chairman Howard Baldwin labeled it a "one-year medical leave of absence."

Both Baldwin and Lemieux made it clear that Mario would not be making any late-season comeback. "I'm not going to play this year, even late in the season or in the playoffs," said Lemieux. The decision was made on the advice of doctors who were treating Lemieux for his chronic back problems and Hodgkin's disease.

Some wondered whether Mario might be finished for good, but he did his best to put an optimistic note in his message. "There's a strong possibility I will be able to come back," he said. "It's just a matter of regaining my strength and working on my back for a year. I still love the game of hockey."

A few days later, Baldwin, upset with some of the negative fallout from the press conference, wrote a letter which appeared in the Op-Ed page of the *Post-Gazette*. Excerpts follow from his defense of Lemieux and the club owners:

"Lastly, a comment about Mario Lemieux and the questions on his courage: Mario Lemieux has been plagued with injury and illness for the past several seasons, but he came back time and time again to try and help his hockey club. There were many nights when he was in such pain, someone had to tie his skate laces. But he went out and played through the pain.

"His performance after his bout with Hodgkin's disease is ample proof of his courage and is one of the most extraordinary efforts by an individual athlete that we will see.

"I cannot imagine that anyone, whether he or she be in the media or a fan, would not want to see Mario receive his financial just due. Remember, this is the Mario Lemieux who turned hockey around in Pittsburgh and led this team to two Stanley Cup championships, one President's Trophy and three division championships...

"... I would hope by now that if this ownership group has proved anything, it is our total commitment to the City of Pittsburgh and to our fans."

AU REVOIR, MARIO

1990-91 Stanley Cup Champions — First row (left to right) Mark Recchi, Joe Mullen, Randy Hiller, Paul Coffey, Wendell Young, Tom Barrasso, Frank Pietrangelo, Bruce Racine, Mario Lemieux, Troy Loney, Brian Trottier, Bob Errey. Second row — John Welday, Jiri Hrdina, Ron Francis, Kevin Stevens, Gilles Meloche, Rick Patterson, Bob Johnson, Paul Martha, Craig Patrick, Scotty Bowman, Rick Kehoe, Barry Smith, Phil Bourque, Paul Stanton, Barry Pederson. Third row — Skip Thayer, Gilbert Delorme, Jamie Leach, Jim Paek, Larry Murphy, Ulf Samuelsson, Jaromir Jagr, Jay Caufield, Grant Jennings, Peter Taglianetti, Scott Young, Gord Roberts, Randy Gilhen, Gord Dineen, Ken Priestly, Steve Latin.

1991-92 Stanley Cup Champions — First row (left to right) Kevin Greenway, Joe Mullen, Brian Trottier, Bob Errey, Wendell Young, Tom Barrasso, Ken Wregget, Mario Lemieux, Kevin Stevens, Troy Loney, Frank Sciulli. Second row – Howard Baldwin, Jr., Tracy Luppe, Gilles Meloche, Rick Patterson, Donn Patton, Tom Ruda, Morris Belzberg, Howard Baldwin, Craig Patrick, Scotty Bowman, Barry Smith, Pierre McGuire, Rick Kehoe, John Gill. Third row – Jim Kittelberger, Jiri Hrdina, Jim Paek, Paul Stanton, Rick Tocchett, Ron Francis, Jaromir Jagr, Larry Murphy, Phil Bourque, Ulf Samuelsson, Gord Roberts, John Welday, Les Binkley. Fourth row – Skip Thayer, Dave Michayluk, Jeff Daniels, Peter Taglianetti, Grant Jennings, Jay Caufield, Kjell Samuelsson, Jeff Chychrun, Jock Callander, Shawn McEachern, Mike Needham, Steve Latin, Greg Malone, A.J. Cagliano.

Who could forget the Gardens?

Old-timers talk about the good ol' days when Hornets played in Oakland

By Jimmy Jordan
Pittsburgh Post-Gazette

February 11, 1970

It doesn't take much of a push to start a few hockey fans gliding over long-melted ice, in an arena hammered off the landscape by the headache ball years ago.

Happened the other night at the Igloo Club at the Civic Arena.

Val Fonteyne had just scored a goal for the Penguins by getting a shoulder in front of a line drive by Bryan Watson. The puck changed course on impact and landed in the back of the Minnesota net.

And that brought back memories of the time Bob Solinger won a Calder Cup game in overtime by steering the puck into the net with his head, which was handier than his stick at the moment.

And memories of how Howie Meeker won the Cup with the help of that victory in his first season as coach of the old Hornets.

And how King Clancy won the first Calder Cup ever for Pittsburgh in his first year as coach in The Gardens out on Craig Street.

And about Charlie Conacher and Roy Worters and Black Jack Stewart and Zero Brimsek and other Hockey Hall of Famers who got their starts in the old car barn out in Oakland, located between St. Paul's Cathedral and Central Catholic High School.

Somebody mentioned that Clancy refereed his first game out there, and Red Sullivan recalled how the rats (they were the biggest, meanest in any hockey rink) ate the armpits out of the Hershey uniforms, etc., etc., ad infinitum.

Then somebody asked about Bob Solinger and his overtime goal.

"It was in Buffalo, the fourth game of the final series," said Jackie Powell, the official Penguins goal judge and unofficial Hornet historian.

"There was no score and it was in the first overtime period. Frank Mathers was winding up for a slap shot, and Solly was skating in, hoping to pounce on a rebound.

"Well, the puck sailed over the goal, hit the wire fence behind the net, bounced straight back, smacked Solinger in the forehead and then rolled over the shoulder of the goalkeeper and into the back of the net. Just like a soccer player heading one into the goal."

That gave the Hornets a 3-1 lead in victories, with the next game to be played in Pittsburgh. The Hornets blew that one in the last period after leading, 3-0 and 4-1, in the first two periods. They won the Cup back in Buffalo on Easter Sunday.

"Bob had about four stitches taken in his head," recalled Andy Barbe, who played on that team. "Somebody kidded him about it and said, 'So what? They're worth about $200 bucks each.'"

And that brought up a memory of the time Andy actually stole a goal off Providence in the old Gardens.

"This guy," someone else said, pointing to Barbe, "was cruising down his left wing without getting much interference along the way. Harvey Barnett was in goal for Providence. Andy sort of ignored him, skated on around the cage. Bennett — he was a tall guy, remember? — must have gotten his shoulder under the crossbar someway, because when Andy was in back of the net he noticed the goal was off the ice about an inch.

"He just poked the puck in from the back. George Coultis was the goal judge and he flipped on the light. He had to. The puck was in the net.

"And the referee — they missed things in those days just like they miss 'em today — allowed the goal!"

And so on, far into the night: the fights with the Cleveland Barons, and the fancy work of Willie Marshall, and the goal tending of Baz Bastien and Gil Mayer, and the big rats, and Mike Gallagher's bar in the joint which was next door to a school and across the street from a church and not 200 feet from either.

My sportswriting colleague Andy Dugo calls it dustin' cobwebs. The wrecker's ball didn't leave any cobwebs, but apparently it didn't destroy the reminiscences.

Reprinted with permission of Pittsburgh Post-Gazette

The Gardens in Oakland was home to the Hornets.

The vigil in the park in Montreal

"He is the one they try to build around. Such a shame."
—Jean Pronovost

By Phil Musick
Sports Columnist,
The Pittsburgh Press

Phil Musick (signature)

Montreal, May 25, 1970

The old men huddle in their colorless wool and leather sweaters, sitting four abreast on an iron bench surrounded by the lush greenness of La Fontaine Park, where last year they raised clenched fists and chortled while the Separatists beat up the provincial police.

They grouse about the foolish vagabond Trudeau and stare sourly at the brazen English girls in their mini-skirts and sniff when the French lasses saunter past, their equally brief fashions fluttering in the spring breezes.

Once each morning, when the sun has eaten away some of the chill, one grumpy old man picks up his cane and hobbles across frantic East Sherbrooke Street to the Notre Dame Hospital, there to inquire about the boy who plays hockey.

"I tell him every day that he should read the newspaper, that I can tell him nothing," says a cute receptionist, her smile and cocky cap and rich Gallic accent breathing life into the cold marble lobby.

"I will call his doctor and I'll give you a number to telephone," she says, parrying an inquiry about Michel Briere, the 20-year-old Penguin center who was critically injured in an automobile accident and now lies in a coma of nine days duration. "You cannot see him, of course."

Two flights up is the office of Dr. Claude Bertrand, a busy, coolly-polite neurosurgeon who has little time for newspapermen who ask the impossible.

"The boy is unconscious, I do not make comments on his condition until he regains consciousness. The damage cannot be estimated until then," he says, inviting and getting an end to the discussion.

Across Montreal in her apartment, Mrs. Jackie Albert, a public relations woman hired by the hospital, is besieged by dozens of telegrams, letters and telephone calls concerning the condition of Briere, hospitalized after his new car flipped on a two-lane highway near his hometown of Malartic and nearly given up for dead 24 hours later.

"Oh, my gosh, I've had days of 20 hours work," she screeches, sounding as if she enjoys her labor. "I get calls from 3 a.m. until past midnight."

Michel Briere

Her answers are pat. Last Thursday, she said Briere was "satisfactory." Yesterday, he was "satisfactory — he's healing, but the coma could go past the weekend. His state of unconsciousness means nothing. The doctor said any brain damage was done before the coma. He is really greatly improved."

Jean Pronovost, who knows what it means to be young and scared and speak only French in a town not particularly noted for its ability to comprehend English, is less assured, less confident.

"He's living," said Pronovost, Briere's linemate and the only other French-Canadian on the Penguins. "Everyone's just waiting. It's all you can do. They say he's in good condition, but they really won't say anything until he comes out of it."

In the blackest hours of the Saturday night before last, Pronovost was at the hospital when it was feared Briere would surely die. Notre Dame is the hospital in Montreal where they take the most critical head cases, and Bertrand is one of the three best neurosurgeons in Canada.

"My sister called me early Wednesday morning and when she told me Michel was at Notre Dame, I knew it was bad," says Pronovost. "We were really scared to lose him Saturday night."

Perhaps what makes the old man leave the park and doggedly ask of Briere is that he is a boy of 20 with much to live for.

"He has the potential to be a super star. He is the one they try to build around," Pronovost says. "Such a shame."

In a language he has to bulldog to handle, Pronovost is eloquent. "That's what people who call me say, 'Such a shame,'" says Mrs. Albert. "Now it is time for prayer."

Briere's fiance, sister and brother-in-law go to Notre Dame Hospital every day, along with the Penguins' scout, Dick Coss, also a busy man.

If Bertrand is irritated and Pronovost saddened by questions about Briere's future, Coss is scared by such inquiries.

Public relations makes him nervous. He is wary that unknown reporters might cause him problems with the front office. "There's been a big improvement, mind you, mister," he says politely on Friday. "Call me tomorrow and I might know something more."

On Saturday he knows nothing. "I've had my instructions to pass inquiries to my superiors in Pittsburgh," he says. "But he's a nice boy, I hope he is soon better."

So does the old man in the park.

Reprinted with permission

Michel's Magic Missing When He Came To A Curve
They believed he would make things hum

"He has style"
—Red Kelly

By Roy McHugh
Sports Editor, Pittsburgh Press

It can't be acquired, they have it or they don't, the quality that sets apart the exciting performer. By one definition, it's chemistry — exactly the right mixture of talent, style and competitive spirit. Quoting the same authority:

"Some players make it strictly because of their competence... and then there's the player who is both competent and competitive, but has a little something extra. He has style. He is colorful. There is something of the showman about him. He is the type of guy who draws standing-room-only crowds because they know he will make things hum."

Michel Briere was such an athlete. Red Kelly first saw Briere at the Penguins' training camp in September of 1969. "He was showing me moves you can't put into a hockey player," said the coach.

Briere skated easily. He skimmed across the ice like a waterbug, not with great speed but with a phantom elusiveness, deftly avoiding body checks, probing and questing for the puck. His shot was quick rather than powerful, coming invariably when the opposition least expected it, preceded as likely as not by a feint, by a drop of the shoulder.

"When he picked up that puck, you knew things could happen," said Kelly last night. "You felt he could take it all the way down, that the puck would end up in the other guys' net." The feeling was a reaction to the chemistry of Briere, to the promise he communicated, for in his only year with the Penguins he scored just 12 goals.

Yet the spectators sensed his possibilities. They believed he would make things hum. Part of his appeal was the way he looked. Slight and dark, with flared nostrils, on the ice Briere called to mind a fugitive fleeing from hunters. While he lay unconscious in a Montreal hospital last summer, his teammate Jean Pronovost said, "He looked like a kid, he looked like a little boy, and he was out there doing great things."

At the start of the season, Kelly tried to protect Briere, keeping him out of matchups with stronger, more experienced centers. On faceoffs it seemed that Montreal's Jean Beliveau beat him to the draw every time — at the start of the season. By the end of the season, Briere was beating Beliveau, getting his stick on the puck before it hit the ice.

The heavies in the league, taking him for a pipsqueak, were impatient to lean on Briere. They would chase him right out of the rink, they told themselves with a smirk, but when the moment came to lean, they'd be leaning, quite often, against nothing. Briere would have slithered away.

In Philadelphia one night, two Flyers took a run at him, collided head-on, and knocked each other out.

Scotty Bowman, the coach of the St. Louis Blues, made it a point last year during the Stanley Cup playoffs to harass Briere with Noel Picard and Bob Plager, his burliest defensemen. From Kelly no countermeasure proceeded. "There he is — there's my little baby," Kelly said. A common sight during the playoff series was Kelly's little baby skating toward the goal while the St. Louis bad boys sprawled on the ice in his wake.

"If they looked at the puck, he'd be gone," said Kelly. "He was slippery, he could shift and make movements, but all the time he was doing this he was still skating. A lot of guys, when they shift, aren't going anywhere. Mike kept on skating at the same rate of speed."

Now he is dead at 21. On trips to Montreal last season, Kelly would visit Briere. "It made you feel kind of bad," Kelly said. "You'd walk in and sit down, you'd take hold of his hand. He'd turn his head toward you and his eyes would open, staring. He couldn't talk. I was always optimistic, but the last time I saw him. . ."

Michel Briere had been only clinically alive since the night 11 months ago when his burnt-orange sports car missed a curve on a road in upper Quebec. Yesterday that life departed. A particular magic blend of talent, style and competitive spirit is gone.

"This kid spent his life playing against and beating boys who towered over him. He played goal for a midget team in Malartic at age 11, and was a forward in peewee at age 12. Michel knew what the other pro scouts were saying about him as a junior — that he was too small. But every summer, he'd go down into the mine or to the saw-mill and build himself up."

—Dick Coss,
Quebec area scout for Penguins
who pushed team to draft him

A Polish Army at The Arena
Bob Woytowich was their man

*"Clap your hands.
Stomp your feet."*

By John Patterson
Feature Editor, The Pittsburgh Press   Nov. 15, 1971

Woytowich's Army is no Polish joke, even though it was inspired by an Irishman.

Three years ago, Tom Niemiec, the man who is now president of the Army, mentioned to sportswriter Jim O'Brien (once a member of *The Press* staff while in high school and college) that he was glad the Pittsburgh Penguins acquired defenseman Bob Woytowich. Knowing that Tom and Steve Kisic and Ken Rusnak and a dozen others were great hockey fans (they were regulars at Hornet games before the Pens arrived in town), Jim suggested they form a fan club for Bob. And they did.

Jim has talked about Bob Woytowich's Polish Army in early morning sports commentaries on WEEP Radio.

It has grown into a full-fledged mob of six dozen regulars and hundreds of irregulars who show up to fill an entire section on Saturdays. One member arranges business trips from Cleveland to sit with the gang. Another comes even farther — from Columbus. They all hoist banners and signs to show their enthusiasm for Woytowich and the Penguins. They sit in the cheapest seats in the building, up high near the ceiling of the Civic Arena.

And the Polish Army is well known in Canada. A bunch of them travel to the Pens training camp at Brantford to watch practice games. They have made their presence known to a Canadian brewery. Two years ago the supply of this company's beer dwindled to nothing while the Army was in town. So an Army "official" wrote to the brewery before this year's training camp opened. He allowed as to how the Army would be in town soon and would they please see that the beer supply was adequate. Everything was arranged.

Probably because an Irishman inspired it, you don't have to be Polish to join the Army. Your name can be Mauro or Furfari, for example.

There are only two requirements. You have to have the money to buy a general admission ticket and you must never say a nice word about any of the Pens' opponents, collectively or individually. As for the officials — well, let's not get into that.

The Army tossed an annual party for the hockey team, more specifically for Bob Woytowich. And last year the hockey team sponsored a party for the Army. Take note that president (how about general?) Niemiec makes sure the under-21 members stick to pop at the parties. At the parties, the Army probably gets a chance to rehearse the printable cheers it shouts at the hockey games. Here's an example:

"Clap your hands.
"Stomp your feet.
"Chicago Blackhawks have flat feet."
And as for Bobby Hull, his head looks like an eagle's nest.
With Polish corn like that, how can the Pens fail to survive?

Reprinted with permission.

Bob Woytowich, who died in his 40s after suffering a heart attack on the way home from work, was one of the most popular of the early Penguins.

Badger Bob Taught Us All How To Live

"Every day is a bonus."
—Bob Johnson

By Ron Cook
Columnist, Pittsburgh Post-Gazette

The telephone call came on a late November day in '91, just as I was sitting down to lunch at Pitt. This was going to be a fun afternoon. I was going to write about one of my favorite events, the upcoming Pitt-Penn State football game. But the call changed that.

"The Badger died," the voice from the office said.

I had been expecting the news for days, ever since the word leaked that Bob Johnson's condition was slipping. I thought I was prepared. I wasn't. Who is ever prepared for the finality of death?

Everyone knew Johnson was very sick. After that horrible press conference three months earlier, everyone knew he wasn't coming back to coach the Penguins. That was the morning team officials announced he had undergone emergency brain surgery the night before.

"I'm devastated," General Manager Craig Patrick said that day. One look at him and you knew what Johnson was facing.

But we all clung to the hope that Johnson would find a way to win the fight for his life. If anyone could, he could, right? If it were a fair fight — his spirit vs. brain cancer — he would win about 8-1. Sadly, the fight against such an insidious disease is seldom fair.

It's easy to be maudlin when someone so young and so vibrant dies an unfair death. I'm not going to do that. I promised myself I wouldn't do that.

I feel great sympathy for Johnson's family, friends and acquaintances. They miss him terribly. But I don't feel sorry for him. How do you feel sorry for someone who lived a tremendous life?

I always envied Johnson, to tell you the truth. I wish I could live my life the way he lived his, but I don't come close. The only person I've ever met who does is former Pirates manager Chuck Tanner. How lucky he is.

To Johnson, every day was something to be cherished. I don't imagine he wasted many. It's why he was able to pack more life into 60 years, eight months and 22 days on this earth than most people do who live to be 100.

I remember one time, maybe the only time, I saw Johnson angry. It was the morning after the Penguins lost Game 5 of their first round playoff series against the New Jersey Devils in the spring of '91. They trailed three games-to-two. The situation looked hopeless. I was in the locker room, convinced the season was over. Johnson noticed my glum expression.

"What are you so down about?" he asked, spitting out the words. To him, it didn't matter the Penguins had to play Game 6 in Jersey without Paul Coffey and Tom Barrasso. He wasn't going to let it ruin his day. And he made damned sure I knew it.

The Penguins came back to win that series, of course. I remember Johnson's response when he was asked after Game 7 how he managed to keep the team, which was encrusted with years of failure and disappointment, on track.

"All you ask for in athletics is a chance to compete." Johnson said. "We had a chance. What are we supposed to do? Feel sorry for ourselves? Life's too short for that. Every day is a bonus, I'll tell you. Ask that poor senator (John Heinz) from Pennsylvania about that. He doesn't have any more bonuses."

I remember Johnson teaching a similar lesson before the Penguins played the Minnesota North Stars in the Stanley Cup finals that same year. He was talking about his daughter, Diane, who was born with cerebral palsy and institutionalized at the State Home for the Mentally Retarded in Union Grove, Wisconsin.

"I don't feel down about the little things. I hear people, players, complaining, feeling sorry for themselves. They should have to spend a day in Union Grove, Wisconsin. They wouldn't feel sorry for themselves anymore."

I like to think a little of Johnson rubbed off on me.

I also like to think he found a little enjoyment at my expense. I was a relative newcomer to the hockey scene for the Penguins' run to the Cup, a novice who could take or leave the sport. But as the playoffs progressed and the games got better, I have to admit I got caught up in that excitement. Hockey played at that level is spectacular.

Johnson noticed my attitude change. I'm convinced that's why he always seemed to find a few extra minutes for me. Converting people to his sport was among his greatest pleasures.

"Hockey tonight, hockey tonight, there's gonna be hockey tonight," he said during one of his strolls through the locker room.

Or, "What would you be covering now if we weren't still playing? Tennis?" I can still hear the way he said "tennis" with detestation.

Even after the Penguins won that final glorious game in Minnesota and he had his greatest treasure, the Stanley Cup, he made it a point to pull me aside in the champagne-soaked locker room. "You know this doesn't happen every year?" he asked. I laughed, but he was serious. "Enjoy this now because you don't know if you'll ever be part of something like this again."

I would see Johnson just one more time, the day a month later when the Penguins went to Washington, D.C. to meet President Bush. "Not a bad few months, huh?" he asked when we parted. "The Stanley Cup and the president. How much better does it get in your job?"

It doesn't.

Johnson is gone now, but I see him every time I look at the banners that hang in the Civic Arena rafters. The Patrick Division banner. The Wales Conference banner. The Stanley Cup banner. They meant everything to Johnson, who constantly talked of building a tradition for the Penguins.

Well, he built one.

I looked at those banners the night after he died, as the Arena grew quiet for a special tribute to the late great coach before a Penguins' game against the Devils. Then, I sat down and enjoyed the hell out of the hockey game.

I couldn't think of a better way to pay my respects to The Badger.

Reprinted with permission of Pittsburgh Post-Gazette

Badger Bob Johnson is flanked by Craig Patrick and Scotty Bowman at press conference where Patrick introduced the two men he was bringing in to help turn the Penguins around before the 1990-91 season.

Lemieux: Too Good to Miss
Who was the best athlete in Pittsburgh?

"... the next day, he'll be gone."

By Dave Ailes
Sports Editor, Tribune-Review

March 29, 1992

Historically speaking, the day will come when every district sports fan is going to wish he or she had seen Mario Lemieux play hockey for the Pittsburgh Penguins.

It won't matter if the fan doesn't know a puck from a plate; if he thinks the only crease is on Uncle Elmer's forehead.

In the year 2020, your family is going to sit down to an Easter ham when somebody's going to pose this question:

Who was the best athlete to play sports in the Pittsburgh district the last half of the 20th Century? Lemieux's name is certain to surface. Early on, in all probability.

You'll feel more confident participating in the inevitable argument if you saw Roberto Clemente run out from under his hat between first and third; if you stood behind the ropes at the 18th when Arnold Palmer hitched his pants over those slender hips; if you saw Tony Dorsett dart through a hole that didn't exist, then show his heels to the secondary.

You can tell your grandchildren, your nieces and nephews about the time Houston double-teamed Joe Greene, then triple-teamed him, down in the Astrodome and the league's biggest, quickest, strongest defensive lineman still caused panic and disorder in the Oilers' backfield.

Or how about those deathly quiet evenings at the Civic Arena when a few hundred fans showed up to watch an unforgettable Connie Hawkins perform for the totally forgettable Rens, then Pipers?

You're sure to have others on your list, but my favorites — from 1950 to the present — are Clemente, Palmer, Dorsett, Greene, Hawkins.

And Lemieux. Always Lemieux.

There's no sense recapping his achievements here. Every NHL history book will start with Wayne Gretzky and Lemieux, not necessarily in that order.

Just as certainly, those who watch Lemieux regularly will tell you nobody in history can handle the puck and pass it with his particular skills. A friend of mine observed that ex-Pen Mark Recchi, a fireplug with legs, seems to be hopping, more than skating. Kevin Stevens, on the other hand, is a grinder.

Lemieux. He glides — like one of those big-winged birds that's suspended in air when it dives to attack an unsuspecting victim.

That's the way Lemieux does it. When you're certain no human being could touch a crazily bouncing biscuit, Lemieux not only stops it with the end of his stick, he nudges it along to a cutting teammate.

This past Thursday, the Pens embarrassed the first-place Vancouver Canucks, 7-3. He not only registered six points on two goals and four assists, he made a couple of passes to Rick Tocchet that gave his new teammate a loaded gun to hold to the goalie's head. On Lemieux's own goals, the goalie was more helpless than an infant. If Mario's shot hit the goalie, it was a stop. If it didn't hit him, there was no time to react.

We've all heard that old line about the guy who was so fast that he could flip the wall switch and be in bed before the light went out. Lemieux's shots appear to travel at the speed of light.

A special athlete, it seems to me, is one who does a lot more than dominate, statistically. Lumbering Dave Kingman used to dominate a baseball game with an occasional home run. What Lemieux can do is establish a game's pace, then alter its momentum. Rare instincts, his.

For the record, heading into Sunday's 8 p.m. matchup with Montreal at the Civic Arena, Number 66 has 30 points in his last 11 games; 100 or more points in seven of his eight seasons.

Without the record, Lemieux is such a dominant force that Pens' fans, typically, take him for granted. One day, he'll be gliding down the boards, waiting to turn a loose puck into a breakaway. The next day, he'll be gone — deciding it hurts too much to bend at the waist.

When the soft-spoken Lemieux says goodbye to the Penguins, and probably adios to Pittsburgh as well, tons of western Pennsylvania sports fans are going to be sorry they never saw him play hockey in person.

He's a show, a special attraction.

"He is a once-in-a-lifetime player with skills you can't believe. Pittsburgh has had some great sports heroes, but none of them top Mario Lemieux."
—Craig Patrick

"I have observed players like Bobby Hull, Bobby Orr, Gordie Howe and Wayne Gretzky traded from the teams where they established most of their records and identity. I never want to be in a position where we have to buy someone else's star player. Our best option is investing our money in Mario Lemieux and keeping him in Pittsburgh where he belongs."
—Howard Baldwin
on signing Lemieux
to 7-year contract

Hockey's Been A Family Affair
From boyhood days in Detroit
Covering NHL rewarding experience

By Bill Heufelder
Publisher, Penguins Report

Although I covered the Penguins for *The Pittsburgh Press* from their maiden season in 1967-68 into the late '70s, my introduction to the sport was as a kid growing up in Detroit.

Olympia Stadium . . . The Production Line of Abel, Lindsay and Howe . . . Black Jack Stewart . . . Terry Sawchuck. I saw Red Kelly play defense for the Detroit Red Wings before he became the coach of the Penguins.

My dad had season tickets behind the goal in what would be considered the B Level at the Civic Arena. There were only six teams in the NHL in those days and, even as a kid, I could feel the tension in the Olympia whenever the Red Wings faced off against Montreal or Toronto.

When I was older and could go to the Olympia on my own, I can remember buying a Standing Room Only ticket and sitting up on the concrete steps of the aisle until an usher chased me up the stairs behind the last row of seats.

I joined *The Press* sports staff in 1963, and I figured all the writers liked hockey or at least followed the sport. After all, the city had the Hornets, a minor league team that, ironically, was the top farm club of the Red Wings. The reality was that nobody on the sports staff much cared for hockey. Even the beat writer looked upon the assignment more as a novelty.

Gradually, I took over the coverage of the Hornets. My enthusiasm for hockey remained as feverish as it was during those trips to the Olympia. When the NHL announced that it would double its size to 12 teams, I prayed hard that Pittsburgh would land an expansion franchise.

I can remember that it was just another day at *The Press* sports department when the scheduled announcement of the new NHL teams was made. But not for me. I hovered over the teletype machine that afternoon and watched as it drummed out the names of the expansion cities until the word Pittsburgh appeared. The city had an NHL franchise and I had a job covering big league hockey.

Until the Penguins became Stanley Cup champions in 1991, their history had been bleak. The early memories are of the raging controversy over the nickname Penguins, the death of the real-life mascot named Pete (of pneumonia), empty seats and mediocre play.

But, in a manner of speaking, I was in the NHL, making the road trips and becoming closer to the sport than I ever imagined.

One of the classic NHL photos is of Bobby Orr soaring across the goalmouth after scoring the overtime goal that gave the Boston Bruins the 1970 Stanley Cup in the playoff finals against St. Louis. Every time I see that photo (it's displayed in Eddie Johnston's game room), the first thought that comes to my mind is that I was there, covering the game.

Although decided underdogs, the Penguins, rather than St. Louis, nearly reached the Cup final opposite Boston that spring. In fact, the highlight of my early association with the Penguins was their performance in the '70 playoffs. They had reached the playoffs for the first time in their brief history, finishing second to the Blues in the West Division.

The Penguins swept the Oakland Seals in the opening round. Les Binkley was superb in goal and the late Michel Briere, a quiet rookie centerman from Quebec, scored an overtime goal in Game 4 to end the series.

The Blues presented a more formidable challenge in the Stanley Cup semifinals. The series went six games, but Binkley, who allowed only six goals in the opening round, was forced out with a knee injury after Game 3.

St. Louis, coached by Scotty Bowman, was loaded with veteran players, including Glenn Hall and Jacques Plante. The organist in the spacious St. Louis Arena would play "When The Saints Go Marching In" as the two Hall of Fame goaltenders led the Blues onto the ice. The packed house would be jumping.

Red Kelly was named Coach of the Year for the job he had done with the Penguins in 1970. They were largely a no-name bunch, a stark contrast to the star-studded Cup teams in Pittsburgh 20 years later. Glen Sather...Bryan Watson...Ken Schinkel...Briere. Dean Prentice was the leading scorer with a modest 51 points.

Hall and Plante each gave up one goal as the Blues won the first two playoff games on their home ice. The Penguins came home and evened the series on a pair of game-winning goals by Briere. However, Plante produced a 5-0 shutout at St. Louis and Hall beat the Penguins, 4-3, at the Civic Arena to end it.

The playoff performance was inspiring for Pittsburgh hockey fans, but few inspirational moments followed before the Lemieux era began in 1984.

Personally, covering the Penguins continued to be a rewarding experience. My two sons, Matt and Todd, spent a lot of Saturday mornings skating at the Civic Arena with the sons of some of the players ... Lane and young Lowell MacDonald ... Eric and Martin Pronovost ... Adam and Jamie Smith, whose father, Al, was one of the most spirited goaltenders in the game.

Eventually, Matt and Todd went on to play a lot of amateur and high school hockey in Pittsburgh. Between them, they were members of four state championship teams at Canevin High School. Matt spent four seasons playing for Duquesne University and was named head coach of the Dukes in 1992. Todd, a goaltender, followed him to Duquesne. It was Badger Bob Johnson who gave him his biggest break.

With his first Penguins training camp just a few days away, Johnson was sitting in the Civic Arena watching some of the early arrivals work out. Todd happened to be the goaltender at one end. After the scrimmage, Johnson asked him about being available as the Penguins' practice goalie.

That season, Todd practiced occasionally with the Penguins and, typically, Johnson treated him like one of the regulars. When the Penguins returned home from New York, having beaten the Rangers to clinch their first division title ever, Badger Bob made certain that his practice goalie got a championship T-shirt.

Even after Scotty Bowman and Eddie Johnston followed Johnson as the Penguins' coach, Todd held onto his small role with the club.

So the Penguins represent more to me than just covering a hockey team. They influenced my life, as well as the way my sons grew up, and they allowed me to make hockey friendships that will last a lifetime.

Indirectly, they were responsible for an especially close relationship that I enjoy today. It was in the late '60s that I met an attractive secretary named Elaine Feith, who worked at the Civic Arena. We were married in 1988.

One of Bill Heufelder's boyhood favorites, Gordie Howe and his wife were honored at Penguins' game at the Civic Arena.

1981 Playoffs Converted Him To Hockey Fan
Nassau Coliseum crowd was deafening

"I never thought I'd say that hockey is my favorite sport."

By John Steigerwald
Sportscaster, KDKA-TV

I was converted in April of 1981. The Penguins and the New York Islanders. I was at the Civic Arena for Game Three of that best-of-five opening round Stanley Cup playoff series. It was far from a sell-out, but it was obvious that virtually nobody had taken Penguins' owner Edward J. DeBartolo up on his offer for a refund.

Even though the Penguins had been totally humiliated in the first two games of the series, and even though Penguins' fans had suffered so much for so long, the fans were there and they started cheering wildly several minutes before the teams came out onto the ice. The crowd helped the Penguins win the next two games and send the series back to Long Island.

I was in the Nassau Coliseum for Game Five and I remember how amazed I was at the atmosphere in that building. The crowd was one fifth the size of World Series and Super Bowl crowds I had seen and heard, but it was five times louder.

It's a cliche now, but it was the first time I had heard the "We Will Rock You" chant, and I couldn't believe how much that building was rocking. I remember wondering what it would be like if the Civic Arena could ever sound like this.

The game was unbelievable. When the Penguins went up 3-1 late in the third period it was the most deafening silence I had ever heard. It wasn't until 1990, at the Civic Arena, that I heard a crowd as wild and loud as that one that night at Nassau Coliseum when the Islanders tied the game and went on to win.

I was hooked.

Not just as a fan, but also as a reporter. I wasn't looking forward to going into the Penguins' locker room, but I'll never forget the first thing I saw when I went through that door. Michel Dion, who had played his third superhuman game in a row, was on the floor, still wearing all of his goalie equipment. He was on his back with his legs elevated and leaning against the back wall of his locker.

Talk about total silence.

The first guy I approached was the Penguins' toughest and most cooperative, media-friendly player, Paul Baxter. Neither he nor any other player in the Penguins' locker room refused to talk. That was my first clue that hockey players are, by far, the most cooperative of all professional athletes.

Boy, was I hooked.

After what we've seen from the Penguins recently, it's hard to imagine, but I received a lot of funny looks when I returned to Pittsburgh and told some of my colleagues that I had just seen one of the best sporting events of my life. Remember, we were only a year-and-a-half removed from a pretty good run of Super Bowls for the Steelers and a World Series win by the ("We-Are-Fam-A-Lee") Pirates.

Something else happened that year that was a major part of my conversion.

My nine-year-old stepson, Brett, started playing hockey. I found that I enjoyed going to his practices and his games.

At 4:30 a.m.

This was a lot different from *saying* I enjoyed going to his baseball games, which consisted of him standing around a lot. I noticed that, in hockey, even with nine-year-olds, there's actually a game going on out there. I remember how angry I was when I left his practices or games. Angry that I had never played the game. The closest we came to hockey when I was a kid was a broom and a tin can on Canonsburg Lake. As Brett learned the game, I learned it, too.

Former Penguin Gregg Sheppard's son, Brent, was the star of my stepson's team, and Gregg and I spent a lot of Saturday mornings together and I learned a lot from Gregg and those nine-year-olds. I later taught myself how to ice skate so that I could better appreciate what my stepson was trying to do. If you've never skated, lace on a pair some day and you'll have a new appreciation for the game at any level.

Then came Mario Lemieux. I remember going back to the WTAE-TV newsroom after seeing Lemieux in his first training camp scrimmage, and telling the producer, Tim Kiely, that at 18, Lemieux was already the most exciting player in the city. Two years later, I raised a few eyebrows in the *Post-Gazette* sports department when I wrote that Lemieux was the best player ever to play any sport in Pittsburgh.

In 1990, I finally got a chance to follow the Penguins on their way to a Stanley Cup championship. I have been pretty lucky in the 17 years that I've been covering sports in Pittsburgh. I covered the Pirates in the World Series and the Steelers in two Super Bowls in the first 13 months of my TV career. Nothing comes close to the Penguins' Stanley Cup run. I remember looking at Kevin Stevens' scarred and bruised face after an early game in the Penguins-Devils series and wondering how he could make it through that series, much less three more.

A Super Bowl is two weeks of hype and one game. The World Series is maybe seven games over ten days. The Stanley Cup is a game every other night for two months and every game is a war. I saw every minute of every game and I made every trip the Penguins made (commercial, not charter) and when it was over I felt like I had taken a few hits into the boards.

It was tiring, but it wasn't work. It seemed like three great stories a day were dumped in your lap. The toughest part was trying to decide which one to use. I had come a long way from my days at KQV Radio back in 1977 when I would sneak up to my brother, Paul, in the press box and ask him what I should ask Coach Johnny Wilson or the players after the game. I like to think that I understand the game a little better now. I like it more every day. I never thought I'd say that hockey is my favorite sport. Now I can't believe it's not everybody's.

And I'm still angry that I never got to play it.

Pittsburgh's legendary sports broadcaster Bob Prince is flanked by Paul, left, and John Steigerwald.

KDKA-TV's John Steigerwald interviews Mario Lemieux after Penguins won second straight Stanley Cup championship.

Penguin Lovers Lived in Birdland
Recalling that first Stanley Cup win

By Paul Steigerwald
WTAE Radio, KBL and KDKA-TV

The Steigerwalds grew up in Birdland. The original Ryan Homes plan, its streets were named after birds. We lived on Raven Drive and when I was thirteen I learned that Jack Riley, the original general manager of the Penguins, lived on the next street over, Grouse Drive.

A friend down the street met Jack's daughter, Barbara, and she made it possible for a group of us to obtain free Penguins tickets from her dad.

Before long, my dad was driving a carload of kids to every game. We would stop at the Riley residence, knock on the door, and Jack's daughter Barbara, or Mrs. Riley would hand us little coupons redeemable for tickets. I went to 33 of the 39 regular season games in 1969-70, and I purchased tickets for all of the playoff games. Jack Riley made me a rabid hockey fan, and I owe my career to his generosity.

I began working for the Penguins in 1980, and for ten long years, I watched the Penguins struggle on and off the ice. Winning the Stanley Cup is a dream for anyone associated with an NHL franchise. But Penguin employees would have been happy just to make it to the third round of the Stanley Cup playoffs.

When we clinched the cup on the night of May 25, 1991, I was doing color commentary with Mike Lange for the telecast back to Pittsburgh. I was on my way downstairs to the locker room for post-game interviews when the final buzzer sounded, so I never saw the Stanley Cup parade on the ice at the Met Center.

When I entered the locker room, Edward J. DeBartolo was there, quietly waiting to greet the Stanley Cup champions. I shook his hand and told him how happy I was for him, because as far as I was concerned, he had been the Penguins' number one season ticketholder, pouring good money after bad to keep the team alive. Now he could boast to his friends who had made fun of his losing team for so many years.

The locker room celebration was a blast. The players' wives and families, media types and front-office employees took part in the fun. Everyone snapped pictures of each other with the Stanley Cup, and the champagne poured and poured.

After a couple of hours in the locker room, we made our way to the buses and the charter flight back to Pittsburgh. Randy Gilhen was in the back of the airplane, tilting the Cup for his teammates and their wives so they could drink champagne. "Suck it back, suck it back," he was yelling. " 'guins win, 'guins win." Halfway home, we learned that nearly 20,000 fans were at the airport, and that traffic was at a standstill all the way back to the city.

This apparently had caught Craig Patrick by surprise, because he had only arranged for school buses to take us to the airport parking lots. When we landed, Patrick announced on the airplane intercom that the buses would take us straight to the Civic Arena instead of the parking lots, and that we would have to pick up our cars in the morning.

I emerged from the jetway to witness one of the most incredible sights of my life. A gauntlet of wild-eyed, delirious hockey fans, five or six rows deep, stacked to the ceiling. We raced through that gauntlet like scared rabbits, and on the way down the escalator, I dropped my bag. I picked it up and hurried to the bus, at which time I realized I had lost my $300 tape recorder. A friend of Mario's, Jimmy Maggs, handed me the recorder a few minutes after I sat down on the bus. That was a relief.

There were several buses, but I was lucky enough to have boarded the one that carried the Stanley Cup. Mario was clutching it between his knees as it rested on the floor at the back of the bus. Tom Barrasso was seated on an equipment rack in front of the emergency door, and I was standing in the aisle, directly in front of him.

The crowds outside the bus were intense, rocking the bus, and reaching into the windows to shake the hands of their heroes. I remember how delighted Barrasso was with the whole scene until he realized that the bus was moving about ten feet for every twenty minutes.

The bus driver apparently hadn't been told of the plan to go to the Civic Arena, and he turned into one of the airport parking lots. We didn't reach the Parkway for about an hour and a half, and the temperature on the bus, which was packed with players, their wives and girlfriends, family members and luggage was well over 120 degrees.

When Bob Errey's wife, Traci, began to hyperventilate, Tom Barrasso's delight turned to anger.

He made his way to the front of the bus and told the driver to turn left instead of right, when he reached the Parkway. An hour later, we pulled up in front of Tom Barrasso's home in Sewickley. The birds were singing . . . the sun was coming up, and we were standing in Tom Barrasso's front yard with the Stanley Cup.

After a few breaths of fresh air, some of us got back on the bus to return to the now peaceful airport parking lots. There were about 15 of us, including Phil and Julie Bourque, and Jay and Alicia Caufield.

We weren't halfway to the airport when the bus ran out of gas. It was now about 7 a.m. on Sunday and we were stranded on the highway, wearing champagne-soaked clothes. Phil and Julie Bourque stuck out their thumbs and hitched a ride back to the airport, and the rest of us waited for the parking lot vans to rescue us. I got home at 8 a.m. and went to bed, with visions of the Stanley Cup celebrations dancing in my head.

The following season began on a terribly sad note with the illness of Bob Johnson. Craig Patrick was devastated, and the players were heartbroken. They received their Stanley Cup rings at a special ceremony at the Igloo Club of the Civic Arena. I introduced Edward J. DeBartolo to those in attendance.

Mr. D. spoke briefly and then Craig Patrick introduced each member of the team one by one. Each one spoke into a camera which was sending the whole ceremony back to Colorado, where a dying Bob Johnson was watching with his family. It was an extremely touching and moving ceremony.

A few weeks later, Mr. D summoned Mike Lange and myself to his headquarters near Youngstown, Ohio. He came into the conference room and talked for about forty minutes, thanking us for our efforts.

Mr. D. was sincerely grateful for the work we had done for his hockey team. He tossed us two small gift-wrapped boxes. We each opened one of the boxes and found our own personal Stanley Cup ring, and put the rings on our fingers. That was the most rewarding feeling I have ever had in my career.

Before we left the room, he told us the story of how he had bought the team from Al Savill in the late '70s. He said he had become a big hockey fan over the years, and that he was reluctant to sell the franchise. We thanked him for the rings, for his hospitality and drove back to Pittsburgh.

There's not a day goes by that I don't think of that first Stanley Cup championship, and my ring is a constant reminder. It certainly makes all the years of losing seem worthwhile.

Paul Steigerwald wore sports uniforms routinely, left at age 10, and right at age 15. "I'd give my daughter Barbara 50 tickets to pass out to kids in our neighborhood before every home game," recalled Jack Riley, the original GM of the Penguins, "and Paul was always first in line at our door."

Why It Took So Long To Win
Hornets, setbacks shape Penguins' legacy

"The names and exploits of those players are still vivid in my mind."

By George Von Benko
Sports Talk Show Host, WASP Radio, Brownsville, Pa.

My earliest memories of hockey in Pittsburgh are those of another time and another team other than the Penguins. In my early youth, I was a big fan of the Pittsburgh Hornets of the American Hockey League. They were not the Hornets of the old Duquesne Gardens. I was only three when that old barn was shut down in 1955. My memories start with the team that came back to town in the sixties.

The Hornets were a minor league team, the farm club of the Detroit Red Wings. The names and exploits of those players are still vivid in my mind. The highlight of any Hornets' season was the annual exhibition game with the parent team, the Red Wings, led by the great Gordie Howe and his linemate, Alex Delvecchio.

Like most Pittsburgh area kids, my hero growing up was Roberto Clemente, but my favorite hockey player was the diminutive former Hornets goalie, Roger Crozier. Some other favorites of mine were Claude LaForge, Ted Hampson, Warren "The Rock" Godfrey, Hank Bassen, Art Stratton, Lowell MacDonald and Bobby Dillabough.

In 1966-67, the Hornets' final season in Pittsburgh, they captured the Calder Cup as league champions. In 1967, the Penguins came into existence and I immediately had some old favorites for which to cheer. They included Les Binkley, whom I had previously seen play for the rival Cleveland Barons, and former Hornets Ab McDonald, Val Fonteyne, Stratton, Dillabough and Bassen. The team's first star was Hall of Famer Andy Bathgate, who was in the final stages of a brilliant career.

That is enough of my reminiscing, and now to the point of my piece. After years of struggling and losing, the Penguins did what I thought I'd never see. They captured back-to-back Stanley Cup championships in 1991 and 1992. Why did it take this franchise 24 years to win a championship?

Many factors played a part, not the least of which was the financial instability that had plagued the team from its inception. But two events stick out in my mind as crossroads for this franchise.

The Penguins did not make their first playoff appearance until

1970. The team finished second in the Western Division behind the St. Louis Blues and notched 64 points for the season.

Leonard "Red" Kelly was named "Coach of the Year" by *The Hockey News* in his first season behind the Penguins' bench. Veteran Dean Prentice paced the Pens in scoring with 26 goals and 25 assists. But it was a rookie, diminutive Michel Briere, who was the sparkplug garnering 12 goals and 32 assists during the season. In the playoffs, Briere spearheaded a four-game sweep of the Oakland Seals, netting the game-winning goal in a 3-2 overtime victory to complete the sweep.

Pittsburgh then faced the hated St. Louis Blues in the semifinals. Yes, I hated the St. Louis Blues in those days. The Blues-Pens rivalry was one of the most heated in the NHL. The Blues had the Plager brothers, Barclay, Bob and Bill. Their roughhouse style along with that of Noel Picard led to many a donnybrook with the Pens' Bugsy Watson, Bryan Hextall, Glen Sather and Tracy Pratt. It was a hard-fought tight series with St. Louis winning 4-3 in Pittsburgh to finish off the Pens, 4 games to 2. The season was a step in the right direction with a young star like Briere, a good mix of veterans and Red Kelly's leadership. The future looked promising.

Fate reared its ugly head when Briere was seriously injured in an off-season automobile accident in May of 1970 near his home in Quebec. Briere lay in a coma for 11 months before he died. Briere's promising career was snuffed out before he could reach his full potential. The team slumped to 62 points and missed the playoffs in 1970-71.

Would Briere have been a catalyst for Penguin success? We can only wonder. Many hockey people I have talked to felt Briere had great potential and would have been a lynchpin for Pittsburgh for years to come. Former Philadelphia Flyer great Bobby Clarke, who broke into the NHL the same year as Briere, thinks Penguins' history might have been very different had Briere lived. How so? It's a question that will never be answered.

The other crossroads in Penguins history came in the 1974-75 campaign. Pittsburgh moved into the Norris Division with NHL realignment. That season the club finished third behind Montreal and Los Angeles in the division. The Pens set a club record for wins (37) and points (89).

This was a high-powered, offensive group. Exciting rookie Pierre Larouche led all NHL rookies in scoring with 31 goals and 37 assists. Jean Pronovost had 43 goals and Rick Kehoe had 32 and Vic Hadfield netted 31. The Pens also had five 20-plus goal scorers, including Ron Schock, who topped the team with 86 points (23 goals, 63 assists) and runner-up Syl Apps had 79 points (24 goals, 55 assists). Apps was also named MVP of the NHL All-Star Game at Montreal. Promising young goalie Gary Inness posted 24 victories, two shutouts and a 3.09 goals-per-game average.

The Pens disposed of St. Louis, 2-0, in the preliminary round of the playoffs and then faced the New York Islanders in the quarter-finals.

Pittsburgh jumped out to a 3-0 lead in the series. Then the Penguins watched in horror as the Isles became the second team in NHL history to storm back from a 3-0 deficit. Game Seven of that Series was played on Saturday, April 16, 1975 in Pittsburgh. In a tight-checking, hard-fought game, Ed Westfall scored a late third period goal to give the Islanders a 1-0 win and the series.

The famous quote uttered following New York's series-tying 4-1 win came from Islanders' forward J. P. Parise, "The workers will beat the fancy dans any day." This win was the first step for the Islanders down a road that would later lead the franchise to four consecutive Stanley Cups.

Pittsburgh made the playoffs in 1975-76, but was ushered out by Toronto 2-1 in a best-of-three preliminary round. Pittsburgh did not win another playoff until 1979. Goalie Gary Inness, who gave up the goal to Westfall, never was the same player. He slumped to 8-9-2 in 1975-76 and was dealt to Philadelphia on March 8, 1976. Pittsburgh management, already having spent playoff earnings they were expecting from advancing past the Islanders, was stuck between a rock and a hard place. The outcome was bankruptcy and the eventual sale of the team.

These were two crossroads in the history of a star-crossed franchise. We can only wonder what might have happened had things gone the other way for the Penguins. Twenty-four years of frustration might have been avoided.

Young George Von Benko, left, joins fellow fashion plates from mid-70s, Bob "Battleship" Kelly and Ken Schinkel.

Losing In Philly Was Routine
It wasn't easy for young fans

"Sometimes it would be frustrating. Sometimes it was infuriating."

By Mike Prisuta
Sportswriter, Beaver County Times

Because they were a Pittsburgh team, they were my team. But because they were the Penguins, they were special.

It wasn't difficult, after all, to root for the Pirates and Steelers if you were growing up in the 1970s. Even if you lived in Philadelphia.

That was the time of Clemente's legend, of Willie Stargell's windmill, of Richie Hebner constantly tugging at the back of his shirt. That was the time of Bradshaw, Lambert, Greene and Noll. That was a decade of dominance that kicked off right about the time "the Immaculate Reception" floated into Franco's fingers.

It wasn't hard to get caught up in it all. Especially if your family had transplanted itself from Aliquippa, as mine had. Dad rooted for the Bucs and Steelers, so naturally, I did, too. And, naturally, once I discovered the game played with long sticks and short pants and that there was a team from Pittsburgh playing it, the Pens became my team as well.

If only more people had approached it that way.

The Pens weren't as accepted on the Pittsburgh sports scene back then. They weren't as successful as the Pirates and Steelers and didn't get close to the same media attention and fan support. The Pens, it seemed, were lucky to have any fans at all back before the Arena added balconies and back when you could sit in D-level seats for $5.75 a ticket and then move down to A-level if you cared to because no one was sitting there, either.

It didn't matter. Dad had taught me baseball and football and basketball, but I had a chance to return the favor with hockey. At first, he feigned interest simply because he knew it meant a great deal to me. Gradually, he became hooked on hockey.

Enough to appreciate Syl Apps and respect Ron Stackhouse. Enough to admire Dave Burrows' talents as a defensive defenseman and Jean Pronovost's ability to put the puck in the net. Enough to love Lucky Pierre Larouche, even though he floated a lot and he didn't score on that breakaway in Game 7 against the Islanders in '75.

Enough to take me to the Spectrum — the Pens' longtime house of horrors — almost every time Pittsburgh was in town.

That wasn't hard to do at the time even though the Flyers were sold out for the season, because most of the Philadelphia faithful had already grown tired of watching the Broad Street Bullies hammer the hapless, flightless Birds. What was hard was watching the Penguins fail to find a way to win over and over again; most times via a blowout.

Sometimes it would be frustrating. Sometimes — like the night in December of 1979 when Behn Wilson kicked a puck past Greg Millen to steal a 1-1 tie and help the Flyers extend an unbeaten streak that would eventually reach an NHL-record 35 games — it was infuriating. Sometimes, when they grew tired of abusing the likes of Apps and Rick Kehoe and Randy Carlyle and Pete Mahovlich, the Philadelphia faithful would yell insults such as "Hey, Pittsburgh, Iron City sucks, too!" It didn't matter. We always went. So often that to this day I believe I've seen the Penguins lose more games in Philadelphia than anyone currently or formerly connected with the organization. It was part of the ritual of hockey season.

Catch a few games at the Arena over Thanksgiving or Christmas. Maybe one at the Capital Centre (got Mike Lange's autograph there once; Tom Bladon's and Ross Lonsberry's, too). And always show up to cheer for the Pens at the Spectrum. Any bandwagon-jumper could root for a multiple Super Bowl or World Series champion, we reasoned. Backing the Pens required a little character. Especially in their building.

There was also little else to look forward to in a hockey campaign. The Pens, certainly, weren't about to win a Stanley Cup. Nor did we expect them to. Back then the best you ever dared hope for was simply making the playoffs each season, and playing enough home games so that the franchise would have enough operating capital that it wouldn't have to move to Hamilton, Ontario, or some other God-forsaken Canadian outpost. Even in 1974-75, the year of The Big Tease, we knew it would end sooner than later. Yes, it was heart-breaking to blow a three-games-to-none lead against the Islanders, but not because doing so abruptly derailed Pittsburgh's Cup run. As we knew better than anyone, the Pens weren't about to beat the Flyers in the next round, anyway. As it turned out, no one was.

But one more win would have meant advancing to the NHL's version of The Final Four and — finally — some respectability for a franchise that surely deserved some. Instead, there was only agony. And more of the same in 1981 against the Blues in double-overtime, and in 1982 against the Islanders (in one overtime this time). And then it really got ugly for a while. But, finally, Mario arrived. And Barrasso. And Craig Patrick. And Badger Bob.

By the time they were skating their way to greatness in the spring of 1991, I had stopped buying $5.75 D-level tickets and started flashing a press pass to enter the Arena. Still, I wasn't about to let this pass unappreciated. Reporters aren't supposed to be fans, but at the same time, I figured, I had this coming. I had earned it. The dues had been paid. Now, it was time to collect. So I called home, collect. After the quotes had been recorded, the champagne had been popped, the stories had been written and the last media bus had left the Met Center in Bloomington, Minnesota, I sought out a hotel lobby pay phone and called Dad back in Philly. He was as ecstatic as I was. And somewhere, we figured, Syl Apps was smiling, too.

Mike Prisuta of Beaver County Times

Guy Junker of KBL

Cleaning Tables To See Penguins
From busboy to Sportsbeat

By Guy Junker
Sportscaster, KBL Sports Channel

An autograph in my high school yearbook reads . . . "To a great kid I met in 7th grade. You have only one fault. You like the Penguins! Ken, Class of '74." You know what Ken? I still do.

We used to make pucks out of wood. I know it sounds crazy, but in the late 60's there were no plastic hockey balls, or inline skates or deck hockey facilities. We were lucky enough in our Baldwin neighborhood to have an old unused basketball gym where we played a primitive form of street hockey. Several of the dads on our street built nets, constructed boards, and even made a penalty box. Since ice hockey pucks would not slide properly across the floor, someone got the bright idea of making a wooden puck in shop class. It worked marvelously and our primitive form of deck hockey reached a new level. We all took turns sneaking scrap wood. We would trace the outline of a rubber puck and then cut it out with a jigsaw. We would make five or six at a time, though, because they would sometimes split in half, especially on a hard slap shot. It kept the goalies on their toes anyway. Many of us played ice hockey, too, but back then, ice was even more scarce than it is now. We would play a few games outdoors at the South Park rink or later at the old Monroeville Mall rink, but it wasn't enough to satisfy our appetite for what at that time was just a cult sport in the Pittsburgh area.

We all loved the Penguins then and would get together somewhere every time they were on television. It was more of an event then because only a few games a year made the tube. Mostly we were disappointed and frustrated by the blunderings of the franchise, but we kept hoping. By the time I was in high school, I was a season ticket holder and supported "my habit" by working as a busboy at Klein's Seafood Restaurant on Fourth Avenue. My mother wasn't thrilled at the late hours I kept downtown, but I always explained that half the money was going into savings for college. The real reason I wanted to do it though was because the other half went for my tickets, shinguards, helmets and ice time.

It's hard to believe that Klein's no longer exists. The building isn't even there now, but then it was the best seafood place in the city. We had many celebrities come in to eat (Lorne Greene of Bonanza, Henry Mancini, Johnny Bench, to name a few I remember). The waitresses would fall all over themselves trying to do a good job when such people were dining there. Most of them never impressed me much although Duke Snider once gave me a five dollar tip. Yet one night in January of 1973, Greg Polis came in to eat. And he could eat. Pens fans later nicknamed him "Porky" because of his general chunkiness. Polis was a pretty good left wing for the Penguins at the time and later that season would be the MVP of the All-Star Game. I couldn't figure out why there wasn't the usual fuss made when an athlete or entertainer dined in the place. As it turns out, I was the only one in the place to recognize him. We weren't allowed to ask for autographs but I must have topped off his water glass 10 times. When he finally left I went to the maitre'd and said, "Do you know who that was?" "No," he replied. I said, "That was Greg Polis." He said, "Who is Greg Polis?" I told him emphatically, "He plays for the Penguins." The maitre'd replied, "I wish I would have known . . . I would have charged him double."

Many of these stories clouded my head on a muggy day late in May of 1991 as I sat in the media bus rolling toward Point State Park for the rally to celebrate the Penguins' first Stanley Cup championship. As a journalist you are supposed to be objective, but I was feeling pretty happy. I thought about my old school friends and teammates who were scattered across the country. One of them had passed away. I remembered the heartbreak we felt when the St. Louis Blues eliminated the Pens in 1970. I still have a goalie stick from that series, autographed by Blues goalie Glenn Hall who is now in the Hall of Fame. I remembered the shock we felt when learning about the death of Michel Briere, and the utter disgust we had when the Pens blew the 3-0 lead to the Islanders in 1975. This was redemption day for anyone ever interested in Pittsburgh hockey. I thought about how today almost any member of the Penguins would be mobbed in a restaurant.

Of course, there was another cup after that and a Presidents Trophy. And where it was once expected that the Penguins find a way to lose, it is now expected that they find a way to win. As a result, hockey is healthy and flourishing in Western Pennsylvania at all levels today. I'm glad for that . . . but I'm also glad that I remember a time when hockey players were not recognized in public . . . a time when pucks were made of wood.

Guy Junker enjoyed riding his bike and playing sports, especially hockey, in his youth back in Baldwin.

KBL's Sportsbeat team: Stan Savran and Guy Junker

"It's a bird, and one of the dirtiest birds in the world. A guy in Toronto sent me a clipping about the habits of Penguins, and they're disgusting."

—Jack Riley
General Manager

These are OUR Penguins
Banquet points up acceptance

"What a grip this hockey team has on this town."

By Stan Savran
Sportscaster, KBL
Guest columnist, Pittsburgh Post-Gazette

Stan Savran

May, 1992

To reach the microphone, Kent Tekulve had to bend his long, thin frame nearly in half. He looked for all the world like one of those goose-necked lamps. Or a lowercase "n." The former Pirates reliever had just finished telling the KBL television audience, and a crowd of 1,800 gathered at the Downtown Hilton for the YMCA All Sports Banquet this past Tuesday night, about the work ethic of the Pirates and the Steelers. But there was a third professional franchise to include in Tekulve's address.

Teke, still bent over like a crane taking a drink of water, intoned, "And our Pens."

What happened next was, and still is for me, a moment frozen in time ... an indescribable experience that I will nevertheless attempt to describe.

When Tekulve said, "and our Pens," he paused. I'm not sure if it was by design, or the reaction of the crowd dictated a pause was necessary. But a ripple, nay, a tidal wave of emotion went through the Hilton's main ballroom. A gentle breeze of a banquet grew into a gale.

A few people applauded, a few more voiced approval. Nearly everybody felt a charge of electricity surge through the room, forcing hairs laying flat on the back of the neck to stand at attention. Throats closed so that swallowing became a conscious action rather than an involuntary reaction.

Pride.

That's the only reason I can offer for the crowd's response. Remember, this was the night after the Penguins had defeated the hooded merchants of violence in Game 5. In New York. A victory of heart and soul more than arms and legs. Or wrists.

The people in that room were so full of emotion, I sensed they wanted to break into a chant of "Let's Go, Pens." They might very well have done so had they not been straitjacketed by the affair they were attending. As a noted hockey sage once said, you had to be there to believe it.

What a grip this hockey team has on this town. This series win over the Rangers rivals anything I have seen during my sweet 16 years here. Super Bowls. World Series. Last year's Cup. Because this was not only a victory, it was a victory achieved the way we like it. Tough, hard-nosed, blue-collar, against all odds. Grind it out. GUT it out. Last year's Penguin highlight film was entitled, "One From the Heart." This year's video should be called, "One From the Gut."

This reminded me so much of the 1976 Steelers. Having watched Joe "Turkey" Jones excavating a tunnel using Terry Bradshaw's head as a drill, the Steelers rallied around and protected rookie quarterback Mike Kruczek by playing perhaps the greatest defense in the history of professional football. They won 10 straight games, allowing just 42 points, and registered four shutouts. Franco and Rocky were human pistons, fueling a boiler-room offense that pulverized opposing defenses into submission. Awesome, it was. Fond memory it is.

Yeah, we like our teams to win. Just like any other town. But unlike other towns, we are especially romanced by, and embrace those teams that not only win, but win in a style to which we relate.

Naturally, a city would be agog over a team that won four Super Bowls in six years. But I have always maintained that the bang-'em-up, bruise-'em-up style the Steelers employed made them even more popular if, indeed, popularity can exceed 100 percent. They were us, and we them. Never before did a team so strikingly represent the personality of its fans and city. Not until now, anyway.

This Penguin team, boy, they're somethin' aren't they? To beat the Darth Vaders of hockey like that? The Rangers had become to the Pens what the Oakland Raiders were to the Steelers. The challenge to beat them is greater, but so is the reward. That's the way we like it. That's the way we want it. And that's why the crowd at the Hilton that night reacted the way it did.

The Penguins have reinforced our region's belief that the spirit fuels the mind, much as the mind commands the body. We believe that sheer will and determination deadens the throbbing pains of life. Reducing them to mere annoyances to be tolerated.

Some will say, "Hey! It's only a game. Don't try to make it more than that!" I say it is more. I say the bond between team and town is real. Strong. A meeting of energies and spirits. The two parties communicate. The fans roar, the players play.

But there is a telekinetic connection as well. We say, "We like what you're doing, and the way you're doing it. You make us proud to be here. We have become a part of you, and you have become a part of us."

Regardless of what happens in the Boston series, or beyond, this hockey team has become a thick fiber in the fabric of our community.

This show may not have been a big hit on Broadway, but it is doing boffo business on Bigelow.

In this morality play, the good guys wear black.

Reprinted with permission of Pittsburgh Post-Gazette

The Name Game
Learning to skate and play hockey

"I would never skate like him, but it didn't matter."

By Goose Goslin
KDKA Radio, Tribune-Review Columnist

It started with the names. I'll never forget the names. Rejean Houle (Ray-jawn Ooo-lay), Yvan Cournoyer (EE-Vawn Corn-why-yeh), Serge Savard, Jean Beliveau (Jawn Bell-ee-vo). It was pure poetry although I would not realize that until much later.

Those wonderful sounds combined with the images of TV character Sgt. Preston of the Yukon to make the country of Canada a wonderful mystery for me as a child and teenager. As a kid fascinated with history and sports, I wanted to travel there. Why did they not come with us during the Revolutionary War? Why were they so much like us north of the border, but yet so different in a charming way?

What was it really like to skate? On ice, that is. Roller skates I knew. I had a pair. Ice skates were something my father wore on the frozen creeks and ponds of Greene and Washington counties in western Pennsylvania when he was a kid. Finally, for my 16th birthday, my dad gave me a pair — figure skates, not hockey skates. Skating was a recreational thing. We didn't play hockey in Pitcairn and Irwin. Baseball, football and basketball were our sports. Hockey was something to watch others do. Besides we had no NHL team in Pittsburgh. Oh, the Hornets were here in the AHL, but they didn't get the media exposure the Pirates, Steelers and Pitt got.

The closest rink was in Greensburg, and there were just too many other things to do and think about to take the time to use those figure skates. I always meant to, but it would be more than twice my 16 years before I got around to it.'

In the meantime, I watched from afar and admired, but didn't get too close. Then, during my senior year at IUP, I met a member of the school's club hockey team. They played forty minutes down the road at Belmont Arena in Kittanning. I went to a game. I loved it.

Shortly after graduation, I landed a job at a TV station in Harrisburg. The Hershey Bears were the only hockey club in the region, the only professional team in the area.

The Bears won the AHL Calder Cup that first season in the state capital, and I was hooked — especially because Pittsburgh now had an NHL team and the Bears were their farm club. Goaltender Denis Herron and defenseman Mario Faubert would go on to play for the Pens, and I would eventually meet up with them again in the early 80's.

Still, I was distracted. The Steelers were having a sensational run in the '70's, and I had played a little football — very little, actually, and not very well, but enough to be totally immersed with Mr. Rooney's team.

Then two seasons I went without hockey in Tidewater, Virginia during my tenure there at a radio and TV station, but in January of 1981 my real march down the aisle began. I returned to Pittsburgh to work. The Pens were still a downtrodden disrespected bunch and that bothered me. My bother was heightened by the fact that my radio station was the flagship of their hockey network. Then came the double overtime loss to St. Louis in the '81 playoffs, the heart-breaking, heart-stopping exit to the Islanders in '82 followed by total collapse the next two seasons. Then came number 66, Mario Lemieux.

The figure skates had gathered a lot of dust in my mother's basement. I was self-conscious carrying them into the Mt. Lebanon Arena. I really didn't know the first thing about what I was doing with them, but there I was, in my mid-30s, about to find out about what I had wondered about for three decades. I had to know just how it is to skate. Even if it was feebly, I wanted to know something of the incredible grace and control this sensational kid from Montreal displayed. Six group lessons later, it wasn't fun. It was passion. It was an experience — almost a way of life. The smell of the rink. The incredible glide. The speed. The freedom. The challenge of making those muscles and those blades do what sometimes seemed impossible. I would never skate like him, but it didn't matter. I bought a used pair of hockey skates, and then a brand new pair.

I had found my hula hoop again. Those silly round things my generation played with ad nauseum as post-World War II baby boomers had taken another form. What removed this game, the skating made for almost constant motion. Forget those NBA guys. They are great athletes, but they couldn't do this. They couldn't literally dance on thin strips of metal and make that little round object do incredible things on the end of a stick.

People talked about other sports being a reflection of life. "Forget about it," I thought. What could be more like the madness of life on this planet than the bumps and grinds, starting and stopping and the sometimes lucky and then unlucky bounces of this game? Nothing I had experienced.

And then came those names again. Where in that Great White North were these guys from for the most part? Yes, there were Americans and Europeans but most of them were Canadians from towns like Guelph and Kitchener and Oshawa, Medicine Hat, Moose Jaw and Viking. Sturgeon Falls and Chicoutimi were in the mix as well not to mention Ville Emard and Laval. Ville Emard, the section of Montreal where Lemieux is from, and the suburb north of Montreal, Laval, where he stirred the interest of a continent playing major junior for La Voisin.

"Voisin (Vuh-wah-zahn)? What's a Voisin?" I wondered. As it turned out, it's not so much a something as it is a somewhere. The closest translation into English would be "the neighborhoods." "The neighborhoods of Laval." Yeah, I liked that. Just like Mr. Rogers' Neighborhood.

It was another connection. It was meant to be. Had to be. How many times does a genius leave the neighborhoods of Laval to play in the place that spawned Mr. Rogers' Neighborhood? It's a classic. He's a classic. These have been classic times. Maybe I'll skate forever.

Stanley Cup belongs in Mr. Rogers' Neighborhood.

Hockey enthusiasts Tom McMillan and Goose Goslin get their kicks from playing their own brand of ice hockey.

Marty Glickman, The Gumper and Leapin' Louie
And how to get hooked on hockey
Pre-Stanley Cup days were more fun

By Doug Hoerth
Talk Show Host, WTAE Radio

I cannot for the life of me recall just how it was I got into hockey. I hung out with a baseball crowd as a kid. In my part of Jersey, we had three teams to root for or against — the Yankees, Giants and Dodgers. Hell, I was born with a fielder's mitt in my mouth!

Football and basketball, too. The Giants and the Knicks. Easy games to play in a field or on the street. But hockey? There were no ice skating rinks in the immediate vicinity. And there were, sure as hell, no ponds. As near as I can remember, my hockey fandom is due to a guy named Marty Glickman.

People in the broadcast biz know the name Marty Glickman. But to the average fan, the name means zip, unless you lived in New York or Jersey, back in the '50s. In my neck of the woods, along with Vin Scully, Red Barber, Russ Hodges and Mel Allen, Marty Glickman was a GOD. He was the voice of the Rangers and the Knicks, did college basketball from the Garden, baseball re-creations, Dodger pre- and postgame shows . . . the guy was great! He was the mentor for Marv Albert of "Yesssss!" fame.

With a very heavy "New Yawwwk" accent, Marty Glickman introduced the game of hockey into my life. The way he said "Ranguuhs" . . . this very clipped play-by-play, Glickman made it as exciting as a Don Dunphy radio call of a boxing match.

The Rangers had no television contract in those days. Hence it was a year or two before I actually saw a game. When I did, it was via a 16-inch Emerson. The voice belonged to Bud Palmer. It was everything Marty Glickman said it was. Marty Glickman did not lie.

The Rangers of my youth were a rather mediocre lot. Six team league. Four in the playoffs, two out. On those rare occasions when the Rangers did get in, they would last, but not long.

Still, they produced several Hall of Fame players, defenseman Harry Howell, goalie Gump Worsley, and forward Andy Bathgate, who, of course, finished up his career in Pittsburgh. That was something a lot of great players did when they were no longer great. Three former Penguins are in the Hall of Fame — notably Bathgate, Tim Horton and Leo Boivin — but they didn't get into the Hall because of what they did in Pittsburgh.

The "Gumper" had a crewcut long before and after they went out of style. The hockey encyclopedia lists him at 5-foot-7. Having met the man I can state categorically that's one helluva stretch. He carried a paunch that put Bobby Layne's to shame, and he had a great thirst for beer. And, of course, he played goalie without a mask. Just like Layne. Gump neither looked nor acted (if the stories of his off-ice exploits are true) like an athlete. But, man, he sure could play goal. He later went on to win several Vezina trophies and Stanley Cup championships with the Montreal Canadiens. And he's in the Hockey Hall of Fame.

They didn't have "goons" in those days. They had fights galore. Far bloodier than the dancing matches of today. Everybody fought their own battles. Hence, if you did Maurice "The Rocket" Richard dirty, sooner or later *he* would retaliate. Gordie Howe's fighting ability is every bit as legendary as his elbows. Even a Lady Byng ("for sportsmanship and gentlemanly conduct") kind of guy like Andy Bathgate would put up his dukes if the occasion called for it. The first honest-to-goodness "goon" I can recall was a guy named Howie Young, who came up with the Red Wings in 1961. His second year, he had the unheard-of total of 273 minutes in the penalty box. This he did in a mere 64 games.

Rangers fans then and now appreciate toughness in a hockey player. Hence, "Leapin' Louie" Fontinato was a Garden favorite. He played hard, he hit hard, fought hard. His most memorable fight was a toe-to-toe encounter with Gordie Howe, one that Rangers fans still talk about today (for the record, Howe destroyed him.) Louie wound up his career as a regular defenseman with the Montreal Canadiens. Six of his fellow "Flying Frenchmen" are today in the Hall of Fame. I mention this, lest anyone attempt to besmirch the memory of Leapin' Louie by referring to him as a mere "goon."

I lost visual contact with hockey from 1973 till late in 1980, when I moved to Pittsburgh from Fort Lauderdale, Florida. How and why I remained a hockey fan those seven long years away from the game I don't know. But I did.

About the time I was offered a job in Pittsburgh, a second offer came along from a radio station in Portland, Oregon. I'd be lying if I said I chose Pittsburgh simply because the city had an NHL hockey team and Portland did not. I'd also be lying if I said it wasn't an important factor in helping me decide which offer to take.

Rooting for a two-time Stanley Cup champion, having an opportunity to see the greatest hockey player in the history of the game on a semi-regular basis . . . great stuff, no doubt about it.

Yet in a way, the pre-Stanley Cup days were a lot more fun. So few people came to the games, you got to know your fellow fans on a first-name basis. The Civic Arena, half filled with a smaller capacity than it's had in recent seasons, was ten times noisier than the sellouts of today. It was a noisy crowd, a raucous crowd, a dungaree (not designer jean) type of crowd. There were a lot of beerbellies consuming a helluva lot of beer. At least one fight-of-the-week in the stands. They were the people who truly loved the game, loved their Penguins. I loved them come hell or high water, loved them win or lose. The dungaree crowd is still around. But they're less in number. The ticket prices took care of that. They've been replaced by guys with three hundred dollar shoes and fifty dollar haircuts. People who come to be seen, many of them, as the Civic Arena has become the place to be. Better dressed. Better mannered. They drink expresso instead of beer. And they think Phil Bourque is the guy who wears No. 77 and plays for the Bruins.

Some of Doug Hoerth's heroes when he was growing up with the New York Rangers were "Leapin' Louie" Fontinato, left, and Gump Worsley, guarding nets below. Toronto Maple Leafs forward Bob Nevin and Rangers' defenseman Doug Harvey are also pictured.

Photos courtesy of New York Rangers

Stanley Cup was a crib for our kid
Winning championships personal thrill

"Most fans came to expect the Pens to win every game."

By Alby Oxenreiter
Sportscaster, WTAE-TV

My first memory of the Penguins comes from the 1970 playoffs. The team was only three-years-old and ready for its first taste of post-season action. I was only nine-years-old, and excited about watching my team in the Stanley Cup playoffs. In the second round that year, the Pens lost to the St. Louis Blues in six games. It was a milestone year for the team, but losing to the Blues was hard for me to swallow. In our backyard patio ice hockey games, I was always the Penguins. My older brother always wanted to be the Blues. So the '70s started with my favorite team losing, in more ways than one.

After college, I lived in three different cities over a five-year period, so my Penguin rooting had to be done from long distance. I think I may have been the only Penguins fan in Grand Junction, Colorado, and I take credit for bringing the nickname "guins" to Harrisburg and Wilkes-Barre, my next two stops.

One of the highpoints to coming back to work in my hometown was getting the opportunity to cover Mario Lemieux and the eventual two-time Stanley Cup champions. It was thrilling to watch their rise first-hand. I still remember one of Lemieux's "breakthrough" games. It was the 1990 All-Star Game, and he sent the Pittsburgh crowd into a frenzy with four goals that earned him the game's MVP award. But Mario's back problems were just beginning. Then, in January 1993, like all Pittsburghers, I felt the shock and the emptiness when Lemieux disclosed that he had been diagnosed with Hodgkins disease. But what I'll remember most was his courageous comeback. Even as he faced a life-threatening situation, Lemieux's demeanor never changed.

And there were the two Stanley Cup titles. The summer of the first championship stirs a lot of memories. Only five weeks after the clinching win over Minnesota, our son Alby, III, was born, and on July 10, 1991, when little Alby was only seven days old, my wife Karen and I dressed him up for his first trip out of the house . . . a short trip to a neighborhood bar — The Korner on Bower Hill Road at Washington Road, owned by Rick Kehoe of the Penguins and his partners — where the Stanley Cup was on display. We put Alby in the Cup for a picture, and it remains one of the most talked-about pictures in our home.

In Chicago the next year, the Pens made it two straight championships. This time, I was there to see it in person. In fact, moments after the win, I was reporting live outside the winner's dressing room, and at the end of the interview with playoff MVP Lemieux, he poured champagne on my head . . . What a thrill! My son was now a year older and too big to sit in the Cup. This time, he stood beside the Cup for another memorable snapshot.

It all happened so fast. The drama of two championships and the summer-long celebrations that followed. It also seemed so easy. The winning came so often that most fans came to expect the Pens to win every game and every series. That's why it's important to never take winning for granted. When your team's on top, savor every moment because they won't be on top forever.

Like any native Pittsburgher, I think of the Penguins as my team. As a sportscaster, I have a different perspective than most but, getting excited about a team I grew up with is what makes my job so much fun. I'd love to see the Pens win another one . . . or two. It would be great to see the Cup make its way back to Pittsburgh, to see Mario lifting it high in the air on Civic Arena ice, and to see my son joined this time by his sister, Abigail, standing beside the oldest sports trophy in North America.

Karen and Alby Oxenreiter cradle Alby III and first Stanley Cup.

The Readers Always Write

*"I am enjoying **MAZ And The '60 Bucs**. I hope you continue your excellent work and write many more books in the future. You have done a great service to Pittsburgh with your books."*
—Eddie Deezen, West Hollywood, Calif.

*"I'm delighted you have written a book, **Remember Roberto**, honoring a real hero of the sports world. My mother, Gertrude McIndoe, has thoroughly enjoyed your other books about 'her Bucs and Steelers,' and I am sure this one will make her equally happy. Mother is 89 years old and has won and lost with the Bucs for most of those years."*
—Beth Hoekje, Portland, Tex.

*"My barber handed me a book and told me I would enjoy it. It was your book, **MAZ And The '60 Bucs**. It really brought back a lot of memories. The pictures of Forbes Field really kind of brought a lump to my throat."*
—Jim Malley, O'Hara Township, Pa.

*"When I read about your book, **Remember Roberto**, I just had to have it. Thank you for making the story of this wonderful man's life available to us, his fans. I sent him a 'birthday' card on three different occasions, and I still have three 'thank you' cards that he sent me in return.*
Regina Jurick, Heidelberg, Pa.

*"**MAZ And The '60 Bucs** is the best book I've read so far about the Pirates. My mom, who is 80 years old, also enjoyed it very much."*
—Randy Butler, Pittsburgh

"I've enjoyed reading all of your Pittsburgh sports books. Over the years, I received some as gifts and some I have purchased while visiting Pittsburgh. Keep the books coming because they are greatly appreciated by Pittsburgh fans. I keep them with my other Pittsburgh sports treasures."

—Al Zdilla, Olney, Md.

*"I recently bought your book, **Remember Roberto**, from a bookstore here and I have to say that I was as excited as a little kid discovering his favorite candy. This book is a jewel! Now I want to get a copy of **MAZ And The '60 Bucs**."*
—Edwin Johnson, San Leandro, Calif.

*"Recently, I finished reading **Remember Roberto** and I loved it! I think that the way you interviewed the people closest to him gave us a chance to really see what he was like. Your book was a moving tribute to a really great guy that I'm sorry I missed. I am only 17 and I, of course, never saw Clemente play, but he has always been a hero of mine. When I finished your book, I truly had a better feeling for what Roberto Clemente, the man, was really about. I hope you continue to write about the terrific sports in Pittsburgh because, as a fan of every Pittsburgh team, I think your books are the best."*
—Lisa Hummel, Altoona, Pa.

*"I just read your books **MAZ And The '60 Bucs** and **Remember Roberto**. They sure bring back many memories. I've ordered your Steeler books and your Pitt book. If they're half as good as your Pirates books they will be great. I have some suggestions for future books, and hope you will write them."*
—Thomas Chuey, San Francisco, Calif.

*"Thanks for sending **Remember Roberto** so promptly. It's a fine read, and brings back a great many memories, both of 'The Great One' himself, and of the people you interviewed."*
—Peter S. Beagle, Novelist
The Innkeeper's Song and
A Fine And Private Place
Davis, Calif.

*"I just finished reading your latest book, **Remember Roberto**, and this, like all your previous 'Pittsburgh Proud' series, was outstanding. I was too young to watch 'The Great One' play, but my dad told me about him and I read a lot of articles and watched every special on him. As I grew up, I wished I could have met this man. Your book reinforced this. Thank you for writing such a book and giving those of us who weren't lucky enough to grow up watching him in action have a chance to feel like we did."*
—Paul R. Donaldson, Jr.
Pittsburgh

Words of Praise

From review of *Doing It Right* by Abby Mendelson:
"It was a sweet time, a time of excellence, of victory, and O'Brien captured it as well as the bittersweet times since. Like David Halberstam's first-rate *Summer of '49*, this book is less a recounting of thrice-told tales than a study of how men came together for a group purpose, driving them to the peak of their abilities.

"Over the years, no one's been a better, more committed sports chronicler than O'Brien. Some may have burned more incandescently, some have remained longer in the trenches, but no one's produced a higher volume of solid reporting.

"*Doing It Right* brought O'Brien back to the players, interviewing them in their homes and offices, bringing himself into the story as Roger Kahn did in the brilliant, elegiac *The Boys of Summer*."

From Matt Marsom of *The Football News*:
"This is the best football book on the market today. It's a unique behind-the-scenes story of what sets the Steelers apart from the pack, yesterday and today. Football fans and non-football fans alike are bound to benefit from the insight into how these men strived for excellence on and off the playing field. Jerry Kramer's *Instant Replay*, which chronicled Vince Lombardi's great Packer teams of the 1960s, has always been my favorite football book. Until now."

From Dave Ailes of *Pittsburgh Tribune-Review:*
"The strength of O'Brien's work — another in a series about the city's proudest sports moments and the athletes who created them — is its scope. He interviewed hundreds of Clemente's teammates, opposing players and Joe Fan. The book, therefore, tells it like it was. O'Brien skillfully wrapped that package in *Remember Roberto*. It's an interesting read."

From Norm Vargo of *Daily News* in McKeesport:
"It looks like the sixth time is the charm for Jim O'Brien. And what timing! O'Brien, a former sportswriter turned author who certainly qualifies as Pittsburgh's self-appointed sports historian, appears to have a real winner in his latest literary effort — *Remember Roberto* — a warm, in-depth look into the life of the late Pirate outfielder who is in the Baseball Hall of Fame at Cooperstown."

From Taylor Scott of Boca Raton, Fla. for *Point* magazine:
"Who said you can't go home again? Each time Jim O'Brien comes out with a book, I am home again. And this is true of *MAZ And The '60 Bucs*. His two previous books that I have read, *Doing It Right* and *Whatever It Takes*, both about the NFL Pittsburgh Steelers, did the same thing. That has always been the uniqueness of O'Brien. He puts you in Pittsburgh. Read this book and you travel through Pittsburgh. You smell it, you feel it, you experience it. Woven throughout is a city and its people and its culture. That's what you get from O'Brien. And you like it."

From *Sports Collectors Digest:*
"If I only had the money to buy one book on baseball besides the *Baseball Encyclopedia*, it would be this book — *MAZ And The '60 Bucs.*"

From Rev. Laird Stuart, San Francisco, California:
"I am getting my baseball 'fix' by reading *Remember Roberto*. It is delightful reading. It is intriguing to discover how this remarkable individual was perceived by different people. Obviously, there were many variables, as there are in the lives of each of us: Clemente changed over the years, the composition of the Pirates changed, each person who knew him has his own changes also, and the times changed, especially regarding racial attitudes. Not surprisingly, therefore, he is perceived differently by different people.

"I think part of your gift is to allow a complex portrait of a complex person to emerge out of the perspectives of so many people. You do not impose an image of Clemente; it emerges.

"It is also fun to read about places and some people I knew, especially Upper St. Clair. As you describe homes and neighborhoods, I can so easily visualize the locale. Even when you describe places I have not been, like Hetherington's in Swissvale, it conjures up images and associations of "the 'burgh" and I enjoy the recollections."

From Jim Kriek, Correspondent, Uniontown Herald-Standard:
"O'Brien is not really in one breath an historian, not really a story-teller, or narrator, or biographer in a single essence of each by itself. Rather, he is a combination of all those attributes who can weave together, and already has done so, memorable accounts of the Steelers glory years, of Bill Mazeroski, and the 1960 Pirates, of Pitt's great years and its all-time athletes, and now of Roberto Clemente. It's a book that is amusing, informative, comical at times, hearty at other times, but always flowing in the narrative, historical style that personifies Jim O'Brien's works. If anybody is looking for a birthday present, a Christmas present, or just wants to personally spend a couple days of enjoyable reading, the baseball lover in the family will thank you deeply if you give him cause to once again 'Remember Roberto.' "

Jim O'Brien joins neighbor Eddie Johnston, the coach of the Pittsburgh Penguins, at a golf outing at Southpointe in Canonsburg in July, 1994.

About The Author

In addition to writing and publishing his "Pittsburgh Proud" series of books, Jim O'Brien writes a weekly column in *The Almanac* and *The Advertiser* in the South Hills of Pittsburgh, and is a contributing columnist to Pittsburgh's *Point* magazine, *Panther Sports Journal* and *The Valley Mirror* in Munhall-Homestead. He also writes for *Street & Smith's Sports Group* in New York.

    Jim was the founding editor of *Street & Smith's Basketball* and served in that position for 23 years. He was also a reporter-columnist for *The Miami News, The New York Post,* and *The Pittsburgh Press*, and a regular contributor to *The Sporting News* and *Sport* magazine. He has taught writing and public relations at Robert Morris College, Point Park College, the University of Pittsburgh, and was extended a special teaching grant to do the same at Carnegie Mellon University.

    He was inducted into the Western chapter of the Pennsylvania Sports Hall of Fame in 1992. He is a frequent speaker and lecturer throughout the tri-state area and conducts writing seminars at schools.